Political Competition, Partisanship, and Policy Making in Latin American Public Utilities

This book studies policy making in the Latin American electricity and telecommunication sectors. Maria Victoria Murillo's analysis of the Latin American electricity and telecommunications sectors shows that different degrees of electoral competition and the partisan composition of the government were crucial in resolving policy makers' tension between the interests of voters and the economic incentives generated by international financial markets and private corporations in the context of capital scarcity. Electoral competition by credible challengers dissuaded politicians from adopting policies deemed necessary to attract capital inflows. When electoral competition was low, financial pressures prevailed, but the partisan orientation of reformers shaped the regulatory design of market-friendly reforms. In the postreform period, moreover, electoral competition and policy makers' partisanship shaped regulatory redistribution between residential consumers, large users, and privatized providers.

Maria Victoria Murillo is Associate Professor of Political Science and International Affairs at Columbia University. She has been a faculty member at Yale University, a Fellow at the Harvard Academy for International and Area Studies, and a Peggy Rockefeller Fellow at the David Rockefeller Center for Latin American Studies at Harvard University. She is the author of *Labor Unions, Partisan Coalitions, and Market Reforms in Latin America* (Cambridge University Press 2001) and coeditor of *Argentine Democracy: The Politics of Institutional Weakness* (2005). Her articles have appeared in numerous U.S. and Latin American social science journals, and she was corecipient of the Luebbert Award for the best article from the Comparative Politics Section of the American Political Science Association in 2004.

T0349302

Cambridge Studies in Comparative Politics

General Editor

Margaret Levi *University of Washington, Seattle*

Assistant General Editor

Stephen Hanson *University of Washington, Seattle*

Associate Editors

Robert H. Bates *Harvard University*
Torben Iversen *Harvard University*
Stathis Kalyvas *Yale University*
Peter Lange *Duke University*
Helen Milner *Princeton University*
Frances Rosenbluth *Yale University*
Susan Stokes *Yale University*
Sidney Tarrow *Cornell University*
Kathleen Thelen *Northwestern University*
Erik Wibbels *Duke University*

Other Books in the Series

Continued after the Index

Political Competition, Partisanship, and Policy Making in Latin American Public Utilities

Maria Victoria Murillo

Columbia University

CAMBRIDGE
UNIVERSITY PRESS

CAMBRIDGE UNIVERSITY PRESS
Cambridge, New York, Melbourne, Madrid, Cape Town, Singapore,
São Paulo, Delhi, Dubai, Tokyo

Cambridge University Press
32 Avenue of the Americas, New York, NY 10013-2473, USA

www.cambridge.org
Information on this title: www.cambridge.org/9780521711227

First published 2009

Printed in the United States of America

A catalog record for this publication is available from the British Library.

Library of Congress Cataloging in Publication Data

Murillo, Maria Victoria, 1967–
    Political competition, partisanship, and policy making in Latin America market reforms in
    public utilities / Maria Victoria Murillo.
        p. cm. – (Cambridge studies in comparative politics)
    Includes bibliographical references and index.
    ISBN 978-0-521-88431-0 (hardback) – ISBN 978-0-521-71122-7 (pbk.)
    1. Power resources – Government policy – Latin America. 2. Telecommunication policy –
    Latin America. I. Title. II. Series.

HD9502.L32M87 2009
333.793'2098–dc22   2008054046

ISBN 978-0-521-88431-0 Hardback
ISBN 978-0-521-71122-7 Paperback

Additional resources for this publication at www.columbia.edu/~mm2140

To my parents

Contents

List of Acronyms

Alianza:	Coalition for Education, Work and Justice
ANTEL:	National Telecommunications Administration
ARENA:	Nationalist Republic Alliance
CFE:	Federal Energy Commission
CNE:	National Energy Commission
CNT:	National Telecommunications Commission
Concertación:	Coalition of Parties for Democracy
COFETEL:	Federal Telecommunications Commission
CRE:	Energy Regulatory Commission
CTC:	Chilean Telephone Company
DC:	Christian Democracy
ENRE:	National Electricity Regulatory Agency
ENTEL:	National Company of Telecommunications
ERSP:	Regulatory Agency for Public Services
FA:	Broad Front
FDT:	Telecommunication Development Fund
FREPASO:	Front for a Country with Solidarity
IMF:	International Monetary Fund
LyF:	Luz y Fuerza del Centro (Light and Power)
NAFTA:	North American Free Trade Agreement
PAN:	National Action Party
PER:	Rural Electrification Program
PRD:	Party of the Democratic Revolution
PRI:	Institutional Revolutionary Party
PROFECO:	Federal Agency for Consumers
PS:	Socialist Party

RN:	National Renovation
SEC:	Electricity and Fuels Superintendence
SEGBA:	Electricity Services of the Great Buenos Aires
SERNAC:	National Agency for Consumer Services
SIC:	Chilean Central Interconnected System
SIGET:	General Superintendence of Electricity and Telecommunications
SUBTEL:	Undersecretariat of Telecommunications
TELMEX:	Mexican Telephones
UCR:	Radical Civic Union
UDI:	Independent Democratic Union

Acknowledgments

It is a great pleasure to thank the individuals and institutions that have provided support during the period of research and writing of this book. I am trying to make my list exhaustive, but I am sure that my memory is not sufficiently good to do justice to everyone whose help and support made this project possible. The institutional support of Yale and Columbia universities was crucial for the research and writing of this book. At Yale, I received a Junior Faculty Fellowship in the Social Sciences, which funded most of the fieldwork for this book along with other funds from the Griswold Committee Fund, the Yale Center for International and Area Studies, the Leitner Program in Political Economy, and the Yale Council on Latin American Studies. At Columbia, I received funding from the Institute of Latin American Studies, the Institute for Social and Economic Research and Policy, and the Center for International Business Education and Research.

My fieldwork benefits from institutional affiliation with the CEPAL in Santiago de Chile, CIDE in Mexico, and the Universidad Di Tella in Argentina. In Chile, Oscar Muñoz, Eugenio Rivera, Hugo Altomonte, Ricardo Ffrech-Davis, Luisa Rangel, and Gonzalo Tapia provided invaluable help. My research in Mexico benefited from the priceless aid of Javier Elguea, Carlos Elizondo, Rafael Fernandez de Castro, Judith Mariscal, Luis C. Ugalde, and Ernesto Zedillo, and it was made more interesting by the friendship of Hilda Rodriguez. In Argentina, I relied on an extensive network of colleagues, among whom I want to mention Manuel Abdala, Marcelo Celani, Juan Carlos Torre, and Carlos Winograd. The help of my father Renato Murillo was also crucial whereas my friends and family made my fieldwork enjoyable. The research assistants who have helped me through the years in Latin America and the United States are Carolina

Curvale, Jorge Gómez, Diego Finchelstein, Barbara Murphy, Constanza Di Nucci, Alejandro Gaggero, Julio Herrera, Catalina Ruiz, Andrés Gómez, Pablo Jammet, Carmen Le Foulon, Cecilia Martinez-Gallardo, Milan Vaishnav, and Virginia Oliveros. Virginia Oliveros bore the weight of helping me finalize the manuscript and producing its index, and I am thankful for her goodwill and good humor through the process. Carmen and Cecilia were also my coauthors in two articles that are partially reproduced with permission from Blackwell and Elsevier in Chapters 2 and 4 of this book: "Political Competition and Policy Adoption: Market Reforms in Latin American Public Utilities," *American Journal of Political Science* 51, no. 1 (January 2007), 120–39, and "Crisis and Policymaking in Latin America: The Case of Chile's 1998–99 Electricity Crisis," *World Development* 34, no.1 (Spring 2004), 1580–96. Ernesto Calvo, Lixin Colin Xu, David Levi-Faur and Jacint Jordana, Manuel Mora y Araujo, Patricio Navia, Carlos Ruffin, James Vreland, Leo Zuckerman, Enrique Zuleta Puceiro and the Project on Elites in Latin America coordinated by Manuel Alcantara were generous in sharing data with me.

Making this research into a book manuscript would have not been possible without the support of Margaret Levi and Lew Bateman as well as the useful feedback of other colleagues who read different versions of this manuscript, under its original name, *Voice and Light*, such as Alison Post, Robert Kaufman, Anna Gryzmala-Busse, Rebecca Weitz-Shapiro, Andrew Schrank (all of whom read it more than once), Stephen Haggard, Bryan Jones, Shannon O'Neill, George Gavrilis, Isabela Mares, Tim Frye, Ira Katznelson, Margaret Levi, Deborah Yashar, Ellen Lust-Okar, and Jeff Wolf. Isabela Alcañiz, Ernesto Cabrera, Ernesto Calvo, Jorge Dominguez, Sebastian Etchemendy, Jeffrey Frieden, Mala Htun, Evelyne Huber, David Levi-Faur, Evan Lieberman, Pauline Jones-Luong, Pablo Pinto, and Mike Tomz read parts of the manuscript and gave me useful comments. Conversations with Alfred Fishlow, John Huber, Ruth Collier, Ernesto Cabrera, Pablo Pinto, and Isabela Mares were crucial in making me clarify my argument. My work also benefited from the feedback received in workshops and seminar presentations at the Departments of Political Science at Rutgers University, Stanford University, Yale University, University of Pennsylvania, University of Chicago, Ohio State University, University of Wisconsin at Madison, University of Michigan, University of Southern California, University of California at Berkeley, ITAM, and CIDE, as well as the Department of Politics at Princeton University, the David Rockefeller Center for Latin American Studies, the Kellogg Institute at the

Acknowledgments

University of Notre Dame, the Watson Institute Colloquium on Comparative Research at Brown University, the Cambridge University Book Workshop at the University of Washington in Seattle, the Group in Politics and Society Workshop, the Conference on Regulation in Latin America: Internationalization and Domestic Politics at CIDE, and the 2004 Meetings of the American Political Science Association and the Latin American Studies Association. I was lucky to have Ruth Homrighaus editing my prose and Emily Spangler helping me with book production. Finally, I acknowledge the Museo Xul Solar-Fundación Pan Klub for granting me the rights to Puerto Azul, the picture on the cover.

As always, my family and friends were crucial in getting me through the exhausting process of writing a book. All my friends were essential in keeping me sane during this extensive process, but I want to mention Mario Pecheny, Pauline Jones-Luong, and Pablo and Dolores Pinto, for their support during the difficult times that coincided with working in this book. As a family, my husband, Ernesto Cabrera, and I were blessed by the arrival of our daughter Anahí while I was working on this project. The unconditional love of Ernesto and Anahí continuously reminded me of what is important in life even when I had to spend weekends in the office working on this manuscript rather than being with them. My mother Susana Rozenblum and my father Renato Murillo have always given me their love and been supportive of my education and work and for that reason, I dedicate this book to them.

Introduction

As democracy was returning to Latin America in the 1980s and 1990s, the citizens of the region's fledgling democracies experienced a paradoxical combination of expanding political rights and shrinking policy choice. Governments of different partisan orientations pursued market-oriented policies. Unsurprisingly, right-wing governments, such as Violeta Chamorro's in Nicaragua or Armando Calderon Sol's in El Salvador, adopted market reforms. Yet, unexpectedly, market-oriented reforms were also accomplished by populist parties that had previously promoted state-led growth and infrastructure nationalization, such as the National Revolutionary Movement (MNR) in Bolivia under Victor Paz Estenssoro, the Peronists in Argentina under Carlos Menem, or Democratic Action (AD) in Venezuela under Carlos Andres Perez. The decline of partisan differences in economic policy making seemed to render the vote inconsequential for economic policy outcomes in the new Latin American democracies.

One of the most symbolic transformations produced by this regional wave of market-oriented reforms was the policy shift of former champions of infrastructure nationalization into privatizers of the same services. Unexpected reformers included political parties that had nationalized public services, such as electricity and telecommunications, claiming the need to defend national sovereignty: nationalization and coverage expansion had been deemed crucial in these two sectors of utmost importance for economic development and the everyday life of households. In the aftermath of the 1980s debt crisis, however, under pressure from financial shortages and technological underinvestment, the formerly populist parties joined their right-wing rivals in seeking to attract private capital and management to these two sectors characterized by capital intensity and technical complexity. In the 1990s, Latin America was the region of the world that

1

moved most quickly in attracting private capital to electricity and telecommunications.

The paradox of apparent policy convergence in the new Latin American democracies provides an opportunity to further our understanding of the effects of partisanship and electoral competition on policy making. Most literature on political parties assumes that linkages between voters and politicians should ideally be based on policy accountability, which requires clear policy differentiation between parties (Hinich and Munger 1994). Hibbs's seminal article (1977) shows how partisan differences on macroeconomic policies (either expansionary for left-wing parties or antiinflationary for right-wing parties), reflecting the interests of constituencies, produced different macroeconomic outcomes in advanced democracies. Alesina (1987) and Alesina et al. (1989) add rational expectations to this partisan theory, thereby predicting that differences in macroeconomic policy should be transitory and should occur immediately after the change of government.

The contemporary literature on globalization emphasizes how increasing capital mobility since the 1970s has reduced the influence of domestic politics on economic policy outcomes by making all countries compete for footloose capital. Following Downs's median voter model (1957), the argument is that politicians are limited in their policy options for fear of creating deleterious economic consequences for constituents that would impinge upon their chances of reelection (Strange 1996; Simmons 1999). Boix (2000) shows how institutional arrangements and increasing capital mobility affect partisan macroeconomic policy effects. Garrett (1998) and Boix (1998) qualify this argument about policy convergence by pointing to partisan differences on economic policy making in advanced democracies into the 1990s, especially with regard to microeconomic policies.

Yet recent studies of policy making in advanced democracies for technically complex and capital-intensive public utilities, such as telecommunications and electricity, emphasize the combination of technological and competitive pressures with institutional effects, and especially the role of technical bureaucracies (Vogel 1996; Thatcher 1999; Bartle 2002; Levi-Faur 2004).[1] Only Schneider et al. (2005) focus on partisanship and

---

[1] Most of these studies of public-utility reforms undertaken in response to globalization pressures in advanced capitalist countries rely on national institutional differences or follow the literature on "varieties of capitalism" (Hall and Soskice 2001), which argues that different institutional configurations generate incentives for economic actors to sustain these diverse equilibria.

find that right-wing governments privatized, whereas left-wing governments defended state-owned telecommunications companies in advanced countries. They conclude that partisan effects declined in the 1990s, however, as privatization became widespread.

When less-developed countries characterized by capital scarcity are included in empirical studies of public-utility policy making, the emphasis shifts to financial incentives (Henisz et al. 2005) and to the role of technocrats – especially U.S.-trained economists – in promoting the diffusion of privatization (Kogut and Macpherson 2004). It seems clear that market-oriented reforms in Latin America were encouraged by financial pressures – including the leverage of international financial institutions and foreign creditors, as suggested by Stallings (1992) – and that they were subject to the influence of experts promoting free-market ideas as a means of access to financial markets (Teichman 2001; Weyland 2005). This study, however, will argue that even when external financial pressures were high, electoral competition and partisan linkages shaped policy making in the reform of Latin American public utilities. That is, electoral choices have implications for economic policy making even when countries are most exposed to the pressures emphasized by the globalization literature, and even in two sectors in which capital intensity and technical complexity heightened the influence of financial markets and expertise, facilitating a worldwide trend toward increasing private participation at the end of the twentieth century (Henisz et al. 2005).

Beneath the veneer of policy convergence, domestic electoral choices did shape policy outcomes in the Latin American reforms of telecommunications and electricity, both at the time of their adoption and in subsequent processes of postreform regulatory change. Credible electoral challenges generated incentives for incumbents to focus on marginal voters. This focus, in turn, favored the status quo at the time of reform and regulatory redistribution to consumers in the postreform period. When their survival in office was not at risk, policy makers focused on core constituencies through partisan policy preferences. These shaped the regulatory content of reforms adopted by cash-strapped incumbents and generated diverse distributive preferences for regulatory change in the postreform period.

To briefly summarize this book's argument, political competition explained the timing of privatization – and reform adoption more generally – whereas the partisan orientation of incumbents shaped the content or design of these policies. That is, the threat of electoral replacement by a challenger who could credibly oppose market-oriented reforms made incumbents less likely to adopt these policies, despite fiscal and technological pressures. In the absence of such a threat (for instance, if the challenger was weak or to the right of the incumbent), Latin American presidents succumbed to fiscal pressures and demands for technological upgrading by adopting market-oriented reforms in public utilities. The content of these policies varied, however, depending on the partisan identity of reformers, because politicians faced different distributive demands from their constituencies, inherited different ideological biases in interpreting technical choices, and relied on different experts for advice. Reformers might be either right-wing politicians who were true believers in the market creed or populists who had previously promoted statist policies for public utilities and pragmatically converted to the new religion only under fiscal strain. In the first case, reforms were more likely to be market conforming, and in the latter, market controlling. An index of regulations regarding foreign investment, entry rules, investment conditions, and degrees of regulatory discretion over pricing and market conflicts provides evidence of this systematic difference in regulatory content.

After market-oriented reforms had been adopted, and regardless of the incumbent's partisan affiliation, electoral competition continued to encourage policy makers to focus on marginal voters when public salience was high, thereby generating incentives for direct regulatory redistribution to residential consumers. At times of low electoral competition, partisanship generated different regulatory preferences for incumbents depending on their role in the initial reform process. The regulatory preferences of the new private providers, in turn, varied according to the original pattern of reform and interindustry technological differences. Political institutions provided diverse forums for and constraints on the articulation of policy makers' and providers' preferences for regulatory outcomes.

Setting the Stage

Latin American policy makers were under dramatic external pressures to adopt market-oriented policies during the last two decades of the twentieth century. Due to the deleterious effects of the 1980s debt crisis on the preexisting model of import substitution industrialization and state-led development, most Latin American countries became avid importers of the new economic policy paradigm associated with market-oriented ideas during this period (Edwards 1995).[2] The effects of capital scarcity were dramatic in this region because the debt crisis closed access to financial markets and triggered capital flight (Frieden 1992). The search for policies to attract scarce capital to fill government coffers fostered the influence of free-market ideas in the policy debate during the 1980s and 1990s, especially in light of the inflationary consequences of financing the deficit through expansive monetary policy. The weight of fiscal deficits, trade imbalances, and debt arrears was so heavy that even politicians who had campaigned on populist platforms often turned into neoliberal presidents after their inaugurations (Stokes 2001). Thus, the pressure of capital scarcity in Latin America and the subsequent adoption of market-oriented reforms across the region seemed to suggest the erosion of partisan policy making and electoral policy influence. Johnson and Crisp (2003), in particular, find that the party of the president had no significant effect on the pace of market reforms in the region during the period from 1985 to 2000. Instead, fiscal deficits and macroeconomic conditions replaced partisan preferences as the variables explaining the pace of adoption of these policies (Stallings and Perez 2000; Weyland 2002a; Corrales 2002).

In analyzing these conclusions, and in particular the incentives and constraints on policy making in Latin America during this period, it is useful to consider reforms in electricity and telecommunications, for a variety of reasons. These two sectors combined capital intensity and technological complexity, which should have increased the influence of two mechanisms identified in the literature as crucial in the diffusion of market-oriented reforms: financial markets and U.S.-trained experts. Moreover, after the debt crisis provoked the largest recession in the region since the Great Depression, politicians found market-oriented policies attracting private investment to these crucial infrastructure sectors appealing. Meanwhile, as electricity and telecommunications services were massively consumed and had a strong potential for expansion due to unmet demand, they provided incentives both for the politicization of prices and access and for the organization of consumers. New democracies allowed elections and the organization of civil societies and thereby opened

---

[2] The countries in the region share a common cultural background that should have facilitated policy diffusion (Simmons and Elkins 2004; Weyland 2005).

both channels for consumers to exercise their voice. Finally, reforms aimed at increasing private participation (through either privatization or new investment) in these sectors generated new political actors – private providers – whose influence on subsequent policy making is crucial to assess the effect of market-oriented reforms on reshaping the patterns of policy making in new democracies.

In choosing to focus on public services, and electricity and telecommunications in particular, for my empirical research, I chose not to investigate other market-oriented reforms that figure prominently in the Latin American literature. Macroeconomic policies did not have such an immediate effect on the organization of new actors, such as consumers, in the newly democratized civil society, and neither did they create a clear set of new private-sector actors, as did the privatization of public utilities.[3] Pension and labor reforms were also subject to policy diffusion but only covered those employed in the formal sector (about half of the regional workforce), thereby facilitating mainly interest group political influence.[4] Health and education were already segmented between private and public provision, and therefore private providers were important policy players, but not players that had been created by market-oriented reforms.[5] Finally, the privatization of water and sanitation services was not as regionally widespread,[6] whereas gas and oil as natural resources were unevenly distributed across countries, thereby reducing the comparability of policy making while generating a more pronounced dynamic in terms of sovereignty perceptions.

Telecommunications and electricity, as capital- and technologically-intensive sectors, had become expensive items in the budgets of financially strapped Latin American states. In particular, massive consumption and heavily subsidized pricing – due to both politicized and antiinflationary policies – made it difficult for state-owned companies to cover the costs

---

[3] Karen Remmer (2002) provides evidence of the effects of partisanship on macroeconomic policy making in Latin America.

[4] On pension reform, see Weyland (2006) for a well-crafted argument on expertise and diffusion and Madrid (2003) for a combination of diffusion and interest group pressures. On labor reform, Murillo (2005) and Murillo and Schrank (2005) combine the effects of diffusion and partisanship through party and transnational alliances of a crucial interest group: labor unions.

[5] The volume edited by Robert Kaufman and Joan Nelson (2004) provides an excellent overview of health and education reforms in the region.

[6] See Post (2007) for an excellent analysis of water privatization in Argentina.

of not only capital investment but also operations.[7] In a context of capital scarcity, attracting private capital to these sectors was appealing for fiscal reasons, as it could stop the drainage of resources and contribute to filling the public coffers, due to the relatively high value of the assets.[8]

Governments around the world used three policies to attract private capital into electricity and telecommunications provision in order to improve supply, facilitate technological development, and reduce the fiscal burden on the state (Levi-Faur 2003, 2004; Henisz et al. 2005):

1. Privatizing by using public sale of shares, transfer of assets, or long-term concession contracts, turning previously state-run companies into privately administered companies.
2. Opening public monopolies to private capital, which generated new Greenfield investments either to supplement limited supply, as in electricity generation, or to provide new services, as in mobile telecommunications.
3. Establishing regulatory authorities to guarantee clear rules for private investors and set standards for service.

According to Henisz et al. (2005), in 1980 only 10 percent of countries in the world had adopted any of these three policies in electricity and 6 percent had adopted any of these policies in telecommunications. By 1991, however, these figures had risen to 41 and 73 percent, respectively. The diffusion of these three reforms in public utilities around the world has been explained by their theoretically positive effects on efficiency (Megginson and Netter 2001), the influence of multilateral agencies pushing for these policies (Henisz et al. 2005), and competitive emulation (Levi-Faur 1999).

---

[7] In the late 1980s, the electricity industry in Latin America was suffering from insufficient incentives for efficiency, price levels that did not cover costs, and lack of investment capacity due to the large fiscal deficits accumulated by state-owned companies (IADB 2001, 165). In telecommunications, because long-term capital investments make up a large fraction of telecommunications costs, the cost of keeping the system running was lower than the cost of making a new investment, contributing to underinvestment by cash-strapped state-owned enterprises in a technologically dynamic sector (Noll 1999, 13).

[8] Telecommunications and electricity provided the two largest shares of world privatization revenues between 1990 and 2000, 36 percent and 16 percent respectively. In Latin America, 75 percent of the value of privatization revenue came from utilities and infrastructure (Chong 2005, 8–9). Noll (1999) argues that the privatization of infrastructure was triggered by its effect on revenues, which could help compensate for the cost of adjustment to market-oriented reforms.

In Latin America, the majority of countries had adopted some of these three policies in both sectors by the end of the twentieth century. The rapid spread of reforms to Latin American publicly owned utilities is not surprising considering the context of capital scarcity and fiscal strain, as well as the increasing influence of international financial institutions as main sources of credit to the region in the aftermath of the debt crisis. Particularly attractive for bankrupt governments was the possibility of meeting the demand for technological modernization and supply expansion while generating fiscal resources through the sale of assets (Noll 1999). Additionally, the potential consequences of these reforms for the average consumer were enormous: for instance, in Argentina in the late 1980s, the availability of a telephone connection determined the price of real estate because the waiting list for new connections was years long, and newspapers published the schedule of daily electricity blackouts so that people could accommodate their lives accordingly.

Even though all Latin American countries suffered similar financial pressures and domestic demands for change in telecommunications and electricity, and even though most of them seemed to react to these pressures in a like manner, there was significant variation in the pace of adoption of market-oriented reforms in these sectors across the region. Not all countries had adopted the three market reforms in both sectors by 2000, and some chose to do so earlier than others. Chile pioneered market reforms in electricity in 1982, for instance, and had started the sale of the main utilities by 1986. In contrast, Mexican policy makers opened electricity generation to private investment in 1992 and set up a regulatory agency in 1995. In 1999 Mexican policy makers attempted to privatize electricity, and they failed in their efforts. Similarly, President Arias in Costa Rica unsuccessfully tried to privatize telecommunications in 1988, the same year in which President Alfonsín failed to achieve a similar goal in Argentina. Yet although the Costa Rican state-owned telephone company remained under public ownership, Argentina privatized its own telephone service two years later.

Reforms also varied in the degree of regulatory control over market outcomes that they established. Although Chile and Mexico privatized telecommunications, Chilean reformers limited regulatory control of market outcomes by avoiding monopolies, restrictions on foreign capital, and investment conditions, thereby choosing a market-conforming regulatory content. Mexican policy makers, meanwhile, attempted to shape market outcomes by establishing a fixed-term monopoly, investment targets, and restrictions on foreign management of the privatized national monopoly, thus preferring a market-controlling reform pattern. Even when opening their markets to private investment and privatizing almost simultaneously, reformers in Panama and El Salvador had different preferences regarding the degree of regulatory control of telecommunications and electricity markets – market controlling in the former case and market conforming in the latter. Panama established monopolies in telecommunications and limits for property concentration in electricity, whereas El Salvador chose to establish no entry rules in either sector.

Finally, after the adopted reform had introduced private providers as important policy constituencies, the degree of redistribution between incumbent private providers, their competitors, and consumers based on pricing, sanctions, and rules governing investment and service varied from one case to another. After privatization, Chile and Mexico reformed their regulation of competition in long-distance communications in the mid-1990s. The increase in competition in long-distance communications (and decline in prices) was much greater in Chile than in Mexico, however, because of different conditions for investment in each country. Similarly, when dealing with crises that affected supply to consumers in the reformed sectors, national responses varied. After privatizing, Brazil, Argentina, and Chile faced electricity blackouts at the end of the 1990s. Brazilian policy makers responded by relying on market mechanisms for rationing. By contrast, the Chilean and the Argentine governments led regulatory efforts to sanction providers and compensate consumers for the scarcity. The scope of compensation consumers received was higher in Argentina than in Chile because the initial Argentine reforms had been market controlling and had thereby given more discretion and sanctioning power to regulators with which to respond.

Implications

Understanding the political dynamics of public-utility reform in Latin America has important implications for our understanding of the political economy of policy reform, distributive politics, and democratic accountability. First, this study improves our understanding of the political economy of market-oriented reforms. It shows the mechanisms by which voters shape the incentives of policy makers in new democracies suffering from capital scarcity. Explaining the adoption and timing of reforms is crucial for understanding the conditions that restrict the policy influence of financial and technological pressures, thereby contributing to a literature emphasizing the survival of domestic political dynamics despite increasing capital mobility. Whereas the literature addressing policy making amid globalization pressures emphasizes either the effects of partisan coalitions (e.g., Boix 1998; Garrett 1998) or institutional incentives (e.g., Hall and Soskice 2001), this book shows that in Latin American new democracies electoral incentives were more influential than institutional effects on policy adoption, whereas partisan coalitions shaped the content of such policy.

These findings may be related to the fragility and flexibility of Latin American institutions vis-à-vis those of advanced democracies (Levitsky and Murillo 2009). In this book, partisanship and electoral competition explains policy choices at the time of market-oriented reforms, as well as subsequent incentives for regulatory redistribution. The mechanisms generating partisan regulatory preferences include not only the distributive consequences of such policies for politicians' constituencies but also parties' ideological legacies and their delegation to allied experts. The role of allied experts, in particular, has been mostly ignored by a literature that focuses on the homogenizing effect of epistemic communities (Haas 1992).[9] The Latin American literature on market-oriented reforms considers experts mostly as agents of policy convergence (e.g., Dominguez 1996; Centeno and Silva 1998; Teichman 2001).[10]

This analysis of partisan policy making is important for the study of Latin American new democracies, which emerged in the context of an economic crisis that sharply restricted their access to capital. In Latin America, partisanship generates incentives for incumbents to devise alternative mechanisms for responding to constituencies' demands and ideological preferences when fiscal constraints limit their ability to follow their original policy preferences. The distributive consequences of partisan institutional choices contributed to easing the reform road by fostering the capacity of unlikely reformers to pursue market-oriented reforms against the expectations of their own core constituencies (Cukierman and Tommasi 1998) while sustaining their linkages to potential reform opponents (Murillo 2001).

---

[9] Studies of earlier periods have looked at the role of experts in generating partisan incentives. See, for instance, Blyth (2002) on the building of social democratic policy options in Sweden since the 1930s.

[10] See Babb (2001) for a more nuanced view of expertise and ideology.

More generally, this book also contributes to the study of distributive politics. In analyzing how electoral incentives shape redistribution, it shows how electoral competition encourages political leaders to favor the preferences of marginal voters. In contexts of low electoral competition, by contrast, the partisan preferences of core constituencies become more influential, as do those of organized interests, such as private providers, in the postreform period. By identifying the conditions under which the preferences of core and marginal voters become influential, this study improves our understanding of democratic redistribution. In particular, it illuminates the role of the middle classes as crucial consumers of public services and marginal voters for right-wing and populist electoral coalitions. Furthermore, it highlights the role of public salience in shaping distributive choices by generating electoral risks for politicians and hindering the influence of private providers in the postreform period, as discussed by Baumgartner and Jones (1993; 2005) in the context of American public policy.

By undertaking a longitudinal comparison of the reform and postreform periods, this work also analyzes policy feedback effects, which have been theorized by the historical institutionalist literature.[11] In doing so, it shows the unexpected effect of technological change in shaping institutional effects on the policy influence of crucial actors. That is, institutional choices, which congealed partisan preferences, shaped the policy preferences of private providers. The effects of these institutional choices, however, depended on the contingency of different available technology in each of the two studied sectors. Hence, in the new Latin American democracies, the impact of institutions was stronger in shaping coordination among economic actors for policy coalitions than in establishing institutional constraints on bureaucratic actors.

Moving beyond political economy, the analysis of electoral incentives on policy choices illuminates our understanding of democratic accountability in a context – that of cash-strapped new democracies – wherein the literature is usually pessimistic about voters' policy influence.[12] This study shows the effect of electoral incentives based on a policy rather than

---

[11] See Pierson (2004) and Thelen (2004) for excellent reviews of the literature, as well as arguments about mechanisms that generate policy feedback effects.

[12] O'Donnell's (1994) seminal study suggested that democratic accountability was weak in the new Latin American democracies, and Stokes (2001) shows that it is limited to retrospective voting – even if it is harsher on policy switchers than for those that kept their word.

a clientelistic calculus between politicians and voters, either marginal or core. Both electoral and partisan policy influences are crucial in providing an accurate assessment of incumbents' avenues of accountability to either marginal or core voters in new democracies.

Finally, by studying policy making in public utilities, this book offers a valuable lens into the politics of market-oriented reforms in Latin America during the 1980s and 1990s, as well as into subsequent changes in public policy preferences. As financial constraints declined, partisan differences started shaping policy adoption again, and the Latin American public began the new century with an increasingly negative view of privatization. This discontent with privatization has been associated with public-utility privatization (Carrera et al. 2005; Bonnet et al. 2006), and with the privatization of telecommunications and electricity in particular (Baker 2007). The negative view of privatization among Latin Americans puzzles the World Bank, as expressed in a study on Latin American infrastructure: "But the public is at odds with the generally positive evaluation of the impact of privatization; in most cases, efficiency has improved, and coverage and quality increased" (World Bank 2005, v). Privatization increased per-capita penetration in telecommunications, reduced the waiting list for the installation of main lines and the faults per main line, and increased digitalization (IABD 2001, 185–6). Private investment in electricity expanded generation capacity, improved the security of supply, and reduced prices for large users (IABD 2001, 165–6). Regardless of the supply and quality of services, though, Baker (2007) finds that increases in the prices of both services explain negative views of privatization. A study by the Inter-American Development Bank, moreover, suggests that regulatory design explains the transfer of rents to private providers in these crucial infrastructure sectors (IADB 2001, 166, 188). In response to this debate, this book provides evidence of how different regulatory choices shaped postreform politics and how public opinion was affected by regulatory redistribution and especially income effects.

Research Design and Road Map

This book employs a research design that treats countries and industries as distinct units of analysis – thereby controlling for national-level and industry-level variation – while using a combination of qualitative and quantitative data analysis. Following the previous literature on public utilities, it studies three market-oriented reforms: privatization, the opening of markets to private investors, and the establishment of regulatory authorities. Yet this study departs from the literature in disaggregating the analysis into the occurrence of reform and its regulatory content in order to assess the extent of external constraints on domestic policy making and to offer a better assessment of the distributive consequences of what is usually perceived as policy convergence. Furthermore, it also compares the process of policy making at the time of reforms (time 1) with that in the postreform period (time 2) to study how the original choices reshaped the political dynamics of policy making – that is, whether the main explanatory variables changed their effect after the adoption of market reforms.

The research design involves theory testing on a dataset including the universe of Latin American reforms in telecommunications and electricity, as well as a comparative research design of case studies in three countries and two sectors. The self-constructed dataset records every instance of privatization, market liberalization, and establishment of regulatory authorities, as well as an index with the general type of reform in both the telecommunications and electricity sectors for all Latin American countries based on the regulations and concession contracts establishing these policies and analyses of their impact. This dataset is used for a quantitative analysis that controls for the effect of different variables measuring external pressures and institutional constraints while assessing the impact of political competition on policy adoption. As the study assumes that all units of analysis were under pressure to adopt market reforms, the use of survival analysis uncovers the factors that shaped the differences in timing across the region.

The comparison of case studies across countries and sectors is based on extensive fieldwork in Argentina, Chile, and Mexico. The comparison controls for the effect of national- and sector-specific factors that have been emphasized by the comparative politics literature on the political economy of market reforms while allowing the identification of causal mechanisms triggered by political competition and partisanship. Being interested in the effect of the partisan identity of reformers, along with the effects of political competition and of earlier choices on subsequent policy making, I chose Argentina, Chile, and Mexico as the cases in order to maximize variation in the independent variable of interest while controlling for political regime and industry-level effects (King, Keohane, and Verba 1994, 139–40). Argentina, Chile, and Mexico are three presidential, middle-income Latin American countries that have similar economic development indicators. Although reformers in these countries had different partisan orientation – political parties with a populist past in Argentina and

Mexico and a right-wing military ruler in Chile – all three were able to impose their policy preferences on content without compromising with the opposition, even though Chile was authoritarian, Mexico was a liberalizing authoritarian system, and Argentina was democratic. Additionally, within each country, national institutions remained constant for the interindustry comparison of reforms. The findings on policy content derived from the case studies in the three countries are confirmed, furthermore, by analysis of the regulations established by telecommunications and electricity reforms in all Latin American countries based on a self-constructed database of reforms in both sectors. More in-depth analysis of the regulations and regulatory content of telecommunications and electricity reforms in two small Central American countries, El Salvador and Panama, provides further evidence that results were not driven by market size in the three middle-income countries studied.

The second part of the book is based on a longitudinal comparison of the same two industries in Argentina, Chile, and Mexico that aims to assess the impact of the original institutional reforms on the political economy of policy making and subsequent regulatory changes until 2005. In the two decades under study (1985–2005), all three countries experienced variation in levels of electoral competition as well as rotation of the party in power, thereby providing longitudinal variation in the values of the main explanatory variables. In the analysis of the postreform period, the comparative case studies are used to test hypotheses about the effect of electoral competition and partisanship on policy makers' preferences and to develop models for the institutional effects of market-oriented reforms on subsequent policy making.

Although these latter factors require further research before the results of this analysis could be generalized, the empirical findings are suggestive, and they provide evidence of which feedback effects were generated by the original policies in combination with contingent technological developments. The longitudinal comparison of the two sectors in three countries is useful, moreover, to test the effects of other factors with potential effects on policy making while keeping national political parties relatively constant. The different institutional settings across the three countries can affect regulatory governance – and the credibility of the original institutions, according to Levy and Spiller (1996) – whereas variation in issue salience and the impact of crises can also affect the policy-making process (Baumgartner and Jones 2005; Henisz and Zelner 2003). Chile and Mexico experienced a transition from authoritarianism to democracy that affected freedom of the press and therefore produced variation in the opportunities for raising the public salience of telecommunications and electricity reform. Argentina and Chile suffered postreform crises of supply in electricity, whereas Argentina and Mexico experienced macroeconomic crises. Hence, the comparison between cases based on the variation of these factors helps illuminate postreform policy-making patterns.

The plan of the book is as follows: Chapter 1 presents the main arguments for explaining policy making at the time of reform adoption and subsequently. Chapter 2 analyzes the effect of political competition on the initial adoption of three market reforms: privatization, the opening of markets to private investment, and the establishment of regulatory authorities. It uses a statistical analysis of all eighteen Latin American countries between 1985 and 2000, which is complemented by case studies of the three policies in the two sectors in Argentina, Chile, and Mexico. Chapter 3 is dedicated to explaining the regulatory content of reforms by using case studies from both sectors in Argentina, Chile, and Mexico, along with a general overview of the region and two shorter case studies from Central America. Chapters 4 and 5 provide in-depth qualitative studies of postprivatization regulatory reform in Chile, where reforms were adopted by right-wing true believers in the free market, and in Argentina and Mexico, where reformers were former populists converted to the market creed. Chapter 6 summarizes the empirical findings while assessesing alternative hypotheses and discussing their implications for the debates on the politics of Latin American policy making. Chapter 7 concludes by analyzing the implications of this study for comparative politics more generally. A full discussion of the data and methodology employed is provided in the electronic appendix to this book at http://www.columbia.edu/~mm2140.

1

Voice and Light

THE POLITICS OF
TELECOMMUNICATIONS
AND ELECTRICITY REFORM

The predominant explanations of market-oriented reforms in Latin America in the late twentieth century emphasize globalization pressures in the form of capital shortages, imported economic ideas, and pressures derived from economic integration. This book incorporates these effects into the analysis of policy making while uncovering the electoral incentives behind reform adoption and content and explaining the evolution of electoral and partisan effects in the immediate postreform period. In so doing, it provides important tools for our assessment of how democratic political processes affect policy making.

This study suggests that citizens' political preferences mattered for public-utility policy making despite external financial pressures at the time of reform (time 1) and, in contexts of high salience, despite the asymmetry of resources and information between residential consumers and private providers in the postreform period (time 2). Political competition and partisan preferences shaped the political dynamics of market-oriented reforms in Latin American public utilities. First, political competition influenced the timing of reforms based on politicians' fear of defection by marginal voters and on the credibility of challengers to provide an alternative policy. Second, the partisan orientation of the incumbent shaped the degree of regulatory control of markets established by reforms based on the demands of core constituencies, politicians' ideological biases, and their delegation to different sets of allied experts. In the postreform period, electoral competition and partisan preferences generated incentives to change the postreform status quo to benefit residential consumers if electoral competition and public salience were high. When they were not, partisanship generated different distributive preferences for

16

policy makers whose regulatory impact depended on how the original reforms and technological developments shaped the preferences of private providers.

The next two sections focus on explaining this argument about electoral competition and partisanship at the time of reform adoption in greater detail, while the following two focus on its application for understanding postreform regulatory redistribution in the electricity and telecommunications sectors.

Disaggregating Market-Oriented Reforms as a Dependent Variable

Unlike scholars who tend to treat market-oriented reforms as discrete historical outcomes, I analyze the policy-making process in terms of adoption and content. Even if both dimensions are simultaneous, each of them entails specific political dynamics for policy making derived from its different potential to affect the public debate. That is, the technically complex choices involved in determining the type of regulations to be adopted are more opaque for the general population than the dichotomous choice regarding whether to adopt a privatization policy.[1] Technical complexity, moreover, requires a larger investment in expertise for electoral challengers, making it easier for politicians to organize their policy positions in a dichotomous way rather than in terms of nuanced technical choices. Hence, there is a theoretical distinction between the adoption and the content or design of public-utility reform based on their potential to have salience with the public and on the influence of expertise in their definition.

The separation between adoption and content also has a methodological explanation. Policy adoption is associated with external financial pressures and domestic demand for services. The stronger the pressures, the sooner reform should be expected to happen. The timing of the occurrence of reform is crucial, as all countries in the region suffered a simultaneous shock, even if the level of the pressures it produced varied across cases (as analyzed in Chapter 2). By contrast, the effect of timing on the regulatory content of reforms is less clear: because there was a lack of

---

[1] As argued by Pierson (1994, 21), "the visibility of effects can also be diminished by increasing the complexity of reforms" to obfuscate voters.

consensus about the best type of regulation, it is difficult to generate hypotheses on whether social learning took place over time.[2]

The next two subsections describe the two dimensions of the dependent variable – adoption and content – as well as the possible range of values they could take at the time of reforms (time 1). Whereas the occurrence of adoption is associated with the coincidence of certain domestic and external pressures at some point in time, the two categories of regulatory content rely on an index of institutional choices made at the time of reform.

Reform Adoption

Policy adoption involves the political decision to "authorize" a reform by either the legislature or the executive (Kaufman and Nelson 2004). As we have seen, this book studies the adoption of three policies in telecommunications and electricity: privatization, the opening of markets to private investment, and the establishment of regulatory authorities separate from the operation of services. By 2000, fifteen of the eighteen Latin American countries had decided to privatize telecommunications (telecommunications in the Dominican Republic had been private since the 1930s), and eleven had private operators in place (including the Dominican Republic). Meanwhile, fourteen countries had taken the decision to sell electricity assets or give them in concession to private companies, and eleven had already privatized them. Sixteen countries had opened the electricity market to private investment. Eleven countries had opened the long-distance telecommunications market to competition among providers different from the original buyers of state-owned assets, and ten had done so for local communications. Finally, the establishment of telecommunications and electricity regulators had been accomplished in all countries, with the partial exception of Paraguay.

As shown in Table 1.1, however, Latin American countries adopted market reforms in public utilities at a different pace. Chile started to adopt the reforms in 1982, while others had not adopted them at all by the end of the century or had dragged their feet in undertaking these policies. The timing of reform is important for distributive and theoretical reasons. These reforms had distributive consequences. For instance, the rate of

---

[2] By 2001, the Inter-American Development bank concluded that although regulation was crucial in the electricity sector, it was unclear how to achieve the right regulations and to make them enforceable, whereas in telecommunications, "traditional regulatory definitions and boundaries [were] out of date" due to technological development (IADB 2001, 178, 187).

Table 1.1. *Public Utility Reform in Latin America**

Country	Privatization Telecom (Law Approved)	Privatization Electricity (Law Approved)	Competition Electricity (Private Capital)	Competition Telecom Local	Competition Telecom Long Distance	Regulatory Agency Electricity	Regulatory Agency Telecom
Argentina	1990	1991	1991	2000	2000	1991	1990
Bolivia	1994	1994	1994	–	–	1994	1994
Brazil	1997	1995	1995	1999	1999	1996	1997
Chile	1982	1982	1982	1982	1994	1978/1985**	1977/1982
Colombia	1994	1994	1991	1998	1997	1994	1994
Costa Rica	–	–	1998	–	–	1996	1996
Dominican Republic	1931***	1999	1999	1990	1990	1999	1998
Ecuador	1993	1993	1998	–	–	1996	1992
El Salvador	1996	1996	1998	1996	1996	1996	1996
Guatemala	1996	1996	1996	1998	1998	1996	1996
Honduras	1995	1994	–	–	–	1994	1995
Mexico	1990	–	1992	1997	1997	1995	1995
Nicaragua	1995	1998	1997	–	–	1995	1995
Panama	1996	1997	1998	–	1996	1994	1995
Paraguay	2000	–	–	–	–	1996	1996
Peru	1993	1992	1994	1999	1999	1996	1995
Uruguay	1991	–	1997	–	–	1997	1993
Venezuela	1991	–	1996	2000	2000	1992	1991

* We only include reforms that happened until 2000, when our dataset ends.

** Deciding which year to use for Chile was complicated by the fact that both the CNE and the Superintendencia have regulatory functions and they were created in different years (1985 and 1978, respectively). Moreover, the CNE had no authority over tariffs until 1982. We decided to use 1985. However, we also ran the regressions excluding Chile (since we do not have data for 1978 or 1982). The results are practically identical.

*** Was private since 1931, when Trujillo sold it to the Compañia Dominicana de Teléfonos (see www.indotel.org.do).

change in the density of telephone lines and electricity consumption per capita in the region increased in most cases after the sale of assets through privatization.[3] Similarly, Chile and Argentina privatized electricity. Seven years later, Chile's generation capacity had expanded by 52 percent and Argentina's by 36 percent.[4] In the latter case, more than 80 percent of the investment in new generation capacity was realized by privatized generators, suggesting that without privatization, investment would have remained stalled.[5] By contrast, Mexico did not privatize electricity but opened generation to private capital in 1992. Ten years later, installed capacity in the public sector grew by 22 percent, with another 6 percent in private generation.

Theoretically, if financial pressures are controlled for, the timing of policy adoption uncovers the conditions that brought some incumbents but not others to make the public decision to authorize market-oriented policies – even when the process of implementation may have lasted longer in some places than others. That is, considering the timing of policy adoption contributes to the literature on globalization pressures on domestic policy making by identifying the conditions that shaped how policy makers responded to similar financial pressures that raised the value of scarce capital. Therefore, this study is crucial to our understanding of policy making in conditions of capital scarcity.

Regulatory Content

The knowledge that policies of a certain type have been adopted in numerous countries often conceals differences in the regulatory content of those policies, and understanding these differences is crucial to any

---

[3] Exceptions are the Dominican Republic in telecommunications and Colombia, Guatemala, and El Salvador in electricity. A difference of means test shows that on average the mean rate of growth for either service among countries that privatized was significantly greater after the public company was sold. This is also true using the number of telephone connections and the level of electricity consumption or the change in these indicators.

[4] In Chile, new installed capacity accounted for 50% of private investment, whereas divestiture was the remaining part (CDEC, http://www.cdec-sic.cl/datos, accessed September 20, 2003). In Argentina, new installed capacity accounted for approximately 25% and privatization for the rest of private investment (IADB 2001, 165) (Informe Annual ENRE 2001, http://www.enre.gov.ar, accessed September 20, 2005).

[5] Murillo and Finchelstein (2004) show that the investment concentrated on the private thermal generation plants, except for the finishing of a hydroelectric plant owned by Argentina, Paraguay, and Uruguay that was not privatized. CRE, http://www.cre.gob.mx/estatidisticas (accessed March 22, 2005).

assessment of the distributive intentions of policy design, as is widely shown by the social policy literature.[6] In defining the content of market-oriented reforms in public utilities, an important dimension relates to the aims of attracting private capital and reducing state involvement in these sectors. Thus, in analyzing policy content, it is important to assess the effect of reforms in undermining or enhancing government capacity to control the industry.[7] The regulations defined at the time of reform are important, moreover, in defining the credibility of the original commitment to private investors, especially regarding the discretion available to governments to deal with subsequent policy making, including their capacity to change supply, price, or quality in the crucial infrastructure sectors of telecommunications and electricity.

This study uses a series of indicators to build two categories based on the degree of government capacity to regulate subsequent outcomes in telecommunications and electricity: "market-controlling" and "market-conforming" regulations. The former emphasizes government regulatory capacity and the latter a lack of government discretion in shaping sectoral outcomes. These two categories also capture an essential ideological variation in attitudes toward the role of states and markets that continued to organize interparty competition at the elite level in most countries of the region into the late 1990s (Rosas 2005) and has reemerged as a focus point of regional politics in the new century (Cleary 2006). The ideological relevance of this divide builds on the traditional coincidence between preferences for a more proactive state and support from constituencies that are more dependent on state subsidies on the one hand and those better-off constituencies that prefer a "guardian state" on the other hand.

Table 1.2 summarizes the indicators used to define each ideal type of reform content. These indicators include regulations that show political preferences sustained at the expense of financial costs, even in a context of capital scarcity. Such market-controlling regulations include restrictions on foreign capital, investment requirements imposed on new investors

---

[6] The literature on welfare states in advanced democracies emphasizes different types of "content" or institutional configuration for social insurance policies based on partisan preferences of incumbents (Iversen and Wren 1998, Esping-Anderson 1990; Huber and Stephens 2001) or policy actors (Mares 2003).

[7] These two categories of government discretion for shaping outcomes in these industries resemble Vogel's (1996, 17) "undermining government control of the industry" and "enhancing government control of the industry."

Table 1.2. *Regulatory Content*

Indicators	Market Conforming	Market Controlling
1. Limits to foreign capital	No	Yes
2. Investment requirements	No	Yes
3. Rules to entry for these markets	No	Yes
4. Regulatory discretion for setting consumer prices	Limited	High
5. Regulatory discretion for setting the cost of interproviders services	Limited	High
6. Regulatory discretion for solving market conflicts between providers	Limited	High
7. Regulatory discretion to solve conflicts between providers and consumers	Limited	High
8. Bureaucratic expansion	Limited	High

(such as quantitative targets or coverage commitments), regulations for entry into the new markets (e.g., rules forbidding vertical and horizontal integration), regulatory discretion in setting consumer prices and interprovider fees (i.e., transmission in electricity and interconnection in telecommunications), and the granting of regulatory powers for solving conflicts between providers or between them and consumers, rather than relying on arbitration or the courts.[8] Such conditions are likely to require a relatively large regulatory bureaucracy to administer the broad regulatory powers they create, and they imply a high degree of regulatory discretion in changing the rules of the game for investors after they have deployed their capital. Regulations of this type, which show distrust in market outcomes, are characterized as market controlling. The opposite set of indicators suggests that governments prefer to reduce their political discretion and rely on market outcomes, thereby solving market imperfections only after they have occurred. They indicate, therefore, a market-conforming regulatory content.

Choices about regulatory content have diverse distributive consequences. The Chilean electricity reforms were market conforming and those of Argentina were market controlling. The lack of entry rules in Chile

---

[8] The first two regulations are associated with the sale of assets; the second and the third to the opening of markets to private investment, which can happen even without the sale of assets; and the latter conditions to the powers of the separate regulatory agency.

produced a higher level of property concentration than in Argentina, where reformers established limits on vertical and horizontal integration. A decade after privatization, the degree of concentration in electricity generation was four times higher in Chile than in Argentina. These levels of property concentration allowed the Chilean provider Endesa to reap higher profits than its competitors in the generation sector except for during two periods of drought (Serra 2003, 35), whereas such a dominant player did not emerge in Argentina.

Voice and Light: The Political Dynamics of Market-Oriented Public-Utility Reforms

This section presents the argument about the effect of political competition and partisanship on policy making for public-utility reform at a time when politicians had little room to respond to electoral pressures and ideological convictions. In doing so, it takes seriously the literature on capital mobility, which points to the constraints on domestic policy preferences in conditions of capital scarcity to explain the convergence of Latin America toward market-oriented reforms in the 1980s and 1990s. It shows that even considering these pressures, political competition influenced incumbents' incentives for policy adoption, whereas their partisan identity shaped policy content. The main hypotheses derived from this argument imply that political competition should have made reform adoption less likely, and the partisan orientation of the incumbent should have shaped reforms in a market-conforming or market-controlling direction.

Political Competition and Citizens' Voice in Policy Adoption

Political competition shapes incumbents' incentives for policy adoption, even considering the external constraints on policy making emphasized by the globalization literature. That is, even when strong financial pressures constrain politicians, political competition gives a voice to Latin American citizens in shaping incumbents' reform incentives. This voice is especially remarkable as Latin American market-oriented reforms have traditionally been explained as products of the influence of international financial institutions, U.S.-trained technocrats, and foreign investors.

International financial institutions, such as the World Bank and the International Monetary Fund (IMF), promoted a policy package of free-market reforms labeled as the Washington Consensus (Williamson 1994). Even policy makers who did not prefer these policies adopted them due to their need for funding (Vreeland 2003).[9] After the debt crisis, these institutions heightened their policy influence in Latin America because they were the main source of credit, their lending opened access to private capital, and their policy conditionality was included in debt renegotiation schemes, such as the Brady Plan (Edwards 1995).[10] Capital scarcity also heightened the influence of financial investors. In particular, they exercised indirect leverage through the credit rating institutions that qualified government bonds, which assessed microeconomic policies in making their evaluations (Mosley 2003, 17).[11] Yet financial institutions and investors were more concerned that Latin American nations raise revenue to meet their debt-service obligations than they were about the specific regulatory content of public-utility reforms.[12]

The Latin American literature on technocrats emphasizes their role as domestic advocates of the same market-oriented reforms across the region, suggesting that their influence on the policy agenda resulted from their linkages to financial institutions and markets that could open doors to credit (Centeno and Silva 1998; Teichman 2001). Governments often used the appointment of technocrats to signal to foreign investors their willingness to undertake market-oriented reforms (Schneider 1998). As discussed in the following text, however, experts' tenure was highly dependent on political appointments, which led to divergence in regulatory options for policy makers.

This study does not deny the strength of financial and technological pressures to bring about reform adoption, but it focuses on political competition to understand how incumbents constrained by fiscal insolvency sometimes failed to adopt the market-oriented policies preferred by

---

[9] The IMF charter grants this agency the ability to seek policy changes in debtor countries, and in the 1990s the actual imposition of conditionality and the average number of terms imposed on borrowing countries rose (Buira 2003).

[10] Callaghy (1997) notes that organizations such as the Paris Club, which organizes creditor countries, required that countries be in good standing with the IMF before debt renegotiation could begin during this period.

[11] Mosley (2003, 124) notes that a good investment record in developing countries is associated with the existence of privatization programs, labor market deregulation, and other microeconomic policies.

[12] Even though technocrats in the World Bank and the IADB cared about regulatory content, they had no power in lending decisions, which were made based on macroeconomic aggregates and then assigned to diverse sectors after negotiations with borrowers.

24

institutions deciding on their access to scarce capital. Political competition affected the process of policy adoption by shaping the distribution of power in the political system, generating a potential electoral risk for incumbents, and increasing the incentives of viable and credible challengers to block the reform.

The institutional effect of power distribution has been widely discussed in the literature on policy making.[13] In particular, when the opposition controls the legislature and when the aggregate preferences of legislators are ideologically distant from those of the executive, an incumbent's policy initiative declines rapidly, making reform adoption unlikely (or at best subject to compromise). Conversely, the larger the legislative contingent of the incumbent party, the easier policy adoption should be, as the party can impose the preferences of a fiscally constrained executive on Congress.

In a presidential system, the president suffers the brunt of financial and technological pressures for policy adoption because he or she is in charge of the budget, regardless of his or her ideological preferences about particular policies. Johnson and Crisp (2003) show that the ideology of the president is not a good predictor of the adoption of market-oriented reform in Latin America. By contrast, challengers (the second largest party) have no fiscal responsibility and can denounce proposed government policies to bolster their calls for replacing incumbents and winning the take-all prize of the presidency.[14] The challenger party has incentives to denounce the executive in order to differentiate itself in the electoral competition. For that reason, the ideology of challengers is important in defining their credibility in providing alternative policies to market-oriented reforms. The electoral credibility of challengers depends on shrinking power differentials between challengers and incumbents and on challengers' relative ideological positions. Shrinking margins between parties increase electoral risks for the incumbent as well as attention to challengers' criticisms. The challengers'

---

[13] Tsebelis (2003) provides a general argument based on veto power, while Haggard and McCubbins (2001) apply this argument to economic policy making in presidential systems. Cox and McCubbins (2001), in particular, consider the effects of political competition in their discussion of the political separation of purpose that complements the structural separation of powers in presidential systems, thereby generating not just the possibility of veto points but also the incentives for actors to exercise their veto power.

[14] Presidential elections are crucial in Latin America because they define the head of office, the main policy direction, and the main source of resources – including fiscal revenue and patronage.

relative ideological position affects the credibility of their attempts to use market-oriented reforms to improve their electoral prospects.

When electoral results reduce power differentials between incumbent and challenger or as surveys announce the proximity of such an outcome, incumbents feel the threat of replacement, which discourages them from adopting market-oriented policies. This inference is based on two assumptions about political competition: (1) that it changes actors' institutional preferences (Moe 1990; Jones and Weinthal 2001; Grzymala-Busse 2007), and (2) that it enhances the policy influence of marginal voters in winner-take-all settings (James 2000; McGillivray 2003). That is, as competition increases, the perception that voters who are discontent with the idea of market-oriented policies may vote against the incumbent constitutes a powerful deterrent for the incumbent against adopting these policies. As challengers' electoral viability grows, moreover, so does their capacity to raise issue salience, potentially increasing electoral effects. That is, viable electoral competition can endogenously increase the public salience of a policy debate and thus the potential electoral costs of policy adoption.[15] Grzymala-Busse (2007) suggests that viability (along with credibility) increases the stakes of challengers in the post-Communist world and amplifies their voice in policy debates.

The preferences of marginal voters regarding utility reform in the early 1990s are hard to assess due to the lack of systematic comparative data, although, as discussed in the following section, a socioeconomic bias seems to have driven privatization views. There is also *ex post* evidence suggesting electoral costs derived from these policies. As Stokes (2001) has shown, strategic politicians prefer to run on populist electoral platforms, even when they adopt market-oriented policies after their inauguration. This behavior was explained by Lora and Olivera (2005) in an analysis of presidential and legislative elections for all eighteen Latin American countries except for Panama in the period between 1985 and 2000. They found that in presidential elections, "the electorate is highly sensitive to one economic outcome – inflation – and strongly rejects the adoption of pro-market policies" (23). They inferred from their findings that the adoption of these policies brought positive electoral payoffs only when implemented in periods of high inflation, as argued by Weyland (1998). These findings suggest that in a context of declining popular

---

[15] I thank Evelyne Huber for bringing this point to my attention.

support, politicians are likely to perceive the introduction of promarket policies as risky.[16]

The ideology of the challenger is important in defining the credibility of political competition to oppose market-oriented reforms, as it provides a signal to voters. Challengers' credibility in denouncing market-oriented reforms is conditional upon their ideological position relative to that of the incumbent and upon linkages to reform losers, such as labor unions, which also provide mechanisms for reform obstruction.[17] The credibility of the challenger is enhanced by being to the ideological left of the incumbent in the policy spectrum and by a lack of previous policy cooperation with the incumbent. In Latin America during the studied period, the ideological reputation of legislators tended to be a reliable predictor of policy adoption (Johnson and Crisp 2003), whereas legislators' surveys from the mid-1990s confirm that the privatization of public services produced divided opinions between left- and right-wing legislators (PELA 2005).[18]

Thus, criticism of market-oriented reforms is more credible when voiced by challengers to the left of incumbents than by right-wing rivals. These center or left-wing parties, moreover, were more likely to be associated with reform losers, such as labor unions, who were willing to mobilize against policy adoption. Additionally, ideological polarization between the incumbent politicians and their challengers is usually an indicator of their prior difficulty in constructing legislative policy coalitions, and thus polarization enhances the challenger's credibility in offering a policy alternative.[19]

---

[16] Politicians could be afraid of price effects, as suggested by their resistance to abandoning cross-subsidies, or of the controversial character of foreign investment in Latin American history given the lack of domestic capital to provide the necessary investment.

[17] Kitschelt (2001) points to the effect of the relative ideological position of challengers on an incumbent's decision to pursue social policy reform in Europe. Additionally, if parties associated with losers, such as labor unions, have an advantage in adopting these policies because they can prevent resistance from their allies (Murillo 2001), the same parties in opposition have an advantage in obstructing these policies based on the organized efforts of the same allies.

[18] In nine of fourteen countries, the difference in means on their views on a three-point scale was significant. The question asked was the following: "Which of the following criteria summarizes better your view on the privatization of public services? I would privatize all public services, I would privatize only public services that are not profitable, I would privatize only those public services that do not affect large portions of the population." The three answers were given values of 3, 2, and 1 respectively.

[19] Frye (2006) shows that ideological polarization undermines economic policy cooperation in the former communist countries by producing policy swings.

(a)

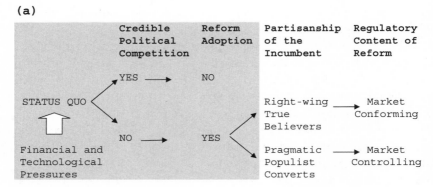

Figure 1.1a Political competition and reform adoption (time 1)

Therefore, the first hypothesis is that credible political competition makes the adoption of market-oriented reforms less likely (see Figure 1.1a). This negative effect can be explained by institutional veto points, by incumbents' fear of electoral costs, and as a consequence of challengers' mobilization against these policies. As a result, we should expect market-oriented reforms to have been less likely to be adopted when a government was divided, the margin between the incumbent party and the challenger (the main party in the opposition in a presidential system) was shrinking, and the incumbent and challenger were ideologically polarized or the challenger was to the left of the incumbent. All these variables can change over time even within the same presidential administration, as shown by the empirical analysis in the next chapter.

Political competition is expected to have a negative effect on policy adoption measured as the occurrence of reform, which is a dichotomous variable. Because between 1985 and 2000 all Latin American countries were suffering external pressures to adopt market-oriented policies, in addition to domestic demand to improve the supply and technology of telecommunications and electricity, it was expectable that the adoption of reforms should have occurred regardless of the partisan preferences of the governments in office. Yet conditions that made reform adoption less likely will be shown to have counteracted these proreform pressures. The timing of adoption in each country is crucial to measure the impact of different factors on policy adoption. That is, *ceteris paribus*, the negative effect of credible political competition should have prevented the authorization of reform in a given year, but as political competition changed over time, reform adoption could happen subsequently, controlling for external proreform pressures, and implementation might have taken even longer. By the 2000s, the regional change in the policy tide, heightened by financial buoyancy due to the improvement of the terms of trade, indicated the weakening of external pressures for reform adoption.

Casting Light on Policy Choice: Partisan Orientation and Policy Content

The consensus of the literature is that incumbents' ideology had no effect on whether market-oriented reforms, including privatization, were adopted in Latin America in the 1980s and 1990s (Johnson and Crisp 2003; Biglaiser and Brown 2003). That is, policy makers on both sides of the political spectrum adopted the same policies, either because they preferred them or because they were subjected to financial pressures – as shown by the empirical evidence in the following chapter. Yet this book shows not only that challengers' ideology mattered for the policy effects of political competition, but also that by casting a different light on how politicians saw their policy choices, the incumbent's ideology shaped the regulatory content of reforms. This effect was further reinforced by policy makers' internalization of constituencies' distributive preferences and linkages with different types of allied experts. This argument implies that two broad types of political coalitions adopted the same policies with different regulatory content in public utilities. When former populists who pragmatically converted to the new creed adopted market-oriented policies, their content was market controlling. Reformers who were right-wing true believers chose market-conforming regulatory content.

The type of reformers can be inferred from their prior policies in public utilities, because these provide indicators of their ideas about sector development and their linkages with organized interests, constituencies, and allied experts. Right-wing incumbents who were true believers in the market had not promoted state intervention in the past. By contrast, former macroeconomic populists who pragmatically converted to the market creed had previously supported state-led development and economic nationalism through state ownership and nationalization.[20]

---

[20] According to Dornbush and Edwards (1991, 9), "economic populism" takes an approach to economics that "emphasizes growth and income redistribution and deemphasizes the risks of inflation and deficit finance, external constraints, and the reaction of economic agents to aggressive nonmarket policies." Economic populism has been pursued by left-wing and political populist governments in Latin America.

Differences in the regulatory content of reforms helped policy makers pursue diverse distributive preferences even when adopting policies with the same name.

The different constituencies, ideological beliefs, and technical cadres resulting from the prereform policy preferences of each political coalition produced partisan differences in policy content. Each coalition has different constituencies with diverse distributive preferences and policy demands.[21] Constituencies' policy preferences depend on the effect of public-utility reform on them. Upper-class voters, such as businesspeople, are more likely to be large users of utilities who favor the adoption of privatization reform. They should benefit from price rebalancing, as they bear the cost of cross-subsidies to residential consumers; benefit from competition, given their size; and be expected to seek improvements in quality and technological upgrading.[22] Middle-class voters include residential users who receive their access to public utilities at subsidized prices and who thus may be hurt by price rebalancing or the price hikes needed to pay for new technology, but these voters may also be willing to pay for access or quality, even if price effects are large relative to their income. These voters, thus, should be the most likely to change their view about the desirability of adopting privatization policies. Finally, lower-class voters usually do not have access to public-utility services, especially to telecommunications services, and should be less favorable to policies that would not benefit them immediately, as they are not attractive as customers and in the case of electricity may endure adverse income effects following privatization reform if they pay subsidized rates or steal energy.[23] Hence, middle-class voters are more likely than upper- or lower-class voters to be marginal voters facing a trade-off of price for access/quality,

---

[21] The literature on partisan policy making in the advanced countries (Boix 1998; Garrett 1998; Huber and Stephens 2001) as well as that of Latin America (Kaufman and Segura-Ubiergo 2001; Remmer 2002) infers partisan effects on economic and social policies based on who the constituencies of the incumbent party are.

[22] Price rebalancing, which ends cross-subsidies and relates prices to cost, is necessary to introduce competition among private providers in these sectors. Due to heavy subsidies to residential users in the prereform period, it implies increasing prices for residential users and those using local telephone service and reducing prices for large users and those using long-distance telephone service.

[23] Hernandez (2007, 88) documents how, in 2003, nontechnical electricity losses caused by illicit consumption and meter manipulation accounted for 15% of the energy produced by Mexican state-owned electricity company Luz y Fuerza del Centro (LyF) serving Mexico City and its surroundings.

and thus their support can be crucial at times of increasing electoral competition.[24]

Public opinion data on the privatization of Argentine telephones from 1989 to 1993 gathered by Ipsos-Mora y Araujo suggests that this assumption is correct. Table 1.3 presents the result of a logistic regression with robust standard errors regarding the likelihood that respondents approved of the privatization of telephone service. It shows that the higher the socioeconomic status of the respondent, the more positive his or her views were about privatization, controlling for measures of political participation, such as party and union membership, and vote choice in the 1989 presidential election. The first model shows that voting for the president, Carlos Menem, increased the likelihood of the citizen's holding positive views of telephone service privatization – even though Menem campaigned on a populist platform – and so did voting for the right-wing candidate, Alvaro Alsogaray, who promised privatization, and feeling optimism about where the country was heading. The second model adds time and regional fixed effects, since the data spans 1989 to 1993 and covers diverse regions in the country. The socioeconomic effect on privatization views is robust to regional and time fixed effects.[25] The third model adds an interaction between voting for Menem and socioeconomic status, which has the expected positive sign (suggesting that the richer his voters, the happier they were with the privatization of telephone service), but it is not significant. The fourth model adds fixed effects. In these last two models, voting for Menem loses its significant effect, but socioeconomic status continues to have significant effects in the expected direction.

The Ipsos-Mora y Araujo data does not allow for a comparison with electricity privatization, because the wording of the electricity question was not whether the citizen agreed with privatization but rather whether he or she agreed with the manner in which the privatization was pursued. The earliest Latinobarometro data on this issue is from 1995 and includes only eight Latin American countries, but it suggests similar trends if we use education as a proxy for socioeconomic status for electricity and

---

[24] As in Baker (2003), the income of the Latin American middle classes will vary across countries, but their place in the income distribution should not vary across countries, as private providers operate within national markets.

[25] The magnitude of effects thus varies across time and location. For instance, in July 1992, a lower-class respondent in the City of Buenos Aires had a probability of agreeing with telephone privatization of 0.36, a middle-class respondent of 0.56, and a high-class respondent of 0.74.

Table 1.3. *Likelihood of agreement with the privatization of telephones in Argentina (Somerc)*

	Model 1	Model 2	Model 3	Model 4
		With Date and Regional Dummies		With Date and Regional Dummies
Socio-economic	0.335	0.354	0.286	0.323
status	[7.44]**	[9.69]**	[6.02]**	[6.59]**
Menem 1989	0.157	0.301	−0.172	0.088
	[3.15]**	[5.57]**	[0.95]	[0.40]
Alsogaray 1989	0.468	0.274	0.438	0.27
	[3.48]**	[2.62]**	[3.07]**	[2.51]*
Party Affiliation	0.03	0.026	0.027	0.024
	[0.83]	[0.93]	[0.78]	[0.89]
Union Affiliation	0.113	0.052	0.116	0.055
	[1.59]	[0.84]	[1.65]	[0.87]
Optimism	−0.717	−0.721	−0.718	−0.72
	[13.98]**	[15.28]**	[13.81]**	[15.06]**
Menem 1989 * SES			0.12	0.077
			[1.82]	[1.01]
Constant	0.876	1.157	1.029	1.258
	[3.05]**	[4.58]**	[3.88]**	[5.21]**
Observations	7009	7009	7009	7009
Pseudo R-square	0.0785	0.1058	0.0792	0.106
Correctly classified	72.71%	73.86%	72.76%	73.98%

Robust z statistics in brackets
* significant at 5%; ** significant at 1%

Note: Model 2 and Model 4 include indicators for region and date of the survey that are not shown in the table due to space limitations. The cities covered by the survey were: Buenos Aires City, Great Buenos Aires, Córdoba, Rosario, Mendoza, Paraná, Rural Tucumán, Urban Tucumán, Bahía Blanca, Salto (left-out category), Olavarría, and Neuquén. The survey was conducted in the following dates: October 1989, March 1990, April 1990, August 1990, December 1990, August 1991, March 1992, July 1992, May 1993, August 1993 (left-out category).

telecommunications. The question asked was whether the respondent preferred private or state ownership of either service. The logistic regressions with robust standard errors in Tables 1.4a and 1.4b show the significant positive effect of education years on the odds that respondents preferred private ownership in both sectors, whether we consider the education of respondents (models 1 and 3) or that of the head of the

Table 1.4a. *Likelihood of Agreement with Private versus State Ownership of Telephones (Latinobarometro)*

	Model 1	Model 2	Model 3	Model 4
			With Country Dummies	With Country Dummies
Respondent's Education	0.29		0.261	
	[6.15]**		[5.95]**	
Head of the household's Education		0.173		0.139
		[4.09]**		[3.62]**
Ideological Self Position	0.004	−0.014	0.003	−0.016
	[0.14]	[0.60]	[0.13]	[0.61]
Country's Future Situation	0.163	0.147	0.14	0.1
	[4.35]**	[3.90]**	[2.47]*	[1.93]
Future Personal Situation	0.096	0.13	0.12	0.156
	[2.25]*	[3.45]**	[2.61]**	[4.66]**
Closeness to Some Political Party	−0.208	−0.221	−0.128	−0.153
	[2.49]*	[2.53]*	[2.74]**	[2.84]**
Pro-Market Views	0.278	0.256	0.233	0.21
	[3.86]**	[3.94]**	[4.32]**	[5.23]**
Political News	0.115	0.079	0.094	0.052
	[1.72]	[1.22]	[1.68]	[0.80]
Constant	−2.836	−2.052	−2.606	−1.587
	[6.84]**	[7.65]**	[7.58]**	[9.32]**
Pseudo R-square	0.0696	0.0447	0.1176	0.0855
Correctly classified	63.31%	60.86%	66.75%	63.99%
Observations	4328	2713	4328	2713

Robust z statistics in brackets
* significant at 5%; ** significant at 1%

Note: Model 3 and Model 4 include country indicators (not shown in the table). The countries covered by the survey were: Argentina, Brazil, Chile, Mexico, Paraguay, Peru (left-out category), Uruguay, and Venezuela.

household (models 2 and 4). Models 3 and 4 include geographic fixed effects. For both sectors, this effect remains significant even when controlling for other attitudinal variables and measures of political participation and awareness. As expected, in both sectors, promarket views (measured by using an index of general views on state intervention) had a significant positive effect, and so did the respondent's optimism about the country and about his or her personal situation, but ideological self-identification and political information had no effect, whereas proximity to any political party had a negative effect.

Table 1.4b. *Likelihood of Agreement with Private versus State Ownership of Electricity (Latinobarometro)*

	Model 1	Model 2	Model 3	Model 4
			With Country Dummies	With Country Dummies
Respondent's Education	0.211		0.192	
	[6.27]**		[6.45]**	
Head of the household's Education		0.141		0.119
		[3.86]**		[3.25]**
Ideological Self Position	0.019	−0.007	0.01	−0.018
	[1.13]	[0.44]	[0.54]	[1.21]
Country's Future Situation	0.096	0.1	0.071	0.074
	[2.87]**	[1.41]	[2.37]*	[1.17]
Future Personal Situation	0.198	0.161	0.196	0.167
	[3.78]**	[2.54]*	[4.15]**	[3.16]**
Closeness to Some Political Party	−0.2	−0.172	−0.105	−0.088
	[3.36]**	[2.91]**	[3.41]**	[2.57]*
Pro-Market Views	0.319	0.282	0.273	0.231
	[4.98]**	[3.97]**	[5.39]**	[4.18]**
Political News	0.137	0.06	0.109	0.029
	[2.08]*	[1.14]	[2.04]*	[0.57]
Constant	−3.177	−2.345	−2.772	−1.835
	[8.42]**	[7.84]**	[8.94]**	[8.61]**
Pseudo R-square	0.0594	0.0388	0.1028	0.0768
Correctly classified	65.06%	63.06%	67.62%	65.88%
Observations	4336	2723	4336	2723

Robust z statistics in brackets
* significant at 5%; ** significant at 1%

Note: Model 3 and Model 4 include country indicators (not shown in the table). The countries covered by the survey were: Argentina, Brazil, Chile, Mexico, Paraguay, Peru (left-out category), Uruguay, and Venezuela.

The magnitude of effects changed by country: In Chile, which had already privatized both telecommunications and electricity, by using the education of the respondent in the model with fixed effects, the probability of preferring private ownership of telephone service was 0.24 for an illiterate respondent but 0.40 for one with an incomplete secondary education and 0.60 for one with a university degree. For electricity, the probabilities of preferring private rather than state ownership were 0.19 for an illiterate respondent, 0.30 for one with an incomplete secondary education, and 0.43 for one with a university degree. In Brazil, which adopted electricity privatization in the year of the survey and passed a law privatizing telephone service two years afterward, the differences are similar.[26] The probability that an illiterate respondent preferred private to state ownership of telephones was 0.22 and 0.24 for electricity. For a respondent with an incomplete education, the probability was 0.38 for telephones and 0.37 for electricity, and for one with a university degree these figures were 0.58 for telephones and 0.51 for electricity.

Constituencies are loyal to parties based on the parties' prior policies – at least until a change in the party system modifies the supply of available options. These prior policies also generate ideological legacies and linkages with allied experts. At the time of reforms, policy makers pay attention to distributive consequences while using their ideological legacies and delegation to allied experts to deal with uncertainty about the future consequences of their policy choices. The effects of ideology and allied experts on dealing with uncertainty contrast to those of "mimesis" – a response to uncertainty emphasized by Di Maggio and Powell (1983) – or even social learning, which requires the passage of time to assess effects. The novelty and technical complexity of public-utility reform generates uncertainty about the medium- and long-term effects of institutional choices on performance (e.g., prices, coverage, quality). As a result, politicians' ideological legacies and delegation to allied experts inform their opinion on the expected distributive consequences of public-utility policy choices.

Ideological legacies provide politicians with prior rules to follow in interpreting the distributive consequences of new choices, even if those are derived from a new menu of available options generated by market-oriented reforms.[27] Ideological legacies help politicians interpret policy choices presented by experts while generating preferences for institutional

---

[26] The proximity to the timing of reform is important because of 1,200 Brazilian respondents, 60% preferred state ownership and 32% favored private ownership for telephones and electricity in this 1995 survey.

[27] Fiske and Taylor (1991) describe the importance of "schemas" as cues for understanding new situations and processing new information in social cognition. Schemas are derived from prior interests, experience, and practices, which in the case of politicians should be related to their prior political experience. Lodge and Hammill show the effect of partisan schemas in processing information and argue that they enable individuals "to make inferences from incomplete data" and "provide the basis for making more confident decisions and predictions" (1986, 506). Therefore, partisan schemas should be useful in interpreting the distributive consequences of novel policies with uncertain distributive effects.

forms similar to the ones they perceive as having worked in the past. As a result, policy makers have different interpretations of the same facts or diverse expectations about the effects of the same institutional choices.

Beyond the clues provided by ideological legacies, politicians delegate to experts the definition of technically complex choices presented to them. Experts share epistemic communities, increasing the homogeneity of their policy views, which makes them ideal as agents for policy diffusion.[28] Yet, as described by Weyland (2006, 46–7), the bureaucracies of the Latin American region diverge starkly from Weberian principles, and technical experts face uncertain tenure. He argues that career incentives make experts rely on inferential shortcuts due to their short time horizons. In the absence of a civil service, their tenure depends on political appointments. These, in turn, generate incentives for experts to internalize the expected distributive effects of policy choices on the constituencies of the politicians who appointed them (and within their time horizons). As a result, the effect of partisanship is reinforced by politicians' delegation to allied experts, whom they trust have internalized their distributive goals based on prior linkages established in political think tanks, during earlier administrations, or through other shared experiences.[29]

Therefore, the two political coalitions have different constituencies, ideological legacies, and allied experts. The core constituencies of right-wing true believers are upper- and middle-class voters, a coalition that is more favorable to market-oriented reforms than the poor and middle-class voters who back pragmatic populist converts. Hence, in setting privatization policies, right-wing true believers are more likely to have a preference for price rebalancing according to costs, which favors large users and promotes competition for investment following market demand because it benefits the most affluent consumers. They are less likely to support

---

[28] According to Haas, "an epistemic community is a network of professionals with recognized expertise and competence in a particular domain and an authoritative claim to policy-relevant knowledge within that domain" (1992, 3). Its members share normative and causal beliefs, notions of validity, and a common policy enterprise.

[29] Politicians are more likely to delegate to experts in a context of high policy uncertainty because the latter have information about technical policies whose consequences are hard for politicians to understand. The use of partisan ties in the selection of technocrats is similar to the application of the ally principle, by which politicians are more likely to delegate to bureaucrats who share their preferences. See the summary of Huber and Shipan (2006) on the effect of policy uncertainty and the ally principle on the incentives for delegating to bureaucrats, which I am applying here to technocrats.

subsidies for poorer users. By contrast, pragmatic populist converts are more likely to prefer subsidized prices, even at the expense of competition, to ensure access to consumers who are not as attractive to providers. They are also likely to prefer coverage expansion to consumers for which demand-driven incentives are insufficient to attract investment.

The policy preferences derived from constituencies' demands are consistent with those derived from their ideological legacies, as processes of redistribution from richer to poorer users had previously relied on state intervention. The ideological legacies of right-wing true believers should make them distrustful of state redistribution, generating preferences for limited regulatory powers and discretion (to reduce the consequences of political capture), limited bureaucracies, and the maximization of market incentives for investment. By contrast, the ideological legacies of former populists, derived from a previous use of the state for redistribution to their constituencies, should make them favor more extensive regulatory powers and discretion, larger bureaucracies, and regulations to control market outcomes according to political goals.[30]

In sum, as true believers, right-wing reformers should favor no entry rules, no investment conditions, no universal service obligations, no discrimination against foreign investors, and a regulatory authority with limited powers and discretion, funding, and personnel. That is, they should prefer a market-conforming content for the market-oriented reforms. By contrast, as pragmatic converts, populist reformers are more likely to prefer the establishment of rules for entry to promote coverage expansion or lower prices, investment conditions to promote access, universal service obligations to subsidize the provision of services to unattractive users, more extensive state regulatory powers and discretion, a larger bureaucracy, and discrimination against foreign capital – that is, a market-controlling content. Therefore, the second hypothesis is that based on the effect of constituencies, ideological legacies, and allied experts, former populists converted to the market creed should prefer a market-controlling regulatory content for the market-oriented reforms, and right-wing true believers should prefer a market-conforming one (Figure 1.1b).

---

[30] By increasing regulatory discretion, these institutional preferences should reduce the credibility of pragmatic converts' new commitment to the market creed. Because pragmatic converts adopt reforms based on fiscal incentives and these institutional choices should entail price cuts in the sale of assets, they only make sense by including political preferences over institutions.

(b)

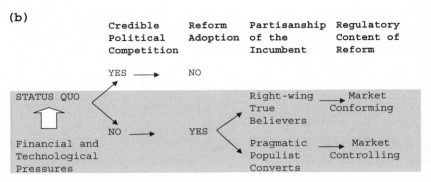

Figure 1.1b Partisanship and reform adoption (time 1)

In addition to the two ideal types of regulatory content predicted by this argument, there are two further testable empirical implications. First, former populists who have pragmatically converted to the new creed should be facing a trade-off between using regulatory content to maintain the credibility of their coalitions despite their policy switch and winning the credibility of international financial markets with their new commitment to the market. As a result, former populists should experience contradictory pressures to appoint neoliberal technocrats, either as preachers of the new creed or signals of their own commitment to it, along with their own allied experts. An implication of the partisan hypothesis, therefore, is that when reformers are pragmatic populist converts, we should observe tensions between neoliberal and allied experts that generate intraadministration conflict over regulatory content. Second, because privatization offers a one-time opportunity for redistribution, partisan preferences should also influence the distribution of compensation to different supporters in each coalition, especially through pricing schemes and the distribution of subsidized assets.

The institutional distribution of power can also shape the content of reform by constraining the preferences of reformers, especially when they need to involve a legislature they do not control. The partisan hypothesis explains reformers' preferences, but the institutional configuration of power provides constraints on their ability to exercise those preferences, including concessions to other partisan preferences with sufficient legislative power. Compromise will be complicated, though, if challengers with sufficient institutional power in the legislature prefer to reject the reform rather than share the blame for it or allow the incumbent to reap its benefits. Thus, the effect of partisanship on regulatory content should be clearer when reformers have unified government or are not required to involve the legislature in the reform process.

Finally, foreign and domestic industry-specific investors – as opposed to portfolio investors concerned about fiscal resources – have preferences about regulatory content and even lobby for them. Yet industry-specific foreign investors had reduced influence during the period under study. Before deploying their capital, foreign investors rely on exit rather than voice to express their preferences, either investing in other places or paying a lower price when policies do not suit them. After deploying their investments, however, the asset specificity of their sunken capital makes foreign investors exercise an active voice in the regulatory policy-making process. Their influence at time 2 (discussed in the following section) is also supported by evidence of contract renegotiation and noncompliance by governments and investors, which suggests that providers were prepared to undertake a relational contracting approach to regulatory structures.[31] By contrast, domestic investors (including large users who can become providers) and the suppliers of state-owned enterprises who needed to be persuaded to accept reform should be more influential at time 1, when privatization takes place. Yet Etchmendy (2009) shows that at privatization, Argentine state suppliers focused on getting compensation through market share rather than regulations in return for their support of reforms.

Postreform Policy Making in Public Utilities

By analyzing postreform policy making in the utilities sector, this book seeks to assess the political consequences of the adoption of market-oriented reforms. First, it is important to assess whether the commodification of public-service provision contributed to its depoliticization as demand and supply replaced political pressure. For Canitrot (1981), Vergara (1981), and Schamis (1991), the depoliticization of public services

---

[31] The World Bank (2005, 17–19) summarizes studies of contract renegotiation in Latin America that suggest opportunistic behavior on the part of new operators and governments. Gomez-Ibáñez (2003) also points to the importance of mutual noncompliance. Post (2007) makes the case for using a relational contracting approach to understanding the interactions between investors and government for water and sanitation and suggests that foreign investors relied on bilateral investment treaties as a last resort when domestic regulatory institutions do not yield favorable results.

was the political goal of neoliberal reforms. Kurtz (2004), for his part, argues that market-oriented reforms generated difficulties for political organization among Latin American citizenry. Alternatively, the reforms could have increased the salience and transparency of policy making and thereby the potential for public controversy. This line of thought is advanced by Post (2007), who suggests that reforms increased politicians' incentives to denounce companies that are not run by their appointees, and Levy and Spiller (1996), who argue that the nature of consumption of public utilities generates incentives for the politicization of prices after their privatization.

Second, reform adoption provides an opportunity to identify whether the establishment of new institutions generated feedback effects that modified subsequent processes of policy making, as the historic institutionalist literature has shown for similar experiences in advanced countries. Answering these two questions is crucial in defining whether market-oriented reforms generated a critical juncture for policy making and, if they did, which were the mechanisms of reproduction for the new political configuration, following the research strategies suggested by Thelen (1999), Mahoney (2003), and Greif and Laitin (2004).[32]

In the postreform period, the external incentives for regulatory redistribution are weak, because income transfers between providers, competitors, and consumers do not have the same fiscal effects as privatization or introducing private investment to replace public expenditures. At the turn of the century, moreover, international financial markets ceased to reward the adoption of market-oriented reforms due to a succession of financial crises in the emerging economies of East Asia, Russia, and Brazil. Finally, the regional wave of market-oriented reforms lost strength following the improvement in Latin American terms of trade beginning in 2003, which transformed capital scarcity into resource abundance, thereby reducing the weight of external incentives to adopt these policies. Although external pressures for policy adoption declined, the original reforms created private providers that have a stake in sustaining the status quo and replaced external pressures as a constraint on the political incentives created by electoral competition and partisanship.

---

[32] Both Thelen (1999) and Mahoney (2003) suggest that searching for the mechanisms of reproduction that generate positive feedback effects is the best way to identify critical junctures. From a game theoretic perspective, Greif and Laitin (2004) similarly propose to identify quasiparameters whose values are affected by the working of the established institutions, which make the institution either self-reinforcing or self-undermining.

Table 1.5. *Categories of Regulatory Redistribution (time 2)*

	Providers Win	Providers Lose
Exchange with consumers	REGULATORY CAPTURE Redistribution from consumers to providers	REGULATORY DOMINANCE Redistribution from providers to consumers
Exchange with competitors	MARKET DOMINANCE Redistribution from competitors to incumbent providers	MARKET COMPETITION Redistribution from incumbent providers to competitors

Regulatory Reform as a Dependent Variable

Regulatory redistribution affecting the income of incumbent private providers is crucial to assessing postreform politics in public utilities.[33] Regulatory redistribution of providers' income can be produced by changing consumer prices, imposing sanctions, modifying quality targets, shifting the costs of intermediate services such as transmission (electricity) or interconnection (telecommunications), modifying the costs of entry into these markets, and so forth. In all cases, these measures redistribute income between first entrants and their competitors or consumers.

The four categories of regulatory redistribution depicted in Table 1.5 have different political implications. The first two categories of regulatory redistribution (in the left column) benefit incumbent providers. In regulatory capture, providers improve their lot at the expense of consumers, which is deemed to be electorally unpopular, whereas in market dominance, competitors foot the bill. In the latter case, providers' rents can be partially shared with targeted groups of consumers and thereby facilitate a short-term electoral gain for politicians.

The other two categories, which redistribute providers' income to consumers or competitors, also have different political effects. Regulatory dominance, which involves regulatory redistribution of incumbent providers' income to consumers, can be targeted to particular groups (of

---

[33] Regulatory redistribution is a better indicator of postreform changes to policy making than analysis of changes in regulatory structure, because the novelty of institutions needed to support a shift to markets in infrastructure sectors makes them more fragile in the developing world than in advanced countries (Victor and Heller 2007, 12).

policy makers' constituents). By contrast, the category market competition involves redistribution from providers to competitors, for instance by using regulation-establishing conditions that reduce their costs or prevent market concentration. Increasing competition, in turn, can lower consumer prices. Yet these price reductions are harder to target to certain groups and usually benefit large consumers, who are more attractive for private providers but less attractive in electoral terms, first. That is, although consumers may benefit, it is harder to make electoral claims about market competition's distributive effects, and these effects can take place during a period longer than the time horizons of politicians.

In studying postreform regulatory change, I separate the factors explaining the preferences of policy makers from the regulatory outcomes. Even when policy makers' preferences are crucial components of the policy process, the final regulatory outcome is also shaped by the policy influence of private providers, the need to compromise with the legislative opposition, and the role of the judiciary in policy making. Policy makers' preferences are crucial, however, to defining regulatory redistribution, and these preferences can be explained in terms of political competition and partisanship.

Competition, Partisanship, and Stakeholders in the Postreform Period

Analyzing the postreform period is important to assessing how market-oriented reforms have reshaped policy making in the two studied sectors. In the postreform period, electoral competition and partisanship have similar effects. The emergence of private providers as crucial stakeholders, however, constrains the effect of partisanship. I present in this section the policy effect of electoral competition and partisanship on policy makers' preferences and, in the following section, the constraints on these preferences generated by providers' policy preferences.

Political Competition and Partisanship in Postreform Policy Making

In the postreform period, political competition, which depends on electoral arrangements, has an effect on the distribution of institutional power in the political system and on the incentives of incumbents and challengers when the issue of regulatory reform is salient enough to enter the electoral campaign. The distribution of power in political institutions, in turn, can shape the final regulatory outcome through the legislative process. Both incumbents and challengers, moreover, are concerned about losing discontented residential consumers as voters, regardless of their ideological positions. Political competition also makes it easier for challengers to raise the salience of regulatory redistribution to inform those voters of their reasons for being discontented.

In the periods before and after reform, the policy incentives generated by political competition are driven by the preferences of marginal voters. As we have seen, marginal voters are more likely to be middle-class residential consumers, because such voters can join either the poor or the rich in political coalitions of pragmatic populist converts or right-wing true believers, respectively. Additionally, the middle class is likely to have access to telecommunications and electricity services but to suffer from the income effects of their relatively high prices once privatization has extended and improved supply. For electricity, due to improved coverage following privatization, the proportion of people in this category should be larger, making it harder to privatize and more likely that regulatory reform will produce redistribution to consumers (regulatory dominance). By contrast, poor and rich voters are more likely to be loyal to either pragmatic populist converts or right-wing true believers and to be less affected by these services due to their lack of access or to the reduced effect of prices on their income, respectively. As discussed in the preceding text, views on privatization in the mid-1990s were biased by socioeconomic status, whereas the post-1998 public opinion evidence shows that postreform discontent with public-utility reform in Latin America was the highest among the middle classes.

High levels of electoral competition should make politicians more favorable to redistribution toward residential consumers if they are paying attention.[34] Yet in the postreform period, the ideology of the challenger is not as important as in the prereform period. Electoral competition makes incumbents and challengers try to please residential consumers, thus heightening these consumers' regulatory influence when the salience of public-utility reform is high enough to have a potential impact on an

---

[34] In a study of U.S. public utilities, Holburn and Spiller (2002) find an institutional effect of consumer policy influence. When consumer advocates are included in public-utility commissions or when commissioners are elected by voters, redistribution of providers' rents to consumers through lower prices is more likely to take place. Elected commissioners are more likely to benefit residential users and consumer advocates more likely to benefit large users, thereby suggesting that electoral incentives favor residential users.

electoral campaign.[35] By contrast, electoral competition is less likely to produce regulatory redistribution to competitors (market competition), because large rather than residential consumers will be the first to perceive income effects from redistribution in this direction. In sum, in the postreform period, the voice of consumers and their ability to benefit from regulatory redistribution is amplified by political competition, assuming contexts of high public salience on the issue.

The public salience of the reform interacts with electoral competition because only when voters pay attention are politicians more likely to associate their decisions with consumer preferences rather than with those of providers, who have better lobbying resources.[36] By heightening the potential electoral consequences of public-utility reform, public salience affects politicians' incentives for regulatory change. Therefore, public salience decreases providers' influence, because politicians are more aware of monitoring by their constituencies. It also increases the cost of expert capture by facilitating the monitoring of regulators through "fire alarms" (either by challengers or by consumer associations), because consumers who are aware of their stakes are easier to mobilize. Hence, public salience increases the likelihood of regulatory dominance and decreases that of regulatory capture when politicians fear the electoral cost of consumer awareness.

Technically complex issues or regulatory decisions with no immediate effect on consumers' income or supply tend to be less salient. Yet electoral challengers or consumer organizations can subsidize the cost of information to the public. Challengers can raise public salience in the context of increasing electoral competition. It is unlikely, however, that they will take on regulatory reform unless some other factor has already put it on the public agenda and they can perceive electoral payoffs from doing so. Baumgartner and Jones (1993; 2005) argue that most citizens are indifferent to the policy process in the absence of high personal stakes

---

[35] This argument is similar to McGillivray's (2003) argument about redistribution to producers in marginal districts through industrial policy at times of electoral competition. However, consumer effects prevail in public utilities due to their weight on the personal income of a majority of voters, in contrast to the limited numbers of employers and employees.

[36] The U.S. literature on policy making emphasizes the importance of public salience in linking problems with solutions, broadening the public debate, and shaping the coherence and intensity of public attitudes to raise the cost of ignoring voters' preferences (Baumgartner and Jones 1993; Kingdon 1995; Manza and Cook 2002).

(a)

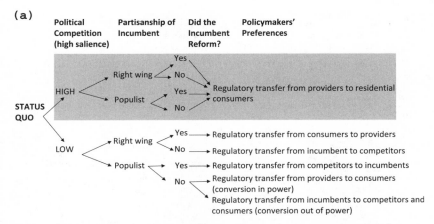

Figure 1.2a Political competition and policy makers' postreform preferences (time 2)

and that politicians do not pay attention to issues until the potential electoral consequences of those issues become evident to them. Consumer associations led by political entrepreneurs can also affect the levels of public salience to promote consumer mobilization by using judicial or media strategies if the regime allows civil society organization.[37]

Alternatively, crises – either microeconomic crises of supply or macroeconomic crises affecting relative costs – should also increase the salience of regulatory reform by affecting both the stakes of individual consumers and media coverage. By increasing consumers' stakes, crises can generate the opportunity for either challengers or consumer advocates to raise the salience of regulatory reform. Henisz and Zelner (2005) argue that crises in public utilities provide a focal point for opponents of the adopted rules to question the legitimacy of the original institutions and build broad coalitions for regulatory reform, and they provide examples from countries that had reformed their electricity sector.

Therefore, the modified first hypothesis for the postreform period is that political competition creates incentives for regulatory redistribution to consumers (regulatory dominance), especially in contexts of

[37] Rhodes (2006) argues that public-utility privatization was crucial in explaining the organization of consumers in Latin America. She adds that these groups used media and judicial strategies for influencing the policy process and especially for shaping the definition of pricing rules in public utilities.

(b)

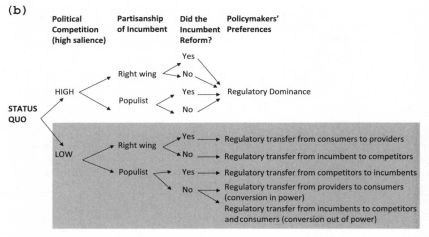

Figure 1.2b Partisanship and policy makers' postreform preferences (time 2)

high salience (Figure 1.2a). These effects should not be affected by partisan preferences, but by changes in electoral competition or public salience.

As in the prereform period, partisan effects are more likely when electoral competition is low, because in such an environment politicians care more about their own constituencies than about marginal voters. Right-wing true believers should prefer to benefit providers (either incumbent or competitors), and pragmatic populist converts should prefer to benefit consumers. Policy makers who have adopted market-oriented reforms and associated their administrations with their success, however, are more dependent on the fortunes of first entrants – either to attract new investors to other sectors or due to linkages emerging from their original decision to invest. Hence, reformers should be more likely to side with the first entrants who have become the incumbent providers.

The process of populist conversion to the market creed affected postreform policy preferences. Those who abandoned statism while out of power were less pragmatic than populists who converted in power under conditions of financial emergency. Hence, populists who converted but did not reform were more trustful of the ability of market mechanisms – such as competition – to benefit their consumer constituencies than those who converted under financial duress. By contrast, populists who did not convert at all (and thereby did not reform) preferred to benefit consumers mainly through the proactive action of the state, that is, with regulatory dominance.

Figure 1.2b summarizes the hypothesized policy makers' preferences considering their partisanship, linkages with first entrants developed by reformers, and patterns of populist conversion inferred from the case studies. Reformist right-wing true believers were more likely to side with incumbent providers and prefer to expropriate consumers (regulatory capture). If they had not reformed, they were more likely to favor competitors and prefer regulatory redistribution from incumbents to their competitors (market competition). Conversely, pragmatic populists who had reformed and were tied to the providers who accepted their political conditions when entering these markets (and trusted in their conversion to the market creed) preferred regulatory transfers from competitors to incumbent providers (market dominance). That is, they favored regulatory redistribution to incumbent providers at the expense of competitors in return for some benefit to consumers in price or coverage. When the converted populists had not reformed, they were not necessarily linked to incumbent providers. If they had converted pragmatically in power, they preferred regulatory redistribution from providers to consumers (regulatory dominance), and if they had done it out of power they were more likely to trust that regulatory transfers from incumbents to competitors (market competition) would also benefit consumers by promoting investment and reducing prices. Although not depicted in Figure 1.2b, uncompromising populists who had never converted preferred regulatory dominance or even reform reversal if possible, as shown by the experiences of the Mexican Democratic Revolutionary Party (PRD) during the studied period and more recently by those of the administrations of presidents Hugo Chavez in Venezuela and Evo Morales in Bolivia.

In short, the second hypothesis on partisan effects is adapted in the postreform period to the following: Right-wing true believers should prefer regulatory redistribution from consumers to incumbent providers if they have reformed and to competitor providers if they have not. Pragmatic populist converts should prefer redistribution from competitors to incumbent providers if they have reformed and to both consumers and competitors if they have not.

Policy makers' partisan preferences do not necessarily shape regulatory outcomes. Their views are constrained during the policy-making process. They should pay attention to private providers' preferences because the latter are crucial stakeholders. In the postreform period, the voice of providers (and their effect over the policy process through lobbying and regulatory capture) is an important constraint on policy makers'

47

preferences. At time 1, decision makers at the international financial institutions and financial markets that had policy leverage cared more about revenue than about the technically complex choices involved in reform design, thereby giving leeway to allied experts in making choices about policy content. As regulatory redistribution affects private providers' bottom lines, they are very active in the policy-making process at time 2. Their influence, in turn, limits partisan effects by creating career incentives for allied experts, through lobbying and donating to politicians, and so on.[38]

In understanding the effect of experts on public-utility regulatory reform, it is important to remember that in Latin America, unlike in advanced countries, the effective independence of regulatory agencies is limited. In advanced countries, the independence of regulatory agencies is formal and effective, thus reducing their politicization, and experts are crucial in defining regulatory initiatives.[39] By contrast, explanations of regulatory reforms that rely on the influence of experts and social learning are less persuasive for Latin America due to the weak effective independence of regulatory agencies in the region.[40] Even when experts are proactive, they need to rely on their linkages to politicians to have the technical decisions delegated to them.

Thus, the lack of an effective civil service politicized the nature of allied experts' tenure-reinforcing partisan incentives for regarding regulatory content in the prereform period. Because experts' career options were heavily dependent on public-sector jobs and political appointments, they had strong incentives to internalize partisan distributive differences. In the postreform period, although bureaucratic careers were still uncertain, experts could choose between jobs in the public or private sector. In the latter case, they were likely to work for regulated companies and be less concerned about partisan preferences. Remarkably,

[38] Corruption may be conceptualized as an "illegal" lobbying strategy in this context.

[39] Thatcher (2002a; 2002b) and Gilardi (2002) show the prevalence of regulatory autonomy in European public utilities. Gilardi explains their delegation to independent regulatory agencies on the need for credibility in these sectors due to their opening to competition and private investment. Eising (2002) argues that European Union (EU) institutions provided opportunities for policy learning to experts and policy makers so as to endogenously change their preferences regarding electricity liberalization in Europe.

[40] In comparing regulatory agencies in Europe and Latin America, Levi-Faur (2004, 19) finds that policy makers in the latter region are reluctant to grant independence to separated regulatory agencies in electricity and telecommunications.

partisan linkages in the prereform period and private-sector careers in the postreform period can generate incentives to weaken the homogenization of expert preferences generated by epistemic communities of academic origin.

Additionally, political institutions are crucial in assessing the impact of partisan preferences, as veto players can preempt regulatory reform or force compromise over its content.[41] The distribution of legislative preferences is crucial for regulatory outcomes that require congressional approval. The capacity and incentives of the judiciary to contradict the executive and the relative access to courts of consumers and providers are also important in the regulatory process. These factors vary over time and across countries. The incentives for legislative compromise are higher when the government is divided, as in Argentina between 1997 and 1999, in Mexico after 1997, and in Chile between 1990 and 2005 (due to the existence of appointed senators). The Argentine judiciary was subservient to the Menem administration – at least until 1999 – according to Helmke (2004) and Gargarella (2008). The politicization of the selection of judges and the weak corporate culture of the judiciary made judges less elitist, however. The 1994 constitutional reform, additionally, opened access to consumer advocates with collective injunctions. In Chile, by contrast, the judiciary became independent with the democratic transition. As the Supreme Court supervises all judicial employees and their promotions, it fosters a corporate judicial culture and sustains elitist linkages that should favor business (Gargarella 2008). Finally, the Mexican judiciary started acting more independently in 1997 (Rios Figueroa 2007), but consumer advocates have limited access to justice, and especially to injunctions affecting regulations because these are costly (Guerrero et al. 2006).

In evaluating regulatory outcomes, it is important to consider the distribution of power in political institutions in the postreform period. Pressure from providers, however, can break partisan legislative discipline and produce outcomes different from those derived from measuring political veto players, even when the forums to exercise such influence vary according to the institutional configuration of each country. I now turn to the factors that affect providers' policy preferences.

---

[41] The arguments of Cox and McCubbins (2001) and Shugart and Haggard (2001) regarding the role of institutional constraints on policy making in presidential systems are applied by Heller and McCubbins (2001) and Haggard and Noble (2001) to electricity regulation.

Providers' Preferences on Regulatory Redistribution

In understanding providers' policy input in postreform policy making, it is helpful to perceive that the choice of original reform content (market conforming or market controlling) was crucial in producing different effects in each sector. These effects resulted from the interaction of the original institutions with technological changes, which generated different first-entrant advantages. Technical complexity, asset-specific investment, economies of scale, scope and density, and mass consumption help the concentration of providers and the dispersion of users. Private providers' stakes are high, because public utilities are regulated companies with large sunk costs and significant asset specificity, and they have abundant resources to defend their bottom lines. By contrast, consumers are harder to organize to defend their diffused interests, because their small individual stakes promote free-riding.[42] Although the difference in resources and stakes between providers and consumers favors the former, private providers have to aggregate their policy preferences into coordinated action, and their own conflicts can generate diverse policy preferences.

The process of preference aggregation depends, as in any sector, on the degree of firm heterogeneity within the industry (Milner 1988). In the case of public utilities, the original reform content and the exogenous shock of technological development has a crucial effect on the coordination of policy preferences at the industry level.

As argued by Olson (1965), the degree of concentration of ownership strongly influences preference aggregation and coordination of policy pressures. In public utilities, concentration affects the relation between the first entrants or incumbent providers and their competitors in terms of the relative power that each has to impose their own policy preferences as those of the industry. Dominant companies can often impose their preferences on representative associations or use informal networks of policy influence, which do not require prior preference aggregation.[43]

In the studied cases, the original reform content had a strong effect on the degree of industry concentration and thereby on the aggregation of

---

[42] Stigler (1971) started off the economic theory of regulation explaining industry capture. Pelzman (1976) broadened its implications by showing that actors other than providers could be part of the dominant distributive coalitions in regulatory policy making. Noll (1989) summarized its political economy applications for understanding public-utility regulation.

[43] On the role of business associations in aggregating policy preferences in Latin America, see Schneider (2004).

providers' policy preferences. This institutional effect was the unintended consequence of a divergent pace of technological development in each sector, which made alternative networks available more rapidly in telecommunications than in electricity.[44] That is, alternative networks allowed the emergence of new providers competing with first entrants in telecommunications, even with consolidation of ownership in the original networks. By contrast, without alternative networks, electricity remained a natural monopoly in distribution and transmission, with only large users reaping the benefits of competitive generation through the wholesale market. As a result, the original reform content produced different effects in each sector.

In telecommunications, market-controlling reforms hindered competition using new technologies, because the use of monopolies to guarantee investment requirements allowed first entrants to retain their advantages. Market-conforming reforms facilitated competition by not hindering the use of alternative networks and by generating more providers with a stake in limiting incumbent advantages. In electricity, market-controlling reforms establishing rules on property acquisition hindered property concentration and the subsequent homogenization of providers' preferences under the hegemony of the strongest. Market-conforming reforms without such rules allowed market consolidation, producing the opposite effect on providers' coordination. Figure 1.3 summarizes the effect of reform content in preference aggregation found for each sector in the studied cases.

Therefore, market-controlling reforms strengthened the policy influence of first-entrant telecommunications providers vis-à-vis their competitors in the postreform period. Dominant providers were more likely to impose their preference for market dominance on their competitors, as they could bear the cost of organizing policy pressure by themselves. Conversely, the same reform content in electricity made the emergence

---

[44] In comparing technological effects on market oriented reforms in infrastructure, a recent study states: "Telecommunications offers the most striking success with reform of a network industry – thanks to a variety of technological innovations that have eased the entry of new competitors and created new products. . . . Electricity is proving to be among the trickiest of all network industries for reformers. The network effects of large power grids, along with the massive economies of scale in modern central power stations, create high barriers to entry that (until recently) had made electricity the epitome of natural monopoly. The prohibitive cost of storing electricity requires that all power systems be managed literally at the speed of light – a characteristic of systems that many had thought would require synchronized central management rather than the looser and decentralized coordination that are the hallmark of most markets" (Victor and Heller 2007, 2).

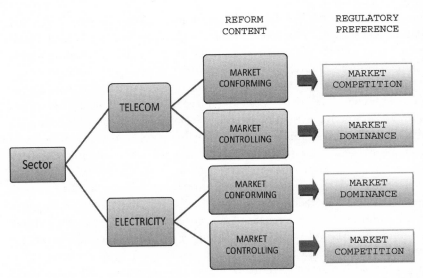

Figure 1.3   Providers' bargaining power and regulatory preferences (time 2)

of dominant providers more difficult by hindering market consolidation, thereby making market competition more likely to prevail as the industry preference, because none of the providers could impose their view on the others. Market-conforming reforms allowed the emergence of more heterogeneous preferences in telecommunications and thereby weakened first entrants (in relative terms to market-controlling reforms) and favored market competition as the industry preference. In electricity, however, the lack of regulation allowed market consolidation and facilitated the emergence of dominant providers who could impose their preferences on the rest of the industry and bear the cost of policy pressure, making market dominance more likely to prevail as the main preference within the industry. These preferences refer to redistribution between providers, as they all agree on the desirability of avoiding transfers of income to consumers.

   This argument emphasizes the empirical effects of first-entrant advantages depending on reform content and thereby complements other general arguments about these advantages in processes of market reform (Hellman 1998) by providing a sector-specific argument for the studied cases. The outcomes are the result of alignment or differences in preferences and compromises during the policy-making process. The effect of institutional choices that congealed partisan preferences about market structure depended on the exogenous shock of technological change. These effects were not path dependent in the sense of reproducing themselves, but they established diverse baselines for politicians to attempt policy reform.

Whereas providers' preferences regarding regulatory redistribution are shaped by reform content and the technological possibilities of each industry, their degree of diversification and the origin of their capital should also affect the policy-making process. Having diversified holdings can allow providers to trade regulatory changes in one industry for benefits in another, as shown by Post (2007) for the water and sanitation sector in Argentina, where domestic firms with diversified operations were less vulnerable to political and economic cycles that affect pricing policies in the utilities sector. Moreover, foreign investors can be subject to the effects of the "obsolescing bargain," as they are less likely to have political connections and more likely to be perceived as illegitimate, especially if they are new in the receiving country and have assets of low mobility (Vernon 1971). That is, investors' bargaining power is high before deploying their capital when developing countries are suffering from financial and technological scarcity. Afterward, their bargaining power declines, as they cannot move their sunken capital to achieve returns on their investments. The weakness of foreign companies in the policy-making process is worsened by crises, argue Henisz and Zelner (2005), because these weaken the legitimacy of the rules adopted to attract foreign investors by generating conflicts with domestic norms of fairness. These effects should decline over time as time horizons lengthen and relations with political actors are developed (Hillman et al. 2004; Henisz and Zelner 2005).

Summary and Implications

This chapter presents a two-part argument about how political competition and partisanship influence public-utility policy making both when market-oriented reforms are adopted and in the postreform period. The argument explaining the original market-oriented reforms in telecommunications and electricity illuminates the diverse political dynamics underlying a process of apparent policy convergence driven by technological and financial pressures. It introduces the policy effects of domestic electoral politics by focusing on both the relative level of political competition and the partisan orientation of incumbents. The distributive logic behind the argument emphasizes the importance of marginal voters when political competition is high and the effect of preexisting partisan linkages when it is low. It underscores the primacy of political survival for politicians, as well as their room for exercising partisan distributive preferences even in shaping the content of policies imposed on them by external financial and technological pressures.

In the postreform period, electoral competition combined with high salience generated incentives for regulatory redistribution to consumers. When electoral competition is low, partisan preferences conditioned on linkages to initial market entrants for reformers prevailed. The hypotheses about the political dynamics based on incentives for political survival are crucial in explaining policy-makers' preferences. Empirically, however, providers' policy demands vary according to the effect of the original reform content on each sector, and these effects must be examined in defining the outcome of regulatory redistribution. That is, politicians' partisan preferences are constrained by a lack of financial capital in the prereform period and by industry-specific investors in its aftermath. This argument provides scenarios that define the conditions for policy outcomes and shows that citizens can have a voice in the policy process, even in technically complex policy processes. Their voice, though, is more effective when exercised through electoral pressures and through partisan linkages than through the organization of consumers as such.

2

Political Competition and Policy Adoption

This chapter focuses on the effects of political competition on the timing of the adoption of market-oriented reforms, given the strong financial and technological pressures on Latin American governments to attract private capital to public utilities from 1985 to 2000. Given those pressures, in any given year in the studied period, political competition made incumbents less likely to adopt policies that might make them lose marginal supporters while amplifying the reach of challengers' criticisms in the policy debate. The first part of this chapter tests this argument for the decision to adopt privatization, the opening of markets to private investment, and the establishment of regulators in electricity and telecommunications in all Latin American countries. Based on a coauthored piece (Murillo and Martinez-Gallardo 2007), it uses survival analysis to show that political competition hindered the adoption of public-utility reforms in all Latin American countries between 1985 and 2000, even when the effect of financial and technical pressures as well as institutional constraints are controlled for. The second part of the chapter illustrates the causal mechanisms behind this argument by using case studies of both sectors in Argentina, Chile, and Mexico.

Political Competition and Public-Utility Reform

Political competition raised the marginal value of discontented voters when power differentials between incumbents and challengers (the most-voted-for alternative party in Latin American presidential systems) were shrinking. Incumbents became more afraid of being replaced due to popular discontent and thereby more risk averse regarding public-utility reforms whose price effects threatened public discontent. Meanwhile, challengers, who were not under financial pressures to adopt market-oriented reforms and whose electoral viability was growing, became more effective in denouncing these policies and making the issue of public-utility reform more salient to voters. Challengers' credibility as providers of a policy alternative, in turn, was greater if they had not previously cooperated on policy making with the incumbent or proposed similar policies. In particular, challengers' credibility regarding market-oriented policies was higher if they were to the ideological left of the government or if they were ideologically polarized from the governing party, making prior policy cooperation less likely.

In Uruguay, for instance, center-right President Luis A. Lacalle proposed a bill to privatize the state-owned telephone company, ANTEL, in 1991. A legislative coalition of Colorados and Blancos passed it into law, but the center-left opposition Broad Front (FA) and its allied union of telephone workers organized a collective demand for a plebiscite against the law in December 1992. The center-left opposition was helped by a constitution that allows citizens to call plebiscites, as well as by increasing political competition, as the country's electoral preferences were divided in thirds among the three main parties. Blanco President Lacalle had only obtained 22.6 percent of votes (although his party obtained 38.9%) in 1989 thanks to an electoral system of single, nontransferable vote. The FA and the union raised the public salience of telecommunications' privatization during the plebiscite campaign. As public opinion against privatization grew, Colorado legislator and presidential hopeful Julio M. Sanguinetti – who had voted in favor of the law – campaigned for its derogation.[1] This about-face served to win him the next presidential election in 1994, when his party obtained 31.45 percent of votes to 30.2 percent for the Blancos and 30.2 percent for the FA. In this case, the center-left FA led the credible opposition to privatization and in a three-party system pulled a large faction of the Colorado Party toward policy obstruction.[2]

In testing the negative effect of political competition on the adoption of market reforms in public utilities, the quantitative analysis in this chapter relies on available proxies for the hypothesized effects on incumbents and challengers. First, to assess incumbents' fear of replacement, it focuses on shrinking power differentials between incumbents and the most-voted-for

---

[1] He had created his faction within the Colorado Party only in 1990 and needed to establish his leadership before the following presidential election (Carlos Moreira, personal communication, July 29, 2005).

[2] Moreira and Narbondo (1998) and personal interview by Moreira and Narbondo with President Luis Alberto Lacalle, Montevideo, May 23, 1995. http://www.georgetown.edu/pdba, accessed March 12, 2009.

other party in the legislature, which captures midterm modifications in power distribution since the last presidential election. A better measure would be one of comparative public opinion, but it is not available across countries for the studied period. Second, to assess the credibility of challengers, this chapter uses ideological polarization between the incumbent and the challenger as a proxy for lack of prior policy cooperation and the relative position on the political spectrum of both as a measure of public perceptions about their opposition to market-oriented reforms.

The effect of challengers in raising the public salience and electoral costs of policy adoption are hard to measure across countries during most of the studied period due to the lack of cross-national and longitudinal measures of public opinion about telecommunications and electricity for all Latin American countries. There are policy conditions that heighten the public salience of an issue, however, such as the scope and magnitude of its effects, its complexity, and its historical resonance. Electricity and telecommunications are public services that reach a large number of citizens, which increases the scope of reform effects. Yet coverage was better in electricity than in telecommunications across all Latin American countries by the mid-1980s. Hence, the potential income effects of electricity reform were larger than those of telecommunications reform, which still held the promise of access for many.[3] In particular, privatization challenged the political control of these utilities' prices and supply, generating important effects for subsidized residential users.

In short, following the first hypothesis, we expect political competition to have made reform adoption less likely. The following two sections present the methodology used for and the results of testing this hypothesis while controlling from the impact of technological demand, financial pressures, institutional constraints, and the incumbent's ideology.

Modeling Policy Adoption and Political Competition

This section presents the modeling strategy and the indicators used to measure the variables of interest, as well as the expectations derived from the argument about political competition and alternative explanations. As discussed in Chapter 1, the timing of policy adoption is important to

---

[3] In 1989, when only Chile had privatized both sectors, there were 5 phones per 100 inhabitants on average in all Latin America countries (save Cuba and Haiti), according to the International Telecommunications Union (ITU), whereas the average coverage of electricity was 60% of households (World Bank and OLADE, 1991).

understanding why some incumbents but not others undertook the passage of public-utility reform policies in telecommunications and electricity, considering the regional impact of financial and technological pressures to do so. The analysis is based on a dataset that covers all eighteen Latin American countries between 1985 and 2000.[4] The values of the dependant variable (reform occurrence) were presented in Table 1.1, which records the year when the government decided to privatize, open the market to private capital, and establish regulators in each sector.[5]

To explain the timing of policy adoption, this study uses survival analysis to explore the factors that affect the probability that a country will choose a particular policy, given that it has not done so up to that point in time.[6] In terms of survival analysis, the individuals in the sample are countries, which are observed when they enter the sample (here the entry point is 1985) and up to their exit from the sample or their failure. (Here, countries fail when they decide to adopt a policy.)[7]

Given the nature of the data, we use a Cox proportional hazards model (Cox 1972), which allows us to model policy reform without specifying *a priori* the relationship between policy reform and time.[8] Importantly, Cox proportional hazards models assume that the relationship between the hazard functions of two countries with a different set of covariates are related to each other through a constant. In practice, however, this is not always the case, because the effect of some variables on the likelihood of policy adoption

---

[4] The statistical analysis excludes Cuba and Haiti, whose peculiar political dynamics prevented them from joining the economic and political policy trends of the region. Chile is excluded from the statistical analysis because its reforms had been adopted by 1985.

[5] Privatization involved transfer of assets with concession or sale of shares. In telecommunications, it involved mainly fixed-line service, and in electricity, it involved assets in generation, distribution, and transmission.

[6] Others have chosen to model the adoption of reforms and not their timing by using logit instead of duration analysis (Henizs et al. 2005). Duration analysis allows us to explicitly model the process of policy convergence that characterized the region and to explain differences in the pace of policy adoption within this general trend. It also allows us to combine the analysis of time-varying covariates (such as growth or GDP) with the analysis of variables that tend to vary less over time within a country (like polarization).

[7] We use robust standard errors in all the models to control for clustering within individuals, i.e., for the possibility that observations within a country are not independent.

[8] Using a more restrictive parametric model would imply imposing a specific structure on the relationship between time and the adoption of policy reform. These models are more efficient only when this relationship is correctly specified. In our case, we have no theoretical reason to choose a specific functional form. We use the efron method to deal with ties, given the small number of cases and the relatively high number of ties.

can change over time and in this sense is nonproportional.[9] Where proportionality issues arose, models were corrected by adding an interaction with time in order to estimate the direct effect of the explanatory variable and control for its effect over time (Box-Steffensmeier and Zorn 2001).

Although testing the effect of political competition on policy adoption, this analysis controls for the incumbent's ideology, institutional constraints (i.e., executive capacity), financial pressures, and technological underdevelopment, which the literature on comparative politics have linked to market reforms. The effect of power differentials between the incumbent and the challenger is measured by the difference in seats between the incumbent's party and the largest opposition party in the legislature as a proportion of the total number of seats.[10] This measure, called *legislative advantage*, is better than the margin of victory, as it captures changes in power differential due to midterm elections, and it should have a positive effect on policy adoption.

Two indicators of relative ideological position measure the credibility of the challenger for using market-oriented reforms to build electoral capital. First, *polarization* measures the ideological distance between the incumbent party and its main challenger in the legislature, which should reflect a lack of prior legislative cooperation between the challenger and the incumbent. Ideological variables are calculated using a five-point scale, where 1 is the left-most score and 5 is the right-most score.[11] If, for example, the incumbent is from a right-wing party with a score of 4.5 and the main opposition party in the legislature has a score of 3, their ideological distance is 1.5. Polarization is a dummy variable that only considers that absolute ideological distance; it takes the value of 1 when such distance is above the average of the sample and 0 otherwise. It is expected to have a negative effect on policy adoption. Second, the relative ideology of the challenger vis-à-vis the incumbent affects the former's credibility as an alternative to market-oriented reforms. Being ideologically to the left of the incumbent should increase the challenger's credibility as an alternative for disaffected voters.

---

[9] We use the stphtest in STATA to test the proportional hazard assumption, and the results are presented below each of the models in Tables 2.1 to 2.5.

[10] When the government is formed by a single party, we take the number of seats held by this party; if the government is a coalition, we use the total seats of all coalition partners. We use data on the Lower Chamber in countries with bicameral legislatures.

[11] The scores are based on party positions from Coppedge (1997) and consultations with country experts. We calculate the average ideology of the government by averaging the scores for all government parties and weighting them by the parties' size.

Thus, *left opposition* is a dummy that takes the value of 1 when the ideology of the main challenger is to the left of the incumbent's and is expected to have a negative effect on policy adoption.[12]

The effects of other variables that the literature has associated with policy adoption, including the ideological preferences of the incumbent, the existence of institutional veto points that hinder policy adoption, the level of financial pressures faced by the incumbent, and the degree of response to domestic demand for services, are also measured.

The effect of the incumbent's ideology on policy adoption is measured by using dummies that indicate whether the incumbent's party is right-wing, center, or left-wing. If ideological preferences matter, as argued by the partisan policy-making literature, the dummy for *Right Incumbent* should have a positive effect on policy adoption. Conversely, ideology should have no effect if financial pressures had muted ideological differences.

Institutional constraints on the executive capacity to adopt a policy regardless of incumbents' preferences are captured by three different variables. Henisz's index of *Political Constraints* measures the effect of veto players on the executive's ability to reform and is expected to have a negative effect on policy adoption.[13] That is, policy reform should be less likely as the political system becomes more indecisive, due to the larger number of constraints on policy change (Cox and McCubbins 2001). Following the extensive literature on presidentialism, an indicator of the government's status, called *single-party majority*, tests the expectation that single-party majority governments face fewer constraints on their ability to adopt reforms than governments that have to negotiate with coalition partners or to bargain with other parties in order to construct a legislative majority. The third indicator (distance) measures the ideological distance between the executive and the median legislator. Following Tsebelis (2003), we expect that as the preferences of the executive and the median legislator grow farther apart, the likelihood of agreement, and thus reform, decreases.

Three control variables that can affect political competition and executive capacity are also included. First, the electoral cycle is likely to play

---

[12] Parties are coded as Right when they score 4 or 5 on the ideology scale. They are coded as Center when they have a score of 3 and Left when they have a score of 1 or 2.

[13] The index goes from 0 to 1 and measures the "feasibility of policy change," taking into account the number of independent branches of government with an effective veto over policy, whether the executive and the legislature's preferences are aligned (e.g., occupied by the same party), and the extent to which preferences in the legislature are heterogeneous. For more details, see Henisz (2002).

a role in the president's political strategy. Thus, the number of years left until the next presidential election (as presidential tenures vary in the region) is used to test whether the timing of elections affects the decision to adopt a reform. This variable was not found to be significant and is not included in the tables presented in the following text. Second, in measuring polarization between the incumbent and the challenger, the effective number of parties serves to control for fractionalization in the legislature and thereby for the relative size of these two crucial players. Third, because the effect of the distance between the executive and the median legislator should be tempered by the size of the government's legislative share, this variable is included as a control for distance.

The literature about international political economy emphasizes the effect of globalization pressures through diverse paths, including direct financial pressures. These include the effect of coercion by international financial institutions, which provide loans with explicit or implicit conditionality (Henisz et al. 2005) and the leverage of financial markets based on the impact of debt service on the current account and the degree of fiscal emergency (Stallings 1992). International coercion is measured by an indicator of whether countries had subscribed to standby agreements with the IMF (*Under IMF*).[14] In telecoms, an indicator of whether the country had a sectoral loan from the World Bank is used as an alternative measure of influence by international financial institutions (IFIs), but no similar indicator exists for electricity. The size of debt service as a proportion of total exports (debt) measures the leverage of foreign creditors, as an increase in this ratio suggests more difficulties in payment and a lower level of creditworthiness.[15] Additionally, the fiscal position of the government (*fiscal position*) – whether the budget was in deficit or surplus – measures its need for fiscal resources. The former three variables are expected to increase the likelihood that reform will take place by

---

[14] We are following Vreeland (2003, 17–18) in using country-years in which a country has entered an IMF agreement, because the influence of international financial institutions is not given only by explicit conditionality but also by its technical assistance, the influence granted to domestic advocates of reform, and their impact in signaling good behavior for other creditors, which can be more important than the amount of the loan (Teichman 2001).

[15] We cannot use sovereign ratings for lack of data. Moody's sovereign ratings do not cover the studied period, as only Argentina, Brazil, Mexico, and Venezuela have been rated since 1985, and the ratings for the majority of Latin American countries started in the mid-1990s. The period covered by Standard and Poor's rating is even shorter, and only Venezuela was rated in the 1980s.

imposing pressures on capital-scarce countries,[16] and the fiscal position should have a negative effect, especially on privatization, which generates revenue for the treasury.

Finally, the domestic demand for reform adoption generates technological pressures based on the capacity of state-owned services to provide an adequate supply of services. Due to the lack of comparative data on quality indicators, these domestic pressures are measured by using *teledensity* (number of telephones per 100 inhabitants) and *electricity consumption per capita* as approximations of the domestic demand for policies that would allow the country to catch up technologically and expand coverage. We expect the density of services in each sector to have a negative effect on policy adoption by reducing the need and increasing the number of consumers affected by potential price hikes. In electricity, though, economic growth (*growth*) should be positively related with electricity demand, as it reflects the energy needs of large users, who should be more concerned with supply than price effects. Technological pressures should have a weaker effect on the establishment of regulators, which has no immediate impact on supply or prices.

Workers for privatized companies, like large users, also have strong stakes in policy adoption, as shown by qualitative studies (Murillo 2001). There is no reliable yearly data on unionization, however, either at the sector level or at the national level, to use as a proxy for labor influence in the quantitative analysis. Moreover, unions' linkages with parties of the Left should reinforce the effect of political competition, especially by increasing the credibility of challengers and their capacity to raise public salience. We also include GDP per capita lagged one year to control for the wealth of the country.[17]

---

[16] It is important to note that we have lagged the financial variables one year to reflect the assumption that financial decisions by the government are made taking into account last year's resources. We have lagged fiscal position two years to take into consideration that we are lumping all reforms in a given year, whether they took place in January or December, and due to the delay that could have occurred between the perception of depleted fiscal accounts at the end of the year and the decision to sell assets to fill them. We include fiscal position in all privatization models because a large literature links privatization with fiscal needs.

[17] To measure how diffusion diminishes the cost of policy adoption for latecomers, Kogut and Macpherson (2004) and Levi-Faur (2004) use the number of previous privatizations. By using event history analysis, we model the dynamic aspect of reform – the factors that affect whether a country is an innovator or a follower – but we do not include the number of previous privatizations in the region, because this variable is perfectly collinear with the country variable. See Meseguer and Gilardi (2005) on measuring diffusion.

Policy Adoption in Telecommunications and Electricity

This section summarizes the results of the quantitative analysis.[18] In interpreting the magnitude of the effects, it is important to keep in mind that the hazard rate refers to the probability that a country will adopt reform at time t, given that it has not done so up to that point. Thus, changes in the hazard rate associated with changes in the independent variables should be interpreted as an increase or decrease in the instantaneous probability of reform. We first present models with economic factors – financial and technological pressures – and subsequently add measures of executive capacity and political competition. We find negative effects of political competition on the timing of policy adoption for the three policies. By contrast, we did not find fiscal deficits to have an effect on the decision to privatize, although they do make the creation of electricity regulators more likely. We find, as expected, that other measures of financial pressure favor policy adoption for privatization and the establishment of regulatory agencies.

Privatization of Telecommunications

Table 2.1 shows the effect of external financial pressures on the privatization of telecommunications.[19] Whereas being under an IMF agreement was not significant, both debt service and World Bank telecoms loans had significant and positive effects. These results indicate the weight of financial pressures on the decision to privatize telecommunications, even if World Bank involvement in the process could result either from the provision of financial incentives for reform or from financial rewards to policy makers for carrying out intended reforms. That is, the stronger the financial pressures, the more likely the country was to adopt privatization reform in a given year. The effect of fiscal deficits on the decision to sell public assets was not significant, however.

The effect of teledensity was nonproportional. Controlling for time, a higher teledensity was associated with an increase of between 12 and 19

---

[18] We have updated the results of Murillo and Martinez-Gallardo (2007) by revising the data in a few instances on the date of privatization and Coppedge's party coding. The results are not substantially different.

[19] We are interested in the political decision to adopt privatization rather than the actual sale of assets, which is affected by available capital and technical issues. Consequently, we focus on the group of countries that had decided to privatize by the end of 2000, even if they were still in the process of implementing the sale of assets.

Table 2.1. *Privatization of Telecommunications (time to adoption of privatization law)*

	Economic Factors		Executive Capacity			Political Competition			
Under IMF	3.104 (1.50)	1.864 (0.93)	5.117 (1.50)	7.180 (1.87)*	2.973 (1.61)	5.241 (1.55)	7.675 (1.94)*	3.102 (1.50)	2.870 (1.23)
Debt	1.056 (3.67)***	1.043 (2.23)**	1.078 (3.86)***	1.071 (3.13)***	1.056 (3.77)***	1.059 (3.39)***	1.060 (2.63)***	1.055 (4.35)***	1.064 (3.19)***
World Bank Loan		9.806 (3.56)***							
Fiscal Position	1.025 (0.16)	0.994 (-0.04)	0.960 (-0.23)	1.191 (0.96)	1.065 (0.36)	1.058 (0.32)	0.964 (-0.25)	1.025 (0.16)	0.995 (-0.03)
Tele Density	1.131 (3.43)***	1.190 (2.76)***	1.277 (3.26)***	1.111 (3.33)***	1.124 (3.43)***	1.225 (3.46)***	1.175 (3.71)***	1.131 (3.36)***	1.105 (2.19)**
Tele Density * LogT	0.946 (-3.28)***	0.929 (-2.63)***	0.900 (-3.38)***	0.955 (-3.08)***	0.950 (-3.24)***	0.914 (-3.70)***	0.931 (-3.52)***	0.946 (-3.19)***	0.957 (-2.03)**
GDP per Capita		1.005 (4.22)***							
GDP per Capita * LogT		0.998 (-4.08)***							
Growth	0.909 (-0.72)	0.865 (-1.00)	1.414 (0.50)	0.842 (-1.18)	0.908 (-0.70)	0.904 (-0.66)	0.942 (-0.48)	0.909 (-0.73)	0.914 (-0.77)
Growth * LogT			0.818 (-0.57)						
Distance			0.318 (-1.52)						

	(1)	(2)	(3)	(4)	(5)	(6)	(7)	(8)	(9)	(10)
Government Share	0.000 (−2.54)**									
Single-Party Majority		4.277 (1.96)**								
Political Constraints			0.263 (−0.87)							
Left Opposition				0.236 (−3.63)***						
Legislative Advantage					0.989 (−0.51)					
Polarization						0.180 (−2.58)***				
Effective Number of Parties							0.946 (−0.29)			
Margin of Victory								1.058 (0.03)		
Right Incumbent									2.101 (0.71)	
Center Incumbent										2.455 (0.74)
Observations	145	141	145	130	145	145	134	131	145	145
Sphtest (Prob > chi2)	0.96	0.43	0.86	0.95	0.93	0.89	0.90	1.00	0.97	1.00
Countries at Risk	16									
Failures	15									

Cox Proportional Hazard Models.
Robust z statistics in parentheses; * significant at 10%; ** significant at 5%; *** significant at 1%.

Table 2.2. *Privatization of Electricity (time to adoption of privatization law)*

	Economic Factors		Executive Capacity				Political Competition		
Under IMF	0.482 (−1.08)	0.524 (−0.90)							
Debt	1.013 (1.08)	1.016 (1.07)	1.015 (1.15)	1.014 (0.96)	1.014 (0.99)	1.012 (0.86)	1.025 (1.33)	1.038 (2.13)**	1.009 (0.68)
Fiscal Position	0.872 (−1.05)	0.918 (−0.75)							0.943 (−0.35)
Electricity Consumption	1.013 (2.13)**		0.999 (−2.26)**	1.013 (2.22)**	1.013 (2.03)**	1.016 (2.39)**	1.016 (2.77)***	1.016 (1.84)*	1.014 (2.30)**
Electricity Consumption*LogT	0.994 (−2.17)**			0.994 (−2.26)**	0.994 (−2.07)**	0.993 (−2.48)**	0.993 (−2.92)***	0.992 (−2.06)***	0.994 (−2.31)**
GDP per Capita		1.007 (2.51)**							
GDP per Capita*LogT		0.997 (−2.46)**							
Growth	0.306 (−2.09)**	0.153 (−2.04)**	0.330 (−2.01)**	0.371 (−1.62)	0.180 (−2.58)***	0.213 (−2.91)***	0.084 (−2.31)**	0.296 (−1.50)	0.233 (−2.25)**
Growth * LogT	1.663 (1.90)*	2.237 (1.95)*	1.605 (1.82)*	1.507 (1.38)	2.062 (2.38)**	1.929 (2.71)***	2.837 (2.05)**	1.704 (1.37)	1.812 (2.11)**
Distance			0.508 (−1.40)						

Government Share				0.024 (−1.47)					
Single-Party Majority					2.000 (1.13)				
Political Constraints						0.143 (−0.93)			
Left Opposition							0.057 (−2.18)**		
Legislative Advantage							0.987 (−0.56)		
Polarization								0.103 (−1.97)**	
Effective Number of Parties								1.691 (2.69)***	
Right Incumbent									0.252 (−1.61)
Center Incumbent									0.271 (−1.01)
Observations	188	188	173	182	188	188	177	174	188
Sphtest (Prob > chi2)	0.79	0.91	0.84	01.00	01.00	0.98	0.52	0.89	0.49
Countries at Risk	17								
Failures	12								

Cox Proportional Hazard Models; Robust z statistics in parentheses; * significant at 10%; ** significant at 5%; *** significant at 1%.

percent in the likelihood of privatization at the outset of the period, but this effect became negative as time went by. This result suggests that technological pressures hit the countries with a higher teledensity first and, as their example took hold, the less-developed countries were more likely to reform in order to catch up. Substituting teledensity for GDP per capita produces similar results.

Among the indicators of institutional constraints, we find only that single-party majority had the expected (and significant) effect. Meanwhile, two of our three indicators of political competition had significant effects in the expected direction. Left opposition was significant, reducing the chance of adopting privatization in a given year by more than 75 percent. Additionally, controlling for the number of parties in the legislature, the measure of ideological polarization was significant, reducing the likelihood of privatization by more than 80 percent. Legislative advantage, however, was not significant.[20] The main effects of political competition thus were a result of the impact of relative ideology on the challenger's credibility. Remarkably, despite the impact of the relative ideology of the incumbent and the challenger on the privatization of telecoms, the ideology of the incumbent alone had no significant effects on the adoption of this policy.

Privatization of Electricity

In the privatization of electricity, financial pressures had weaker effects than in telecommunications as shown in Table 2.2. There were no significant effects derived from either debt service or being under an IMF agreement, and there is no direct measure of electricity loans available like the one available for telecommunications. Although the effect of fiscal budgets was in the expected direction – a fiscal surplus has a negative effect on policy adoption – it was not significant at standard levels.

Electricity consumption per capita did have a significant effect on the likelihood of privatization adoption. As in the privatization of telecoms, however, this effect was nonproportional. The direct effect (at $t = 0$) of electricity consumption on the likelihood of privatization was positive, but it became significant and negative, so that between 1993 and 1994 a higher level of electricity consumption translated into a smaller likelihood that

[20] The effects of left opposition and legislative advantage hold if they are included separately.

privatization would occur.[21] As in telecoms, it seems that countries with higher per capita consumption were more likely to adopt privatization at the start of the period, while poorer countries were more likely to do it later on in an effort to catch up. Similarly, the effect of growth was nonproportional – that is, it was negative until the mid-1990s and positive thereafter.

Regarding the effect of institutional constraints on executive capacity, neither Henisz's political constraints index nor government status had significant effects on the probability of adopting privatization laws. As in telecommunications, the results confirm the hypothesis about the effects of political competition. Even though the president's legislative advantage had no significant effect, both left opposition and polarization – which measure the credibility of challengers – had significant effects in the expected direction. Controlling for the number of effective parties in the legislature, polarized governments were more than 90 percent less likely to privatize than governments that were not polarized, whereas left opposition reduced the hazard of reform by more than 90 percent. Finally, the ideology of the incumbent had no significant effect on policy adoption in this sector either.

In sum, the results provide support for the first hypothesis that political competition reduced the likelihood of privatization in both sectors. In particular, the effects of challengers' credibility to oppose reforms – measured through the relative ideology of the incumbent and his or her main challenger – were significant in both sectors. These effects hold when controlling for financial pressures for policy adoption through World Bank loans in telecoms and fiscal deficits in electricity. These results, though, provide limited confirmation of the effect of institutional constraints on executive capacity. Finally, lending credence to the idea that privatization was driven by pragmatism rather than by sheer ideological conviction, the results show that the ideology of the executive alone did not affect the likelihood of policy adoption in either sector. We tested an alternative measure based on prior policies in public utilities, which classifies parties based on whether they nationalized or created companies in these two sectors, in order to separate formerly populist parties from the rest (not reported here). Yet we found that an incumbent with a populist past had no effect in explaining the likelihood of privatization in either sector, further

---

[21] The effect of electricity consumption if we do not add an interaction with time is negative. We used electricity losses as an alternative measure, but it was never significant, and we did not include the results in our tables.

Table 2.3. *Timing of Decision to Open Up Electricity Markets to Private Investment*

	Economic Factors		Executive Capacity			Political Competition			
Under IMF	1.302 (0.42)	1.252 (0.38)	1.392 (0.50)	1.323 (0.44)	1.400 (0.54)	1.238 (0.33)	1.421 (0.56)	1.281 (0.41)	1.270 (0.40)
Debt	0.933 (−0.34)	0.910 (−0.49)	0.941 (−0.29)	0.933 (−0.34)	0.974 (−0.13)	0.950 (−0.25)	0.952 (−0.26)	1.039 (2.13)**	0.860 (−0.86)
Debt* LogT	1.048 (0.50)	1.062 (0.68)	1.044 (0.45)	1.047 (0.50)	1.026 (0.27)	1.038 (0.39)	1.038 (0.42)		1.091 (1.09)
Fiscal Position		0.982 (−0.16)							
Electricity Consumption	0.999 (−0.31)		0.999 (−0.18)	0.999 (−0.31)	0.999 (−0.32)	0.999 (−0.32)	0.999 (−0.20)	1.004 (0.89)	1.002 (0.39)
Electricity Consumption* LogT	1.001 (0.48)		1.001 (0.30)	1.001 (0.48)	1.001 (0.51)	1.001 (0.35)	1.001 (0.36)	0.998 (−0.84)	1.000 (0.19)
GDP per Capita		1.000 (2.62)***							
Growth	0.701 (−0.33)	0.907 (−0.11)	0.646 (−0.42)	0.680 (−0.35)	0.605 (−0.48)	0.659 (−0.42)	0.725 (−0.30)	0.690 (−0.33)	0.870 (−0.11)
Growth * LogT	1.238 (0.47)	1.119 (0.30)	1.238 (0.55)	1.254 (0.49)	1.324 (0.64)	1.277 (0.57)	1.223 (0.45)	1.267 (0.48)	1.156 (0.27)
Distance			0.454 (−0.95)						
Government Share				1.309 (0.21)					

Single-Party Majority					1.565 (0.50)				
Political Constraints						0.406 (−0.43)			
Left Opposition							1.795 (0.81)		
Legislative Advantage							1.026 (2.05)**		
Polarization								0.203 (−2.00)**	
Effective Number of Parties								0.118 (−0.60)	
Effective Number of Parties*LogT								2.944 (0.70)	
Right Incumbent									9.244 (1.74)*
Center Incumbent									5.295 (0.87)
Observations	181	181	183	193	201	201	183	184	201
Sphtest (Prob > chi2)	0.99	0.93	0.49	0.97	0.24	0.28	0.97	0.12	0.99
Countries at Risk	17								
Failures	15								

Cox Proportional Hazard Models; Robust z statistics in parentheses; * significant at 10%; ** significant at 5%; *** significant at 1%.

reinforcing the view that incumbent ideology did not matter for policy adoption during this period.

The Opening of Markets to Private Investment

In telecoms, market liberalization, which opened markets to private investors beyond those buying the privatized assets (and allowed them to compete for the same customers), was often scheduled at the time of privatization. In this sense, the opening of the telecoms market to private investment cannot be taken as an independent decision. Instead, in many countries, when privatization laws were adopted, legal monopolies were also established in order to increase the value of assets, promote investment, and smooth the end of cross-subsidies. These conditions are analyzed in Chapter 3, but they limit the empirical analysis of policy adoption to the opening of electricity markets to private investment. This decision did not always coincide with the sale of assets in the sector, and it typically included different investors from the ones that purchased state-owned assets. As before, survival analysis is used to estimate the factors that affected the likelihood that a country would allow private investment without transfer of assets.

Our results show that political competition had some influence on the adoption of private investment policy, but we find little effect from other variables (Table 2.3). We do not find effects derived from economic or technological pressures or even from measures of executive capacity – which may be explained by the fact that in many countries the decision was made by a unilateral presidential decree or through changes in concession rules rather than by an act of Congress. Perhaps this same reason explains why right-wing incumbents were nearly nine times more likely to adopt a policy of market liberalization than their left- or center-leaning counterparts, whereas the relative ideological position of the challenger was not significant.

Two measures of political competition were significant (see Table 2.3). The effect of competition on the incumbent's incentives is clear from the significant positive effect of legislative advantage, whereas the negative effect of *ideological polarization* captures the capacity of the challenger to use policy adoption to his or her advantage. An increase of 1 percent in legislative advantage between the incumbent and the challenger made reform approximately 2 percent more likely (or 81 percent more likely for each change of one standard deviation) in a given year, while the existence of ideological polarization made reform more than 85 percent less likely, controlling for the number of parties in the legislature.

In short, political competition affected the opening of electricity markets to private investment, but other variables had weaker effects, whereas the ideology of the incumbent became significant. A possible reason for the lack of significant findings regarding economic pressures might be that the opening of electricity markets to private investment has a weaker effect on revenue than does the sale of assets. The lack of findings on executive capacity could be related to the possibility that the reform could be made effective without the help of the legislature. This political strategy might also explain why the ideology of the incumbent mattered for the adoption of this policy, in contrast to both privatization and the establishment of a regulator, discussed in the following subsection.

The Establishment of Regulatory Agencies in Telecommunications

Because regulatory agencies do not bring or liberate fiscal resources, financial pressures should have weak effects on their establishment. Henisz et al. (2005) argue, however, that international coercion explains their creation to please international financial institutions. As shown in Table 2.4, debt service had no consistent effects whereas neither fiscal deficit nor debt service had consistent effects on the establishment of regulatory agencies in telecommunications in Latin America. In line with Henisz et al., however, both IMF agreements and sectoral World Bank loans in telecoms had significant effects in the expected positive direction. Again, it is hard to determine whether this result measures encouragement or rewarding, but it does suggest that the World Bank played some role in the policy process. As in privatization, teledensity had a significant effect on the establishment of regulators in the sector, but this effect was strongly nonproportional. Although its effect was negative when included alone, when an interaction with time is included, its effect was positive at the beginning of the period, while around 1992 and 1993 it became significant and negative.

The effect of political competition was stronger for the capacity of credible challengers to oppose reforms. Polarization and left opposition had statistically significant and substantial effects: controlling for the number of effective parties, a polarized political system made the establishment of regulators more than 80 percent less likely, and having a challenger to the left of the incumbent made reforms more than 70 percent less likely in a given year. Among the variables measuring institutional constraints on executive

Table 2.4. *Timing of Decision to Establish Regulatory Agency for Telecommunications*

	Economic Factors			Executive Capacity				Political Competition			
Under IMF	4.966		3.821	6.425	3.505	4.182	4.345	5.096	10.210	3.982	3.548
	(2.70)***		(2.57)**	(2.03)**	(1.93)*	(2.12)**	(2.22)**	(1.63)	(2.43)**	(2.15)**	(2.15)**
Debt	1.012	1.008	1.019	1.014	1.015	1.011	1.010	1.014	1.018	1.011	1.009
	(1.18)	(0.73)	(1.69)*	(1.28)	(1.54)	(1.08)	(0.94)	(1.44)	(1.77)*	(1.04)	(0.84)
World Bank Loan		8.035									
		(3.26)***									
Fiscal Position	1.159	0.988	1.169								
	(1.69)*	(−0.11)	(1.82)*								
Tele Density	1.123	1.159		1.121	1.168	1.119	1.127	1.166	1.145	1.126	1.121
	(3.59)***	(2.97)***		(3.21)***	(3.12)***	(3.54)***	(3.35)***	(2.92)***	(2.59)***	(3.62)***	(3.39)***
Tele Density * LogT	0.947	0.938		0.947	0.933	0.949	0.945	0.933	0.939	0.946	0.948
	(−4.27)***	(−3.16)***		(−3.75)***	(−3.51)***	(−4.15)***	(−4.06)***	(−3.19)***	(−2.71)***	(−4.31)***	(−4.01)***
GDP per Capita			1.004								
			(6.19)***								
GDP per Capita * LogT			0.998								
			(−7.17)***								
Growth	0.848	0.810	0.870	0.911	0.896	0.902	0.889	0.919	0.915	0.902	0.897
	(−1.61)	(−1.57)	(−1.52)	(−1.22)	(−1.35)	(−1.36)	(−1.50)	(−1.03)	(−1.25)	(−1.31)	(−1.27)
Distance				0.478							
				(−1.70)*							
Government Share					0.027						
					(−1.25)						

74

	(1)	(2)	(3)	(4)	(5)	(6)	(7)	(8)	(9)	(10)	(11)
Single-Party Majority						1.531					
						(0.78)					
Political Constraints							3.079				
							(0.85)				
Left Opposition								0.259			
								(−2.38)**			
Legislative Advantage								0.982			
								(−1.32)			
Polarization									0.187		
									(−4.19)***		
Effective Number of Parties									0.947		
									(−0.26)		
Margin of Victory										0.605	
										(−0.36)	
Right Incumbent											0.917
											(−0.15)
Center Incumbent											0.495
											(−0.57)
Observations	162	160	162	165	174	182	182	169	166	182	182
Stphtest (Prob > chi2)	0.98	0.89	0.83	1.00	1.00	1.00	1.00	1.00	0.98	1.00	0.99
Countries at Risk	17										
Failures	16										

Cox Proportional Hazard Models; Robust z statistics in parentheses; * significant at 10%; ** significant at 5%; *** significant at 1%.

Table 2.5. *Timing of Decision to Establish Regulatory Agency for Electricity*

	Economic Factors		Executive Capacity				Political Competition		
Under IMF	2.458 (1.25)	2.909 (2.10)**	3.876 (2.33)**	3.367 (1.86)*	3.217 (2.36)**	2.563 (1.76)*	3.285 (2.32)**	5.514 (2.02)**	3.072 (2.18)**
Debt	1.026 (2.10)**	1.026 (2.26)**	1.025 (1.93)*	1.026 (2.04)**	1.028 (2.51)**	1.027 (2.26)**	1.021 (1.99)**	1.032 (2.18)**	1.031 (2.48)**
Fiscal Position	0.777 (−3.31)***								
Electricity Consumption	1.017 (4.20)***		1.012 (2.43)**	1.014 (2.14)**	1.004 (1.93)*	1.006 (3.07)***	1.011 (2.78)***	1.013 (1.90)*	1.004 (1.52)
Electricity Consumption*LogT	0.993 (−3.91)***		0.995 (−2.36)**	.994 (−2.05)**	0.998 (−1.63)	0.998 (−2.29)**	0.995 (−2.71)***	0.995 (−1.73)*	0.998 (−1.28)
GDP per Capita		1.000 (0.12)							
Growth		2.059 (1.26)	0.525 (−0.52)	0.388 (−0.77)	2.123 (1.51)	1.958 (1.41)	0.291 (−1.20)	0.409 (−0.70)	2.059 (1.22)
Growth * LogT		0.776 (−1.11)	1.330 (0.57)	1.509 (0.83)	0.757 (−1.42)	0.789 (−1.24)	1.717 (1.28)	1.507 (0.80)	0.772 (−1.09)
Distance			0.498 (−1.38)						
Government Share				1.018 (0.01)					

Single-Party Majority					1.794				
					(1.21)				
Political Constraints						0.026			
						(−2.88)***			
Left Opposition							0.268		
							(−2.02)**		
Legislative Advantage							1.009		
							(0.71)		
Polarization								0.239	
								(−2.27)**	
Effective Number of Parties								0.743	
								(−0.96)	
Right Incumbent									0.863
									(−0.27)
Center Incumbent									0.615
									(−0.57)
Observations	171	192	173	183	192	192	177	174	192
Stphtest (Prob > chi2)	0.74	0.98	0.68	0.83	1.00	0.99	0.74	0.24	0.99
Countries at Risk	17								
Failures	16								

Cox Proportional Hazard Models; Robust z statistics in parentheses; * significant at 10%; ** significant at 5%; *** significant at 1%.

powers, the ideological distance between the executive and the median legislator had the expected negative effect, decreasing the hazard by nearly 50
percent for every increase of one point in distance.[22] Yet other measures of
institutional capacity had no effect. Finally, the ideology of the incumbent
had no significant, direct effect on the establishment of regulators.

The Establishment of Regulatory Agencies in Electricity

The results in Table 2.5 regarding the establishment of regulatory agencies
in electricity suggest that financial pressures also had a strong effect on the
adoption of regulatory authorities in this sector, as argued by Henisz et al.
(2005). Both being under an IMF agreement and debt service had significant and positive effects, although the effect of Under IMF was slightly less
robust. Remarkably, fiscal position had a significant effect in the expected
direction – that is, greater deficits increased the likelihood of reform adoption, even though creating a new bureaucracy had no positive effect on the
budget. As in privatization, electricity consumption had a significant effect
on the establishment of regulators in the sector, but this effect was strongly
nonproportional and sensitive to model specification. Although its effect
was negative when included alone, when an interaction with time was
included, its effect was positive at the beginning of the period, but around
1995 it became significant and negative.

The effect of political competition was again stronger in terms of the
credibility of the challenger than of power differentials. Whereas legislative
advantage had no significant effect on policy adoption, polarization and left
opposition had significant effects in the expected negative direction,
decreasing the likelihood that a regulatory agency would be established
for the electricity sector by more than 70 percent in a given year. Finally,
institutional constraints had some effect on policy adoption for the establishment of regulatory authorities, as political constraints had a significant
negative effect on reform adoption. Henisz's measure of political constraints decreased the hazard rate of reform adoption by almost 50 percent
for every increase of one standard deviation in the index. Although these
effects suggest a link with the need for legislative action to create new
regulatory authorities, they do not explain why we do not find them in
telecommunications.

[22] The effect of distance holds if we leave the government's share out. The government's
share of seats, however, is not significant if included alone.

Summary of Results

To sum up, the analysis of the three policies shows that the ideology of the incumbent had practically no effect on policy adoption (with the exception of the opening of electricity markets to private investment), suggesting that pragmatism dominated the adoption of market-oriented reforms in Latin American public utilities. When testing the impact of political competition on policy adoption, we controlled for the effect of financial pressures emphasized by the literature on globalization and policy diffusion and for the effect of institutional constraints, which are the focus of the literature on domestic policy making.

Table 2.6 summarizes the expectations and findings of this section regarding the analyzed variables. External fiscal pressures mostly had the expected effects, even with varying significance. There is no strong support

Table 2.6. *Summary of Results*

	Expected Effects	Privatization		Market Opening	Regulatory Authority	
		Telecom	Electricity	Electricity	Telecom	Electricity
Under IMF	+	+	−	+	+	+
World Bank Loan	+	+	NA	NA	+	NA
Debt	+	+	+	−	+	+
Fiscal position	−	+	−	−	unclear	−
Distance	−	−	−	−	−	−
Government Share	+	unclear	−	+	−	−
Single-Party Majority	+	+	−	−	+	+
Political Constraints	−	−	−	−	+	−
Effective Number of Parties	−	+	+	+	−	−
Left Opposition	−	−	−	−	−	−
Legislative Advantage	+	+	+	+	+	+
Polarization	−	−	−	−	−	−
Right Incumbent	+	+	−	+	−	−
Center Incumbent	unclear	+	−	+	−	−

Statistically significant results are shaded.

for the expected effects of institutional constraints on executive capacity, however, which depend on the power distribution produced by electoral competition. As expected, the ideology of the incumbent had no effect on policy adoption – with the exception of the opening of electricity markets to private investment, which was more likely under right-wing governments. The first hypothesis about political competition is supported by these results. Interestingly, challengers' placement on the ideological spectrum relative to incumbents, which affected their policy credibility, had stronger effects than shrinking power differentials, which captured the incumbent's fear of replacement. Our proxy for those power differentials is based on prior electoral results, however, and thus is not as good a proxy as public opinion about an upcoming election would have been.

Policy Adoption in Argentina, Chile, and Mexico

This section describes the political context for the adoption of free-market reforms in telecommunications and electricity in Argentina, Chile, and Mexico in order to demonstrate the incentives generated by political competition for policy adoption even when controlling for regime features, which varied across the three countries at the time of the reforms. The literature on the effects of regime on policy making emphasizes the responsiveness of incumbents.[23] By contrast, this study focuses only on regime effects on political competition, which, in turn, triggered incentives for incumbents and challengers that affected policy adoption. The three studied countries had different political regimes at the onset of reforms. Chile had an authoritarian military regime, Mexico had a liberalizing authoritarian regime until at least 1996, and Argentina was fully a democracy during the whole period. Although each country had different institutional constraints on electoral competition due to its different political regime, credible political competition was low in all three nations at the time of reform adoption – due to either repression of challengers or the popularity of incumbents.

Chile: Policy Adoption with Repressed Political Competition

Chile was a pioneer of market-oriented reforms in public utilities, and their adoption occurred under a regime that constrained political competition.

---

[23] Przeworski et al. (2000) show how responsiveness generates different patterns of growth – either labor- or capital-intensive, depending on regime. Haggard and Kaufman (1992) associate regime with different macroeconomic policy, and Etchemendy (2009) with patterns of policy making for market-oriented reforms.

A right-wing authoritarian government of true believers who were not constrained by fiscal pressures pursued these policies. The establishment of the offices that would become the regulatory authorities dates from 1977 for telecommunications and from 1978 for electricity. Decree laws of 1982 privatized both industries, opened market competition, and defined the powers of regulatory authorities in both sectors. These policies were adopted after three years of fiscal surplus (1979–81) and after six years with an average rate of growth of more than 7 percent (1976–81) (Meller 1996, 187–8).

The Chilean telecommunications system before privatization was composed of two main state-owned companies: the Chilean Telephone Company (CTC) and ENTEL (the National Telephone Company).[24] CTC had been owned by ITT (International Telephone and Telegraph) until its nationalization by the Socialist administration of Salvador Allende in 1971, and it provided local communications and domestic long distance in the central region of Chile. ENTEL was created by a decree of Christian Democratic President Eduardo Frei in December 1964 under the tutelage of the state-owned holding CORFO (Production Development Corporation). The aim of the state-owned company was to provide long-distance telecommunications service and to cover the areas not serviced by ITT. As a result, ENTEL provided local service in a small region in the south of Chile, as well as domestic and international long-distance services.

In electricity, the Chilean Central Interconnected System (SIC) concentrates more than two-thirds of installed energy in the country; the Northern Interconnected System (SING) accounts for 20 percent of installed capacity; and two separate systems in Patagonia provide the rest (Inostroza 1995). Prior to privatization, there were two main companies in the SIC: Chilectra and Endesa. Chilectra had been created at the turn of the century with American capital for the central area of the country (including the metropolitan area of Santiago) and was nationalized in 1970 by the administration of Salvador Allende. In 1941, the Popular Front coalition, which included the Socialists, created Endesa as a state-owned company under CORFO to serve the areas of the country not covered by Chilectra. Both companies were

[24] The state-owned Telex-Chile (Chilean Telegraphs) provided services of telex and telegrams and would later be privatized as Chilesat, a provider of long-distance telecommunication services. Two small public companies – which were privatized in 1981 – provide local service in Patagonia while three small private companies provided it to certain areas of Santiago and the central region. The military government retained CTC investment in the wealthy areas served by these companies and made state-owned companies provide interconnection to promote the development of private providers (Melo 1993, 77).

vertically integrated, thereby concentrating generation, transmission, and distribution, although they served different areas of the SIC.[25]

Chilean public-utility reformers were right-wing true believers who repressed electoral competition and the dissent of Socialists and Christian Democrats, who had previously promoted public ownership in telecommunications and electricity. In the late 1970s, regulatory authority was separated from operations and established in the Undersecretariat of Telecommunications (SUBTEL) and the National Energy Commission (CNE). Decree laws of 1982 approved the privatization of assets, opened the market to private investment, and defined regulatory powers for both sectors.

The Chilean military regime of 1973 to 1990 restrained political competition by outlawing political parties and constrained the salience of policy issues by censoring the press. The regime had evolved from a collegial executive in the form of a military junta into a one-man rule when General Augusto Pinochet obtained the presidency and gained veto power by imposing a rule of unanimity on the military junta, which retained legislative functions.[26] To gain legitimacy, Pinochet called a plebiscite in 1980 to approve a new constitution, which established a timetable for regime transition depending on the outcome of another plebiscite to be held eight years later.[27] In a context of limited electoral competition, he received two-thirds of the vote. By 1983, however, the debt crisis had triggered

---

[25] The process of delivering electricity includes these three stages. Generation absorbs about 51% of total costs of the process. Transmission of electric power absorbs 11% of the cost, and distribution of power the remaining 38% (Hachette and Luders 1993, 149). Before privatization, the Chilean state controlled 90% of generation, 100% of transmission, and 80% of the distribution of electricity (Moguillansky 1999, 174).

[26] Decree Law 527 of 1974 established that the military junta had constitutional and legislative powers and that the executive power was exercised by the president of the junta, whose title was changed to "President of the Republic" by Decree Law 806 of 1974. Pinochet's supremacy was definitively established in 1978 when he ousted General Brigadier Gustavo Leigh from the military junta by accusing him of a lack of patriotism based on an interview to a foreign press journalist (Arriagada 1988, 36–7). Leigh was the main military opponent to shock therapy and excessive privatization, as well as to Pinochet's power personalization and extended authoritarian rule (Schamis 2002, 71).

[27] The 1980 constitution included 120 permanent articles establishing a "self-protected democracy" with republican institutions and 29 transitory dispositions, which took precedence over the permanent articles during the first presidential term until the 1988 plebiscite. Regardless of the outcome of the plebiscite, the constitution established the end of military rule in March 1990, when a civilian congress would be inaugurated, although the path to it would differ depending on whether the government or the opposition won the plebiscite (Barros 2002, 169–70).

a wave of popular protest against the regime, which interrupted the privatization of public utilities. The failure to achieve democratic transition wore down protesters as economic recovery started in the mid-1980s, and consequently the process of privatization was reinitiated in 1986.[28]

In short, Chilean reforms were adopted before the government started facing political competition, which heightened in late 1987 when support for a coalition of Socialist and Christian Democratic parties campaigning for the end of the regime in the 1988 plebiscite gained strength. Even though the Pinochet regime's fear of replacement started to grow and was confirmed by electoral defeat in the plebiscite of 1988 and in the subsequent presidential election of 1989, market-oriented reforms had already been adopted.

Mexico: Successive Reform Efforts under Political Liberalization

Unlike in Chile, Mexican reformers belonged to a party, the Institutional Revolutionary Party (PRI), which had promoted state intervention in the telecommunications and electricity sectors. Mexican populists converted to the market creed under external financial pressures. In Mexico, the reforms were pursued gradually and simultaneously with a process of political liberalization. Thus, incumbents faced varying levels of political competition as the regime evolved from a competitive authoritarianism into a democracy. In 1990, President Carlos Salinas (1988–94) privatized the state-owned telecommunications monopoly (Telmex [Mexican Telephones]) while establishing the rules for the subsequent opening of the long-distance telecommunications market to other investors. The regulatory authority was created only in 1995, however, by his successor, President Ernesto Zedillo (1994–2000). President Salinas also opened electricity generation to private investment in 1992, while the creation of the electricity regulatory authority was undertaken by President Zedillo in 1995. The latter also tried unsuccessfully to privatize electricity in 1999. Although both presidents were from the PRI, the sequence of reforms coincided with growing levels of political competition since 1997 and with the replacement of the ruling party for the first time in seventy years in the 2000 election.

---

[28] The protests against the regime started in May 1983 and finished around July 1986, when it became obvious that the regime would not fall, even though more than 100 lives were lost in the process. Although at the onset the protest enjoyed middle- and upper-class support, this support dwindled as the lower classes joined the movement (Arriagada 1988, Chapter 7).

The telecommunications industry in Mexico before privatization was concentrated in Telmex, a monopolistic state-owned enterprise. Telmex originated in the merger between two private companies of American and Swedish capital in 1947, which included capitalization by the users. Since 1956, Telmex had undergone a "Mexicanization" process by which foreign private owners were first pressed to merge into a single monopoly and then to sell to Mexican nationals in the 1960s. The company was finally nationalized in 1972, when the Mexican state acquired 51 percent of its shares (Petrazzini 1995, 107–9; Székely and Del Palacio 1995, 46–8). Although coverage grew rapidly in the 1970s, the 1982 crisis and the 1985 Mexico City earthquake had a dramatic effect on the company's operating capacity.

The Mexican electricity sector was dominated by two publicly owned companies – the Federal Energy Commission (CFE) and Luz y Fuerza del Centro (LyF), which were vertically integrated from generation to distribution but covered two different geographical regions. In 1937, PRI President Lázaro Cárdenas sanctioned the law that created the CFE, which started to buy private electricity companies around the country and invest in new services to expand coverage. In 1960, the PRI government nationalized LyF, which was privately owned until then, by purchasing 95 percent of its shares.[29] In that year, a constitutional amendment established a public monopoly over the provision of electric energy. Whereas the financial situation of LyF had been fragile since the 1970s, CFE installed capacity grew until the debt crisis of the 1980s.

The pragmatism of the conversion of PRI to the market after having nationalized both sectors can be explained by financial pressures. Mexican reformers converted under the financial strain provoked by the debt crisis, which began with Mexico's unilateral moratorium on debt payments in August 1982. The year before Salinas privatized Telmex, the fiscal deficit had reached almost 5 percent of GDP. Although it declined thanks to privatization, it grew again to 1.5 percent in 1998, the year before Zedillo attempted to privatize electricity. In December 1994, moreover, the year before the adoption of regulatory authorities in both sectors, a financial crisis was solved by a U.S. bailout, which fostered financial pressure from U.S. investors. Mexico's cost for international borrowing, as expressed by Moody's credit ratings, followed a similar trajectory. Its rating was

[29] The purchase of remaining shares was completed by President Salinas in return for the support of the union of that company for his candidacy.

withdrawn from February 1983 to December 1990, when it received a Ba3, which was raised to Ba2 only in 1996.[30]

Despite fiscal pressures that brought President Zedillo to propose electricity privatization, the incentives generated by political competition aborted this reform. Even when the formal powers of Mexico's presidents were weaker than those of Chile or Argentina (Shuggart and Carey 1995), their informal powers to select successors, along with partisan discipline and unified government until 1997, allowed both PRI presidents to obtain the approval of most of their bills until 2000.[31] Even after 1997, the number of executive bills approved only dropped to 87.5 percent (Saiegh 2006). The failure of the electricity privatization bill, however, was caused by PRI legislators, who refused to bring it to the legislative floor, rather than by gridlock between the president and Congress.

Changes in political competition modified the potential for increasing the salience of reform, amplified challengers' voices, and raised the electoral risks for incumbents. In the 1988 and 1994 elections, the PRI won a bare majority in the Lower Chamber – although it improved its share to 61 percent in the midterm elections of 1991. In 1997, the PRI obtained only 39 percent of votes for Lower Chamber representatives. The vote margin between the PRI and its main challenger, moreover, which had increased from 33 percent in 1988 to 44 percent in 1991, dropped to

---

[30] The highest quality obligations are Aaa, followed by Aa1, Aa2, and Aa3 as risk progresses. Then A1, A2, and A3, which involve some long-term risk. As risk grows the rating of obligations moves to Baa1, Baa2, and Baa3 and when the credit quality is considered questionable, their grade comes down firtst to Ba1, Ba2, and Ba3 and then to B1, B2 and B3 when they are considered subject to high risk. Extremely poor credit quality puts obligation rating down to Caa1, Caa2, and Caa3, with Ca involving speculative investment usually in default of deposit obligations and C as the lowest rating for bonds typically in default and with low potential recovery values. Electoral competition grew thanks to an electoral reform that granted independence to the Federal Electoral Commission and controlled campaign financing, thereby guaranteeing free and fair elections. This crucial institutional reform ended a protracted process of liberalization and brought democracy to Mexico (Magaloni 2006). It also facilitated the heightening of political competition, especially after the PRI conceded the results in the 1997 election.

[31] This informal power included the president's designation of a successor and control of the party hierarchy in charge of deciding candidacies. Because the constitution prohibited reelection for legislators, these informal powers granted the president control over politicians' future careers, whether in executive or legislative positions, and eased the approval of presidential initiatives in Congress (Weldon 1997; Casar 1998). From 1988 to 1997, more than 95% of executive initiatives were approved in Congress (Casar 1998, 128), whereas the annual budget sent by the executive was always approved with only minor changes (Ugalde 2000, 158–9).

24.5 percent in 1994 and 12.5 percent in 1997 in a three-way race. After 1997, political competition grew stronger, and the PRI started to fear losing the presidency. This fear seemed ever-present during the 2000 presidential campaign, in which the National Action Party (PAN) and PRI candidates were tied in surveys for three months before the election was won by PAN candidate Vicente Fox (Lawson 2004, 9).[32] Moreover, the PRI was confronting the right-wing PAN and the center-left Party of the Democratic Revolution (PRD), which obtained almost as many votes as the PAN in the 1997 legislative elections. The PRD provided a credible alternative to voters who were discontent with market-oriented reforms, as its core was constituted by former PRI politicians who refused to convert to the market creed.[33] Therefore, the increase in political competition – both by generating a replacement threat for the PRI and presenting a credible challenger in the PRD – made policy adoption increasingly difficult when President Zedillo attempted to privatize electricity in response to financial pressures in 1999, especially as both the PRI and the PAN would need to attract PRD voters to win the 2000 election.

In February 1999, President Ernesto Zedillo submitted a bill to Congress proposing to privatize electricity to deal with increasing demand and the growing fiscal cost of public guarantees to private investment. Large industrial users concerned about supply and the CFE labor union called Single Union of Electricity Workers of the Mexican Republic (SUTERM), which expected job creation, supported the reform, while the LyF labor union called Mexican Union of Electricity Workers (SME) rejected it.[34] Although Zedillo could not run for reelection, the high level of political competition altered the incentives of PRI politicians concerned about their electoral futures, including presidential hopefuls.

---

[32] The PAN was founded in the 1950s as a reaction to the electoral fraud and anticlericalism of the PRI. While the regional base of the PRD is in the south, that of the PAN is in the north of Mexico.

[33] The PRD emerged from a 1988 electoral front created by former PRI politician Cuauhtémoc Cardenas, which had an unexpectedly strong showing in the presidential elections of that year, and claimed that electoral fraud deprived him of the victory.

[34] There were two unions in the sector: SME, which represented LyF workers, and SUTERM for CFE workers. Because SME workers had better conditions, which would have imposed higher labor costs in the rest of the sector due to labor regulations, the two unions never merged. The PRI controlled the SUTERM, whose leader claimed that the reform would create more jobs (*El Informador*, March 10, 1999). The SME was controlled by left-wing leaders with short-term horizons due to two-year electoral cycles and a rule against immediate reelection (Murillo 2001).

The incentives for political competition were heightened by the public salience of the reform, which was the highest of all six reforms reported in Table 2.7. Higher salience was facilitated by increasing freedom of the press due to democratization and by market competition in the media since the mid-1990s (Lawson 2002).[35] Newspapers published 273 articles about the reform between January and December 1999 and 108 articles in the peak month of February. The left-wing PRD and its labor allies in the LyF union mobilized to raise the salience of reform, thereby increasing the electoral stakes for PRI politicians concerned about being replaced. Forty percent of articles on the reform denounced it, and the source of criticism was almost equally divided between the LyF union on the one hand and PRD and discontented PRI politicians on the other. The PRD and the SME criticized the reform, emphasizing the loss of national sovereignty and the negative price effects on consumers that would result from it.[36] The public salience of the reform increased its potential electoral consequences for the incumbent and the challenger, especially as public opinion surveys showed that electricity privatization was one of the few policy issues considered by voters as they weighed the candidates in the presidential election (Magaloni and Poire 2004, 294).

Although the main challenger was to the right of the PRI and the main opposition to reform came from the PRD, PRD and PRI voters were more likely to oppose the reform than PAN voters. Support for privatization had a positive effect on the probability of voting for Fox and a negative effect on the probability of voting for either the PRD candidate, Cuauhtémoc

---

[35] Press coverage provides a good indicator of salience, as radio reports often reproduce newspaper articles, and there was more freedom of the press in written media than in televised media due to the larger number of outlets. All studies of press coverage in Mexico were done by using the archives of PRODATO, which selects articles by topic in *La Jornada, El Universal, Uno mas Uno, El Financiero, Proceso, El Nacional, Excélsior*, and *Reforma*. I report the month with the highest number (peak) because the intensity of information is crucial for assessing public salience.

[36] SME union leader Rosendo Flores opposed privatization based on arguments of national sovereignty (*Excélsior*, February 16, 1999), the surrendering of public policy to international financial institutions (*Excélsior*, February 16, 1999), and its effect on consumer prices (*Novedades*, February 28, 1999). PRD legislator Sergio Osorio Romero accused the proposal of being a NAFTA imposition with a negative effect on consumer prices even before its formal presentation (*La Jornada*, January 29, 1999). PRD leader and future major of México City Andrés Manuel López Obrador denounced the proposal as the result of negotiations between the PRI and the PAN to sell out the electric industry to private capital, both domestic and foreign (*El Economista*, February 15, 1999).

Table 2.7. *Public Salience of Market Reforms in Mexico (number of newspaper articles)*

Policy	Monthly Average	Peak month
Privatization of telecommunications	3	15
Opening of telecommunication market	2.5	12
COFETEL (regulator)	3	7
Privatization of electricity	**25**	**208**
Opening of electricity market	0	0
CRE (regulator)	0.3	1

Source: archives of PRODATO based on El Universal, La Jornada, Uno mas Uno, El Nacional, El Financiero, Reforma, Expansión and Excelsior.

Cardenas, or the PRI candidate, Francisco Labastida (Magaloni and Poire 2004, 304–8). As PAN and PRI candidates needed to attract PRD voters, their position on electricity reform was important.

As expected, political competition decreased the likelihood of reform adoption in 1999. PRI politicians were afraid of supporting the reform. Soon after Zedillo introduced the bill, PRI politicians from the hinterland publicly voiced their opposition, whereas PRI legislators claimed that the proposal could not be discussed until the following legislative term. The PRI legislative delegation and the presidential hopeful and government secretary Francisco Labastida, who was in charge of achieving PRI legislative discipline, did not support the reform and kept it from reaching the floor for consideration, fearing its negative electoral consequences.[37] Moreover, even PAN candidate Vicente Fox, who favored electricity privatization (as did most of his party's voters and legislators), changed his position to attract PRD voters, who hated the PRI more than the PAN (*La Jornada*, February 4, 1999). During the electoral campaign, he further promised not to privatize electricity, whereas PAN legislators withdrew legislative support for reform. As the left-wing PRD and its labor allies were effective in raising the salience of the reform, the PRI and the PAN decided not to support this policy.

Other electricity reforms had been passed at a time of low political competition. In 1992, with a fiscal surplus of 4 percent of GDP, but under pressure to comply with the energy chapter of North American Free Trade

---

[37] Labastida's preferences were reported in confidential interviews one and two (with high officials in Zedillo's administration), October 9, 2002 and February 12, 2004.

Agreement (NAFTA), President Salinas sent a bill to Congress to reform the 1975 Law of Public Electricity Service. The PRI passed his reform despite opposition from the PRD for ideological reasons and the PAN, which objected that the law was of dubious constitutionality. This reform allowed private investment in electricity under different schemes, such as independent power production, cogeneration, self-supply, and small-scale generation, limiting sales to 30 megawatts a year to one of the two state-owned firms. The investment in new installed capacity under these arrangements required substantial public guarantees (Carreón Rodríguez et al. 2007). The public salience of this reform was very low, as there was no press coverage of it – and no price effects for residential consumers, because the new supply of energy was to be sold to the state-owned CFE. Low public salience, along with unified government, facilitated policy adoption. Additionally, in 1995, and under Zedillo, low public salience, a low level of political competition, and a unified government facilitated the approval of a law creating the electricity regulatory authority, or Energy Regulatory Commission (CRE): there were only three articles in the press about the issue during the period of the legislative debate between January and October 1995 (Table 2.7).

Institutional constraints amplified the incentives generated by low political competition when PRI President Carlos Salinas pursued telecommunications reforms. When he announced the decision to privatize Telmex and open the telecommunications market to private investment, he did not need to involve the legislature, which at the time was controlled by his party. He could revise the concession terms based on the previous legislative delegation of the prerogatives to buy and sell companies in the Law of State-Owned Enterprises (Rogosinski 1997, 109).[38] The executive also decided unilaterally to open only the domestic market to private investors, keeping the long-distance market closed until August 1996.[39] Additionally,

---

[38] The Organic Law of Public Federal Administration defines two types of state-owned enterprises: decentralized organizations, which can be created by either the legislative or the executive branch, and companies of majority state participation, where the state owns at least 51% of the shares, but there is private participation. The Law of State-Owned Enterprises gives the executive power the right to sell or transfer state-owned shares in the latter on the stock exchange (art. 32) and gives the Secretary of Finance control over the process (art. 68). Because Telmex was a company with majority state participation, as President Echeverría bought 3% of its stock to make the state the main shareholder in 1972, the executive did not need legislative intervention to divest it.

[39] The opening of the local market was not made effective, however, because the secretary of communications did not grant licenses for operation to those demanding them until 1995 (confidential interview three, January 17, 2001, and personal interview with Axtel manager Carlos Escalante, January 19, 2001).

the competitive authoritarian regime made it difficult to raise public salience about the reform. There were fifty-two articles on telecommunications privatization in the major newspapers between June 1989, when the sale was announced, and November 1990, when it took place; that is, there were three monthly articles on average and fifteen in the month with the highest coverage (Table 2.7). Not only was the media coverage surprisingly scant, but none of these articles mentions opposition to privatization. Furthermore, the telephone workers' labor union was controlled by a political ally who supported privatization in exchange for compensation for workers and the organization (Murillo 2001).

On the decision to postpone the liberalization of the long-distance market for six years – thereby granting a monopoly to the buyers of Telmex – public salience was slightly lower than for privatization, as there were 43 articles published during the same period in the press, or 2.5 per month, with 12 in the month with most coverage (Table 2.7). The third market reform in telecommunications – the establishment of a regulatory authority – was postponed until 1995, when Congress passed the Federal Telecommunications Law mandating the creation of the Federal Telecommunications Commission (COFETEL). In 1995, the PRI continued to control both chambers of Congress, and the issue had a low public salience. There were only eighteen articles in the Mexican press about COFETEL from January to June 1995 – the period of legislative debate over the Federal Telecommunications Law – that is, three per month on average and seven articles in the month with most coverage (Table 2.7). Thus, we may conclude that the lack of credible challengers with the capacity to raise public salience facilitated reform adoption.

In sum, Mexican telecommunications reforms, as well as the initial electricity reforms, were adopted in a context of restricted political competition. Whereas financial pressures prompted both telephone and electricity privatization, the latter failed because high levels of political competition generated incentives for PRI politicians and the PAN presidential hopeful to avoid this reform, lest it cost them dearly in future elections.

Argentina: Democracy with Changing Political Competition

Whereas Mexican changes in political competition coincided with regime transition, Argentina's case studies show how varying levels of political competition within a constantly democratic regime generated incentives affecting policy adoption. Argentina returned to democracy in 1983 after seven years of military rule.[40] It had a two-party system, with a relatively high level of legislative discipline and a president with strong, proactive powers (Jones 1997; Mustapic 2002). Both parties, the Peronist Party (PJ) and the Radical Civic Union (UCR), had previously promoted populist policies in public utilities but pragmatically moved to pursue market-oriented policies to deal with the country's fiscal shortfall.

Fiscal pressures explain the adoption of market-oriented reforms in Argentina. In 1983, the Radical candidate, Raúl Alfonsín, won the presidential election. The Peronist candidate, Carlos Menem, was elected in 1989 and reelected in 1995. Presidents Alfonsín and Menem were the main initiators of efforts for the adoption of privatization. President Alfonsín failed to privatize telecommunications in 1988, but his successor accomplished the task two years later while postponing competition in that market and establishing a regulatory authority two years later. In December 1991, moreover, Menem achieved the approval of a bill, which privatized, opened the market to investment, and created the regulatory agency in electricity.

The Argentine telecommunications industry was born as a private industry in the nineteenth century and consolidated under American capital by 1929. Perón nationalized it in 1948, and it was renamed ENTEL in 1956.[41] Its coverage was the second most extensive in Latin America after Uruguay: in 1985, the number of phones per 100 inhabitants (teledensity) was almost nine, which was approximately double that in Chile and Mexico.

The state-owned Argentine electricity industry was concentrated into three vertically integrated state-owned enterprises: SEGBA (Electricity Services of the Great Buenos Aires) for Buenos Aires and its suburbs, Hidronor for the Northern Patagonia rivers, and Agua y Energía for the rest of the country.[42] Perón had created Agua y Energía in 1947, whereas

---

[40] The 1976–83 military regime produced a proposal for the privatization of long-distance telecommunications in February 1982 at a time when increasing political opposition brought military rulers to embark on a war with Great Britain to recover domestic legitimacy. The regime faced a successful general strike in March 1982 and started the war on April 2. Its military defeat prompted democratic transition and killed the proposal.

[41] The company served 92% of the market, with a private provider, the Argentine Company of Telephones, owned by Ericcson (CAT), serving 7% – concentrated in the interior – and cooperatives 1% (Petrazzini 1995, 56).

[42] Some provinces, like Buenos Aires, Córdoba, and Corrientes, also had their own distribution companies, and two utilities were owned by the state in association with the Paraguayan and Uruguayan states.

SEGBA had been nationalized by Radical President Arturo Frondizi, who also created Hidronor by using oil royalties (Sabato 1971).

Presidents Alfonsín and Menem attempted to introduce market-oriented policies under financial pressure. Alfonsín was facing a fiscal deficit that surpassed 3 percent and 2 percent of GDP in 1987 and 1988, respectively. After Menem started to privatize, it declined to 0.35 percent in 1990, according to the IMF's International Financial Statistics.[43] Argentina's cost of international financing – expressed by Moody's credit rating – imposed further constraints on former populists. In November 1986, it received a Baa3 grade, which declined to B3 in May 1989 and was only raised to B1 in July 1992. Hyperinflation caused real prices to plunge, moreover, and along with the fiscal crisis brought public services to the brink of collapse.[44] Electricity companies suffered from underinvestment, which provoked daily blackouts in major metropolitan areas.[45] Financial pressures provide a good account of why two formerly statist presidents attempted to adopt market reforms, as explained by both Llanos (2002) and Margheritis (1999).[46]

Although President Alfonsín faced a divided government from 1987, his reform attempt did not drown in legislative deadlock, because the concession contract with Telefónica of Spain proposed by his minister of public works did not require congressional approval. However, he faced opposition from PJ politicians and the PJ-controlled labor union while finding it hard to persuade his own troops in a competitive presidential election season. The UCR had won 48 percent of the legislative vote in 1983 and

---

[43] The Ministry of the Economy of the Argentine government reported a deficit of 4% of GDP for 1987 and 1988, which reached 12% of GDP in 1989.

[44] When Menem was inaugurated in 1989, telephone residential prices had reached their lowest historical levels – they dropped 830% due to hyperinflation in that year alone – whereas lack of investment due to continuous deficits since 1984 had brought the completion of local calls to a mere 49% success rate and long distance calls to 30%. The international standard was 95% and 85%, respectively (Petrazzini 1995, 58–9).

[45] Installed capacity in generation had grown by less than 12% between 1984 and 1990 (Spiller and Viana Martorell 1996, 95), and by 1991 the unavailability of thermal generating units in the interconnected system had reached 50% (Bastos and Abdala 1995, 41). The public management had calculated that without privatization, they would have needed to increase the price of electricity by 64% to provide the investment necessary to met demand in 1992 (Bastos and Abdala 1995, 92).

[46] The large outstanding financial obligations of the public sector would bring Menem to swap debt for privatized assets to increase the country's financial credibility. Moreover, the state-owned companies had been given as collateral for foreign loans, and creditors needed to authorize their sale, increasing their leverage over the process (Margheritis 1999, 140).

44 percent in the 1985 midterm elections, thus keeping its electoral margin over the Peronist Party at 10 percent and 9 percent, respectively. In the 1987 legislative elections, however, support for the Radicals dropped to 37 percent, while that of the Peronists rose to 41 percent, thereby shrinking their power differentials. Radicals became afraid of the replacement threat, which materialized when the Peronists won the 1989 presidential election. The Peronist Party won again in the 1991 and 1993 midterm elections, further increasing its electoral dominance over the Radicals and enhancing its legislative influence. President Menem was reelected in 1995 by a larger electoral margin than in 1989.

In early 1988, Alfonsín committed to the privatization of telecommunications under financial pressure, which had also brought him to sign a standby agreement with the IMF in July 1987 (Llanos 2002, 56). Although he was able to achieve some telecommunications reforms of low salience – including mobile telecommunications and data transmission (Decrees 1950/87 and 1757/87, respectively) – he failed to privatize ENTEL. Because public opinion opposed ENTEL's privatization, minister of public works Rodolfo Terragno decided to increase the public salience of the reform in an effort to persuade skeptical Radicals, Peronists, and the general public.[47] He made television cameras follow his six-hour testimony to the Senate (Llanos 2002, 57–60, 65). In his testimony, he pointed to fiscal pressures as the main reason for reform, because state-owned enterprises accounted for half the fiscal deficit, even when they were unable to meet demand. He also emphasized the pragmatism of the decision against Peronist accusations that he was contradicting the Radical electoral program, which defended state ownership based on the essential character of public services (Senado, Diario de Sesiones, April 27–8, 1988, 3208, 3218, 3264).

Although fiscal pressures explain Alfonsín's privatization attempt, political competition made it impossible for the attempt to succeed. The UCR faced a dramatic reduction in power differentials with the Peronists after losing the October 1987 legislative elections; Terragno claimed that he pushed for privatization with the aim of regaining political terrain (personal interview, February 19, 2008). Radicals were afraid of the electoral

---

[47] In a personal interview, Terragno said that he ordered a survey in 1987 that showed the public's opposition to privatization, in particular if the buyers were foreign. He claimed that ENTEL was the company that generated the most privatization opposition. Therefore, he decided to go to Congress to sell the reform and modify public opinion, which turned positive over time (Buenos Aires, February 19, 2008).

Table 2.8. *Public Salience of Market Reforms in Argentina (number of newspaper articles)*

Policy	Monthly Average	Peak Month
Privatization of telecommunications (Alfonsín)	5.5	9
Privatization of telecommunications (Menem)	9	29
Opening of telecommunication market	7.3	7
Regulatory Agency (CNT)	2.4	7
Privatization of electricity	5.6	22
Opening of electricity market	2.7	11
Regulatory agency (ENRE)	2.5	11

consequences of an uncertain reform, whereas the Peronists, who had nationalized telephones, were credible in their opposition to reform. Peronist legislators denounced the proposal, arguing that "national sovereignty cannot be sold," disapproving the sale of the national firms to foreign capital, and defending the importance of keeping monopolies in public services even if they were not profitable.[48]

Terragno's effort at increasing public salience raised the stakes for both parties. During the six months between the agreement with Telefónica over privatization and the public introduction by Terragno of the policy in Congress, 33 articles on the issue appeared in the press, for a monthly average of 5.5 articles, peaking at 9 in March 1988, the month when the agreement was signed (Table 2.8).[49] Although this coverage was not as extensive as that of Menem's reform, increasing political competition heightened the misgivings of Radicals and the Peronist legislative resistance.[50] That combination killed the project, especially as the Peronists – like the Mexican PRD – had the credibility, granted by their statist past, to denounce the Radicals' plan in order to improve their electoral prospects. Defending state ownership, for instance, PJ senator Romero referred to the public management of ENTEL during Perón's first two presidencies as having been crucial for the expansion of service (Senado, Diario de Sesiones, April 27–8, 1988, 3273).

---

[48] See, in particular, the speeches by PJ senators Eduardo Menem (brother to future president Carlos Menem) and Juan C. Romero (Senate, April 27–8, 1988, 3222, 3273).

[49] The analysis of press coverage in this chapter is based on the archives of *Clarín* newspaper and includes all major national newspapers.

[50] The Radical presidential candidate disagreed with the type of privatization, which excluded public bidding (Terragno, personal interview, February 19, 2008).

Though political competition hindered privatization under Alfonsín, financial and technological pressures continued to generate incentives for reform adoption. After Menem's election in 1989, political competition diminished, while hyperinflation made both the public and Peronist politicians more supportive of whichever policy would stabilize prices (Palermo and Torre 1992; Weyland 1998).[51] In 1989, the annual rate of inflation surpassed 3,000 percent, and public opinion considered inflation to be the main problem of the country (Llanos 2002, 66). Thus, privatization as a solution to the fiscal deficit became increasingly attractive: a May 1989 survey by Ipsos-Mora y Araujo found more than 60 percent support for the privatization of ENTEL. Hyperinflation also facilitated the legislative approval of the State Reform Law of 1989, which delegated the privatization of several state-owned companies – including ENTEL and SEGBA – to the executive power (Acuña 1994; Palermo and Novaro 1996). Weak political competition combined with favorable public opinion facilitated policy adoption in telecommunications at the onset of Menem's first term, although this was the most publicly salient of all reforms in Argentina (Table 2.8). Between June 1989 and July 1990, 117 articles were published about ENTEL privatization. These were more or less evenly distributed across months, with a monthly average of eleven articles, a median of fifteen monthly articles, and a peak in March of twenty-nine articles. The delegation of authority to the executive by the beleaguered Radicals, however, restricted policy resistance to a minority faction of workers, because the union was controlled by a Peronist leader who was appointed as undersecretary of communications and who promised to deliver compensation to telephone workers in return for their support for the reform.[52] Finally, not only were the political power differentials favorable to Peronists, but also the Radicals had no credibility to oppose a reform they had introduced onto the public agenda.

Presidential decrees established the conditions for opening the market to private investment and the creation of a regulatory authority (the National Telecommunications Commission, or CNT). These reforms were simultaneous with privatization but less publicly salient. Between June 1989 and July 1990, ninety-six articles appeared about the entry rules

---

[51] In a two-party system, the electoral margin in the presidential election had widened to 16% in favor of Peronists in 1989 from 12% in favor of Radicals in 1983.

[52] The labor union divided between supporters and opponents, and internal rivalry fostered militancy against the reform. However, government compensation, an employee-owned stock program, and organizational concessions for the union gained union approval of the privatization (Murillo 2001).

(peaking in March with twenty-three articles, and in April there were twenty-two) and thirty-two articles about the regulatory authority (peaking in April with seven articles) (Table 2.8). This differential in public salience and the lack of credible electoral competition also prevented the opposition from shaping the policy adoption process for these two reforms associated with privatization.

In electricity, the three reforms were simultaneous and established by Law 24,065, in contrast to the use of presidential decrees that characterized the telecommunications reforms. The legislative debate took place in 1991 and ended with the approval of Law 24,065 in December of that year; it was sanctioned the following month. Law 24,065 established the unbundling of the sector in into generation, transmission, and distribution; the conditions for transferring assets to private providers; the rules for entering each segment; and the regulatory authority. The Radical legislators in the opposition did not compromise over content but instead voted in dissent to the bill and presented their own minority bill, which was more statist.[53] The Peronist legislators supported the reform: they were not afraid of replacement, because the power differential between them and the Radicals had grown after the October 1991 legislative election.[54]

As in telecommunications, privatization was the most publicly salient of the three electricity reforms, followed by the opening of markets and the creation of a regulatory agency. Between September 1989, when privatization was announced, and August 1992, when the sale of assets started, 129 articles were published on the privatization of SEGBA (and 18 on the privatization of Agua y Energía), with a peak of 22 articles in December 1991, when Law 24,065 was approved (Table 2.8). By contrast, there were sixty-three articles on the opening of the market (eleven in the peak month of December 1991) and fifty-eight articles on the establishment of the regulatory authority, the National Electricity Regulatory Agency (ENRE), with fourteen articles in the peak month of December 1991. Yet in the absence of political competition, the challenger could not capitalize on these levels of public salience. Therefore, resistance to policy adoption

---

[53] The Radicals did not support the law and presented a minority proposal to the energy commission that was rejected on the floor. Their proposal considered generation as a public service and established that price regulation should protect users and that provinces should have a more relevant role in the process through the Federal Electricity Council (CFEE) while opposing the privatization of Hidronor and Agua and Energía.

[54] The legislative margin between the Peronists and the Radicals increased from 12% in 1989 to 16% in 1991.

was limited to a faction of the labor union that was militant in its rejection; as in telecommunications, the majority of the union was controlled by a Peronist leader who supported the process in return for compensations benefiting workers and the organization (Murillo 2001).[55]

In sum, the experience of Argentina with policy adoption confirms that external financial pressures generated strong pressure on the incumbents to adopt these policies and convinced Alfonsín and Menem to abandon their statist past. It also shows that even controlling for regime-type variation in political competition produced the hypothesized change in policy makers' incentives.

Conclusion

This chapter has provided empirical evidence of the effect of political competition on policy adoption based on a duration analysis of all Latin American countries, while illustrating with case studies of market-oriented reform of the electricity and telecommunications sectors in Argentina, Chile, and Mexico the incentives that competition generated. The analysis controls for the effect of financial pressures, which were crucial in explaining the adoption of market-oriented reforms in Latin America, especially in the cases of populists who pragmatically converted to the market creed. It shows that even when facing financial pressures for reform, political competition makes incumbents fear that pushing market-oriented reforms would lead to their replacement. Political competition, moreover, gave challengers the ability to oppose the reforms when they could provide a credible policy alternative. Through these two mechanisms, in addition to its institutional effects, political competition reduced the likelihood of reform adoption. These effects were captured by legislative power differentials and the relative ideological position of the incumbent and challenger in the duration analysis. The case studies showed the success of reforms in cases of limited political competition and their failure when credible challengers opposed them in the context of shrinking power differentials, which occurred in Argentina in 1988 and Mexico in 1999.

---

[55] As in telecommunications, the militant faction that resisted privatization eventually abandoned its Peronist affiliation, but the national labor federation controlled by Peronist union leaders was able to obtain compensation for workers, employee-owned programs, and organizational concessions for the organization – including the purchase of assets, financial support, and especial conditions to enter the privatization of pensions (Murillo 2001).

The effect of policy positioning in the proposal of policy alternatives by challengers – indicates that ideology still matters for prospective evaluations of challengers. The relative ideological position of the challenger, determined by using either polarization or left opposition as indicators, is the most significant measure of political competition, probably because challengers do not bear the brunt of pressure for policy adoption, as incumbents do. In Latin America, during the studied period, privatization never took place in either sector when a left-wing incumbent faced opposition to his or her ideological left, and there was only one case in which a center incumbent successfully pressed for privatization although he had an opposition from the left (Fernandez Reyna). Hence, our results for left opposition indicate that right-wing incumbents facing a left-wing opposition are substantially less likely to reform than all other incumbents (without opposition to their left), and especially less likely to reform than right-wing incumbents without opposition to their left. The ideological credibility of the challenger is essential, then, in making privatization less likely.

The case studies show that market-oriented reforms in telecommunications and electricity were successfully adopted in Argentina, Chile, and Mexico, although the incentives for pursuing these policies were ideological for right-wing true believers in Chile and financial for pragmatic populist converts in Argentina and Mexico. Yet high levels of political competition amplified the opposition of credible challengers, reducing the likelihood of policy adoption by risk-averse converts in the case of telecommunications in Argentina and electricity in Mexico. In Argentina, the opposition that rejected the 1988 attempt at privatizing telecommunications was a prostate intervention Peronist Party, which would later convert to the market creed. In Mexico, the pull of the unconverted left-wing PRD on marginal voters brought the PRI and the PAN to reject electricity privatization.

In sum, this chapter shows that political competition affected incentives for policy adoption across the region in the context of external financial pressures for convergence toward market-oriented reforms. The effects of political competition on policy adoption are important to consider in linking the role of competitive politics to market reforms. By focusing on the process of policy adoption, however, one loses track of other important political components of the process. That privatization policies were adopted across Latin America does not mean that they all had the same regulatory design. As Chapter 3 will show, the study of policy content is crucial to uncovering the resilient diversity of partisan policy preferences hidden behind apparent policy convergence.

3

Casting a Partisan Light on Regulatory Choices

This chapter shows how the content of market reforms in public utilities varies depending on who adopts these policies. Reformers can be either right-wing governments of true believers in the market as the best way of allocating resources or populists who pragmatically converted to the market creed under financial pressure. Which sort of politicians implement privatization reforms has a crucial effect on policy content due to their different constituencies, prior beliefs about state intervention, and allied experts. These factors reinforce each other in producing different preferences for the ideal degree of government control of private investors and for the distributive effects expected from privatization. As a result, the regulatory content of reforms generates different beneficiaries and institutional choices depending on the partisan identity of the reformers. When right-wing true believers are in charge, we should expect reforms to be market-conforming, and when pragmatic populist converts adopt reforms, we should expect them to be market-controlling. This partisan variation in policy content has been ignored by most studies of market reforms in Latin America due to the less publicly salient character of this dimension of policy making as compared with initial policy adoption.[1]

Partisanship: Constituencies, Ideas, and Experts

Partisan preferences about policy content are based on constituencies, ideological legacies, and allied technocrats. Partisan constituencies generate distributive demands, ideological legacies provide a lens with which to interpret the distributive consequences of policy choices under new

---

[1] Murillo (2002) presents an early version of this argument.

circumstances, and politicians' linkages to allied technocrats define to whom they will delegate technically complex choices based on a shared understanding of distributive goals.

Following the theory presented in Chapter 1, incumbent reformers are classified based on the public-utility policies they have adopted in the past. These original policies should reflect what their distributive goals are in the absence of external financial constraints. These earlier public-utility policies, moreover, should have been justified by diverse views regarding economic nationalism and state intervention.[2] Such policies also allowed experts to develop their prior careers in public utilities and were crucial in defining experts' linkages to politicians.

Original policies affect the subsequent demands of constituencies, the ideological biases of politicians, and linkages with experts to whom they can delegate technical decisions. The legacies of prior policies in public utilities, therefore, justified diverse policy content in the 1985 to 2000 period based on who made up politicians' constituencies, how politicians perceived the distributive consequences of their institutional choices, and who they appointed to make technically complex choices. These mechanisms promote variation in policy content even when politicians are adopting the same basic policies. Whereas the literature on partisanship has explained the effect of partisan constituencies in generating diverse policy preferences, it has paid less attention to the effects of ideological legacies and of delegation to allied experts. The demands of different constituencies generate incentives to maximize certain short-term goals regarding the price, coverage, and quality effects of reforms – as well as the use of subsidized shares to compensate employee stakeholders – based on the assumptions that right-wing true believers target the middle and upper classes and that pragmatic populist converts have poor and middle-class constituencies.

Price effects are easier to figure out than rules for competition and technically complex regulations for constituencies and politicians.[3] Hence, policy makers form their opinions based on ideological legacies and delegation

---

[2] Economic nationalism legitimated the nationalization of public utilities (Gomez-Ibáñez 2003). Attitudes toward state distribution of resources (decommodification) have traditionally defined distributive preferences over economic policies between left-wing and right-wing politicians in advanced democracies, and Rosas (2005) shows that they defined patterns of interparty competition at the elite level in most Latin American countries during the studied period.

[3] According to Petrazzini, "people generally recognize a private provider's responsibilities toward customers. Instead, they do not understand so clearly what may be the impact of market liberalization on the price structure of basic services" (1995, 18).

to experts whom they trust. The influence of ideological legacies is based on perception bias. As argued by Weyland (2004) in his analysis of Latin American pension reform, the urgency with which decisions had to be made and the pressure of information overload, as well as uncertainty about policy effects, favored the use of inferential shortcuts.[4] Politicians base their judgments regarding uncertain reform effects on their ideological backgrounds and their views of state institutions (which are based on their prior distributive effects). Ideas about economic nationalism and state intervention that they formed in the past generate different views regarding restrictions on foreign investment, nationalization of foreign-owned utilities, creation of state-owned enterprises with subsidized pricing schemes, trade protection, and subsidies for domestic capital. Populists in Latin America had earlier pursued economic nationalism and promoted state intervention in the economy, including public utilities, whereas right-wing true believers have trusted the market as a good mechanism for the allocation of resources and have been more reticent about state intervention.

Experts, who owe their tenure to politicians due to the lack of an effective civil service in Latin America, internalize the distributive preferences of the latter when policy choice is delegated to them – even within the constraints of their own epistemic communities – because there is dissent regarding the medium-term effects of microeconomic policies. Hence, the combined effect of constituencies' demands, ideological biases, and delegation to experts who are political appointees provides a better explanation for partisan patterns of policy content than the bureaucratic dynamics shown to affect the same policies in advanced countries (Vogel 1996).

The political factors discussed in the preceding text generate two different ideal types of regulatory content for market-oriented reforms in public utilities. Market-controlling regulatory content favors the establishment of political goals to shape investment decisions. Limits on the investment of foreign capital, even if capital scarcity is driving the reforms, reflect a political preference for domestic ownership or management – assuming either that profit would be reinvested locally or that establishing

---

[4] Similarly, Pop-Eleches (2008) shows that partisan ideology shaped politicians' interpretation of crisis causes and solutions and therefore their propensity to accept IMF programs in Latin America during the 1980s. He finds that different partisan interpretations apply to inflation but not to low levels of foreign reserves, for which there was less uncertainty about the effect of IMF standby loans.

"national champion" companies under domestic management would strengthen the international position of the country.[5] The existence of investment targets suggests government-imposed conditions for capital allocation in order to achieve coverage and quality goals set politically rather than determined by markets. Entry rules are used as a tool for fostering developmental goals different from what market demand might have achieved. The state uses its regulatory power and its creation and expansion of bureaucracies to impose prices and resolve intraindustry conflicts; these become crucial mechanisms by which it shapes market outcomes. In creating regulatory authorities, moreover, the decision to establish a larger bureaucratic structure, personnel, and budget reflects an institutional preference that originates in prior reliance on and trust in state development agencies. Larger regulatory discretion enhances the flexibility of regulators to react to unforeseen circumstances and to cover different aspects related to the development of the sector, but it also increases the potential for regulatory expropriation, especially as regulatory independence is harder to enforce than restricted regulatory powers.

By contrast, a market-conforming regulatory content limits regulatory discretion explicitly and therefore circumscribes the capacity of governments to control private investment. That is, reforms include no limits on foreign capital, market incentives drive investment decisions, markets are opened without entry rules, and negative market externalities are resolved *ex post* and treated as market imperfections. As a result, when market-conforming regulatory agencies are established, the size of public bureaucracies and their regulatory discretion are limited.

Beyond the effect of partisanship on policy content, the effects of reformers' preferences have other empirical implications for the process of policy making. First, when pragmatic populists convert to the market creed, they are torn between their distributive preferences, reflected in their appointment of allied experts, and the need to have neoliberal technocrats in their administration to signal their commitment to financial markets. For that reason, pragmatic populist converts to market-oriented reforms are more likely to experience intraadministration conflicts af-

---

[5] FDI is attractive due to its positive externalities for technology, managerial skills, and higher resilience to crisis than portfolio investment (Fernandez-Arias and Hausmann 2000). Eicheengreen and Fishlow (1998) and Stallings (1992) argue that attitudes toward FDI in Latin America are associated with balance of payment difficulties and capital availability; thereby, we should expect no restrictions on foreign capital, considering the capital shortages and balance of payment deficits during the reform period.

fecting policy content. Second, the identity of reformers should lead to policies that produce diverse sets of beneficiaries of subsidized assets during privatization, as privatization provides a one-shot opportunity for redistribution that is more likely to be used by reformers to benefit the core constituencies of the governing coalition.

The rest of this chapter provides evidence of differences in the regulatory content of market-oriented reforms (either market controlling or market conforming) by showing the effect of the three mechanisms derived from partisanship. It uses comparative case studies of the electricity and telecommunications sectors in Argentina, Mexico, and Chile, as pragmatic populist converts reformed in the former two countries and right-wing true believers in the latter. It also shows how pragmatic populist converts were subject to more intraadministration conflict over policy content between allied experts and neoliberal technocrats. Case studies of market-oriented reforms in two smaller Latin American economies – El Salvador and Panama – provide a control for the effect of market size, whereas an analysis of patterns of regulatory content in all Latin American countries that privatized either sector provides further evidence of partisan effects.

Reformers' Preferences in Argentina, Chile, and Mexico

The incumbent reformers in Argentina, Mexico, and Chile had different constituencies, ideological legacies, and allied technocrats. The military government of General Augusto Pinochet was a right-wing administration of true believers, whereas the Argentine Peronist Party and the Mexican PRI had pursued a strategy of state-led growth. Prior administrations of both parties had nationalized public utilities, and they only converted to the market creed under fiscal strain. Therefore, we should expect to find market-conforming reforms in Chile and market-controlling reforms in Argentina and Mexico.

Chilean true believers pursued policies of state retrenchment in reaction to the Socialist administration of Salvador Allende (1970–3). During Pinochet's tenure (1973–89), the number of publicly owned companies in Chile shrank from 594 to 43, and public employment dropped by more than 35 percent (Hachette and Luders 1993, Appendix A and p. 117). Additionally, the Pinochet regime pursued dramatic trade liberalization by setting uniform 10 percent tariffs and established nondiscriminatory conditions for foreign investment through Decree Law 600 and Law 818 of 1974 (Hachette and Luders 1993, 104–5).[6] These policies were associated with the preferences of Pinochet's supporters and with the ideological legacies and allied experts of this administration.

The political coalition behind the Chilean military regime included the armed forces, members of which had staged the coup against Allende, as well as civilian supporters who would later form a new political party, the Independent Democratic Union (UDI); it also included the personnel linked to the traditional conservative party, which was reorganized and renamed the National Renovation (RN). The core of civilian personnel for the regime included two groups whose personal linkages were based on their prior militancy against university reform at the Catholic University: the *gremialistas* and the "Chicago Boys" (Huneeus 2000a). The former built Pinochet's political program and were responsible for the 1980 constitution, and the latter were the technocrats – most of whom pursued graduate studies in the Economics Department of the University of Chicago – to whom economic policies were delegated. These neoliberal technocrats, who viewed the market allocation of resources as essential to development, served as a link between the military rulers and their business supporters, the main financial conglomerates (Silva 1991; Schamis 2002). Their macroeconomic success made them popular with the upper and middle classes, who supported Pinochet in reaction to the Socialist rule of President Salvador Allende (Fontaine Aldunate 1988; Silva 1991). The support of these groups would later transfer to the vote for Pinochet in the 1988 plebiscite and to subsequent electoral support for the two right-wing parties emerging from the regime, the UDI and RN.

Both civilian groups increased their influence with Pinochet after the failure of traditional economic policies and the exit of Christian Democrats from the support coalition in 1974 (Kurtz 1999). As Pinochet adopted the neoliberal ideas put forward by the technocratic Chicago Boys, consolidating his regime's control of the armed forces and achieving macroeconomic stability, their influence grew (Schamis 2002). Their rejection of state intervention and economic nationalism appealed to Pinochet after the Socialist policies of Allende.

---

[6] Pinochet abolished nontariff barriers, reduced tariffs to an average of 10 percent, and cut tariff dispersion (Meller 1996, 63). Conservative President Jorge Alessandri (1958–64) had already attempted a modest process of trade liberalization and state retrieval, showing the long-term commitment of the Chilean right to the market as the best method for resource allocation.

Also in reaction to that experience, the *gremialistas*, under the lead of Jaime Guzmán, were crucial in reshaping the political system through the 1980 constitution, which justified state retrenchment as a public policy. The 1980 constitution not only guaranteed the right to private property but also established immediate compensation in cash in case of expropriation, which can only be decided by law. Moreover, article 19, precept 21 requires the adoption of a law by a qualified quorum to allow the state to engage in any entrepreneurial activity, and precept 22 curtails regulatory activity by banning granting privileges or the creation or imposition of taxes or duties that imply any form of discrimination among economic sectors, activities, or regions (Schamis 2002, 73).

The ideological bias of policy makers was evident in their framing of public-utility reform. In 1985, Pinochet's finance minister, Hernán Büchi, justified the privatization of telecommunications and electricity in terms of the importance of private property to a market economy, the efficiency gains generated by private control, the stabilization effect of deepening the stock market, and the spread of ownership (Bitrán and Sáez 1994, 342).[7] Büchi went on to become the right-wing presidential candidate in the 1989 elections, and his electoral platform explicitly stated his support for the market as the best method for resource allocation and advocated a nondiscriminatory approach toward foreign investment, thereby demonstrating the right-wing continuous distrust of state intervention and economic nationalism after the adoption of reforms.[8]

In short, the Chilean reformers were true believers with constituencies that included voters in the middle and upper classes, financial conglomerates, and military officers. They delegated economic policy making to neoliberal technocrats, and their ideological legacies were marked by the rejection of state intervention in the market, which was associated with the prior Socialist experience. We ought to expect this combination to have

---

[7] According to Sigmund, "Privatization was not carried out because of a need to relieve the burden of state enterprises' deficits; that problem was resolved relatively quickly after the 1973 coup. Rather, the Chicago boys were committed to a vision of a decentralized and privatized economy as morally, politically, and economically superior to the long Chilean tradition of state intervention" (1990, 359–60).

[8] In his electoral program, "Lineamientos Fundamentales del Programa de Gobierno" (Santiago 1989), former economy minister and presidential candidate Hernán Büchi emphasized the achievements of the military regime in terms of expanding economic freedoms and efficiency based on the development of the market economy and found no fault in the regulation and privatization of public utilities, despite the criticisms in the electoral program of his contenders (Documentos La Epoca 1989).

led to a market-conforming policy content in electricity and telecommunications.

Unlike in Chile, the Argentine reformers belonged to a populist labor-based party, the Peronist or Justicialista Party. The prior Peronist policies of state intervention and nationalization of public utilities generated ideological legacies and ties to allied experts. When nationalizing telecommunications in 1948, President Perón argued that telephone and telegraph services were strategic for economic and national security reasons (Petrazzini 1995, 111). Perón also created a nationwide electricity company, expanded public-sector employment as he enlarged the regulatory functions of the state, subsidized domestic manufacturers, and increased trade barriers.[9]

These policies favored the Peronist electoral coalition, which included the lower and middle classes – even when these were urban workers in the industrialized regions – and the rural poor and local bosses in the hinterland (Mora y Araujo 1980a; 1980b). The Peronist appeal to the lower classes – defined in terms of their lack of wealth and education – continued after the 1983 democratic transition (Catterberg 1989). This electoral support, along with the alliance with organized labor, continued even when President Menem switched from being a populist to become a neoliberal (Gervasoni 1998; Murillo 2001). The party's support base was strong in the poorer regions of the Buenos Aires province's industrial suburbs and in the less urbanized peripheral provinces (Gibson and Calvo 2000).

The ideological legacies of Perón's policies were the result of his own framing of them. He argued that Peronist goals were to achieve "a nation with social justice, economic freedom and political sovereignty." In his view, the role of the state was crucial for promoting industrialization and guaranteeing national sovereignty (Altamirano 2002, 216), even when he welcomed foreign investors in oil and manufacture in the 1950s.[10] For instance, article 40 of the 1949 constitution – promoted by Perón and cancelled by the military that ousted him – granted the state the power

[9] McGuire (1997) describes Perón's expansion of public employment from 203,300 to 394,900 jobs and of credit to industry, as well as his increase in trade tariffs and nationalization of foreign trade to direct foreign exchange to the industry through a state agency called the Argentine Institute for Trade Promotion (IAPI) (58). He also describes the effect of labor regulations on increasing wages and improving work conditions and social benefits.

[10] Perón tried to attract foreign capital to promote the development of an automotive industry and also signed petroleum exploration contracts with Standard Oil in 1955, which were highly criticized by nationalist groups but, according to him, compatible with the search for economic freedom (McGuire 1997, 71–2; Altamirano 2002, 238).

to intervene in the economy, monopolize an economic activity for the purpose of protecting the general interest, and establish conditions for the nationalization of energy and public services, including criteria to compensate private owners (Altamirano 2002, 237). These goals were also reflected in economic policy making during Perón's last period of tenure in the early 1970s (Sturzenegger 1990).

After his pragmatic conversion, Peronist President Menem sustained these ideological legacies in his view of the state's role in development. According to Menem and his former minister of public works, Roberto Dromi, "It is not possible to privatize public services and some of the strategic activities of the state by depriving it of the powers of police [control] and *planning* [orientation]."[11] Menem coined his own term, "popular market economy," to frame the adoption of neoliberal policies within the legacies of the Peronist tradition. A popular market economy was "popular" because it rewarded work and guaranteed social and distributive justice while preserving state intervention, state orientation, and state planning to ensure the public good. It was a "market" approach because it guaranteed economic freedom, private initiative, and competition while demanding efficiency (Menem and Dromi 1997, 42–3).

The ideological legacies of the PJ promoted the delegation of reform planning to allied experts like Minister Dromi. It generated tensions, however, with the more neoliberal views of technocrats appointed to signal Menem's promarket commitment, such as finance minister Domingo Cavallo. This intrabureaucratic conflict reflected the halfhearted conversion of Peronism to the market creed. Even when the PJ only experienced a minor split over market reforms at the onset of Menem's first administration, Levitsky (2003) points out that a majority of party activists did not support market reforms except on pragmatic terms.[12] Gervasoni (1998), meanwhile, found that half of those who voted for Menem in his 1995 reelection campaign adhered to statist views. As late as 1999, the PJ platform proposed state regulations to promote universal coverage in water,

---

[11] Menem and Dromi (1997, 109). Translation by the author; italics in the original.

[12] In a 1997 survey of thirty-nine PJ National Council members and eighty-seven PJ legislators, Levitsky (2003, 151) found that around 40% were pragmatists, who supported reforms as a pragmatic solution to the crisis, and a third were critics, who thought that some reforms were necessary but that Menem had gone too far. In a survey of 75 local party leaders and 100 punteros, or ward bosses, he found one-third pragmatic supporters, one-third pragmatists, and one-third critics (152). In both cases, only 20% were neoliberals who thought that reforms were necessary and had to be continued.

electricity, and telecommunications.[13] These more statist tendencies of the PJ would become prevalent after the PJ electoral defeat in the 1999 presidential election and even more apparent after the dramatic crisis of 2002, as described in Chapter 5.

In sum, the Peronist constituencies included the lower and middle classes, and there was a regional tension between the metropolitan areas and the hinterlands. The Peronist ideological legacies involved a history of encouraging state intervention and economic nationalism that generated ties to allied experts at a time when the party also had a need to appoint neoliberal technocrats in order to demonstrate a new promarket commitment. Therefore, we should expect Argentine reforms to have been market-controlling in electricity and telecommunications but torn by intrabureaucratic conflict between allied experts and neoliberal technocrats.

Like its Argentine counterpart, the Mexican PRI was a populist, labor-based party that had previously promoted state-led development, including heavy state ownership, trade protectionism, and subsidies for domestic capital (Aspe 1993, 137–9).[14] Additionally, after foreign direct investment had successfully promoted a deepening of industrialization in the 1950s and 1960s, the PRI government imposed restrictions on foreign capital in the 1970s (Gereffi and Evans 1981; Lustig 1992, 244). In public utilities, prior PRI administrations had advocated for nationalization and the creation of state-owned enterprises. PRI President Lázaro Cárdenas had created the CFE in 1937. In 1960, the PRI nationalized the remaining private companies with a constitutional amendment establishing a public monopoly over electric energy. In telecommunications, the PRI had induced two private companies to merge into Telmex in the 1940s and then forced foreign owners to sell to Mexican nationals. In 1972, the Mexican state acquired a majority stake in Telmex.

PRI constituencies, which included the lower and middle classes – including urban workers and public employees in the metropolitan regions, as well as peasants, the rural poor, and local bosses in the hinterland – favored these policies (León 1990; Gibson 1997). After the shift toward promarket reforms in the 1980s, the PRI sustained labor unions' loyalty

---

[13] See Partido Justicialista. "Plataforma Electoral: 10 compromisos y 100 medidas para una Argentina mejor," Buenos Aires, 1999. Yet there were no explicit links to national sovereignty, as in Mexico.

[14] For instance, in the 1970s, President Echeverría established 160 state-owned companies, and his successor created 98 more (Lustig 1992, 244).

and kept its support among the poor and in the less developed region (Gibson 1997; Burgess 2004).[15] Camp shows that the PRI had better electoral results among poorer voters and in the low-income states in all presidential elections between 1976 and 2000 (2003, 198).[16]

The ideological legacies of the nationalization policies, which were shared by the statist experts who had previously run the telecommunications and electricity sectors, came into conflict with the views of more neoliberal technocrats appointed to signal the conversion to the market. Experts were divided between those of a more nationalist and statist tradition and neoliberal technocrats. Babb (2001) describes the conflict between statist and nationalist experts – who had run these sectors in the state-led period, were trained mainly in the public universities (especially the National Autonomous University of Mexico, or UNAM), and did their graduate studies in Europe – and the more neoliberal technocrats, who were trained increasingly in private institutions (especially the Autonomous Mexican Technological Institute, or ITAM) and acquired their graduate degrees in the United States.

According to Centeno (1994), even technocratic presidents internalized these divisions. Presidents Salinas and Zedillo, who had PhDs from Harvard and Yale, respectively, promoted market-oriented reforms while wishing to maintain a guiding role for the state. This was especially true of Salinas, who emphasized continuity with traditional party ideology by framing market-oriented reforms as "social liberalism." Centeno cites Salinas: "If the free functioning of economic mechanisms implied the achievement of national goals, planning would be unnecessary. . . . [T]he evidence indicates the inexistence of automatic equilibria and of spontaneous social harmony" (194). Centeno concludes that the Mexican national development model was not Chilean, but that of Taiwan and Korea, as Salinas believed "the government should not directly control the economy but rather serve as an overseer that would impose the discipline, order and efficiency the system required" (195).

---

[15] In the 1994 election, PRI votes increased among the less educated and the poor (Domínguez and McCann 1996, 203).

[16] In rural areas and smaller towns, the PRI obtained more than its national average, whereas other parties received less than their national average, and the same pattern was apparent among voters with only a primary school education and low income (Camp 2003, 200). Klesner (2004, 114–17) shows that even for the 2000 election, the PRI voters were poorer and less educated.

The divisions between experts parallel the internal strife in the party caused by the policy shift.[17] These tensions started when President Miguel De La Madrid (1982–8) initiated market-oriented reforms and brought the PRI to a split in 1988, leading to the formation of the left-wing PRD. The exit of faithful populists from the PRI weakened the statist faction in comparison to its Peronist counterpart. The signing of NAFTA, however, generated tensions around economic nationalism.[18] PRI politicians, allied experts, and especially legislators from the labor sector were concerned about policy options that hindered economic nationalism, such as regulations on foreign capital.[19] As a result, the PRI electoral platforms for the presidential campaigns of 1994 and 2000 still maintained that public-sector control of strategic sectors (including electric energy) was necessary for national sovereignty. Its 2000 electoral platform proposed to strengthen state capacity to regulate and control important sectors of the economy, as well as its directive economic role (PRI 2000, 6.2.5). After the 2000 electoral defeat, the antimarket factions became more influential as the party recovered a more nationalist and statist discourse in opposition, as discussed in Chapter 5.

In short, PRI constituencies in the lower and middle classes – and their regional tensions between the urbanized metropolitan areas and the hinterlands – were similar to those of the Peronist Party in Argentina. The PRI's ideological legacies also involved state intervention and economic nationalism, and it also experienced tensions between allied experts and neoliberal technocrats. Therefore, we should expect a market-conforming content for reforms in telecommunications and electricity.

The following two sections describe the reforms of the electricity and telecommunications industries that actually took place in all three countries

---

[17] Reveles Vazquez (2003) describes the political conflict within the PRI and how it shaped the process of selecting presidential candidates for the party. For instance, the 1996 party conference banned presidential candidates without prior electoral experience as a way to preempt technocrats from gaining the presidential candidacy.

[18] De la Garza Talavera (2003, 336) analyzes the transformation of PRI ideology under Salinas. He shows that Salinas understood national sovereignty in the context of globalization as combining economic integration with keeping political independence. There was nonetheless no dramatic turn on foreign policies, as the government did not break its ties to Cuba and with the left-wing revolutionary groups of Central America, as the PAN would do after 2000.

[19] Personal interviews with former secretary of communications and transportation Carlos Ruiz Sacristán (January 18, 2001), former PRI secretary general and senator Genero Borrego, and former secretary of government and senator Manuel Barlett (October 9, 2002), and confidential interview 2 (October 9, 2002).

in order to examine whether the identity of reformers shaped the policy content of the reforms in the way predicted by the second hypothesis on partisan effects. They also assess how partisan incentives shaped the process of reform, especially looking for intrabureaucratic tensions in the case of pragmatic populist converts and at the targeting of compensation to different groups of core supporters.

Regulatory Content in Electricity Reform

In Chile, true believers who implemented electricity reforms chose a market-conforming content for those reforms with no investment requirements or rules for entry, prevented bureaucratic expansion, restricted regulatory discretion, and guaranteed nondiscriminatory conditions for investors based on the origin of their capital. The 1982 decree law on electricity forbade discrimination against foreign capital, investment conditions, or entry rules while providing for vertical unbundling of the industry. Investors in generation had no need of licenses and no supply obligations, whereas distributors were given nonexclusive concessions based on predefined criteria and the obligation only of serving their areas of concession (Serra 2002, 16). The law promoted the unbundling of the industry into generation, transmission, and distribution. It established no rules regarding property acquisition, allowing that the partition of assets resulted in a subsequent concentration of property vertically and horizontally (Berstein 1995, 32; Bitrán and Serra 1998, 939–40).

This decree law also prevented bureaucratic expansion and restricted the discretion of the regulator. Instead of creating a new agency, the 1982 law granted regulatory authority to the preexisting CNE and restricted its pricing discretion by defining a preestablished methodology for calculating distribution prices in the law.[20] As transmission monopolies were abolished, the cost of transmission fees was left to the agreement of the parties or arbitration in case of disagreement rather than being set by the regulator.

---

[20] Because the wholesale market only applied to large users, small consumers were captured clients of distribution companies, and their prices had to be regulated. The law was very specific about the use of long-term incremental marginal costs and a boundary of 10% difference with the wholesale market price to limit the discretion of the regulator (Spiller and Vianna Martorell 1994; Bernstein 1995). By contrast, the 1959 electricity regulation established a Tariff Commission to define prices. This commission was composed of representatives of the president, the companies, and consumers, and was headed by the director of the Office of Electric Services. This commission was perceived as amenable to consumers (Spiller and Viana Martorell 1996, 116).

Additionally, the regulator had no role in and very limited information about the working of the independent dispatch operator, or Economic Load Dispatch Center (CDEC).[21]

Bureaucratic expansion was kept to a minimum, as the CNE depended upon the presidency and was run by an executive secretary appointed by the president, along with delegates of seven ministries. It lacked its own budget and only had twenty-four personnel. Distrust of state intervention also explains the delay in passing Law 14,410 until 1985. This law transformed the Superintendency of Electricity, Gas and Telecommunications into the Electricity and Fuels Superintendency (SEC) in charge of overseeing the quality and safety of electricity installations. According to neoliberal technocrats Renato Agurto and Sebastián Bernstein, who drafted the 1982 reform, they ignored the SEC because its bureaucracy was incompetent and bureaucratic strengthening was not a government priority (personal interviews, March 27, 2001). Consequently, this controller was granted a very limited budget, and its 158 employees were immediately cut to the 132 already employed, leaving some functions vacant (Inostroza 1995).

According to Bernstein, the intrabureaucratic debate over electricity reform was very limited, as only the technical personnel in Endesa and Chilectra resisted their partition because they preferred the consolidation of the industry into a large state-owned company following the model of Electricité de France. The main source of resistance was external and came from experts in the Inter-American Development Bank and the World Bank, who were concerned about the novelty of the reforms (Bernstein 1995).[22]

The government's upper- and middle-class supporters benefited from the improvement in supply and quality of service even at the expense of higher prices, which had stronger income effects on the poor. Price rebalancing, which started in 1974, resulted in hikes of more than 700 percent

---

[21] The CDEC coordinated prices in the competitive wholesale generation market for large consumers (those with a demand in excess of 2 megawatts). All generators can make supply contracts with clients and are required to purchase any shortfall from other members at the marginal costs of peak power (the annual cost of increasing installed capacity during peak demand periods by 1 kilowatt). The CDEC coordinates supply and demand of energy. Its board was to be controlled by operators with at least 2% of the total generation, which were Endesa, Chilgener, Pehuenche (also controlled by Endesa), and Colbún after privatization (Mines Ministry's Supreme Decree 6 of 1985).

[22] The proposal was presented by Decree Law 1 of 1982 establishing the General Law of Electric Services, and it established for the first time a methodology to regulate by incentives, while price caps became public in the Stephen Littlechild report on regulation in 1983 (Serra 2002, 14).

for the residential price of electricity by 1982, when the reform abolished cross-subsidies (Spiller and Viana Martorell 1996, 120). Company managers and public officials (including military officers and managers of the companies) received shares with voting rights and paid for with loans that used the dividends of the same shares as collateral (Moguillansky 1999, 178). Among the government officials who benefited were the managers of the three largest electricity corporations emerging from privatization: Enersis, Chilquinta, and Gener. The head of the Enersis group, José Yuraszeck, had been in the government planning agency and was then appointed as CEO of Chilectra before its privatization. The head of Gener, Bruno Phillipi, had led the CNE in charge of electricity privatization (Moguillansky 1999, 190). Gonzalo Ibañez Langlois from Chilquinta collaborated with Jaime Guzmán in the drafting of the 1980 constitution (Schamis 2002, 66). Company employees received shares to pay for accumulated state pension obligations and severance payments, generating incentives for them to leave the companies. The remainder of the shares were acquired by taxpayers without fiscal debts and by pension funds, thereby furthering the electoral loyalty of middle-class voters. Thus, as expected, the content of Chilean reforms was market conforming, and the process involved limited intrabureaucratic tensions. Moreover, the one-shot redistribution through privatization was used to benefit regime constituencies and personnel.

By contrast, the electricity reforms in Argentina were market controlling. Even though these reforms did not limit investment by foreign capital, they established rules for entry and investment requirements, necessitated bureaucratic expansion, and gave the state broad regulatory discretion. As in Chile, the Argentine law promoted the vertical disintegration of the electricity industry into generation, transmission, and distribution, but it was more proactive regarding entry rules. Investment conditions in generation included security, environmental, and dispatch rules. In distribution, there was an obligation to provide services within the area of concessions, with quality requirements and service levels to be defined by the regulator; achieve quality targets (e.g., reduction in length and frequency of service interruptions, speedy reconnections, and improvements in public safety); provide street lighting; and invest in the modernizing and maintenance of the network. Moreover, the state was given a proactive role in controlling property concentration during and after the sale of privatized assets. Rules for property acquisition forbade transmission companies from purchasing distribution assets (art. 32) and required that the regulatory authority oversee ownership changes that might lead to either horizontal or vertical integration.[23]

In establishing a new regulatory authority, the reform expanded bureaucratic capacity and delegated broad powers to the National Electricity Regulatory Agency, or ENRE (art. 54). The ENRE regulated transmission and distribution in the area of Buenos Aires – other regulators were established in the provinces – and its broad functions included defending consumer rights, establishing thresholds of consumption for large users, overseeing property acquisitions, and defining transmission fees and distribution prices (art. 2). The agency's directors were appointed by the president after a competitive process for overseeing candidates' credentials.[24] The agency also had its own budget financed by taxes on the industry, nearly 100 personnel, and procedures that included holding public hearings with consumer participation.

The expected intrabureaucratic tensions emerged during the reform process. The first reform proposal was drafted by allied technocrat Juan Legisa with the support of the labor union and the PJ-controlled CFEE. Yet after Cavallo's appointment as minister of the economy, he replaced both Legisa and his proposal with one drafted by his neoliberal team headed by Carlos Bastos. The ability of Cavallo to control macroeconomic stability gave him increasing influence, as it allowed the PJ to win the 1991 midterm elections. Not only did Legisa continue to advise PJ politicians, however, but he was also appointed with congressional support as the first head of the regulatory agency – although Cavallo vetoed the choice and appointed the man in charge of SEGBA's privatization, Carlos Mattauch.[25]

---

[23] To avoid horizontal concentration in the privatization of distribution in the area of Buenos Aires, the government established a clause forbidding the same company to acquire more than 10% of the installed capacity at the time of asset privatization (Ambito Financiero, May 13, 1992).

[24] Their terms were fixed and did not overlap with those of the executive. PJ legislators included provisions requiring congressional agreement with the appointments and giving provinces the right to propose two directors.

[25] Legisa had run a state-owned utility during the 1970s PJ administration and was an advisor to PJ legislators during that of Alfonsín. Mattauch had worked in Cavallo's think tank, Fundación Mediterránea, before his appointment as SEGBA's privatizater. Legisa's replacement, which was forced by Cavallo, did not follow formal procedures established in the law. Moreover, the regulatory agency started to function a year later than supposed and with only three of its five directors, as the remaining two directors were to be elected by the provinces, and the PJ-controlled Federal Electricity Commission, which did not agree with Cavallo and Bastos regarding procedures for choosing them.

PJ politicians, whose support was crucial to obtaining the legislative approval of the reform, curtailed Cavallo's influence.[26] PJ legislators included veto power for the state in the dispatch operation (*Clarín*, December 19, 1991) and established that the prices should entail a "fair and reasonable" profitability rather than a specific rate of return on investment (*La Prensa*, December 21, 1991). They established a National Energy Fund to subsidize users in provinces where energy costs were higher and to promote energy development in the interior of the country (art. 70) (personal interview with former secretary of energy Carlos Bastos, December 19, 2000). During the legislative debate, moreover, PJ legislators defended the market-controlling powers of the state from the criticism of the Argentine Industrialists Association (UIA) and right-wing legislators. The former preferred to copy the Chilean CNE, and the latter wanted to curtail the broad powers of the ENRE (e.g., in defining the threshold for large users) and the secretary of energy (e.g., approval of exports and imports, approval of licenses for generation, and veto in the dispatch operation).[27]

The demands of PJ constituencies were also considered in the reform process. The government cut taxes on electricity service, which amounted to 10 percent of prices, to limit negative price effects on consumers.[28] Moreover, privatization included granting subsidized assets to provincial cooperatives and workers – all part of the original PJ coalition. Workers were granted 10 percent of shares to be paid for with dividends, which were to be administered by their labor union until paid off; these shares only accrued to employed workers and could only be sold if all of the workers agreed. The labor union also acquired four small generators and two regional transmission companies at subsidized prices (Murillo 2001, 160–4). Additionally, to keep the support of Peronists in the hinterland, provincial governments received the ownership of generation and distribution

[26] PJ legislators also institutionalized the future influence of provincial interest by imposing on the bill the need of congressional approval of the budget and provincial directors in the ENRE, and by transferring ownership of many utilities to the provinces.

[27] The Peronist legislative majority in the Lower Chamber gave additional powers to the secretary of energy in addition to its veto power in the independent dispatch operator called Company for the Administration of the Wholesale Electricity Market (CAMMESA), which regulated the spot price based on marginal costs and seasonal demand for the wholesale market. CAMMESA's board was equally divided among representatives of the associations of generators, transmission companies, distributors, large users, and the secretary of energy, who retained veto power (Decree 1192/92).

[28] Price increases in 1989 and 1990 were hard to track due to hyperinflation, and prices decreased in 1991 before privatization started (Bastos and Abdala 1995, 36; Fiel 1999, 484; Arza 2002, 102).

companies (personal interview with technocrat Manuel Abdala, July 20, 2000).[29] Hence, following our expectations, the Argentine reforms had a "market-controlling" design, involved intracoalition tensions (including neoliberal and allied experts and PJ legislators), and took advantage of privatization to benefit crucial players in the Peronist coalition.

In contrast with the other two countries, Mexico was unable to privatize electricity. The limited electricity reforms it did pass, however, and even the failed proposal to privatize, were market controlling in nature. They kept constraints on foreign capital as well as entry rules established by the CRE for self-generators, and they left investment conditions up to the state-owned companies while promoting bureaucratic expansion through the creation of a relatively powerful regulatory authority.

The 1992 reform opened generation to private capital, but only for self-consumption or for selling to the state under long-term contracts. In 1995, a PRI-controlled Congress created the CRE. The CRE regulates the supply and sale of electricity to public-service costumers, private-sector generation, import and export of electricity, acquisition of electricity for service to the public, transmission services between permit holders, and public-service agencies. It is a decentralized agency with 137 personnel, its own budget, and technical autonomy in decision making (Carreón-Rodriguez et al. 2007); in 1996, its budget was U.S.$6.3 million.[30]

In 1999, Zedillo unsuccessfully tried to privatize electricity generation and distribution. His reform established an investment plan for new entrants while including entry rules and broad powers for the regulatory authority. In the proposed reform, the public sector would have continued to control the generation of nuclear energy and the operation of the national transmission grid. The secretary of energy would have been in charge of planning the expansion of the transmission system and the incentives for an efficient development of the electricity sector. The secretary of energy would have also appointed the nine members to the governing board of the independent dispatch operator and enjoyed the power to veto the

[29] During the legislative discussion, the Energy Committee led by the oilworkers' union leader and PJ legislator Antonio Cassia curtailed the assets to be privatized by transferring the ownership of hydroelectric utilities to the provinces. Although negotiations limited the size of the cut, the provinces retained most hydroelectric and some thermal utilities. Additionally, binational public utilities were excluded from privatization (*Clarín*, December 19, 1991).

[30] Secretary of Finance and Public Credit, http://www.shcp.sse.gob.mx/contenidos/contabilidad_gubernamental/temas/informe_cuenta_publica/1997/infsec.html (accessed February 20, 2005).

general director selected by those members. The proposal contained entry rules to prevent vertical integration and allowed the regulator or any interested party to denounce practices of horizontal integration to the Anti-Trust Commission. In this proposal, the regulatory agency (CRE) would have regulated transmission and distribution prices, investment conditions, and the quality of services (including subsidies for residential consumers), as well as transmission concessions. It would also have granted permits for generation subject to legal, technical, and financial requirements to be defined by the law (Secretaría de Energía 1999). Thus, the failed reform was market controlling in character, entailing entry rules, investment conditions, bureaucratic expansion, and regulatory discretion – though there was no mention of discrimination against foreign capital.

This reform proposal divided the PRI and generated opposition from other political parties. Partisan discipline got the PRI vote for the 1992 reform (which was presented to PRI legislators as a condition for signing NAFTA) against the opposition of the PAN and the PRD. The 1995 CRE law was opposed by PRD legislators, whereas PAN legislators tried to improve its procedural transparency to limit regulatory discretion.[31] Moreover, intrabureaucratic tensions grew when Zedillo attempted privatization. Neoliberal technocrat and Secretary of Energy Luis Tellez said, for instance, that he had expected limits to foreign capital to be added to the reform by PRI legislators had the bill been discussed (personal interview, October 9, 2002). In spite of his willingness to concede on issues such as foreign investment and the fact that he spent six months trying to persuade PRI politicians and allied experts to support the reform, a large number of PRI legislators continued to oppose it (personal interviews with PRI senators Manuel Barlett and Genaro Borrego).

Constituencies' demands, especially regarding price effects, were also crucial in the policy debate.[32] The government continued to fund fiscally expensive cross-subsidies benefiting residential and agricultural users, who

---

[31] They suggested the inclusion of collective decision making by the CRE board and public audiences for general rules into the law. They also proposed a public registry of the internal discussions and administrative decisions as well as the use of arbitration to settle disagreements between users and the regulator. These proposals were rejected by the PRI majority. For the debates, see Diario de Debates de la H. Camara de Diputados, Legislatura LVI, 2nd year, No. 11, October 8 and 10, 1995, and Diario de Debates de la H. Camara de Senadores, Legislatura LVI, 2nd year, No. 12, 13, 14, November 19–24 and 26, 1995.

[32] Trying to diffuse opposition to the reform, CFE director Elías Ayub promised that the government would control prices until the benefits of the reform brought them down and would keep subsidies for low-income users (La Jornada, 2/9/99).

paid 50 percent and 30 percent of the cost of electricity, respectively. By contrast, industrial users paid about 90 percent, and commercial users were overcharged by between 5 and 30 percent in the 1995 to 2002 period (Carreón-Rodríguez et al. 2007, Table 5.5).[33]

In sum, partisan expectations about the content of electricity policy reform held in the three countries. In Chile, prices increased sharply with the abolition of cross-subsidies, and the sale of subsidized assets benefited mostly government officials and potential voters. The content of reform was market conforming, as there were no entry rules, investment conditions, or limits to foreign capital, while bureaucratic expansion and regulatory discretion in price setting were sharply limited. In Argentina and Mexico, the government was more cautious with price effects, even when cross-subsidies were abolished in the former country. The sale of subsidized assets benefited organized labor and provincial governments in Argentina, and reform was market controlling even without discrimination against foreign capital, because it imposed entry rules, investment conditions, bureaucratic expansion, and broad powers for regulatory authority over prices. In Mexico, where the reform was limited to the opening of markets to private investors subjected to the approval of the CRE, the regulatory agency nonetheless had relatively broad powers and discretion, and it was relatively large in size.

Policy Content in Telecommunications Reform

The patterns observed in electricity reform were repeated in telecommunications in all three countries. The cross-sectoral comparison shows that partisan incentives were stronger than those derived from industry-specific features. In Chile, right-wing true believers shaped telecommunications reforms with a market-conforming content. They established no entry rules or investment conditions, banned discrimination against foreign capital, and established a small regulatory authority with limited discretion. Supreme Decree 423 forbade monopolies in concessions and imposed the obligation of interconnection for public services while defining nondiscriminatory conditions for foreign capital (Ministry of Transportation and Telecommunications, 1978).

---

[33] Residential users account for 88% of CFE's 16.5 million clients and 25% of its sales of energy, while large industrial users account for 1% of its clientele but 60% of sold electricity (CRE, http://www.cre.gob.mx/estatisticas, accessed March 12, 2005). According to former PRI secretary of energy Jesus Reyes Heroles (1996–8), the 1995 inflation reduced the real price of electricity, but it was politically difficult to increase it (personal interview, October 8, 2002).

The General Telecommunications Law (Law 18.168) of 1982 also forbade monopolies (art. 13) and established the obligation of interconnection (art. 25). Despite this obligation, however, the law failed to grant power to the regulatory authority to either set interconnection prices or address the lack of price agreements between parties. Pinochet's undersecretary of telecommunications, Gustavo Armas, justified the regulatory vacuum in terms of the government's intention "to deregulate" (personal interview, March 3, 2001). Thus, competition remained facilities-based and resulted in the reproduction of networks until 1994. Moreover, the lack of investment conditions produced an initial increase in unmet demand in this sector.[34]

The influence of ideological biases was especially obvious in the structure and powers of the regulatory authority. The 1982 telecommunications law (DFL No. 1) granted regulatory powers to the Undersecretariat of Telecommunications (SUBTEL) of the Ministry of the Economy rather to the existing superintendency or a separately created body. In 1987, a proposal was made to create a new superintendency following the British model of Oftel, but the government decided against it to "reduce state intervention," according to former undersecretary of telecommunications Gustavo Armas (personal interview, March 3, 2001). SUBTEL structure was very limited and so was its discretion in price setting. Consumer prices were subjected to a very specific methodology, and interconnection prices were left to the agreement of the parties involved.[35]

The debate over policy content did not generate intrabureaucratic tensions, and the armed forces' concerns about the security implications of privatizing telecommunications were calmed with the distribution of subsidized assets. The navy received 10 percent of CTC shares, and the army received the same proportion of ENTEL shares.[36] Like in electricity, other beneficiaries of privatization included public officials and company

---

[34] A 1987 telecommunications law gave providers ten years to operate before becoming subject to the application of maximum terms of three years to connect users in their self-defined areas of concession, although they could charge customers in advance for the cost of investments necessary for the installation of services, and no provision was made for enforcement. The demand for telephone services increased after privatization, in particular between 1988 and 1992 (Melo 1993).

[35] The methodology used the incremental long-term costs of an ideal efficient firm as the basis of its calculation. The costs' floor avoided cross-subsidies (art. 30) with information provided by the companies.

[36] These were supposed to be used in building an alternative military communication infrastructure (personal interviews with former undersecretary Gustavo Armas and neoliberal technocrat Gustavo Aburto, March 3 and 27, 2001).

managers, taxpayers without fiscal debts, and pension funds. This targeting of supporters and potential voters in the middle and upper classes was matched by the distribution of benefits from price increases, which, due to the abolition of cross-subsidies, benefited large users. Between 1981 and 1988, CTC residential prices increased by 33 percent, while commercial prices dropped by 22 percent and large users' by 59 percent. Although the latter paid ten times what residential users paid in 1981, this differential had fallen to three times as much in 1988 (CTC Oficio No. 2877, December 19, 1988, cited by Melo 1993, 123). The variation in the fixed cost of service was even more dramatic, for it grew by 84 percent for residential users while remaining the same for large users (124). The evolution of ENTEL's long-distance prices during the same period was in the opposite direction, with costs per minute of calls within up to 20 kilometers dropping by 32 percent and those of calls to places more than 3,250 kilometers away by 82 percent (126).

By contrast, in Argentina, pragmatic populist converts adopted market-controlling reforms in telecommunications. They included rules for entry, investment targets, bureaucratic expansion, and broad regulatory powers for price setting, but they placed no limits on foreign capital. ENTEL was divided into two vertically integrated companies serving the north and south of the country, and each was sold with a seven-year monopoly on local and long-distance communications. These monopolies were conditional on the companies' meeting investment targets defined in the original bid, which were subject to change by the regulator. Decree 62/90 defined coverage targets for every Argentine province and imposed the obligation to serve more than a thousand unconnected towns defined by the regulatory agency, along with targets on digitalization and service improvement (e.g., fewer interruptions, more finalized calls, quicker repairs).

The ideological legacies of state intervention are again obvious in the shape taken by the regulatory agency. Decree 1,185/90 created a separate regulatory authority, the CNT, which had broad powers, 127 personnel, and a large budget derived from a tax of 0.5 percent on telecommunications revenue and charges for the use of the radio spectrum that were defined by the agency.[37]

---

[37] Originally, the CNT had powers to define the taxes in the sector that would provide its budget after approval of the finance minister. The unused funds were to be used in the development of the sector. In 1992, the CNT raised revenue of U.S.$30 million, its approved budget was U.S.$17 million, and its expenses were U.S.$12 million (Abdala and Spiller 1999: 45). The president appointed its five commissioners in a competitive process to fixed terms, which did not overlap with those of the president. Commission decisions could only be appealed to the executive.

The CNT's powers included the application, interpretation, and enforcement of regulations; granting and revoking licenses; controlling fulfillment of the investment targets defined for licenses and those for the extension of the seven-year monopoly for three more years; resolving conflicts among companies about interconnection prices; controlling property concentration; approving regulated prices and equipment standards; and signing international agreements.

The Peronist reform considered the effects of privatization on the party's main constituencies. To soften price hikes, reformers cut taxes and postponed the abolition of cross-subsidies in the two vertically integrated monopolies. Moreover, the government had to reverse a 433 percent increase in telephone prices planned for May 1990 due to popular protests supported by Peronist politicians (Petrazzini 1995, 84–6; Arza 2002, 103). In distributing the subsidized assets of privatization, the labor-based party favored domestic business, the labor union, and provincial cooperatives. Former state suppliers were allowed to enter the two purchasing holdings on special terms, employed workers in the sector received 10 percent of shares at lower prices to be paid for with dividends and administered by the labor union until paid off, and 5 percent of shares were reserved for purchase by provincial cooperatives at subsidized prices.[38]

As expected from pragmatic populist converts, there were intrabureaucratic tensions about reform content. These were contained within the executive, however, as the reform did not require legislative approval because it had been included in a general State Reform Law. The main intraadministrative conflict involved ENTEL CEO neoliberal Maria Julia Alsogaray and allied expert and minister of public works Roberto Dromi.[39] The former was appointed to signal the administration's reform commitment to the business sector (Abeles et al. 2001, 57).[40] Dromi's ministry

---

[38] Law 23,696 of 1989 and decrees 59 and 62 of 1990 established the transfer of companies to the provinces as well as subsidies that benefited cooperatives, employees, and producers of products or services in the industry (former suppliers to these companies). The union administered the trust fund in charge of buying blocs of shares until their purchase by employees, appointed a director to the board, and charged administrative fees to the fund.

[39] Minister Dromi had his own plan for the privatization that had previously been agreed upon with the union and telecommunications undersecretary and union leader José Guillán (Margherites 1999, 164–5). In a 1991 interview cited by Margheritis, Maria Julia Alsogaray said she did not know whether the government was really committed to privatize ENTEL when she was appointed, which generated tensions, as she had a "liberal" agenda (172).

[40] She had been appointed based on her technical skills and her links to the business community to instill credibility to the reform, according to former minister of the economy A. E. Gonzalez (interview cited by Margheritis 1999, 163).

housed the Undersecretariat of Telecommunications, and he had drafted the State Reform Law and decrees that allowed the reform. He was a recognized administrative lawyer and long-term loyalist to President Menem of the government Celeste faction. He vied with Alsogaray over the reform content and even the preference for American or European investors. Dromi justified the monopolies to promote investment and argued that publicly owned European investors were more in tune with the consumer and regulatory culture prevailing in Argentina than were private U.S. investors (personal interview, Buenos Aires, August 20, 1998). Alsogaray sought to increase competition by dividing ENTEL into more companies, and she was perceived as more favorable to privately owned American capital and a competitive regulatory structure (*Mercado*, no. 873, July 28, 1990). Dromi prevailed in defending monopolies to maximize fiscal revenue and meet investment goals.[41]

As in Argentina, Mexican reformers were pragmatic populist converts. Similarly, they adopted market-controlling reform that included rules for entry, investment requirements, and limits to foreign management, along with broad regulatory powers and bureaucratic expansion – the latter delayed because it required legislative approval. To guarantee domestic management for the privatized telecommunications company, the government created different types of shares. Shares with management rights could only be acquired by Mexican nationals and could not be sold during the fixed-term monopoly period. As in Argentina, the entry rules were tied to investment conditions. The six-year monopoly on long-distance telecommunications was conditional on investment targets defined in terms of expanding coverage (at 12 percent per year), reducing connection time, increasing the number of pay phones, digitalizing the network, providing service in every town with more than 2,500 inhabitants and pay phones to those with 500 people, and meeting quality-of-service goals (Skelezy and Del Palacio 1995, 58). Although local competition was not legally forbidden, it was deterred by the broad discretion of the regulator in (not) granting licenses.[42]

---

[41] He was helped by a study of financial viability by Coopers and Lybrand that suggested that the final division into two areas, each of them including Buenos Aires, would be more effective in maximizing revenue and future competition.

[42] In spite of the absence of a legal monopoly on local services, when the preexisting mobile company (Iusacell) demanded a concession to provide local service through fixed wireless technology before 1997, the secretary of communication and transportation denied it, arguing that it was technically difficult to assign a new spectrum and that local service was not ready for competition given local tariffs (Mariscal 2002, 80). The then-manager of a company called Iónica recalled that when he demanded a concession for local service in 1994, the secretary never responded (confidential interview 3, January 17, 2001).

Because new bureaucracies required congressional approval, the regulatory authority could not be created in a reform process that by-passed legislative intervention. The Secretariat of Communication and Transportation (SCT) retained broad discretion as the regulatory authority until 1995. In that year, Congress created the Federal Telecommunications Commission (COFETEL) as a separate regulatory body that, although dependent on the secretary for final decision making, had technical and budgetary autonomy – that is, it had control over its budget, which was U.S.\$2.2 million in 1996.[43] COFETEL had a large bureaucracy and a mandate to produce technical plans and auction radio-electric spectrum; conduct technical, legal, and financial assessments for the granting of concessions; and oversee and control providers' quality of service.[44] Because it was only created in 1995, however, when a private provider (Telmex) had a strong stake in the status quo, the preferences of Telmex had to be considered in the regulatory design.

The influence of private Telmex grew as it agreed to protect government constituencies from price hikes by postponing price rebalancing to contain inflation during a macroeconomic crisis. A high technical official in charge of drafting the law claimed that Telmex's influence on the regulatory design was crucial (confidential interview 4, December 6, 2000). The government had also been concerned about the price effects of privatization at the onset. Thus, as in Argentina, it cut taxes and postponed price rebalancing until after privatization to keep cross-subsidies, so that increases in nominal prices in 1990 for domestic long-distance were five times as large as those for local service, while the connection price remained untouched (Szekely and Del Palacio 1995, 56, 98). As expected of a labor-based party, PRI reformers also granted subsidized shares to Telmex's employees (who received 4.4 percent of shares, syndicated and administered by the labor union until they had been completely paid for), although there were no compensations for the hinterland like those made by the Peronists in Argentina.

Finally, the pragmatic populist converts faced intrabureaucratic debate on reform content, though this debate was restricted to the executive power because privatization did not require legal reform. The debate engaged

---

[43] Secretary of Finance and Public Credit, http://www.shcp.sse.gob.mx/contenidos/contabilidad_gubernamental/temas/informe_cuenta_publica/1997/infsec.html (accessed February 12, 2005). Its personnel for 2002 was 528. COFETEL, http://207.248.166.91/cofetel/informe/006.pdf (accessed April 1, 2005).

[44] The board is directly appointed by the president, reducing its political autonomy and weakening the regulatory authority.

neoliberal technocrats in the Trade Secretariat and nationalist allied experts in the SCT and Telmex (along with the labor union). The secretary of commerce and industry led the opposition to quantitative targets and monopolies proposed by the SCT to generate a national champion firm and promote coverage, according to a former advisor to the trade secretary (confidential interview 5, January 21, 2001). By contrast, allied expert and former undersecretary of telecommunications Carlos Mier y Terán claimed that the monopoly was crucial to achieve a national champion, facilitate meeting coverage commitments, and allow the postponement of price rebalancing (personal interview, April 29, 2005).[45] The treasury solved the dispute by siding with allied experts on the ground that monopolies not only facilitate national champions and investment but also increase fiscal revenue (Mariscal 2002, 50–6).[46]

The ideological legacies of the PRI were also apparent in the framing used by President Salinas when announcing the privatization of Telmex. He claimed that privatization had five objectives: guaranteeing the state's control of the telecommunications sector, radically upgrading telephone services, guaranteeing the rights of workers, conducting research and development to strengthen national sovereignty, and maintaining telecommunications under the control of a Mexican company (Mariscal 2002, 75). Hence, his view of the process coincided with his support for the position defended by allied experts.

In sum, partisan expectations about the regulatory content of telecommunications reform, patterns of intraadministration debate over this content, and the distribution of costs and benefits held in the three countries. Chilean right-wing true believers chose a market-conforming content without discrimination against foreign capital, entry rules, or investment conditions discretion in the establishment of the regulatory authority. They also favored their future core constituencies and compensated their military supporters. By contrast, in Argentina and Mexico, the pragmatic conversion of

---

[45] Secretary of Commerce and Industry Jaime Serra Puche had a PhD in Economics from Yale, whereas his telecommunications advisor had an ITAM BA and Stanford PhD. By contrast, Carlos Mier y Teran had studied at UNAM and the London School of Economics. These scholarly trajectories, as suggested by Babb (2001), match those of neoliberal technocrats and nationalist experts, respectively.

[46] The resulting single privately owned and vertically integrated monopoly was effective in creating a "national champion," as Telmex is the single Latin American transnational in telecommunications that expanded across the region and became a strong contender to Telefónica of Spain, the other large telecommunications player in Latin America (Mariscal and Rivera 2005).

former populists led to a market-controlling content for telecommunications reform, although only Mexico discriminated against foreign capital. Both countries chose to establish entry rules in the form of fixed-term monopolies that would help to guarantee that investment conditions were met, and both created large bureaucracies to fulfill regulatory tasks. Even though the CNT had more discretion than COFETEL, budgets and personnel were larger for the latter than the former. Both maintained discretion over price setting by refusing to establish an explicit pricing methodology. As in electricity, both countries experienced intrabureaucratic tensions over policy content, and, differently from Chile, both cut taxes to reduce price hikes and postponed price rebalancing to protect their constituencies from sudden price hikes. Like the Chileans, they used subsidized assets to compensate their core constituencies, which in these cases included workers and the telecommunications labor union, as both the PRI and the PJ were labor-based parties.

The following section provides further evidence for partisan effects on reform content by considering the general trends of the region in electricity and telecommunications reforms, while also adding case studies of both sectors in two smaller Central American economies: Panama and El Salvador. The general picture of the region is based on a dataset on regulatory content for the original reform in each sector for all eighteen countries that is based on the original legislation, concession contracts, and regulatory agency Web pages. The case studies of Panama and El Salvador also involve secondary literature.

Market Size and Regional Patterns

The importance of policy makers' preferences – even if constrained by institutional configurations – suggests that identifying reformers in Latin America should give us an approximate idea of what type of reform content to expect. By using a self-collected dataset on the political identity of reformers and eight indicators of reform content, this section's analysis compares patterns of reform in countries that effectively privatized both sectors with those that did not. The indicators of reform content used are as follows: limits on foreign investment; entry rules; investment requirements; regulatory discretion for setting consumer prices, setting intraprovider prices (for either interconnection or transmission), solving conflicts between providers, and solving conflicts between consumers and providers; and regulatory capacity to tax the industry in order to provide an operating budget for the regulatory authority. The values used to build the two indexes of reform type – either market-conforming or market-controlling – are

125

provided in Tables 3.1a and 3.2a, which encompass market-controlling, market-conforming, and nonprivatizing countries. The categories used to construct these codings are presented in Tables 3.1b and 3.2b.

The identity of the reformer was defined by using as a proxy whether the reformer's party had promoted state intervention or nationalization of public utilities in the past, with the coding of Peru being indeterminate because although President Fujimori was elected as a populist and promoted market-oriented reforms, he had no party legacy with which to trace his prior beliefs. As can be seen in Tables 3.1a and 3.1b, which describe the ranking and coding for telecommunications, and Tables 3.2a and 3.2b, which describe the ranking and coding for electricity, in the following text, using 4 as a cut-off point on the 8-point scale to distinguish market-conforming from market-controlling policies, we observe that most reforms adopted by former populist governments were market controlling and that most reforms adopted right-wing true believers were market conforming. A difference in the means test of the index shows that there is a statistical difference in the type of regulations created in each sector depending on whether reforms were adopted by pragmatic populist converts or right-wing true believers. On average, however, there is no statistically significant difference between the regulations of sectors privatized by former populists and those that did not effectively privatize. There are some cases that do not conform to the prediction and in which institutional constraints explain the inability of policy makers to impose their policy preferences.

Table 3.1a. *Degree of Market Control in Telecommunications*

	No Effective Privatization	Pragmatic Convert	True Believer
	Costa Rica 8	Argentina 6	Chile 0
	Paraguay 5	Bolivia 5	Ecuador 7.5
	Uruguay 4	Brazil 4.5	El Salvador 0
		Colombia 6	Guatemala 0.5
		Honduras 6	Nicaragua 5
		Mexico 7	Dominican Rep. 1
		Venezuela 5.5	
		Panama 7.5	
		[Peru 4.5]	
AVERAGE	5.66	5.94	2.33
AVERAGE Including Peru	5.77		

Yet on average the expectations derived from the influence of political identities on policy preferences were more likely to have been met than not.

A detailed analysis of the policy content of market reforms in electricity and telecommunications in El Salvador and Panama provides an additional test of partisan policy effects in two smaller and poorer Latin American countries than the three subjects of the previous case studies – and of countries that were much more dependent on foreign aid and exposed to international pressures.[47] Additionally, these two countries had traditionally been more open to trade and to U.S. pressures than had Argentina, Chile, or Mexico, due to their prior economic relations with the United States.[48] As trade exposure, capital integration, and U.S. hegemony are associated with economic liberalization (Simmons 1999), it should have been harder for these small, open economies to withstand globalization pressures than it was for their larger neighbors.

Panama and El Salvador adopted market reforms in telecommunications and electricity in the mid-1990s under governments of different partisan orientation, suggesting the strength of external pressures in promoting these policies. Salvadorian reformers were true believers under the helm of President Armando Calderón Sol from the right-wing party the Nationalist Republic Alliance (ARENA). By contrast, Ernesto Pérez Balladares of the formerly populist and statist PRD adopted market reforms in Panama.[49]

---

[47] Argentina, Chile, and Mexico are middle-income countries with a GDP per capita equal to purchasing power parity (PPP) 12,106, 10,277, and 9,168 respectively for 2003. Their respective populations in that year were 38 and 104 million. By contrast, El Salvador's GDP per capita in 2003 was PPP 4,781 and Panama's was 6,854, and their populations were 6.6 and 3.1 million, respectively (UNDP, http://www.undp.org, accessed February 20, 2005). Moreover, whereas electricity coverage in 1989 had reached 95% in Argentina, 91% in Chile, and 86% in Mexico, it only reached 48% in El Salvador and 58% in Panama (Olade 2003). Teledensity per 100 inhabitants in that year was 9.6 in Argentina, 5 in Chile, and 5.7 in Mexico, versus 2.3 in El Salvador and 8.5 in Panama (ITU).

[48] In 1985, the degree of openness (export and imports as a percentage of GDP) was 6% in Argentina, 10% in Mexico, 26% in Chile, 30% in El Salvador, and 33% in Panama (IMF 2005).

[49] ARENA is right-wing party founded in 1981 to oppose the reformist military junta that was ruling El Salvador at the time. Although its founder was linked to death squad murders, in the peaceful post–civil war environment the party functions with complete legitimacy as a normal right-wing party with support from the business sectors. The PRD was designed to unify the political groups and forces that had supported General Omar Torrijos. Proclaiming itself the official supporter and upholder of Torrijismo, the vaguely populist political ideology of Torrijos, the PRD included a broad spectrum of ideologies ranging from extreme left to the right of center. The prevailing orientation was left of center. Like the PRI in Mexico, the PRD has managed to co-opt much of the Panamanian left, thereby limiting and undermining the strength of avowedly Marxist political parties. At times, the PRD also has claimed a social-democratic orientation, and in 1986 it acquired the status of a "consulting member" in the Socialist International.

Table 3.1b. *Telecommunications Index of Regulatory Content*

Indicators	Argentina	Bolivia	Brazil	Chile	Colombia	Costa Rica	Ecuador	El Salvador	Guatemala	Honduras
Limits to FDI	0	0	0.5	0	0	1	1	0	0	1
Investment requirements	1	1	0	0	0.5	1	1	0	0	1
Rules to entry	1	1	1	0	0.5	1	1	0	0	1
Regulatory discretion for network prices	0	0	0	0	1	1	1	0	0	0
Regulatory discretion for consumer prices	1	1	1	0	1	1	1	0	0	1
Regulatory discretion for solving conflicts between consumers and providers	1	0	?	0	1	1	1	0	0	1
Regulatory discretion for solving conflicts between providers	1	1	1	0	1	1	1	0	0	1

Bureaucratic taxes for regulator on regulated rather than general budget	1	1	1	0	1	1	0	0	0.5	0
Independent RA	0.5	1	1	0	0	1	0	0.5	0	0
Date of privatization	1990	1994	1997	1982	1994	N/A	1993	1996	1996	1995
Effective privatization	Yes	Yes	Yes	Yes	No	No	No	Yes	Yes	No
Date of opening to competition	2000		2002 LD, 1996, mob.	1994	1997	0	2002	1996	1998	2005
Coding	6	5	4.5	0	6	8	7	0	0.5	6
Party	PJ	MNR	PSDB	PiNochet	PL		PUR	Arena	PAN	PLH
Government type	Pragmatic Populist	Pragmatic Populist	Pragmatic Populist	True Believer	Pragmatic Populist		True Believer	True Believer	True Believer	Pragmatic Populist
Government share of lower chamber the year of privatization decision	0.48	0.61	0.56	1	0.48		0.23	0.46	0.54	0.48

(continued)

Table 3.1b. *(continued)*

Indicators	Mexico	Nicaragua	Panama	Paraguay	Peru	Dom. Rep.	Uruguay	Venezuela
Limits to FDI	1	1	0.5	0	0	0	0	0
Investment requirements	1	1	1	0	1	0	0	1
Rules to entry	1	1	1	0	1	0	0	1
Regulatory discretion for network prices	0	0	1	1	0	0	1	0
Regulatory discretion for consumer prices	1	0	1	1	0	0	1	1
Regulatory discretion for solving conflicts between consumers and providers	1	1	1	1	0.5	0	1	0.5
Regulatory discretion for solving conflicts between providers	1	1	1	1	1	0.5	0	1

Bureaucratic taxes for regulator on regulated rather than general budget	0	0	1	0	1	0.5	1	1
Independent RA	0	0	1	1	1	1	0	0
Date of privatization	1990	1995	1996	2000	1993	1931	1991	1991
Effective privatization	Yes	No	Yes	No	Yes	Yes	No	Yes
Date of opening to competition	1997	2005	1996	1995	1999	1990	2001	2000
Coding	6	5	7.5	4	4.5	1	4	5.5
Party	PRI	UNO	PRD	ANR	Cambio 90	PRSC		AD
Government type	Pragmatic Populist	True Believer	Pragmatic Populist	Pragmatic Populist	Unclear	True Believer	Pragmatic Populist	Pragmatic Populist
Government share of lower chamber the year of privatization decision	0.48	0.55	0.48	0.48	0.55	0.35	0.48	0.48

Note: The indicators were given 1 when the rules were present and were given 0 otherwise. A few cases had rules of more limited reach and were given 0.5 as a value.

131

Table 3.2a. *Degree of Market Control in Electricity*

	No Effective Privatization	Pragmatic Convert	True Believer
	Costa Rica 8	Argentina 6	Chile 0
	Paraguay 3.5	Bolivia 4	Nicaragua 1
	Uruguay 4	Brazil 5.5	El Salvador 0
	Ecuador 4.5	Colombia 5	Guatemala 1.5
	Honduras 2	Panama 7	
	Mexico 7	Dominican Rep. 2.5	
	Venezuela 4	[Peru 5.5.]	
AVERAGE	4.8	5	0.62
AVERAGE Including Peru	5.07		

The hypothesis of partisanship should lead us to expect a market-conforming content in the reforms of Salvadorian right-wing true believers and a market-controlling one in those of Panamanian pragmatic populist converts.

In telecommunications, the Salvadorian right-wing true believers drafted the 1996 reform law with a market-conforming content. It established no limits on foreign capital – despite demands in that regard from the left-wing opposition party, Farabundo Martí National Liberation Front (FMLN).[50] It did not establish entry rules or investment conditions associated to licenses, either. Reformers' distrust of state intervention became clear in the design of the regulatory agency, called the General Superintendency of Electricity and Telecommunications (SIGET), which covered both sectors. SIGET had limited discretion in telecommunications, with no power to set interconnection prices and strict rules defining the allocation of spectrum and price regulation. Price regulation was based on the recommendation of an external consultant, and conflicts regarding interconnection prices were to be resolved by arbitration. It had no functions regarding the regulation of competition, planning, licensing conditions, or policy making. According to the IADB, its personnel and budget are insufficient.[51]

---

[50] As the FMLN fared better in midterm elections, subsequent laws forced ARENA to compromise on reform content by including compensations and equity participation for workers and investment requirements in underserved areas, as well as limits to invest in wireless companies and then use the proceeds for social or infrastructure projects. However, the original law provides a better measure of the partisan preferences of the ARENA government, which at the time controlled the unicameral Congress.

[51] The Power Sector in El Salvador, report by the IADB, http://www.iadb.org/sds/doc/1880eng.pdf (accessed March 11, 2006).

132

By contrast, pragmatic populist converts in Panama chose a market-controlling content. Panama's Law 5 of 1995 limited the sale of the tele-communications monopoly to 49 percent of shares, with the state maintaining the right to repurchase them should the private provider wish to sell and with limits on the participation of companies a majority of whose shares were owned by foreign states (art. 18). The entry rules included ten-year monopolies for fixed lines and for the two mobile bands (art. 7), which were matched with investment conditions that defined targets for coverage, service quality, and attention to clients, as well as a program of investment and modernization to be supervised by the regulatory agency.

The ideological bias toward state intervention in Panama's program was apparent in the design of the regulatory agency, called the Regulatory Agency for Public Services (ERSP). Due to economies of scale, it covered telecommunications and electricity, along with sanitation. Yet, unlike its Salvadorian counterpart, it had broad powers, including the power to impose taxes on the public-service companies to fund itself and the capacity to take over companies and appoint trustees, to resolve interconnection conflicts, define regulated prices, establish and modify investment targets, approve the extension of monopolies, and control anticompetitive behavior and mergers that would result in market concentration (Law 26 of 1996).

In electricity, neither Salvadorian right-wing true believers nor Panamanian populist converts imposed limits on foreign capital, and both kept transmission in the public sector. Salvadorian right-wing true believers chose a more market-conforming content, however. They allowed energy trading and left the expansion of transmission to be paid for by the market actors. They established market mechanisms based on a formula for setting prices and imposed no investment conditions (except that information be supplied to the regulator) or entry rules, thereby allowing vertical integration as long as accountancy was separated.[52]

By contrast, Panamanian pragmatic populist converts chose a more market-controlling approach to electricity privatization. They established investment conditions and entry rules: distribution companies have obligations to meet in the provision of service and specific targets for expanding coverage, street lighting, and quality in performance and customer service. They also have to follow clear rules limiting property acquisition, so that generators cannot control distribution companies or ask for new

[52] Ibid.

Table 3.2b. *Electricity Index of Regulatory Content*

Indicators	Argentina	Bolivia	Brazil	Chile	Colombia	Costa Rica	Ecuador	El Salvador	Guatemala	Honduras
Limits to FDI	0	0	0	0	0	1	1	0	0	0
Investment requirements	1	1	0	0	1	1	1	0	0	0
Rules to entry	1	1	0.5	0	1	1	1	0	0	0.5
Regulatory discretion for network prices	1	0	1	0	1	1	0	0	0	0.5
Regulatory discretion for consumer prices	0	0	1	0	1	1	0	0	0	1
Regulatory discretion for solving conflicts between consumers and providers	1	1	1	0	0	1	0	0	0	0
Regulatory discretion for solving conflicts between providers	1	0	1	0	0	1	0.5	0	0.5	0

Bureaucratic fees with self-taxation on regulated companies rather than general budget	1	1	1	0	1	1	1	0	1	0
Independent RA	1	1	1	0	0	1	0	0.5	0.5	0
Privatization date	1991	1994	1995	1982	1994	N/A	1993	1996	1996	1994
Effective privatization?	Yes	Yes	Yes	Yes	Yes	No	No	Yes	Yes	No
Opening to competition date	1991	1994	1995	1982	1991	1998	1996	1998	1996	N/A
Coding	6	4	5.5	0	5	8	4.5	0	1.5	2
Party	PJ	MNR	PSDB	Pinochet	PL			Arena	PAN	
Government type	Pragmatic Populist	Pragmatic Populist	Pragmatic Populist	True Believer	Pragmatic Populist	Pragmatic Populist		True Believer	True Believer	Believer
Government share of lower chamber the year of privatization decision		0.61	0.56	1	0.55			0.46	0.54	

(continued)

Table 3.2b. *(continued)*

Indicators	Mexico	Nicaragua	Panama	Paraguay	Peru	Dom. Rep.	Uruguay	Venezuela
Limits to FDI	1	0	0	1	0	0	0	0
Investment requirements	1	0	1	1	0.5	0.5	0	1
Rules to entry	1	1	1	1	0	1	1	0.5
Regulatory discretion for network prices	1	0	1	0	1	0	1	1
Regulatory discretion for consumer prices	1	0	1	0	1	0	1	0.5
Regulatory discretion for solving conflicts between consumers and providers	1	0	1	0	1	0	0	0
Regulatory discretion for solving conflicts between providers	1	0	1	0	1	0	0	1

Bureaucratic fees with self-taxation on regulated companies rather than general budget	0	0	1	0.5	1	1	1	0
Independent RA	0	1	1	1	0	0	0	0
Privatization date	1992	1998	1997	N/A	1992	1999	N/A	N/A
Effective privatization?	No	Yes	Yes	No	Yes	Yes	No	No
Opening to competition date	1992	1997	1998	2006	1994	1999	1997	1996
Coding	7	1	7	3.5	5.5	2.5	4	4
Party		PLC/AL		PRD	Cambio 90	PLD		
Government type		True Believer		Pragmatic Populist	Unclear	Pragmatic Populist		
Government share of lower chamber the year of privatization decision		0.45		0.42	0.55	0.44		

concessions if they serve more than 25 percent of domestic consumption (Law 6 of 1997, art. 69).

The regulatory agencies are the same as in telecommunications for both countries, as noted in the preceding text. Regulatory powers are more limited in El Salvador than in Panama, however. In El Salvador, there is no policy-making body for electric energy. The SIGET set the criteria for operating the wholesale electrical market and maximum rates for low-use residential customers only for a transitory period, after which market rules applied to all prices.[53] Its discretion to regulate noncompetitive prices and resolve conflicts over transmission fees was severely limited.[54]

In contrast to the lack of policy-maker agency in Salvadorian regulation, the Panamanian Energy Policy Commission served as the policy-making body in addition to the regulatory agency, the ERSP. Law 6 of 1997 allowed the intervention of the ERSP to guarantee the quality of service, expansion of coverage, efficiency of provision, promotion of competition, establishment of prices, and expansion of coverage in unprofitable areas (art. 4). The regulatory agency could also set subsidies for low-income users, resolve conflicts between actors in the sector, and impose a tax to fund its budget. Moreover, the regulator had the power to use sanctions to punish anticompetitive behavior and control property sales that might produce market concentration. It was given discretion in establishing rules for electricity concessions and for the use of networks, as well as in defining the criteria used in regulating prices.

Partisanship thus is crucial to understanding the technical choices made by policy makers who privatized the telecommunications and electricity sectors in El Salvador and Panama. These regulations can be understood in the context of a right-wing Salvadorian party with middle- and upper-class supporters that was emerging from a civil war against a formerly socialist-leaning guerrilla group. By contrast, Panamanian populists had a base of lower- and middle-class constituencies. In particular, the effect of policy makers' ideological legacies is clear in their own interpretations of

---

[53] http://www.saprin.org/elsalvador/research/els_sum_privatization.pdf (accessed March 12, 2006).

[54] Distribution prices were to be set by SIGET only for thirty-six months, after which they were to become equal to the market price plus a discount rate of 10%, using a predefined formula (Ley General de Electricidad, ch. 7, sec. 1, art. 88). In the event of a conflict over transmission fees, the SIGET can appoint an expert, and the parties provide information to the expert, along with two final proposals. The SIGET selects one of the two proposals, which ought to be the one closest to the expert's report. The SIGET cannot take a position different from the ones proposed by the parties (Ley General de Electricidad, ch. 7, sec. 2).

technical options. The account of two Salvatorian ARENA technocrats – Alfredo Mena Lagos, who headed the Presidential Commission for the Modernization of the State, and Juan José Daboub, who was the president of the state-owned company ANTEL – regarding the choices they made in the reform of telecommunications highlights this effect. In particular, Mena Lagos liked the idea of having disputes about interconnection fees subject to arbitration in order to render unnecessary the establishment of a regulator with a high level of discretionary power, a notion he particularly disliked. As described by Bull (2005, 70), in a personal interview, Mena Lagos explained how he chose the most market-conforming regulatory model he was presented with: "I asked my assistant from the commission to give me all of the offers for technical analysis on the law and I wanted to go through them, and I read through them on the flight and I discovered that the one that came closest to a free market model was the offer that Pablo Spiller had made, so I asked Manuel to go over that with me and you know, then we decided upon Pablo Spiller."

In sum, this section has drawn on regional patterns of reform content, which included compromise in many instances but nonetheless reveals the persistence of the expected partisan effects. To control for the effect of market size, it provided further evidence by drawing on the regulatory content of reforms in both sectors in two smaller and more exposed countries. This analysis further confirmed the existence of partisan effects even in small economies. The following section discusses alternative explanations for the policy content of privatization reform and their complementarities with the political incentives generated by partisanship.

Alternative Hypotheses Explaining Policy Content

By emphasizing policy makers' preferences rather than the constraints on their choices, this chapter's focus on partisanship has provided an account that explains a great deal of policy content in cases where political competition was restricted, allowing the adoption of reform with little compromise. Constraints, though, are the focus of explanations emphasizing the impact of technological pressures, international diffusion of ideas, economic preferences of foreign investors, and influence of policy-making institutions. This section reviews these alternative approaches to explaining reform content, assessing their complementarity with the partisan explanation of policy preferences.

First, technological pressures were different in each sector, as technological change generated the possibility of alternative networks in telecommunications more rapidly than in electricity. At the same time, the coverage of electricity services was much more extensive than that of telephone services when reforms seeking to bring private capital to these sectors began. These differences suggest that reform content should have followed industry-specific patterns, in particular with faster convergence on policy content in the telecommunications sector, where technological pressures were stronger (Levi-Faur 1999, 2003; Bartle 2002). Sector-specific conditions certainly define the boundaries of what policy makers could do and, as discussed in subsequent chapters, shape the way in which reform content affects the subsequent bargaining power of private providers. The previous two sections have shown, however, that reform content did not follow sectoral patterns in the three studied countries. That is, Chilean right-wing true believers chose a market-conforming content in electricity and telecommunications, whereas Argentine pragmatic populist converts preferred a market-controlling content in both sectors.

Second, studies of the international diffusion of ideas focus on technocrats sharing the same epistemic community (often U.S.-trained economists). Their transnational linkages across countries and with their peers in international financial institutions facilitate the spread of similar policy models (Kogut and Mcpherson 2004). A less rational approach suggests that these experts may be imitating what they perceive as a successful and feasible policy proposal, such as the pioneering Chilean experience with pension privatization (Weyland 2006). Weyland explains this process of policy isomorphism using policy makers' perception biases, which brought them to copy Chilean institutions, even if adapted to their local context. He does not identify cross-national patterns of local adaptation, however.

Chile was also a pioneer in privatizing public utilities, and its model could have been copied by Mexican and Argentine policy makers making decisions about reform content. Allied and neoliberal technocrats in Argentina paid close attention to the Chilean experience with electricity reform.[55] That is, prior experiences were considered in defining possible options.

---

[55] Allied expert and undersecretary of energy Juan Legisa, who produced the first reform proposal of a more statist nature, sent a mission to Chile to study the reform in 1990 (Pagina 12, August 23, 1990). Cavallo's electricity reform team of neoliberal technocrats also studied the Chilean experience (personal interview with Domingo Cavallo, New York City, May 6, 2003).

Policy makers, however, also had their own partisan biases when interpreting those experiences. As a result, Argentine populist converts chose a different content for their electricity reform than that of Chilean right-wing true believers whereas Salvadorian right-wing reformers chose a similar one. As the Argentina reform preceded that of El Salvador, an unbiased process of social learning, should have considered the lessons of that reform as well.

In Chile, true believers established no rules restricting entry or acquisitions in the reform of electricity. As a result, the generation sector was heavily concentrated as well as vertically integrated under private ownership a decade after privatization (Bitrán and Serra 1998). Argentina reformed its electricity sector after Chile, and its technocrats, under a converted Peronist administration, established entry rules that set limits to horizontal and vertical integration, which prevented a similar outcome in terms of market concentration. Five years after the Argentine privatization, El Salvador reformed electricity under the true believer administration of Calderón Sol with the advice of the two Chilean consultants who had been responsible for designing the Chilean reform (Sergio Bernstein and Renato Agurto), and its policy makers chose to impose no limits on vertical integration or horizontal concentration. By 2001, the concentration of the three largest providers in the generation market was three times higher in El Salvador than in Argentina (Inter-American Development Bank 2001, 171). Ideological biases, thus, seem to have trumped social learning in this case.

The Chilean experience of reforming telecommunications provides similar indicators that the experts interpreted facts differently based on their partisan biases. Whereas Chile opened its telecommunications market to competition early and later established rules to make competition more effective, Argentine and Mexican policy makers instead chose to adopt gradual liberalization in this sector. Former Argentine regulator Roberto Catalán defended the 1998 limited liberalization of the telecommunications market, arguing that cutthroat competition in Chile was ineffective in promoting investment and expanding coverage because it weakened the private providers (personal interview, May 11, 1999). Similar arguments were used by the former Mexican secretary of communications Carlos Ruiz Sacristán to defend the 1995 decision to pursue a gradual approach in the liberalization of the long-distance telecommunications market (personal interview, January 18, 2001). Yet Chile's rate of growth in teledensity outperformed Mexico's and Argentina's within a few years of the reform. Therefore, whereas the literature on expertise emphasizes homogenization through social learning, it is important to include in this equation the bias of experts – whether it is generated by their career options in terms of political tenure or their prior institutional experiences – in order to assess their technical choices.

Third, the general adoption of market reforms in the region has been associated with policy makers' need to access international financial markets (Edwards 1995). Stallings (1992) argues that foreign capital becomes more influential when countries are more cash strapped, and therefore we should expect foreign investors to affect reform content in countries under financial duress. The Chilean electricity and telecommunications reforms were designed at a time of fiscal abundance – the budget surplus was 2.9 percent of GDP in 1981 (Meller 1996, 195) – and international financial institutions were suspicious of electricity unbundling and privatization, as discussed in the preceding text.

Even for the pragmatic populist converts for whom financial pressures were crucial, however, it is important to remember that financial markets were more interested in debt repayment than in the details of reform design. Industry-specific multinational corporations looking for future investment options paid more attention to the fine print, but until they have sunk their capital, the latter can easily choose the next country. Due to the low mobility of their assets, it is only when they have deployed their capital that their stakes increase, along with their investment in policy influence.

It is also important to look at domestic investors, whose influence has been pointed to by the literature on foreign investment as derived from political connections (Henisz and Zelner 2003) or from the need of competitive regimes to build consensus for their policies (Etchmendy 2008). In Argentina and Mexico, foreign investors vied with domestic investors, whose assets were less mobile and who were looking for compensation in exchange for reforms that reduced their role as state suppliers. Domestic businesses were the owners of a scarce resource whose returns declined as capital inflows increased, so that they did not necessary share the preferences of foreign investors. In Argentina and Mexico, the preferences of domestic capital holders were able to override those of foreign investors regarding reform content, as they demanded compensation for market reforms by using political linkages. In Argentina, for instance, Unión Fenosa, Eléctricité de France, and Endesa of Spain, which were potential investors in electricity distribution for the Buenos Aires area, publicly opposed the partition of SEGBA before it was divided into Edenor, Edesur, and Edelap.[56] Similarly, Southern Bell, AT&T, and Telefónica of Spain opposed the division of ENTEL before it was split into two vertically integrated companies.[57] In contrast to foreign multinationals, domestic investors, which were former state suppliers, wanted a smaller-scale privatization to maximize their own opportunity to acquire assets.[58] Foreign investors would only become more influential after deploying their capital, especially as reformers tied their luck to the success of early reform experiences to attract further investment.

Fourth, the literature on institutions and policy making emphasizes how the distribution of political preferences in a particular institutional configuration generates veto players who can induce compromise over policy content (Cox and McCubbins 2001; Tsebelis 2003). This literature takes policy makers' preferences as given and does not investigate them, whereas the partisan hypothesis does, thereby making both approaches complementary. By analyzing cases with few veto players, such as telecommunications reforms delegated to the executive, the impact of preference on policy content becomes obvious. The hypothesis should work, however, even with a larger number of veto players. That is, partisanship can explain the preferences of policy makers before the start of the policy-making process, in which compromise may produce a different policy content.

Conclusion

The widespread adoption of market-oriented reforms in public utilities across Latin America reduced the effect of partisanship in defining policy divergence. Yet partisan differences continued to affect policy making by shaping the design of market-based utilities reforms. Policy makers' constituencies, prior beliefs, and allied experts influenced lawmakers' diverse regulatory choices and upheld the policy identity of partisan coalitions, sustaining the loyalty of politicians, activists, and experts. Interrogating the content of these reforms helps to clarify how pragmatic populist

---

[56] "Privatización de SEGBA. Los vientos vienen de España." *Informe Industrial*, no. 124, año XIII, December 1990, 30–1.

[57] Personal interview with former deputy undersecretary for communications Raúl Parodi (February 8, 2000); *El Cronista Comercial*, August 16, 1989.

[58] Domestic companies, such as Bridas, Macri, and Pescarmona, favored partition to maximize their opportunity to participate in the privatization of smaller assets. *Clarín*, August 18, 1989; *Ambito Financiero*, September 13, 1989; *Clarín*, September 17, 1989.

converts in the opposition were able to move back to more statist policies in the twenty-first century. Moreover, it highlights three mechanisms by which partisanship shapes policy making: the ideological legacies of politicians, demands of constituencies, and delegation to experts who internalize political preferences to sustain their career options.

This chapter provides evidence of the explanatory power of partisanship by assessing the testable implications of the hypothesis on indicators of regulatory content, as well as on the immediate impact of reforms on different types of constituencies as consumers or recipients of subsidized assets in three middle-income countries: Argentina, Chile, and Mexico. Furthermore, policy makers' preferences are reflected in the general trends of policy content across the region, while a comparison of the reform content in two small-size economies controls for the effect of market size. Thus, this chapter shows that the explanatory power of partisanship in policy preferences is not limited to middle-income countries in the region.

The implications of these findings are limited by the scope of the cases, and further testing is necessary to establish their larger external validity. The chapter's findings do cast important doubts, however, on prior conclusions about the death of ideological preferences – especially with regard to policy implications – in Latin America. The survival of ideological policy preferences has often not been perceived because their effect was not as strong on policy adoption as it was on the less publicly salient dimension of reform content. Preferences sustained prior linkages, which resulted from the original distributive policy preferences of incumbent governments. Incumbents, even converted ones, could try to benefit their supporters within the restraints imposed by a financial shortage by delegating to experts whose proposals would more likely reflect politicians' ideas about the need to control or rely on market allocation of resources. These legacies are telling, as the outliers in terms of policy content, like Bolivia's MNR or Venezuela's AD, are political parties that subsequently could not return to their populist backing when the commodity boom of the 2000s reduced fiscal constraints. The following two chapters discuss the distributive dynamics derived from privatization policy choices and the political effects they had in terms of postprivatization regulatory reform.

4

Postreform Regulatory Redistribution in Chile

In analyzing the consequences of market-oriented reforms, private providers emerge as crucial stakeholders in the defense of the conditions under which they decided to make their original investment decisions. This study focuses on the preferences of policy makers, as opposed to relational and institutional approaches to the study of public utilities, which focus on private investors' preferences, but it includes providers' preferences and bargaining power as constraints on policy makers' actions.[1] This chapter and the one that follows have two goals. First, they test the explanatory power of the two main hypotheses for the postreform period; that is, taking advantage of longitudinal changes in electoral competition and partisanship within the same national context. Second, they seek to assess the institutional effects generated by the market-oriented reforms of public utilities in Argentina, Chile, and Mexico, with a focus on policy makers' and providers' preferences in explaining subsequent regulatory outcomes.

The dependent variable in both chapters is regulatory redistribution, which is measured using the four categories introduced in Chapter 1. These categories capture redistribution between the first entrants who became privatized incumbent providers and either their potential challengers or consumers. The four categories include "regulatory capture," involving redistribution from consumers to providers; "regulatory dominance," which generates redistribution in the opposite direction; "market dominance," where redistribution goes from competitors to incumbent providers; and

---

[1] See Gomez-Ibanez (2001) and Post (2007) for a relational take on the postprivatization dynamics between both parties and Levy and Spiller (1996) for a more institutionalist view. The incentives for regulatory redistribution are similar in both approaches, but institutions are considered to have a stronger capacity to constrain actors' bargaining power in the latter.

"market competition," a case in which competitors benefit at the expense of incumbent providers.

These two chapters trace how the preferences of policy makers and private providers led to these various regulatory outcomes in telecommunications and electricity in Argentina, Chile, and Mexico, following the argument presented in Chapter 1. That is, political competition creates incentives for regulatory redistribution to consumers (regulatory dominance) for incumbents and challengers in contexts of high public salience. The effect of partisanship is shaped by the role of incumbents in the initial reform process, which generates ties to first entrants. Right-wing true believers should prefer regulatory redistribution from consumers to incumbent providers if they have reformed and to competitors if they have not. Populist converts should prefer regulatory redistribution from competitors to first entrants if they have reformed – usually in exchange for targeted benefits to groups of consumers – and from first entrants to competitors and consumers if they have not reformed. Finally, private providers' preferences depend on the original regulatory content of reforms and on technological differences: market-controlling reforms strengthened first entrants in telecommunications and facilitated their imposition of market dominance as the industry preference. The same reform content in electricity made the emergence of dominant providers more difficult, facilitating market competition as the industry preference, because no provider could impose its view on the others. By contrast, market-conforming reforms weakened first entrants in telecommunications and favored market competition as the industry preference, whereas they allowed market consolidation in electricity, facilitating the emergence of dominant providers that imposed market dominance as the industry preference.

Due to the small number of observations, the research strategy in the following chapters focuses on tracing causal mechanisms derived from the main hypotheses and defining common patterns regarding policy feedback effects for inductive theory building. To keep institutional effects constant, each of the two chapters analyzes postreform regulatory instances in the same type of institutional legacy – either market conforming or market controlling – while comparing across industries. Therefore, Chapter 4 focuses on a longitudinal comparison of Chilean regulatory reforms in electricity and telecommunications, holding constant the market-conforming institutional legacy. The same longitudinal analysis and interindustry comparison is made for regulatory reforms in Argentina and Mexico – holding constant the market-controlling institutional legacy – in Chapter 5. This research design takes advantage of the longitudinal variation in levels of political competition and in the identity of the incumbent policy makers within each country.

By focusing on the postreform Chilean experience, this chapter provides a baseline for evaluating the instances of regulatory redistribution in the following chapter while allowing for an interindustry comparison (considering the different pace of technological reform) along with an evaluation of the effects produced by changing levels of electoral competition. However, this chapter maintains constant not only the institutional legacy of market-oriented reforms but also the partisan identity of the postreform governments, which is nonetheless different from that of the reforming government. The next chapter focuses on Argentina and Mexico and shows the effect of variation in the partisan preferences of incumbents during the postreform period.

Political Competition, Partisanship, and Institutional Legacies in Postreform Chile

This section describes the evolution of the main independent variables – political competition and partisanship – along with the impact of institutional legacies on market structure and their expected effects on preferences for regulatory redistribution. In the cross-national comparison of partisanship, the analysis of partisan policy preferences uses the regulation of consumer rights as an indicator of ideas about market-state relations as well as preferences for favoring either consumers or providers. Legislative debates on laws explicitly protecting consumer rights are useful indicators of policy makers' preferences because they illustrate general views about the role of the market in the allocation of resources that are not limited to public utilities.

Political Competition

The sale of Chilean telecommunications and electricity assets was finalized in 1988, the same year Pinochet was defeated in the plebiscite for democratic transition. Democratic elections were called for the next year, and the Pinochet administration focused on establishing institutions that would tie the hands of its successors (Boylan 2001). Between 1990 and 2005, the presidency was held by the Concertación of Political Parties for Democracy (hereafter the Concertación), which brought together Christian

Democrats, Socialists, and Radicals. The level of political competition varied, however, during the first three Concertación administrations under presidents Patricio Aylwin (1990–4), Eduardo Frei (1994–2000), and Ricardo Lagos (2000–6).[2]

Political competition remained at low levels until 1999 and then declined again after 2001. In the 1989 presidential election, the Concertación candidate, Patricio Aylwin, received 55.17 percent of the vote, whereas the right-wing candidate, Hernán Büchi, obtained 29.4 percent; the legislative candidates of Concertación and the right-wing coalition received 51.5 and 34.2 percent of the vote, respectively. The electoral margin increased in the 1993 presidential election, when the Concertación candidate received 58 percent of the vote and its right-wing contender only 24.4 percent. This result signaled a decline in political competition, which was softer in the legislative elections, as Concertación received 55.4 percent of the vote and the parties in the right-wing coalition 36.7 percent. This electoral margin narrowed slightly in the 1997 legislative elections, when Concertación received 50.5 percent and the right-wing coalition 36.2 percent. In early 1999, however, presidential approval ratings bottomed out (see Figure 4.1), and in the first round of the presidential election the Concertación candidate, Ricardo Lagos, received 47.96 percent of the vote to 47.51 percent for his right-wing rival, Joaquín Lavín; Lagos won the second round with 51.31 percent to Lavín's 48.69 percent. As presidential approval ratings recovered under Lagos, electoral competition declined slightly in the subsequent legislative elections of 2001, as Concertación gathered 47.9 percent of the vote and the right-wing coalition 44.27 percent (see Figure 4.1).

During the studied period, electoral competition peaked in the first round of the 1999 presidential election, when the distance between the winner from the incumbent party and the challenger was less than 1 percentage point. In that year, moreover, there was an exogenous shock to the electricity sector in the form of a supply crisis but none to the telecommunications sector, generating different costs for raising the public salience of regulatory reforms in each sector and therefore making regulatory dominance more likely in the former than the latter.

---

[2] The first administration under Christian Democratic president Patricio Alwyn was shortened to four years as a result of agreements between the outgoing military regime and its democratic opposition after the victory of the latter in the 1988 plebiscite on democratic transition.

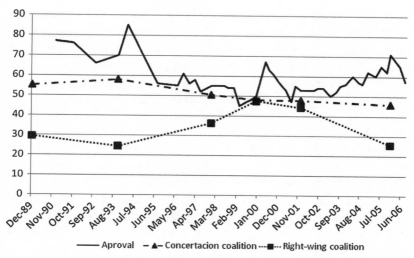

Figure 4.1 Public Opinion on the President and Presidential Vote (1990–2005)
Notes: 1997 and 2001 are legislative elections, and the results used for the presidential elections correspond to the first round. In the 2005 election, Sebastian Piñeira is considered the right-wing candidate.
Source: Political Database of the Americas, http://www.pdba.georgetown.edu (accessed March 30, 2009).

Partisanship

The partisan identity of the incumbent changed in the immediate aftermath of reforms with the replacement of Pinochet by a center-left coalition, which was continuously reelected to the presidency in 1994, 1999, and 2005. This coalition involved former populists, who we might expect to have preferred to defend redistribution to consumers. Because they had converted to the market creed while out of power, however, they should have been more likely to believe in the virtues of market competition than their Latin American peers who adopted reform when the state was on the verge of fiscal collapse, making market competition a more likely outcome.

Right-wing true believers adopted market reforms in Chile, whereas the political parties that would later form the Concertación denounced them. Two parties emerged from the cadres of the right-wing military regime: UDI and Renovación Nacional (RN). Huneeus (2000, 616–17) has shown the overlap between UDI and RN elected representatives and the officials of the regime. Among the UDI representatives elected between 1989 and 2001, for instance, 48.3 percent had been mayors and 24.1 percent had been

149

government officials under military rule, whereas among RN representatives, 31.4 percent had been mayors and 23.5 percent had been government officials during that period. In the first Congress, moreover, all eight UDI senators and nine of the fourteen RN senators had participated in the Pinochet administration.

By contrast, the Concertación included the Christian Democrats (DC) and the Socialist Party (PS), as well as its offspring, the Party for Democracy (PPD), all of which had promoted state intervention in public utilities in the past, as discussed in Chapter 2. The Concertación parties had accepted the main principles of the free-market economic model established by the military rulers, however, and had thus converted to the market while out of power. Their conversion had a certain degree of pragmatism, because during the negotiations regarding the democratic transition, they had to agree not to revise the privatization of public utilities.[3] The 1989 electoral program of the Concertación explicitly stated, "Considering the agreements made by the Concertación regarding the privatization of public assets following the plebiscite, it is necessary to end with property instability in the country – either for private or public property. In the future, any nationalization or privatization would be supported by a broad national consensus expressed in Congress" (La Epoca 1989, 13).

The conversion of the Concertación, however, was not only driven by pragmatism, but also, even before the transition, the left-wing parties in the coalition had undertaken a process of ideological renovation that included the acceptance of market mechanisms (Hite 2000). The Socialists tried to differentiate themselves from their revolutionary predecessors to keep the support of their middle- and lower-class constituencies while providing strong guarantees of property rights.[4] As a result, Concertación administrations emphasized human capital and social policy (i.e., health and education) while promoting competition and consumer rights as an alternative to unchecked market forces. Because they converted while out of

---

[3] According to the former director of communications of the General Secretary of the President during the Frei administration, Cristian Toloza, in the negotiations that took place between the 1988 plebiscite and the 1990 transition it was agreed that privatization was not going to be revised (personal interview, June 5, 2005).

[4] The Socialist administration of Salvador Allende (1970–73) had promoted nationalization, land reform, and other radical policies. Yet the limits to the social goals of the Concertación government were particularly dramatic during the first democratic administration (1990–94), which wanted to avoid confrontation with the business sector that had supported Pinochet's coup against Allende (Boylan 2001).

power, Concertación technocrats were likely to believe in the use of regulation to promote competition in order to benefit residential consumers. Personal interviews with two allied experts and undersecretaries of telecommunications under Alwyin exemplify this view. Jorge Rosenbluth said that Concertación experts involved in the regulation of public utilities were firm believers in the power of regulation to achieve competition among multiple providers in all network industries (June 27, 2005). Meanwhile, Gregorio San Martin emphasized the regulators' role in teaching Concertación politicians about the need for regulation to promote competition in areas where it was possible, such as telecommunications (November 10, 2000).

The influence of allied experts was heightened, moreover, by the introduction of partisan quotas on political appointments of regulators and the establishment of civil service reform, which privileged a combination of expertise and partisan ties during the Frei administration (1994–2000) (Rehren 2000, 161–4). The Frei administration established that competition was a crucial mechanism for modernization; his electoral platform explicitly promised to promote consumer organization and blamed the regulatory weakness of privatized public services on the "ideologized" character of privatization under Pinochet while promising to revise regulatory frameworks to promote competition and strengthen regulatory authority (Concertación 1993, 72–3). Genaro Arriagada, then chief of staff, argued that regulating privatized sectors to increase transparency and competition was a crucial mechanism for providing an alternative to state intervention and the sheer power of business (personal interview, March 29, 2001).

Lagos's 1999 presidential platform promised to strengthen competition and consumer protection and emphasized the need for a transparent process of price definition in public utilities, as well as the need for regulators with sufficient power to monitor and sanction in these sectors (Lagos 1999, 8). Similarly, Bachelet promised in 2005 to strengthen procompetition institutions, including the national economic prosecutor and the new Anti-Trust Court, to defend the "welfare of consumers, citizens, and the weak" (Bachelet 2005, 40). She even promised to focus regulatory efforts on telecommunications operators with significant market power, establish a mechanism for resolving interconnection conflicts, and establish a universal service fund (49).

The contrasting ideological views on market-state relations between the Concertación and its right-wing rivals in the postreform period became apparent in the legislative debate about a 1993 executive bill on consumer rights. All Concertación representatives in the Lower Chamber supported the creation of the National Agency for Consumer Services (SERNAC) to regulate the defense of consumer rights. Concertación parties only differed on whether consumer or neighborhood associations should represent residential users – with the Socialists and PPD supporting the former and the Christian Democrats the latter. By contrast, RN legislators denounced those powers as strong enough to challenge the tenets of a competitive, free-market economy. They claimed that an unregulated free-market economy was the best defense for consumer rights. UDI legislators also decried the "excessive" delegation to the SERNAC and the idea of active state regulation (BCN 1993, 89–125). Echoing their concerns, the right-wing legislative think tank Instituto Libertad y Desarrollo criticized the bill for promoting state intervention in the economy and reversing the deregulation implemented by the military regime (Libertad y Desarrollo 1993a).

Similarly, the electoral platform of Arturo Alessandri – the presidential candidate of the right-wing Alianza in 1993 – did not mention consumer rights and emphasized the need to privatize the remaining state-owned companies, including the copper-producing Codelco, in order to promote private investment and expand private ownership. When Joaquin Lavín was the presidential candidate of the Alianza in 1999, his electoral platform did not mention consumer protection either. In 2005, the main right-wing candidate was Sebastian Piñeira from Renovacion Nacional, and his electoral platform stated that competition was a tool for increasing efficiency rather protecting certain groups from others (Piñeira 2005).

The partisan preferences of Concertación policy makers were constrained by the institutional configuration of the polity. The 1980 constitution established a president with the strongest, most proactive powers of any president in the world, which should have facilitated regulatory reform (Shuggart and Carey 1992). Yet Concertación presidents did not resort to using these strong presidential powers to impose their will on the legislature. During the first three democratic administrations, their consensual behavior was promoted by the binomial electoral system, which made it difficult to transform electoral majorities into legislative majorities; the lack of unified government; and the Concertación's reluctance to use presidential powers to overcome legislative stalemates (Siavelis 2002; Aninat et al. 2004, 16). In particular, the intentions of the Concertación to promote regulatory reform had to overcome the right-wing veto in the Senate until the end of the Lagos administration, when a constitutional reform abolished the nonelected senators. For instance, in a compromise over the 1993 consumer rights bill, right-wing senators forced the government to weaken SERNAC regulatory powers while making it difficult for consumer associations to represent consumers, according to Francisco Fernandez, former director of SERNAC (personal interview, March 20, 2001).

Regulatory Legacies and Market Structure

In electricity, the market-oriented reforms resulted in the division of Chilectra and Endesa, the two vertically integrated companies in the SIC in which 80 percent of installed capacity was located. Before its privatization, Endesa was divided into six regional distributors and four generators, and the transmission grid was sold, with the main generator called Endesa (later operated as Transelec). Chilectra was divided into one generator (Chilgener, later Gener) and two distributors (Chilquinta and Chilectra) (Moguillansky 1999, 173–5).

The original reforms were market conforming, thereby granting only weak powers to the regulator. Weak regulatory powers favored Endesa's influence. The regulatory authority had to cope with information asymmetry, a lack of qualified personnel and adequate infrastructure, and the possibility of industry capture: there was no ban on regulators' working in regulated companies after their tenure with the regulatory authority came to an end (Inostroza 1995; Bitrán 1998; Bitrán and Serra 1998; Bitrán and Saenz 1994). Bitrán and Serra (1998) argue that the major regulatory shortcoming of the electricity sector was the weakness of regulators.[5]

The absence of rules for entry allowed property reconcentration and vertical integration. The holding company Enersis, which owned the distributors Chilectra and Rio Maipo, gained control of Endesa in 1993 and later purchased the generator Pehuenche, which had 10 percent of installed capacity. Property concentration in generation, along with vertical integration, reduced incentives for entry in generation and thus facilitated price discrimination against Endesa's competitors (Bitrán and Saenz 1994; Bitran and Serra 1994; Bitrán 1998).

Endesa's ability to discriminate against its competitors based on its control of the main grid was heightened by the absence of rules about

---

[5] Both authors were Concertación technocrats: Eduardo Bitrán was advisor to the finance minister and CORFO's president and in 2006 was appointed minister of public works when Pablo Serra also became the executive director of CNE.

transmission fees (left to agreement between parties), the ambiguities in transmission pricing rules, and uncertainty about transmission fees paid by unregulated consumers located in the franchise area of distribution firms. The influence of Endesa promoted inefficient duplication of investment to avoid Endesa's discrimination in the use of transmission networks (Bitrán and Serra 1994; Bitrán et al. 1999; Serra 2002, 32). The three largest companies controlled the board of the independent dispatch operator, or CDEC, and the information on which its decisions were based came from a subsidiary of Endesa called Ingendesa. Due to a unanimity requirement for its decisions, moreover, Endesa enjoyed veto power on the board (Bitrán and Serra 1998).

Hence, in the aftermath of privatization, the concentration of the electricity market was high. According to Serra, the main three economic holdings concentrated 96.1 percent of the installed capacity in the SIC by 1996 (2002, 27). Moreover, two distributors concentrated two-thirds of electricity demand in the SIC: Chilectra (40%) and Chilquinta (20%). The main actor across the three segments of the industry was Enersis, which along with its subsidiaries concentrated 62 percent of installed capacity in the SIC (mainly through Endesa and Pehuenche), owned the transmission grid (Transelec), and controlled 40 percent of distribution – including Chilectra and Rio Maipo (Altomonte 1996, 60). Vertical integration reduced conflicts between providers in diverse segments, while limited differentials in profit facilitated the coordination of common regulatory preferences by the two largest holdings, Enersis and Gener, under the predominance of the former. This market structure facilitating Enersis predominance favored an industry preference for market dominance.

In telecommunications, there was an informal agreement, which gave most of local communications to the CTC and the long-distance ones to the ENTEL, although the former had a license for domestic long-distance in the central region and the latter for local communications in the south.[6] The agreement was kept after the privatization of the two companies. The market-conforming reforms allowed competition but did not regulate

---

[6] This division of labor originated with the creation of ENTEL to provide long-distance service with a publicly financed microwave network to cover what was perceived as the failures of CTC after an earthquake in 1967 (Melo 1993). The DFL 1 of 1987 allowed CTC to provide long-distance services with the infrastructure it had already installed (art. 26), while decree 202 of 1982, which had not been derogated, permitted CTC to provide long-distance service through third-party infrastructure.

interconnection prices or conflicts. This situation allowed facilities-based competition, which included these companies and other minor ones resulting from privatization (Chilesat) or investment in the sector (e.g. Manquehue) but generated numerous judicial conflicts due to the lack of regulation of interconnection.[7]

Telecommunications reforms also produced a weak regulatory authority with little ability to demand information from companies or to penalize them. Regulatory discretion was limited by a formula that included providers' own estimates of their long-term marginal costs (Law 18,168, art. 30A). Additionally, because the companies provided the result but not the input used for the calculus, the regulator had to deal with an information asymmetry (Tabja 1996; Melo and Serra 1998).[8]

Thus, in the aftermath of reforms, the telecommunications sector was characterized by facilities-based competition and overlapping areas at the local level, where CTC competed with smaller providers. Coordination difficulties between providers generated incentives for competitors to support market competition as a regulatory option. Because CTC controlled 94 percent of the local market and ENTEL most of the long-distance market until de facto competition in 1993 reduced its share to 75 percent of domestic and 55 percent of international long distance (BCN 1994, 4898), the companies had incentives to compete in both markets. Large profit differentials between CTC and ENTEL heightened CTC's will to enter the lucrative long-distance market.[9]

In short, the legacy of market-conforming reforms in Chile favored the hegemony of Enersis in electricity, and thereby the predominant industry preference was market dominance, which implied sustaining the status quo. By contrast, in telecommunications, the development of alternative networks along with profit differentials increased incentives for conflict within

---

[7] Among the cases mentioned during the legislative debate because they involved the intervention of the Anti-Trust Commission were denouncements against CTC by CMT, Manquehue, and Sertel (BCN 1993, 1037–8).

[8] For instance, SUBTEL had difficulty in getting the necessary information from CTC for the 1994 price regulation decree, because the regulator had no power to sanction the company for its refusal to provide traffic projections (Fischer and Serra 2003, 30).

[9] The returns were particularly high in international long-distance communications because there was a difference between the number of incoming and outgoing calls that produced an excess profit appropriated by the long-distance carriers. The CTC profit over equity ranged from 12.7% in 1988 to 23% in 1993. In the same period, ENTEL's ranged from 73.6% to 37.4% (Fischer and Serra 2003, 23). In 1990, profits were 13% for CTC, 53% for ENTEL, and 22% for the smaller long-distance provider Chilesat (Fischer and Serra 2003, 23).

the industry (especially between CTC and ENTEL) and made providers' coordination at the industry level difficult, thereby fostering their preference for new regulatory reforms that would facilitate market competition.

Providers' influence was attenuated, however, by consumer demands. Whereas providers' coordination was shaped by the impact of institutional legacies on market structure, the relationship between consumers and providers was not only affected by the political incentives described in the preceding text (i.e., electoral competition and partisanship) but also by consumers' stakes in the regulatory process. The stakes of residential consumers based on the income effects of public-service prices should have been higher in telecommunications than in electricity because the increase in coverage and price was larger in the former sector. By 1987, 98 percent of urban households had electricity (though only 88 percent of the total population, due to sparser rural coverage), whereas there were less than 5 phones per 100 inhabitants (Fischer and Serra 2003, 18, 57). This difference in coverage generated a socioeconomic bias in access to telecommunications services.[10] The large unmet demand in telecommunications brought a significant expansion of coverage, so that the number of fixed lines more than doubled between 1988 and 1994 and more than quadrupled by 2000, thereby allowing coverage for sectors for which the income effect of prices was sizeable.[11]

Consumers' policy pressure, however, is shaped by their perception of the stakes, which is affected by the public salience of the issue in question. In the case of Chile, consumer organization was relatively weak due to the legacy of an authoritarian regime (Rhodes 2006), making an endogenous increase in the public salience of utilities regulation reform less likely.[12] Although the democratic transition of 1990 reduced the negative incentives on organization and increased the freedom of the press, only in the electricity sector did a crisis of supply heighten the public salience of electricity reform at a time of high electoral competition. The crisis heightened politicians' attention to the electoral costs of ignoring consumer concerns and eroded providers' capacity to resist redistribution in favor of consumers.

---

[10] By 2000, only 25% of the people in the lower decile of income had a fixed telephone line in urban areas, whereas 95% of those in the top decile had one (Fisher and Serra 2003, 26).

[11] The number of CTC fixed lines grew from 592,000 in 1988 to 1.5 million in 1994 and 2.7 million in 2000 (Fisher and Serra 2003, 19).

[12] The largest consumer association, CONADECUS, had about fifty members at the time, according to its president, Ernesto Benado (personal interview, March 27, 2001).

Regulatory Reforms in Electricity

The Concertación's policies sought to benefit consumers through direct and indirect regulatory redistribution. That is, its preferences for regulatory reform included regulatory dominance and market competition, because its members were populists who converted while out of power. Electoral incentives, however, increased the prevalence of regulatory dominance as the policy preference of the Concertación and its right-wing challengers. The policy preferences of the Concertación should be expressed in terms of executive policies, the actions of the economic prosecutor (appointed by the president), and regulatory proposals, due to the right-wing veto in the Senate.

In 1992, the government's preference for market competition led the economic prosecutor to sue Endesa and Transelec for vertical integration in order to prevent noncompetitive behavior and thereby to demand the divestiture of Transelec. In 1997, the Anti-Trust Commission dismissed the case but recommended that the government pass legislation regarding the use of transmission lines and that Transelec open itself to participation by other firms (Resolution No. 488 of July 1997) (Basañes et al. 2002, 12–13; Serra 2002, 32).[13]

Executive actions also reflected regulatory preferences for market competition. First, in seeking to promote competition with Endesa in generation, the government backed the construction of a pipeline for importing Argentine gas to reduce the cost of inputs for thermal utilities, such as Gener and Colbún (Rivera 2000). Colbún (the remaining large state-owned utility in the SIC) also was an active litigator against Endesa in regard to issues of vertical integration.[14] In 1996, the Concertación government privatized Colbún while establishing an entry rule that excluded existing private companies from the process, with the goal of promoting

---

[13] The Anti-Trust system had two commissions: the Preventive Commission and Resolutive Commission. The decisions of the former commission, which were indicative, could be appealed to the latter, whose decisions were binding and could only be appealed to the Supreme Court.

[14] For instance, Colbún sued Chilectra, Endesa, and Pehuenche in 1992 for discrimination and predatory practices. Due to the lack of regulation on transmission fees, Colbún could not reach an agreement with Endesa on transmission fees to supply energy to Chilectra in 1990. After failed arbitration, Colbún decided to build its own private transmission line, which prompted Endesa to reduce its fees. However, Colbún built two 220KVh transmission lines (refusing to use Transelec facilities even as a backup), generating an inefficient multiplication of investment (Basañes et al. 2002, 16–17; Serra 2002, 32).

Table 4.1. *Daily Press Coverage of the Main Electricity Reforms*

Newspaper	Time Period	Administrative Reform of 1997	Law 19,613 (1999)	Law 19,940 (2004)
La Nación	Month of Congress			
	Approval	0.06	1.5	0.00
	One Month before	0.00	1.9	0.00
	Two months before	0.00	0.5	0.00
El Mercurio	Month of Congress			
	Approval	0.03	0.5	0.10
	One Month before	0.00	0.4	0.10
	Two months before	0.00	0.4	0.10

Sources: El Mercurio (pro-opposition) and La Nación (pro-government).

competition rather than maximizing the price of electricity (Eugenio Rivera, director of regulation of the Ministry of the Economy, personal interview, November 6, 2000). Colbún was acquired by a consortium of the Belgium Tractabel in association with the Chilean holding Matte, introducing a new private provider in generation.

The government established a program to expand coverage in nonprofitable rural areas called the Rural Electrification Program (PER). The PER increased the rate of rural electrification from 3.45 percent annually in the 1982–92 period to 5.13 percent in the 1993–2003 period (Saavedra 2005, 10), so that coverage of rural households grew from 46.6 percent in 1992 to 85.7 percent in 2002 (Fisher and Serra 2003, 44–6). Yet it was paid for from the general budget, thereby reducing its redistributive effect within the industry.

The DS 327, an electricity statute approved by administrative reform in December 1997, provides another indicator of market competition preferences. The original proposal of 1994 sought a stronger regulator but avoided going through Congress in order to limit the public salience of the reform, as requested by providers and preferred by experts, who feared delays caused by legislative intervention. Yet, favored by the low salience of regulatory reform (see Table 4.1), private providers' demands, led by Endesa, delayed the approval of the reform until the end of 1997 and watered down its content considerably.[15] The DS 327 modified the

---

[15] Personal interview with former CNE executive director Maria Isabel González (November 7, 2000) and director of planning in the Ministry of the Economy Eugenio Rivera (November 6, 2000).

working of the CDEC board. It allowed the representation of all firms with capacity for generation higher than 9 megawatts (down from 60 megawatts before the reform), imposed a professional board paid for by the firms, and established majoritarian – rather than unanimous – decision making for the board, which weakened Endesa's veto power. The board decisions were binding unless the Ministry of the Economy opposed them within a period of 60 days (previously, the authority had 120 days to resolve CDEC conflicts). It gave power to the CDEC to propose areas for transmission fees but left conflicts to resolution by arbitration. It also obligated distribution companies to bid on their supply from generators (to avoid preferential buying within the same business group), created a methodology to determine the available energy in generation, and specified the means of calculating distribution prices (Diaz, Galetovic and Soto 2000; Serra 2002). That is, the compromised reform slightly favored competition in generation.

In the studied period, there were two important legislative reforms in the electricity sector, the 1999 electricity law and the 2004 Short Law. Because these laws included a legislative debate in which the partisan preferences of the government had to confront those of the opposition as well as the lobby of providers, they are useful cases for analyzing the hypothesized policy dynamics in the postreform period. Additionally, the 1999 reform coincided with a crisis of supply and was passed in the year of a competitive presidential election, which heightened the stakes for politicians regardless of their partisan preferences and should have favored regulatory dominance, as no party wants to lose the votes of unhappy consumers. Conversely, providers' policy pressures should have been more influential in the 2004 Short Law, which was passed in a context of low electoral competition and limited public salience.

The 1999 Electricity Reform

The 1999 reform was triggered by an electricity crisis and was sanctioned six months before the most contested presidential election since the return of democracy.[16] The energy shortage resulted from a harsh drought combined with technical problems that delayed the opening of a major new generation plant in 1998. When a thermoelectric plant failed on November 11, power shortages in the SIC prompted the government to pass a rationing decree the next day. The crisis of supply peaked in 1999, however: the

---

[16] This subsection relies heavily on Murillo and Le Foulon (2006).

energy deficit reached 7.6 percent in April before falling to 6.1 percent in May and 3.6 percent in June 1999 (CNE 1999, 12). Press coverage of the crisis was widespread from the onset. From November 11, 1998, until the end of the month, two major newspapers (the right-wing *El Mercurio* and the government-owned *La Nación*) covered the electric crisis almost every day (see Table 4.1).

The high public salience of the electricity shortage heightened the electoral impact of electricity reform, as a substantial part of the population considered the electricity crisis to be a major national crisis: in May 1999, a third of the population (28.9%) in the metropolitan area of Santiago and 24 percent of the total population considered electricity shortages to be the most important problem of the country (CEP 1999). In a personal interview, the former communications director of the chief of staff, Cristian Toloza, claimed that the electricity crisis was the main challenge confronted by the Concertación during the presidential campaign (June 5, 2005).

The potential impact of consumer unhappiness was magnified by public discontent with the country's economic performance and by the lowest presidential approval rating in the studied period, at 45 percent in March 1999 (Figure 4.1). In May 1999, 78 percent of the population considered the country either stagnant or in decline, twice as many people blamed the government for the economic malaise (CEP 1999), and two-thirds of the Santiago population felt harmed by electricity rationing (MSGG, May 1–2, 1999). Half a year before the election, moreover, the Concertación candidate, Ricardo Lagos, had the anticipated support of 32 percent of voters versus 21 percent for his challenger, Joaquin Lavin, whereas half a year before the prior presidential election, President Eduardo Frei had a 52 percent support to 5 percent for his main challenger (CEP 1993; 1999). As electoral competition continued to grow – the candidates' vote totals were separated by less than 1 percent in the first round of voting of December – it generated incentives for the government and the opposition to blame private providers and promote regulatory dominance as a response to the crisis.

First, the government accused providers of giving false information about their capacity and disregarding the general interest. The progovernment newspaper *La Nación* titled its front page story "Government Accuses Endesa" on November 15, 1998. The executive secretary of the CNE, Maria Isabel González, publicly stated that the firms had privileged their private interests over the public interest, hiding information (*El Mercurio*, November 15, 1998). This campaign was successful. Two-thirds of the metropolitan population perceived the government as helping to solve the crisis, but only one-third thought the same of providers (MSGG, May 1–2, 1999).

Second, on December 16, 1998, the executive introduced an electricity bill to Congress that increased sanctions on providers and strengthened regulatory powers. Electoral incentives for redistribution were combined with partisan goals of increasing regulatory power. CNE head Oscar Landerretche explicitly said the crisis provided an opportunity for structural reform in the electricity industry (Rozas 1999, 45). Concertación legislators suggested using the reform to ban vertical integration and to strengthen regulatory powers for promoting competition and consumer interests (*La Tercera*, March 15).

The government bill strengthened the oversight powers of the SEC and augmented the value of its sanctions (BCN 1999, 2). More important, the bill catered to residential consumers by including rationing for all users (regardless of the type of supply contract they had) and consumer compensation for any type of service interruption, even under force majeure.[17] A prior drought and electricity crisis in 1989 had resulted in the establishment of a force majeure exception to benefit Endesa, providing an example of regulatory capture in the final year of Pinochet's tenure in line with our expectations about right-wing reformers siding with first entrants, as discussed in Chapter 1.

Residential consumers were supportive of the bill: 83 percent of the metropolitan population favored even rationing, 89 percent backed compensation for consumers, 97 percent agreed with higher sanctions for companies, and 93 percent supported the strengthening of regulatory powers (MSGG 1999). As consumer pressures muted providers' resistance, the president used his proactive powers to accelerate the approval of the bill on May 19, 1999.[18] The bill was sanctioned as Law 19,613 on June 2.

---

[17] President Frei speech, "Sobre la crisis eléctrica, 26 Abril de 1999," BCN 1999, 82, 211, 213, 216, 219, 223, 227, 231, 242–3, 255–8.

[18] The president can accelerate the legislative process by imposing different types of urgency status that limit the time allotted to Congress to debate and vote on a bill. The three categories are "simple urgency," which establishes a thirty-day limit, "high urgency," which defines a ten-day limit, and "immediate discussion," which imposes a three-day limit. Moreover, when the bill is in the Conference Committee that resolves differences between the Lower and Upper Houses, the time limits apply to the committee and to the chambers. President Frei once requested "simple urgency," twice "high urgency," and three times "immediate discussion" to accelerate the law. These actions forced a simultaneous discussion of the details of reform and the reform as a whole in the Lower Chamber followed by a vote after a single day of debate in the Senate.

The impact of electoral incentives in a context of high public salience predominated over those of partisanship. Thus, even though right-wing legislators resisted the expansion of regulatory powers, they also demanded redistributing the cost of the crisis to large users and providers by defending consumer compensation and even rationing (BCN 1999, 66, 73–82). Socialist representative Antonio Leal, president of the Mining and Energy Commission at the time, said that the social pressure generated by the crisis was crucial in allowing the modifications to article 99bis for even rationing and for compensation in all events (personal interview, June 27, 2005). Similarly, providers decried the electoral incentives behind the reform.[19]

Residential consumers benefited from even rationing for all users (because they lacked long-term contracts) and consumer compensation for shortages even in the case of force majeure. Large users opposed even rationing because they had paid for contracts that guaranteed energy provision (Basañes, Saavedra, and Soto 2002; Díaz, Galetovic, and Soto 2000). Electoral incentives were clearly behind the introduction of this provision, which was not included in the original bill but was added during the legislative discussion following the suggestions of a legislative report on the crisis (Cámara de Diputados 1999). Consumer compensation was established for both authorized (i.e., rationing) and unauthorized electricity cuts. The predominance of electoral incentives over partisan differences was reflected by the fact that the only disagreement in the legislature was about whether the treasury (as proposed by the executive) or the users (as demanded by right-wing legislators) ought to collect the compensation for unauthorized cuts. The latter view, which was electorally more appealing, prevailed in the final law (art. 16B of Law 18.410) (BCN 1999, 317–18).

Partisan differences emerged, however, during the legislative debate on regulatory powers that had no direct redistributive effect on consumers. Concertación legislators supported stronger sanctioning power for the regulator by increasing fines on companies that failed to comply with quality and information demands. They also made companies pay the fines as a security deposit before appealing them judicially.[20] Opposition legislators contested this latter requirement and obtained a reduction in the

---

[19] In personal interviews, Endesa general manager Pablo Inhen claimed that Congress lacked technical capacity and politicized the reform (March 29, 1001), whereas Gener manager Felipe Cerón evaluated that the 1999 electricity reform responded to political pressures generated by the crisis (April 16, 2001).

[20] The modification increased the value of fines 240 times.

amount that had to be paid up front for appealing from the 100 percent first proposed by the government to 50 percent in the Lower House and ultimately to 25 percent in the Senate.[21] Yet right-wing legislators gave into other ideologically driven demands due to the pressure generated by the crisis to approve the reform. As a result, the law augmented the SEC's discretion in interpreting and implementing rules (art. 3, inc. 34 of Law 18.410) and in limiting electricity consumption during rationing (inc. 38). The bill also established the SEC's right to demand information from companies and to require companies to pay an independent auditor when it had doubts about the information they provided (modifying art. 3B of Law 18.410). In sum, electoral incentives in a context of high public salience favored the approval of a law increasing regulatory dominance with the support of both Concertación and right-wing politicians, as all policy makers sought to please consumers who were unhappy with electricity rationing.

The 2004 Reform

Unlike the 1999 law, this reform was not conceived in a context of electoral competition but one of economic slowdown, which made the government more attentive to the concerns of providers and large users, especially as installed capacity only grew by 0.6 percent between 1999 and 2002 (Fischer and Serra 2003, 50). According to Eugenio Rivera, Director of Regulation of the Ministry of the Economy under Lagos, the new administration prioritized investment in the electricity sector (personal interview, November 6, 2000). Similarly, Enersis manager Juan Manuel Kindelan said that the Lagos administration was more attentive than its predecessors were to providers' concerns (personal interview, November 8, 2000). As in the case of the 1997 statute, the low public salience of this reform in comparison with the 1999 law also favored providers' influence (see Table 4.1).

The original reform content sought to redistribute from the main provider (Endesa) to its competitors and large users (a case of market competition). The executive sought to ban vertical integration, define transmission prices, and establish incentives for the expansion of transmission networks by changing the division of costs for their construction,

---

[21] See BCN 1999, 40, 90, 208, 236.

creating a new spot market to replace the CDEC, faciliating electricity commercialization, and changing the calculus of distribution prices. The expansion of transmission networks and the definition of transmission prices – which was a concern of competitors and large users – became the major issue of the reform, however, and the government had to compromise on the ban on vertical integration and to abandon electricity commercialization, the spot market, and the changes in the definition of distribution prices. Large users were the most affected by the three abandoned issues, although they were compensated with a reduction in the threshold to enter the wholesale market from a consumption level of 2 megawatts to one of 500 kilowatts.

In the reform process, providers and large users lobbied policy makers, especially regarding transmission costs. In the original proposal, generators would pay transmission fees according to their use of transmission networks. Endesa opposed this division of costs because it was farther from consumption centers than other generators, and it proposed instead to divide costs in half with wholesale consumers (either large users or distributors). A compromise was reached for the law, with the cost of transmission fees divided so that generators (those introducing energy into the transmission lines) paid 80 percent and those retiring energy from transmission lines – either large users or distributors – paid 20 percent. The joint opposition of Gener, Colbún, and large users to what they perceived as a subsidy to Endesa was crucial to shaping this regulatory compromise. Endesa was also able to weaken regulations fostering competition, however, based on its remaining dominance of the market and the weight of its investments in the economy.

Providers exercised their influence in the executive – the CNE included them in the preparation of the bill – and in the legislative debate. There were accusations of regulatory capture of different Concertación officials by Enersis and Gener. The minister of the economy was accused of lobbying in favor of Gener, his former employer, whereas the CNE executive director was accused of pro-Enersis sympathy because her husband worked for the holding and she was a close friend of the president of Chilectra, with whom she participated in a new Concertación think tank called Expansiva. She eventually resigned over her disagreements with the minister on this issue. Large users opposed Endesa and demanded more competition. Their lobby was influential because they were represented by the president of the industrialists' association, who was also the head of the main peak employer organization, which was involved in macroeconomic policy making (personal interview with former CNE executive director Vivianne Blanlot, October 25, 2005).[22]

The legislative debate focused on technical issues, and independent experts participated as legislative witnesses to a much larger extent than in 1999. The technical debate gave informational advantages to providers and large users. Right-wing legislators, however, supported Endesa's positions, as expected from their role in the reform process, even though the original owners had already sold the company to Endesa-Spain. Based on their ideological rejection of state involvement, they opposed the CNE role in planning the expansion of transmission networks and public participation, which assumed that transmission was a public service.[23] Due to the need for supermajorities and the role of the Senate, the compromise was that the regulator would define the transmission fees, coordinate the plans for network expansion, and establish public bidding criteria for construction. The right-wing opposition also resisted the resolution of conflicts over transmission by the Ministry of the Economy and compromised on the creation of an Experts' Panel. In another compromise, vertical integration regulation was only to apply to future ownership when transmission companies would require incorporation as public companies, at which point they would face limits on purchasing in the other segments of the industry. The reform limited to 40 percent the total participation in transmission of firms related to the electricity sector: power generation firms, distribution firms, and those related to the unregulated sector. This limit did not apply to existing transmission lines (art. 7 of DFL 1) or to the property links between generation and distribution, such as those between Endesa and Chilectra.[24] This compromise shows Endesa's influence despite the coalition of its competitors. Yet the formation of such a coalition, which weakened Endesa's influence, resulted from policies that had changed the market structure of the industry, such as the sale of Colbún and the expansion of gas pipelines for thermal generation.

---

[22] The large users' association ACENOR, established in 1997, was too weak to play an important role in the reform.

[23] For instance, RN senator Prokuriça and UDI senator Orpis demanded a reduction in bureaucratic involvement and centralization in the management of the sector by CNE and proposed greater involvement of private actors.

[24] This law also introduced public authorization for the transfer of property in distribution, which similarly did not apply retroactively (art. 46 of DFL 1).

Regulatory Reforms in Telecommunications

As in electricity, Concertación's policies in postprivatization telecommunications reform sought to benefit consumers through direct and indirect regulatory redistribution, that is, through regulatory dominance and market competition, as expected of populists who converted while out of power. Unlike the electricity sector, however, the market structure of the telecommunications industry fostered conflicts between the main providers that also generated pressures for market competition as a regulatory outcome.

In the immediate aftermath of privatization, conflicts between CTC and its competitors arose due to lack of regulation of interconnection and to large profit differentials between segments, which prompted CTC to ask for a long-distance license after Bond sold it to Telefónica of Spain in 1990. Given Telefónica's participation in ENTEL as well, SUBTEL consulted with the Anti-Trust Commission on ownership concentration and vertical integration. A ruling of the Anti-Trust Commission forced Telefónica to sell its participation in ENTEL, which occurred in 1992; it also resulted in a request to the government to regulate vertical integration. Meanwhile, SUBTEL had given long-distance licenses to Chilesat in 1992 and VTR in 1993, whereas new technologies allowed ENTEL to bypass the local network in serving large users, thereby fostering competition in long-distance and local services. While waiting for SUBTEL's license, CTC made an agreement with Chilesat to carry long-distance traffic, sharing their profits (BCN 1993, 1502).[25] The subsequent decline in ENTEL's long-distance market share and profits furthered providers' pressures for regulation of vertical integration.[26]

Competition between providers generated a demand for regulatory reform fostered by a ruling of the Anti-Trust Commission. On April 16, 1993, its Resolution 389 allowed vertical integration with a multicarrier system for access-code dialing rather than long-term contracts; this decision reaffirmed the commission's prior Resolution 332 of 1989, appealed by ENTEL and sustained by the Supreme Court. The resolution also

---

[25] At the time, customers could not choose their long-distance carriers, whereas ENTEL and Chilesat had international partners to carry long-distance communication. Chilesat also recognized CTC's right to vertical integration in this agreement.

[26] In 1993, ENTEL's market share declined to 75% of the domestic long-distance and 55% of the international long-distance markets. As a result, ENTEL's profits from equity declined from 49.7% in 1992 to 17.2% in 1994 (Fischer and Serra 2003, 23).

mandated the division of companies into different subsidiaries for each segment of the market and gave SUBTEL eighteen months to implement the system, thereby prompting the government to send a regulatory bill to Congress.

Although this reform was not mentioned in the Concertación electoral program, since 1991 the Concertación administration has established a working group to define the government's telecommunications policy, which included allied experts Alejandro Jadresic, Gregorio San Martin, Jorge Rosenbluth, and Ricardo Pool. The group determined that regulation – of interconnection prices, for instance – was necessary to promote competition. These views were reflected in the government response to providers' conflicts regarding vertical integration. The government tried to take advantage of providers' demands for market competition also to pursue its partisan preference for strengthening regulatory powers that could be used to redistribute to either consumers or competitors. The resulting bill sent to Congress regulated vertical integration (requested by CTC) and interconnection fees (demanded by CTC's competitors and important for the government) in order to promote competition. Additionally, and seeking to promote a more market-controlling regulatory framework, the bill strengthened regulatory powers by creating a superintendence, increased regulatory sanctions to foster access to company information necessary in setting regulated prices, established more rapid judicial procedures for dealing with consumer complaints, and proposed a Telecommunication Development Fund (FDT) to expand coverage in areas with low teledensity.[27] The FDT was added by Concertación legislators to the executive bill, showing that legislators were also keen on regulatory redistribution (especially as it could be geographically advantageous to their districts).[28]

In introducing the bill, the government emphasized consumer benefits either through competition (market competition) or regulation (regulatory dominance), thereby framing the reform as a response to the needs of consumer constituencies rather than to providers' conflicts. Minister of Transportation and Telecommunications Germán Molina said: "The government telecommunications policy aims, especially, at allowing access to

---

[27] The program sought to reduce regional disparities. The FDT provided public telephones for 6,059 rural communities by 2000 (Fischer and Serra 2003, 14).

[28] Personal interviews with Socialist legislator Carlos Montes, March 27, 2001, and former undersecretary of telecommunications Jorge Rosenblut, June 27, 2005, confirm the legislative origin of the idea.

telecom services for consumers at the minimum possible cost. . . . [I]t seeks telecom services with reasonable prices for the largest share of the population as well as increasing their geographic coverage." He added, "The state has a fundamental and indispensable role in the promotion of competition and the regulation of natural monopolies and externalities in telecommunications. It should also create the incentives necessary to expand coverage and penetration of basic telephone service to the sectors that do not have it, and where market incentives do not work" (BCN 1994, 1063).

Even though providers disagreed on how to regulate competition, they did agree on their opposition to the granting of regulatory powers to the state that could be used to redistribute their income to residential consumers. All providers rejected the creation of a superintendence, the informational provisions, and the FDT program for expanding coverage.[29] Telecommunications providers fiercely attacked the FDT and opposed its financing with rents derived from the difference in price between incoming and outgoing international calls, which were being appropriated by long-distance carriers.[30] Right-wing legislators joined in opposing this program as a form of state intervention and an unconstitutional earmark tax on the industry.[31] In a Senate compromise, Concertación legislators agreed to cut the program's term from seven to four years and to fund it from the general budget.[32] Similarly, the government had to sacrifice the

---

[29] The regulated providers prefer the absence of a regulator, according to personal interviews with ENTEL's Regulation Manager Cristian Maturana (March 22, 2001) and CTC's strategic Vice-President Raimundo Beca (November 6, 2000).

[30] "The opinion of telecom companies to the Lower Chamber Telecom Commission was opposed to the creation of the Telecom Development Fund." CTC representatives mentioned their preference for market allocation of resources, while ENTEL denounced the public nature of the fund and, along with Chilesat, criticized the funding system, which affected the returns on long-distance communications. VTR criticized the use of subsidies for the expansion of coverage as well as the use of public funds (BCN 1994, 590–1).

[31] The most vocal among right-wing legislators were Federico Ringelin (RN), who opposed the fund because it increased the size and responsibilities of the state, invading an area that could be served by the private sector (BCN 1994, 1,018), and senator Miguel Otero (RN), who also opposed it because it promoted state intervention (personal interview, March 26, 2001). The publications of the right-wing legislative think tank Libertad y Desarrollo provided further arguments against the fund based on accusations of state intervention (Libertad y Desarrollo 1993b).

[32] The vote in the Telecommunications Commission of the Senate was divided along partisan lines, with two UDI senators, three RN senators, and four institutional (nonelected) senators voting against and two PS senators, one PSDC senator, eight DC senators, and one institutional senator voting in favor.

new superintendence, the informational powers of SUBTEL, and the faster track in justice for telecommunication consumers.

Even though the government compromised on most of the clauses opposed by providers, neither these concessions nor the proactive powers of the Chilean president were sufficient to get the bill passed into law until the government and providers reached an agreement in December 1993.[33] The crucial point in this agreement exchanged ENTEL's consent to vertical integration in return for transitory market quotas in the long-distance market, which included enforcement sanctions, along with a timeline for the implementation of access code dialing and the transfer of infrastructure to subsidiaries (BCN 1994, 3616). The bill was approved shortly thereafter in early 1994, suggesting the importance of this agreement. Further confirmation is derived from the fact that a similar proposal of market quotas by Concertación legislators had previously been defeated in the Lower Chamber.[34]

Another indicator of providers' influence in the regulatory process was the erosion of partisan discipline, in the ranks of the Concertación and in those of its right-wing rivals. The Concertación legislative delegation divided, as legislators from the Socialist Party, the Party for Democracy, and the Radical Party supported the government proposal of regulated vertical integration requested by CTC, whereas a group of Christian Democratic representatives opposed it, following ENTEL's position. Similarly, the majority of right-wing representatives sided with ENTEL, but most senators and their legislative think tank, Libertad y Desarrollo, favored regulated vertical integration.

Beyond the erosion of partisan discipline, the legislative minutes report numerous criticisms of continuous (and unregulated) business lobbying of legislators, further suggesting that providers' influence was high during an election season in which legislators faced electoral competition even when the presidential election was not competitive (BCN 1993; 1994). For legislators facing competitive elections, the marginal value

---

[33] President Aylwin used the "high urgency" status six times during the legislative debate and the "simple urgency" status once. According to Oscar Guillermo Garretón, former CTC CEO (personal interview, November 3, 2000), the agreement was crucial for the approval of the law. The timing of the approval suggests that his evaluation was correct.

[34] The modification was proposed as a transitory article by representatives Montes (PS), Yunge (DC), and Faulbaum (PR). According to RN representative Vilches, the lobby from the CTC was crucial in this proposal's rejection (Rep. Carlos Montes, personal interview, July 2005).

of campaign contributions from these companies was high.[35] Additionally, CTC and ENTEL had ties to political parties. CTC's CEO was Socialist Oscar Guillermo Garretón, who had been Allende's minister of the economy, and the CEO of CTC's long-distance subsidiary was Christian Democrat Cristian Nicolai, who would be the electricity and telecom regulator under subsequent Concertación administrations.[36] ENTEL, by contrast, was led by Colonel Ivan Van de Wyngard, who had been CTC's CEO under Pinochet, and Juan Aristía, who had been the superintendent of pension funds of the military regime and had close ties to right-wing politicians.

The comparison between this law and the 1999 electricity reform is telling. In both cases, politicians were brought to regulate due to exogenous pressures, but the different degree of public salience and electoral competition affected the relative policy influence of providers and consumers. Whereas consumer pressure accelerated the 1999 reform, providers' pressure was crucial to securing the fast approval of Law 3-A (19,302), which was introduced on June 22, 1993 and passed on March 2, 1994. The speed of this bill's passage was similar to that of the 1999 electricity reform, even though the issue commanded a much lower level of public salience (see Table 4.2). In contrast to the 1999 electricity reform, moreover, press coverage of Law 3A was broader in the right-wing *Mercurio* than in the government-leaning *La Nación* (Table 4.2). This difference suggests that commercial users (with long-distance needs) were more aware of the regulatory reform and its price effects than residential users (with local communication needs). The preference for market competition had the expected effect. The reform caused ENTEL's share of the long-distance market to decline dramatically to around 40 percent of long-distance calls in 1994, whereas the CTC share of the local market only declined from 94 percent in 1993 to 89 percent in 1997 (Fischer and Serra 2002, 63–5).

---

[35] Socialist representative Carlos Montes argued that lobbying was pervasive to the point of having providers' employees writing the modifications for legislators in the corridors of Congress (personal interview, August 8, 2005). Carlos Carmona, a former government official in charge of legislative relations in the secretary general of the presidency at the time, said that although the presidential election was not competitive, the legislators needed funds to pay for their own campaigns. As the law was discussed during the electoral campaign, it increased the leverage of companies as donors to those campaigns (personal interview, June 6, 2005).

[36] Additionally, Telefónica of Spain was publicly owned until 1997, and the incumbent Socialist Party of Spain had both an influential director on the board and informal links with the Chilean Socialists.

Table 4.2. *Comparison of Daily Press Coverage for Publicly Salient Reforms*

Newspaper	Time Period	Law 19,613 (Electricity)	Law 3 A (Telecommunications)
La Nación	Month of Congress		
	Approval	1.5	0.2
	One Month before	1.9	0.16
	Two months before	0.5	0.1
El Mercurio	Month of Congress		
	Approval	0.5	0.3
	One Month before	0.4	0.53
	Two months before	0.4	0.5

Sources: El Mercurio (pro-opposition) and La Nación (pro-government).

The executive also sought to promote market competition in telecommunications through SUBTEL. In 1997, SUBTEL allowed ENTEL to bid for more than one band of a new mobile technology (Personal Communications Systems, or PCS). As ENTEL won two bands, it built its recovery around mobile communications. Its share of that market grew from less than 20 percent in 1998 to almost 40 percent in 2001 (Fischer and Serra 2002, 66). Similarly, SUBTEL's 1999 price regulation decree was based on Resolution 515 of the Anti-Trust Commission requested by ENTEL, which mandated unbudlling the local loop and the definition of smaller interconnection segments. As a result, interconnection costs for CTC competitors and regulated local prices declined. On average, local prices dropped by 11 percent, whereas interconnection fees declined 72 percent. In a personal interview, the undersecretary of telecommunications at the time, Juanita Gana, argued that the regulator had to guarantee that the market had sufficient actors for competition to be effective (November 8, 2000). Christian Maturana, ENTEL's regulation manager, agreed that both her tenure and that of her predecessor, Gregorio San Martin, were characterized by efforts to regulate in a way that would foster a more competitive market (personal interview, March 22, 2001).

The price decree also established the "calling party pays" system for mobile telephones (the total bill was applied to the initiator of the call), which had been judicially resisted by CTC, fearing its negative effects on the volume of traffic from local to mobile phones. This system, along with the approval of prepaid calling cards the prior year, had a dramatic effect on the expansion of the mobile telecommunications market, because poorer users could buy them just to receive calls: the number of mobile phones grew by more than 400 percent between 1998 and 2001 (Fischer and Serra 2003, 58). ENTEL profits, which had been negative in 1998, became positive in 1999, whereas those of CTC moved in the opposite direction, in contrast to what happened in 1994 (73). That is, the Concertación did not side with one of the two main providers but tried to promote competition between them.

In response to increasing market competition, CTC threatened to withhold investment, appealed the new interconnection fees, and sued ENTEL for lack of fulfillment of the conditions in the PCS bid.[37] Telecommunications investment dropped in 1999, although it had been stagnant for the previous two years (18).[38] Conflicts over interconnection and the obligation of the local company to charge consumers the long-distance fees of other providers (including the suspension of services for lack of payment of those services) were particularly acute, although SUBTEL established a single telephone bill to promote the payment of long-distance fees along with local ones. CTC challenged this practice judicially and allowed consumers to pay only their local bill when they had used other long-distance providers, prompting further judicial actions from ENTEL. The high level of judicial litigation in the industry shows the difficulty of coordinating common policy preferences.[39]

Judicial litigation and Anti-Trust rulings forced the government to regulate. Based on an Anti-Trust Resolution of September 2003, SUBTEL's 2004 price regulation established referential rather than maximum prices, granted price flexibility to CTC, and increased interconnection fees. Despite complaints from CTC's competitors, residential prices declined 6 percent (Subsecretaria de Economia 2004, 22), whereas competition by local providers – especially from VTR, a cable television provider – continued to grow. CTC's share of the local market declined to 71 percent in 2005 and 65 percent in 2007, whereas VTR's has grown to 11 percent in 2005 and 17 percent in 2007.

---

[37] According to former undersecretary of telecommunications Juanita Gana, CTC started firing employees to put pressure on the Ministry of Labor in the context of an economic slowdown (personal interview, November 8, 2000).

[38] CTC's director of strategic planning, Raimundo Beca, said that efforts of the Frei administration to reduce the prices of public services had caused the losses of CTC and the halt of investment (personal interview, November 6, 2000).

[39] According to Christian Maturana, ENTEL's regulation director (personal interview, March 22, 2001), and to Gabriel Chomalí from a smaller carrier called GVT and formerly from Chilesat (personal interview, March 21, 2001), ENTEL served as a de facto representative of all CTC competitors. SUBTEL, http://subtel.cl, accessed March 20, 2008.

Efforts at regulatory dominance were modest, though. In 1999, Under-secretary of Telecommunications Juana Gana sent a bill to Congress imposing the new regulated prices retroactively as of the date of their official publication to prevent delays in the application of price declines due to litigation.[40] This reform received no press coverage and resulted from lobbying by consumer associations.[41] Additionally, the Lagos administration achieved the approval of Law 19.724 in March 2001, which extended the already expired Telecommunications Development Funds and allowed their use by different telecommunications services to promote Internet penetration. It implied no redistribution from providers, however, because it was paid by the treasury, as was the original 1994 fund.

Regulatory Redistribution, Political Incentives, and Institutional Effects

The previous two sections described the patterns of regulatory redistribution in electricity and telecommunications in postreform Chile. The preferences of Concertación policy makers were similar for both sectors: they wanted to redistribute to consumers indirectly (through market competition) and directly (through regulatory dominance) while trying to strengthen regulatory controls. By contrast, the right-wing opposition that had adopted the original privatization reforms supported the original providers and rejected government attempts to redistribute to consumers. The combination of their veto power in the Senate and providers' resistance weakened government efforts at regulatory dominance except in the case of the 1999 electricity law, which was passed at a time when public salience and electoral competition persuaded politicians in the government and the opposition to favor consumers. The role of the Chilean Anti-Trust Commission was also unique, as it could force the government to regulate at the request of providers, thereby introducing an institutional venue for regulatory conflict among providers that did not exist in the other cases.

---

[40] Senate Record for the 19th session of the 339 legislature, January 20, 1999 (http://www.senado.cl, accessed March 30, 2009).

[41] Ernesto Benado, president of CONADECUS, said that in 1999 his association, along with Adecua and Consumer International, brought the issue of regulated prices that were not applied due to judicialization in both sectors to regulators Oscar Landerretche (electricity) and Juana Gana (telecommunications) seeking a solution to this problem (personal interview, March 27, 2001). Former undersecretary Juana Gana confirmed that consumer associations had called her attention to this problem (personal interview, November 8, 2000).

The other electricity reforms were not publicly salient and were mostly aimed at fostering market competition. The predominant provider tried to protect its market power, however, weakening these reforms to some extent, as had happened with the DS 327. Nonetheless, government policies helped modify the market structure without changing the rules for the dominant provider (Enersis). The effect of changes in market structure on providers' policy coordination was perceived during the discussion of the 2004 Short Law, wherein Endesa could not impose its position due to the resistance of its competitors and large users. Therefore, the impact of the institutional legacies in electricity was not necessarily path dependent, even when it established a skewed baseline for subsequent policy making.

Regulatory dominance was a more unlikely outcome. Although residential prices for electricity declined more than telecommunications prices between 1989 and 2004, in neither sector were price regulation processes crucial in defining trends, as shown by Figure 4.2, which notes the years in which price regulation was in effect. This difference in prices also coincided with higher profits for telecommunications providers than for their electricity peers, suggesting no income redistribution to consumers.[42] Additionally, the rural electrification program was paid for from the general budget, and only the 1999 law, produced by the combination of high public salience and a competitive election that increased consumers' influence, allowed a regulatory dominance outcome despite providers' resistance – expressed in litigation against sanctions that prevented the payment of compensation to consumers at least until 2005.

In telecommunications, by contrast, regulatory reforms fostering market competition were predominant, because providers' own conflicts generated a preference for such an outcome. Most regulatory actions responded to rulings of the Anti-Trust Commission resulting from inter-provider conflicts. As in electricity, declines in residential prices resulted mostly from competition, and the absence of any exogenous shock raising consumer awareness prevented major outcomes of regulatory dominance. As in electricity, the attempts to increase regulatory control or promote

---

[42] For the first four years of democracy, profits were on average 8.2% for Gener, 10.3% for Endesa, and 12.9% for Pehuenche in the competitive wholesale electricity market (Fischer and Serra 2003, 54). The electricity distribution companies – with captured residential customers – fared better. The largest four of them reached an average of 21.5% of returns/equity during the same period (55). In telecommunications, profits were also sizeable, although long-distance provider ENTEL received larger profits (47.5% on average) than CTC (17.8%) in that period.

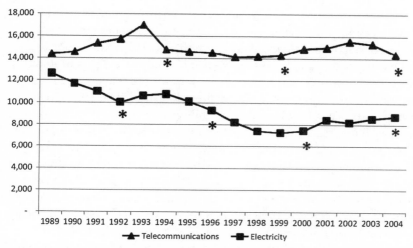

Figure 4.2   Residential Price Evolution for Electricity and Telecommunications on the Santiago Metropolitan Area
Source: Subsecretaria de Economia (2004: 23, 25).
Note: The stars mark the years of price regulation decrees.

regulatory dominance were hindered by providers – and their right-wing allies – as shown by the compromises that took place in preventing the creation of a superintendence and in changing the type of FDT funding.

The mechanisms of policy making in Chile's postreform telecommunications and electricity sectors show the sustained impact of initial partisan differences between the Concertación and the Alianza, especially regarding the degree of regulatory control in each industry and the defense by right-wing reformers of the first entrants into these markets. The effect of partisanship is apparent in the legislative debates, although it was weakened by electoral competition with high public salience in the case of the 1999 electricity law. Moreover, providers eroded partisan effects – either through lobbying in Congress or through career incentives. Changes in the original postprivatization management facilitated the latter mechanism for Concertación experts, as is shown with CTC, which was sold to Telefónica in 1990. Providers also used judicial litigation (and especially the Anti-Trust Commission) to advance their policy preferences.

In contrast to providers, residential consumers had less at stake and fewer organizational and informational resources. Although the 1999 electricity crisis increased the stakes of residential consumers, their associations did not organize collective action to protest or to demand regulatory reform.[43] Consumer influence was mostly restricted to representation by political parties seeking to win their vote through the 1999 electricity reform.

The origin of capital in these companies and their diversification are important but insufficient factors to account for the tendencies in regulatory redistribution described in the preceding text. The main providers were industry specific and had little ability to trade regulatory favors in another policy area. Moreover, the foreign nature of the industries' ownership is not sufficient to explain either their policy preferences or the regulatory outcomes. In electricity, foreign capital entered as an important actor in 1996 with the government sale of Colbún, which had the specific goal of fostering competition. Endesa of Spain acquired a majority control of the Enersis holding in 1999 and U.S.-based AES of Gener the following year. The breakdown of the original linkages favored the hiring of Concertación experts but did not seem to erode those with right-wing legislators in the 2004 legislative debate, thereby suggesting a weakening of partisan effect through allied experts. Moreover, as Enersis and its competitors became foreign owned by that year, this factor cannot explain the weakening of its veto power.

In telecommunications, CTC was originally sold to an Australian group in 1988 and bought by Telefónica of Spain in 1990, while ENTEL sold a minority stake to Telecom of Italy in 1996 and a majority stake in 2001. As mentioned in the preceding text, the sale to Telefónica facilitated linkages to Concertación experts at a time when these were more tenuous in ENTEL. Yet the Concertación kept supporting market competition not just in the 1994 reform that favored CTC but also in subsequent reforms that were denounced by that company.

Finally, the experience of postreform Chile illuminates the empirical effects of the original institutional choices of regulatory control on market structure and their subsequent impact on providers' policy influence. Yet even when institutional legacies shaped providers' playing fields and defined diverse starting points for the regulatory game, their effects were not necessarily permanent. The market structure of the regulated industries could be modified by gradual policies or by dramatic shocks, usually produced in contexts of high public salience and heightened electoral

---

[43] In spite of consumer concern, there were no organized protests, and only 340 of the 3 million users of the SIC filed complaints with consumer associations or the SERNAC (National Consumer Committee) (*La Tercera*, May 2, 1999).

incentives. As a result, even when the government kept regulatory preferences continuous, relative changes in providers' preferences modified the regulatory outcome. Original institutional choices thus have important distributive effects in the policy-making arena, but they are not path dependent in the sense of closing options for regulatory redistribution. Both crises that heighten consumer influence combined with electoral competition and a succession of gradual policy decisions can reshape the policy-making field and weaken the original institutional effects, even when the game is played on a slanted field.

5

Postreform Regulatory Redistribution in Argentina and Mexico

This chapter focuses on regulatory redistribution in Argentina and Mexico, where populist converts had adopted market-oriented reforms with a market-controlling content, in contrast to the market-conforming Chilean reforms. In addition to assessing the effect of institutional legacies, the analysis of postreform policy making in these two countries provides longitudinal variation in the main political variables of interest. In both countries, reformers remained in power in the postreform period but were replaced by presidents of another political party. Thus, it is possible to assess the hypothesized effects of having adopted the reforms and the partisan preferences of incumbents. Like Chile, both countries experienced bouts of electoral competition around the turn of the century, and Argentina experienced an electricity crisis simultaneous to the Chilean one. Unlike Chile, however, these countries suffered deep macroeconomic crises in the postreform period. These conditions permit testing the effects of electoral competition and the impact of exogenous shocks on public salience. In contrast to Chile and Mexico, Argentina had well-organized consumer associations that had the ability to endogenously raise the public salience of telecommunications and electricity regulation issues. As in the Chapter 4, the cross-sectoral comparison within country serves to control for industry-specific factors.

Political Competition, Partisanship, and Institutional Legacies in Postreform Argentina

This section presents the expectations derived from the main hypotheses of Chapter 1 for regulatory preferences in postreform Argentina. That is, it describes the evolution of the main independent variables – political competition and partisanship – along with the impact of institutional legacies on market structure and their expected effects on preferences for regulatory redistribution.

Political Competition

Argentina's President Menem adopted market-oriented reforms in the early 1990s. Subsequently, the Peronists won the 1993 legislative elections and, after a constitutional reform allowing his second term, President Menem was reelected in 1995 by a larger electoral margin than in 1989. The reform also shortened the presidential tenure from six to four years and caused an exit of voters from the Radical Party in reaction to an agreement between former president Alfonsín and President Menem that allowed the reform to occur. As a result, many non-PJ voters supported José O. Bordón from a new center-left party called Front for a Country with Solidarity (FREPASO), and Bordón finished as the runner-up in the 1995 presidential election. The Radical candidate, Horacio Massaccesi, finished third (see Figure 5.1). Electoral competition increased in the midterm elections of 1997, won by an electoral coalition of the Radicals and FREPASO called the Alliance (Alianza) for Education, Work and Justice (hereafter "Alianza") with 46 percent of the vote to the Peronist 36 percent (Figure 5.1). High-level electoral competition continued, and the Peronists lost the 1999 presidential election to Alianza candidate Fernando De La Rua, who received 48.5 percent of votes to the 38 percent received by Peronist Eduardo Duhalde (Figure 5.1). The parties' legislative vote shares were 40.5 and 33 percent, respectively.

President De La Rua (UCR) had a short honeymoon, as his coalition lost the 2001 legislative elections with 23 percent of valid votes to the Peronists' 37.4 percent. A quarter of ballots were null or black. Voters' disappointment with economic performance and with a corruption scandal that brought Vice-President Carlos Alvarez (FREPASO) to resign in October 2000 was forecast by a steep decline in public support from late 2000 (Latintrack 2000). The 2001 electoral result triggered a deep economic and political crisis. To sustain the fixed-exchange-rate regime established in 1991 for controlling hyperinflation, the government imposed limits on bank withdrawals. As a result, the middle classes lost access to their savings, and the cash-dependent informal economy that sustained most of the poor collapsed. Food riots and street protests forced the resignation of De La Rua in December 2001. With the PJ controlling both

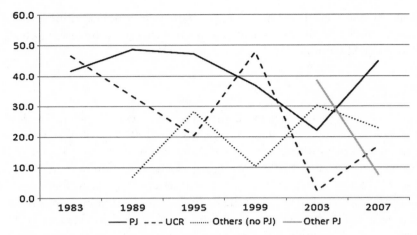

Figure 5.1 Electoral Competition on Presidential Elections

chambers of Congress, his successors were two Peronist interim presidents: Rodolfo Rodriguez Saá, who lasted for a week, and Eduardo Duhalde, who finished his mandate in May 2003.

The political collapse of non-Peronist parties (especially the UCR) heightened electoral competition within the Peronist factions, so that in the 2003 presidential election the vote was divided between three Peronist candidates: former presidents Menem and Rodriguez Saá, along with Nestor Kirchner, who was a little-known governor of a sparsely populated Argentine province and was supported by the incumbent, Duhalde. Although Menem won the first round of votes with 25 percent to Kirchner's 23 percent, he did not run in the second round, as surveys announced Kirchner's victory. Electoral competition remained high until the 2005 legislative election, when Kirchner's PJ faction defeated Duhalde's faction.[1]

In short, the electoral campaigns of 1999, 2003, and 2005 were competitive (Figure 5.1). Two exogenous shocks coincided with these periods: the 1999 electricity crisis, which happened before a presidential election, and the 2002–3 macroeconomic crisis, which was the deepest in recent history

---

[1] In the 2005 election, of a Lower Chamber of 257 representatives, Kirchner obtained 112 PJ legislators and 10 non-PJ legislators from allied parties, along with 8 Radical allied legislators. Moreover, most of the forty-two non-Kirchnerist PJ legislators migrated to his camp in the aftermath of the election, and so did various Radical legislators.

180

(Levitsky and Murillo 2003). The coincidence of these shocks raised the stakes for consumers of telecommunications and electricity matters, thereby increasing the potential public salience of these issues. This situation, in concert with a competitive electoral arena, should have made regulatory dominance more likely in these particular periods.

Partisanship

The partisan preferences of PJ and UCR/Alianza depended on their linkages to different constituencies and ideological legacies. Yet unlike in Chile, both parties had a populist past that led them to prefer regulatory control of markets. Because Menem had adopted the reforms, we should expect the Peronists to have shifted their preferences from regulatory dominance to market dominance due to their commitment to the first entrants who trusted their conversion and responded to privatization calls. We should also expect, however, to find the presence of intraadministration tensions about these preferences due to the Peronists' delegation to both allied and neoliberal experts, who were appointed to increase the PJ's international credibility as a convert to the market creed. After the 2001 crisis, the influence of neoliberal experts vanished, and PJ administrations began their return to the original creed, moving toward a preference for regulatory dominance. By contrast, we should expect the UCR/Alianza, having converted mostly out of power, to have preferred market competition and regulatory dominance. As in the Chapter 4, policy preferences are observed in the parties' electoral platforms, public-utility policy debates, and discussions about regulations for consumer protection.

Although PJ and UCR had a populist past, the former had poorer and less-educated constituencies whereas its electoral strongholds were in the interior of the country and the poor (formerly industrial) suburbs of Buenos Aires. By contrast, the UCR/Alianza was stronger in the City of Buenos Aires and in the richest, most populated, and most urbanized provinces (Córdoba, Santa Fe, Buenos Aires, Mendoza) (Calvo and Murillo 2005). Hence, UCR/Alianza were more likely to care for the residential consumer who already had access to services but suffered from price effects, especially in telecommunications, given that more than 90 percent of households had electricity before privatization (Arza 2002, 122). Conversely, we should expect PJ policy makers to have cared more about extending telephone services and keeping electricity prices low.

UCR views on public utilities reflected the party's preferences for market competition and regulatory dominance. And the party accepted the privatization of all but the hydroelectric utilities while proposing further regulation of privatized utilities to promote competition and consumer rights. Its 1995 electoral platform included proposals for an antitrust law, consumer participation in regulatory agencies, and the increasing independence of regulatory agencies. The center-left FREPASO, which included disaffected Peronists, promised independent regulatory agencies and consumer participation in the regulatory authorities, along with periodic reviews of regulatory frameworks and the establishment of consumer courts in its 1995 electoral platform.

The 1999 presidential platform of Alianza (a coalition of UCR and FREPASO) promised policies fostering market competition and regulatory dominance in public utilities. Its platform stated, "An adequate regulation of public services and policy for the defense of competition are necessary tools for improving equity" and "our unavoidable commitment with consumers is to pursue policies that promote competition, because they would generate lower prices and better quality." It continued, "Moreover, where competition is not possible, our commitment is to modify regulatory frameworks based on the best international practices and prioritizing the public interest and the interest of consumers. This goal requires the existence of strict, fair, transparent and autonomous regulatory agencies, which include the participation of users and consumers" (Carta a los Argentinos, 11–12). Once in office, the Alianza institutionalized its preferences with the creation of the secretary for the defense of competition and consumer rights in the Ministry of the Economy.[2]

In the PJ, it is important to distinguish the Menem administration, which adopted the initial privatization reforms and suffered from intra-administration conflicts between allied and neoliberal experts, and the post-2001 PJ administrations, under which the collapse of the fixed-exchange-rate regime established under Menem curtailed the influence of neoliberal technocrats. After 2001, allied experts prevailed as the party returned to its more populist roots, emphasizing its search for regulatory dominance.

---

[2] An allied technocrat, Pablo Gerchunoff, was crucial in the creation of the new secretary and in linking competition and consumer rights (personal interview with Edith Schmukler, advisor on consumer issues to the secretary, October 26, 2000).

Intraadministration tensions on public-utility regulation continued to be intense in the postreform period under Menem. Menem's 1995 electoral platform emphasized the achievements of his privatization policies and the fact that consumer rights were added to the 1994 constitution but only proposed to create an office for the defense of consumers – a promise that was quickly forgotten after his reelection. The tensions within the PJ, however, had become apparent already in December 1994, when a bill drafted by allied expert Roberto Dromi requested the creation of a legislative commission for controlling regulatory agencies. The bill also included profit ceilings and price definitions based on the quality of services, as well as company comptrollers and consumer representatives in the regulatory authorities, and it called on regulators to defend users rather than providers (*Clarín*, December 27, 1994). The bill was never approved, but PJ legislators resuscitated it in 1996, 1997, and 1999, raising criticism from business and the neoliberal ministers of the economy. (Domingo Cavallo was succeeded by another neoliberal: Roque Fernandez.) Additionally, Duhalde's electoral platform of 1999 promised universal access to public services, such as water and electricity, along with regulatory reform and lower prices in telecommunications and transportation. It lacked any specific proposals on how to improve competition or consumer rights in public utilities, however. These tensions reflected the preference of neoliberal experts in the executive, more tied to providers, whereas allied experts and PJ legislators preferred regulatory dominance in line with their partisan legacies.

The tensions within the Menem administration, in contrast to the more homogenous policy preferences of the opposition, were apparent in the debate over the Law on Consumer Rights, approved in 1993. The original bill was introduced by UCR senator Luis León in 1988 but was not approved. The bill was resuscitated with bipartisan support in 1991. The main modification was the exclusion of the Consumer Court proposed by León and the addition of state subsidies and broader powers for litigation for consumer associations (added by another Radical legislator), as well as sanctions for public-utility companies charging consumers rates in excess of 50 percent higher than in the previous year. Radical senator León emphasized the need to defend consumers due to their weakness in market relations and asked that this bill be supplemented with regulation promoting competition. Radical senators also defended the right of consumer associations to litigate in defense of consumers.[3]

[3] Diario de Sesiones, Lower Chamber, 8a Meeting, 1st ordinary sessions, June 16, 1993.

Peronist preferences for regulatory dominance emerged in the Lower Chamber. PJ representative Becerra focused on the role of consumer associations in controlling companies and promoting civic participation. PJ representative Cafiero, meanwhile, explicitly argued that the law would put a limit on the monopolistic power of privatized companies, for example, telephone prices.[4] The intra-PJ tensions became apparent after the approval of the law, when President Menem used his partial veto power in a decree signed also by neoliberal minister Domingo Cavallo on the clauses pertaining to overbilling by public utilities and the ability of consumer associations to litigate for consumers (Decree 2089/93).

After the 2002 macroeconomic crisis, interim Peronist president Duhalde and elected Peronist president Kirchner returned to their statist roots. The collapse of the fixed-exchange-rate regime, which had allowed Menem to control hyperinflation, eradicated the influence of neoliberal technocrats and allowed allied experts and pragmatic politicians to revert to their old creed. In the 2003 election, all three PJ candidates, including Menem, campaigned on low public-service prices for residential users. The Kirchner platform was consistent with the policies of interim president Duhalde, who had anointed him, and expressed their preferences for regulatory dominance. It explicitly promised to defend residential consumers, ensure transparent regulation of public services, apply competition regulation, and subsidize prices for the poor (Frente para la Victoria 2003). Whereas Rodriguez Saa's twelve-point platform lacked specific proposals, Menem's had a chapter on public services that highlighted the change in context. In his "Ten Proposals to Overcome the Crisis," he promised contract revision to guarantee service for consumers and consumer protection – including class actions in public services by consumer associations, which he had vetoed as president. Moreover, he promised to make regulatory agencies independent to establish new regulatory frameworks by law for the services wherein regulation had been decreed (by himself) and to enhance provincial participation in the provision of energy services (Frente para la Lealtad 2003).

Finally, the Argentine 1994 constitution granted quasilegislative powers to the executive through the use of decrees. During the period under study, these powers were supplemented by congressional delegation of legislative

---

[4] See Diario de Sesiones, Chamber of Representatives, 8th Meeting, First Ordinary Sessions, June 16, 1993, and Diario de Sesiones, Chamber of Senators, 37th Meeting, September 9, 1993.

powers. Presidents Menem and Kirchner made ample use of decrees, and the former also made use of partial vetoes, suggesting the leeway of the executive in policy making, which reduced its incentives to compromise in the legislature while increasing the stakes for intraadministration tensions.

Regulatory Legacies and Market Structure

Two vertically integrated regional monopolies called Telefónica (in the northern region) and Telecom (in the southern region) emerged from the privatization of ENTEL. The former was managed by Telefónica of Spain and the latter by France Cable and Radio and the Italian Telecom. Their monopolies were to last for seven years for local and long-distance communications, with a possible extension of three more years if the two companies fulfilled their investment requirements. There were also two providers of mobile telecommunications – Movicom (owned by Bell South), serving the Buenos Aires metropolitan area since 1989, and Telephone Company of the Interior (CTI) (owned by General Telephone and Electronics Corporation, or GTE), covering the interior since 1993 – in competition with the mobile services of the two main providers in their respective geographic areas. The fixed-term monopolies and identical license conditions made provider preferences easier to coordinate, as Telefónica and Telecom did not compete with each other.

By contrast, in electricity, market-oriented reforms created a multiplicity of actors in the Argentine Interconnected System (SADI). In 1993, there were twenty-five generation companies, six main transmission companies (Transener in charge of the main grid and Transba, Transnoa, Transnea, Transcomahue, and Distrocuyo managing regional grids), and twenty-one distribution companies (some of them still owned by provincial governments), although three of them (Edelap, Edenor, and Edesur) concentrated around two-thirds of total consumption (Romero 1999, 70). All these actors were represented in the board of Cammesa, along with large users and the secretary of energy (with veto power).[5] As entry rules limited acquisitions to prevent both vertical and horizontal integration, the electricity industry was more competitive than telecommunications. By 1998,

---

[5] The interest of small and large consumers generally coincided due to the absence of cross-subsidies, according to experts in the large users' association Aaguera (personal interviews with Engeneers Calcrain and Arias on August 26 and 30, 1999).

the Herfindahl-Hirschmann index of concentration, based on economic holdings for the Argentine interconnected system, was 0.092, in contrast to the 0.43 of the Chilean SIC (ENRE 2003). The large number of smaller actors in each segment of the electricity sector made policy coordination more difficult, thereby reducing their influence on regulatory decisions in comparison with the main telecommunications providers. Thus, in contrast to Chile, the market structure of the Argentine telecommunications industry facilitated coordination and regulatory influence more than that of electricity. Therefore, we should expect providers' preferences to have favored market dominance in telecommunications and competition in electricity, and we should expect both to have resisted redistribution to consumers.

Providers' influence, though, is limited by consumers', which in turn depends on their stakes. As in Chile, telecommunications coverage grew faster than did coverage in electricity, and so did prices for residential users. In 1985, only 38.9 percent of households had telephone service, whereas 90.3 percent had electricity. By 1996, 67.5 percent of households had telephone coverage, and 99.8 percent had electricity (Arza 2002, 122). The expansion of coverage had different distributive effects, as it benefited mostly the highest deciles of income in telecommunications and the lowest in electricity (120). In addition to access, the quality of services improved in both sectors.[6] Between 1993 and 2001, the proportion of consumers with positive views about their electricity service grew from 74 percent to 85 percent, while those who approved of their telecommunications service swelled from 48 to 68 percent (Observatorio de Servicios Públicos, OPSM-Enrique Zuleta Puceiro), suggesting that there were stronger pressures for redistribution to residential consumers in telecommunications than in electricity.

Argentine consumers should have been better prepared than Chilean residential users to foster their stakes through collective action because Argentina had a larger number of consumer organization that focused on public utilities. In 2000, I administered a survey that was answered by eleven of the thirteen consumer associations registered with the secretary

---

[6] Gerchunoff et al. report that the waiting time for telephone repairs dropped from ninety days on average before privatization to less than two days by 1994 (2003, 21). The energy losses in distribution also declined from 22% before privatization to 15% by 1996 (Romero 1999, 66). The average number of interruptions in service per year per user declined from thirteen to three in the 1992–8 period for the distribution company Edenor and from thirteen to four for Edesur (Abdala and Spiller 1999, 128).

of defense of competition and defense of consumers. The oldest had been formed in 1956 and the newest in May 1997; only two of the associations existed before 1991, and only one of them was headquartered outside the Buenos Aires metropolitan area (in Salta). Their membership ranged from four hundred to a few thousand, and all of them had a strong connection with public-utility users. They had different views on privatization of public utilities but agreed that it had improved the provision of public services. Yet they all claimed to be working on the demands of their users, especially regarding telephone billing. These consumer associations had the capacity to endogenously increase public attention to public-utility reform by using a combination of judicial and media actions.

Independently of actions by consumer associations, crises could increase the salience of public-utility regulations and consumer stakes on public-utility prices and supply. Argentina suffered a crisis in the supply of electricity in 1999 and a macroeconomic crisis affecting the impact of prices in both sectors in 2002. The 1999 electricity crisis generated a shortage of supply, which caused damage to users and drew continuous media coverage during a competitive presidential campaign. The 2002 macroeconomic crisis increased the stakes of consumers in both sectors, as a devaluation generated dramatic price effects on their income, whereas the political fluidity produced by the collapse of non-Peronist options increased electoral competition. The combination of high salience and contexts of heightening electoral competition should increase the likelihood of regulatory dominance in those periods.

Regulatory Redistribution in Electricity

In the postreform period under Menem, there was no legislative reform in electricity. Regulatory changes were ruled either by the secretary of energy or by the ENRE, which regulated distributors Edelap, Edenor, and Edesur and federal transmission companies. The ENRE was a locus of intraadministrative tensions, although it was considered the most independent of Argentine regulatory agencies (Urbiztondo et al. 1998; Vispo 1999). Cavallo had originally vetoed the choice of allied technocrat Juan Legisa as ENRE's first president and appointed instead neoliberal technocrat Carlos Mattauch. Mattauch resigned with Cavallo in 1996 and, after a brief interim period under another allied expert, was succeeded by Legisa in a move characterized as the "Peronization" of ENRE (*Clarín*, May 11, 1997).[7] The intraadministration tensions continued in the postreform period around the degree of market control involved in the liberalization of electricity markets and the expansion of transmission networks. Surprisingly, as De La Rua had to call Cavallo back, they persisted into the Alianza administration.

Under Mattauch, the ENRE used its discretion to reduce the thresholds for entering the wholesale market for large users with a demand of 5,000 kilowatts (with long-term contracts for half of it) in the original reform to those with a demand of 1,000 kilowatts (in 1993) and then 100 kilowatts (in 1994). In September 1998, the Secretariat of Energy, headed by neoliberal expert Alfredo Mirkin, passed Resolution 423. This resolution further reduced the threshold for entering the wholesale market to allow large users with an annual demand of 50 kilowatts while announcing a liberalization of the market in energy trading, originally rejected by PJ legislators as part of Law 24,065. Distributors complained about the loss of captured clients and threatened judicial action (Urbiztondo et al. 1998, 22; Azpiazu 1999, 83). That year, César McCarthy, who had just finished his tenure as PJ senator, replaced Mirkin and halted further liberalization.[8]

McCarthy also shifted gears regarding the mechanisms for the expansion of transmission networks, which had not grown as demand required after privatization. Numerous studies had pointed to the lack of incentives to expand the transmission network (NERA 1998; Abdala and Spiller 1999; Shoetters 1999; Romero 1999; Gerchunoff et al. 2003), and most actors in the market agreed with this evaluation.[9] Generation companies and large users were concerned, as they suffered the cost of congestion charges and shortages (Arias and Damonte 1998; Badaraco 1998). The original reform allocated the expansion costs to users based on the

---

[7] The interim head, Alberto Devoto, was a Peronist technocrat who would occupy the positions of secretary of economic planning and secretary of energy during the interim presidency of Peronist Eduardo Duhalde (2002–3).

[8] His undersecretary of electric energy was allied technocrat Luis Sbértoli, who had been responsible for planning the energy sector under Juan Legisa until 1991 and had worked as an expert in Agua y Energia during the Peronist administration of the 1970s.

[9] Personal interviews with Cristian Nadal, general manager of Edenor (November 23, 2000); Ing. Ernesto Badaraco, president of the generators' association AGUERA (December 12, 2000); Ing. Silvio Resnick, president of the Association of Transmission Providers and manager of Transener (December 18, 2000); Carlos Bastos, former secretary of energy (December 19, 2000); and Ing. Ramon Saenz, vice-president of Cammesa (August 26, 1998).

identification of prospective beneficiaries, conditional on the approval of more than 70 percent of them, which was very unlikely given the diversity of interest in the electricity sector. Because generators paying for the expansion were not guaranteed the use of the networks – others with lower marginal costs could be dispatched first – they had few incentives to fund their expansion.

Mirkin had commissioned a study by National Economic Research Associates (NERA) in 1997 to seek competitive mechanisms for expanding the transmission network. The study identified the absence of transmission rights as a major problem and suggested a "risk-bearing expansion" method (Littlechild and Skerk 2004, pt. II, 3). By contrast, McCarthy's Resolution 657 of 1999 established that the Electricity Nacional Fund – financed by a tax for each transaction in the wholesale market that was to be increased from $2.40 to $3.00 per megawatt-hour – would pay for network expansion (Littlefield and Skerk 2004, pt. II, 32). McCarthy also approved interconnecting the SADI with the Patagonic system (which benefited his own province) and the Mining Line interconnecting northwestern provinces, benefiting crucial members of the PJ peripheral coalition. The PJ-dominated CFEE, which overrepresented the interior provinces, provided technical support for Resolution 657. The debate occurred in a context of low public salience – in the five months prior to and the month after the passage of all these resolutions, there were no articles about them in *Clarín* newspaper. Thus, the government responded to the limitations identified by first entrants who had responded to its privatization calls, even when divided about the degree of market control necessary to meet their needs.

By contrast, ENRE's Resolution 292, which imposed regulatory dominance on providers, was publicly salient because it was adopted in response to a rationing crisis and during a competitive presidential campaign. As in Chile, this combination made the incumbent and the challenger prefer regulatory dominance. The crisis started on February 15, 1999, when a fire in a substation of Edesur in the City of Buenos Aires left more than 150,000 users (approximately 450,000 people) without electricity for more than ten days. The public salience of the resolution was high. In the month after the blackout started, *Clarín* published 135 articles on the electricity crisis (4.7 daily articles on average), 33 of them on the front page. In addition to spontaneous protests, consumer associations organized public demonstrations and brought judicial charges against the company, along with the city and national ombudsmen. Public demands to punish the company rapidly gained momentum.

The competitive nature of the presidential campaign increased incentives to demand consumer compensation to the point that providers' experts and managers denounced the electoral politicization of the event (*Clarín*, February 25 and 28, 1999).[10] President Menem called two emergency cabinet meetings to discuss the crisis and scolded the secretary of energy and the "independent" regulatory agency. He claimed the crisis was giving an opportunity to the opposition to criticize the government and demanded immediate compensation for consumers (*Clarín*, February 19 and 26, 1999). By February 23, the government was threatening to cancel the concession based on an ENRE technical resolution that found Edesur guilty of negligence under the conditions established in the concession contract. In early March, Vice-President Carlos Ruckauf demanded the cancellation of the concession (*Clarín*, March 1, 1999), while PJ legislators presented bills to increase legislative control over regulatory agencies and consumer participation on their boards.

The opposition also requested consumer compensation while blaming the government. Fernando De La Rua, Buenos Aires mayor and Alianza presidential hopeful, blamed Edesur, the national government, and the regulatory agency while demanding the cancellation of the concession (*Clarín*, February 24, 1999). Alianza legislators requested an immediate solution from the Edesur general manager, and Alianza experts demanded market-controlling regulation.[11]

On February 19, the ENRE issued Resolution 292, which provided that, in view of the exceptional characteristics of the event (electricity supply was suspended for longer than the ten-hour limit defined in the concession contract), the provisions of preexisting sanctions had been exceeded, and consumers had to be compensated for extraordinary damages beyond those established in the concession contract.[12] Although the ENRE

---

[10] In May 1999, after the PJ and the Alianza had selected their presidential candidates, surveys showed a 1.9% margin between them (*Clarín*, July 11, 1999).

[11] For instance, Jorge Lapeña, former secretary of energy under Raúl Alfonsín, argued that an electricity provision was a service of "public interest" for which the state retained a responsibility even after privatization. He added, "Market rules are not entirely appropriate: the active control of the state before, during and after the delivery of public service is necessary" (*Clarín*, March 15, 1999).

[12] The resolution established a uniform minimum amount in estimated damages to which all residential users were entitled without making claims or offering evidence of damage in the amount of U.S.$90 for those who lacked electricity for less than twenty-four hours and U.S.$100 plus U.S.$3.75 per hour for those who suffered the shortage for a longer time. Receipt of such compensation did not limit the freedom of consumers to take judicial action to demand damages, moreover.

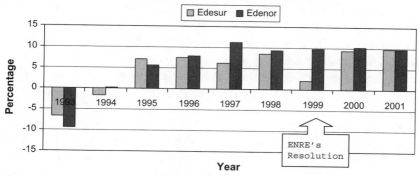

Figure 5.2 Profits by Electricity Providers
Source: Company balances provided by ENRE.

claimed that this resolution sought to avoid the administrative chaos of dealing with more than 100,000 consumer claims (Legisa 1999; ENRE press communiqué of February 2000), the regulator also changed the subsequent application of quality regulations. It started imposing sanctions for all service interruptions instead of only for those above the ten-hour limit, as it had done before (Urbiztondo 2000).[13] The resolution had a high public salience: it was covered by forty-seven articles (1.7 daily articles on average), eleven of them on the front page of *Clarín*, in the month after it was issued.[14] Hence, as in Chile, the combination of public salience and electoral competition favored regulatory dominance. Unlike Chile, though, the regulatory agency already had the sanction power to impose fines due to the market-controlling content of the initial reform, and Edesur paid compensation to consumers although it had initially appealed the requirements of the resolution.[15] Their negative effect on Edesur's profit is shown in Figure 5.2.

---

[13] An Edenor's manager said that changes in the application of quality regulations resulted in higher value of sanctions and their use as examples when blackouts became publicly salient (confidential interview, June 30, 2006).

[14] In December 1998, only 38% of people in the Buenos Aires metropolitan area knew about the ENRE, but in March 1999, 66% did, while 91% demanded more control of public-service providers (Observatorio de Servicios Públicos, OPSM, Enrique Zuleta Puceiro).

[15] Edesur appealed Resolution 292 and refused to pay the total amount of the sanctions until it changed owners at the end of March and accepted the fines shortly thereafter.

Alianza president Fernando De La Rua was inaugurated in December 1999. Having converted to the market creed while out of power, the Alianza combined preferences for market competition and regulatory dominance. De La Rua appointed allied expert Daniel Montamat, who favored regulating natural monopolies, as secretary of energy.[16] Before his appointment, Montamat said that markets where the demand uses a network required state intervention to simulate the conditions of competition, which are absent in natural monopolies (*Clarín*, February 28, 1999). On June 30, 2000, he announced the Federal Electricity Transmission Plan, which essentially implemented McCarthy's Resolution 657. Under his program, the state would auction network expansion rights to the lowest bidder, delegating to the secretary of energy the decision whether the expansion would be socially beneficial.

Providers, save for generators near consumption centers, reacted positively to this program, which solved the potential problems of service obligations for distributors, supply prices for large users, and cost for generators far away of consumption centers discussed in the preceding text.[17] Its expansions did not require the lowering of total costs, and new regional lines were identified that would also link the radial system into a meshed network. In defending state regulation for its ability to promote competition, increase supply, and lower consumer prices, Montamat said that the state's investment was being made "because the market incentives have not worked with adequate speed in the expansion of the network" (*Clarín*, July 13, 2000). The dramatic recession and fiscal crisis faced by the government, however, brought De La Rua to call Cavallo back to the Ministry of the

---

[16] Montamat was an allied technocrat to the Radical Party. He was an expert on energy educated in the United States who had been director of the state-owned gas and oil companies during the Alfonsín administration.

[17] Edesur manager Silvia Molinari said that the fund was expected to allow the expansion of the networks that generators required, fulfilling their quality of service obligations. She added that they required the investment badly, even if it involved state intervention (personal interview, November 21, 2000). Edenor general manager Cristian Nadal also said that state initiative was necessary to solve the problems of expansion in the transmission network that increased the risks of generators (personal interview, November 23, 2000). The president of the transmission companies' association and Trasnener manager Silvio Resnick had a positive evaluation of the fund, arguing that market competition in electricity required networks (personal interview, December 18, 2000). However, the president of the generators' association, Ernesto Badaraco, had a less positive view of the fund, because it involved a tax to subsidize those generators that were far away from consumption centers, and nobody was responsible for the quality of transmission (personal interview, December 15, 2000).

Economy in March 2001. The latter brought neoliberal expert Carlos Bastos to the Ministry of Public Works. Bastos drafted Decree 804 of June 2001 – based on the delegation of legislative powers to the executive for confronting the economic crisis – to modify Law 24,065.

Decree 804 abolished the Federal Electricity Transmission Plan and established a new market-oriented investment system wherein network expansion would be free and at risk, with "congestion rights" accruing to those investing in expansion, in addition to a transmission charge (*Mercado Eléctrico* 3, no. 98: 4–5). Decree 804 also allowed energy trading in competition with distribution companies.[18] Distribution companies such as Edelap, Edenor, and Edesur opposed energy trading, claiming that traders had made no investment (*Clarín*, June 23, 2001). Large users represented by the UIA and the Association of Large Users (AGUEERA) protested that trading would increase wholesale prices, and they filed judicial injunctions against the decree (*Clarín*, August 18, 2001). That is, a difficult-to-coordinate industry, including providers and large users, unified in their opposition to the decree. Additionally, PJ and Alianza legislators rejected it, arguing that energy trading would increase consumer prices, traders had no investment commitments, and halting the Federal Electricity Transmission Plan would be detrimental to interior provinces. Congress derogated Decree 804 just before the abrupt end to De La Rua's administration.

In sum, electricity regulation under both Menem and De La Rua was subject to tensions between allied and neoliberal technocrats about the best means to promote competition and supply, although the reasons for these tensions were different in each administration: Menem had adopted the reforms, and De La Rua was trying to survive a macroeconomic crisis by calling neoliberal experts back to office. Despite the fragmentation of the Argentine electricity market, providers unanimously rejected Decree 804, which also inspired the opposition of PJ and Alianza legislators concerned about its potential effects on large and residential users, though it was not very salient. Press coverage was almost null for all of De La Rua's reforms; there was a single article on the Federal Electricity Plan, and Decree 804 inspired three articles per month in *Clarín* in the period from its sanction to

---

[18] Prior to his appointment, Bastos was working for Enron. He criticized the Federal Electricity Transmission Plan as a return to state planning and suggested that a competitive system with transmission rights as incentives for taking on the risk of expansion would be better (personal interview, December 19, 2000).

its derogation (peaking at its derogation), whereas residential consumers were absent from the debate.

Regulatory Redistribution in Telecommunications

Because Menem had adopted the reforms, his administration was tied to the original providers who responded to his privatization calls and generated a concentrated market. As a result, providers and policy makers preferred market dominance, although the latter were subject to intraadministration conflict. By contrast, the Alianza administration had no ties with the original providers and preferred market competition and regulatory dominance.

The first regulatory challenge faced by Menem in the postreform period was produced by Cavallo's 1991 program for macroeconomic stabilization, which established a fixed exchange rate and made money supply dependent on monetary reserves in the Central Bank while banning price indexation. Because the rate for privatized telephones services included an indexation clause due to the high level of inflation at the time of privatization (Abeles et al. 2001, 98), providers protested the change of rules. They requested price dollarization, the establishment of an indexation mechanism, and an 11 percent hike in compensation for March 1991 inflation. The government rejected the price hike but allowed peak hours, when prices were higher, to be expanded (*Clarín*, December 4, 1991), and it also issued Decree 2,858 on December 6, 1991. This decree established the dollarization of telephone prices and their indexation according to the U.S. Consumer Price Index (CPI), which would become higher than the Argentine one in 1995. Figure 5.3 shows that residential telecommunications prices went up more quickly than electricity prices (Gerchunoff et al. 2003, 23, 32). It also shows the impact of the dollarization decree, which produced a redistribution that favored providers at the expense of consumers (regulatory capture).

Providers' influence was favored by the low public salience of telecommunications regulations reform. In the six months between July 17, 1991 and January 17, 1992, there was an average of three articles per month in *Clarín* on the price negotiations, peaking in the month of November with eleven articles. Remarkably, none of these articles ever mentioned the decree. Allied experts in the regulatory agency CNT resisted the decree and requested a price freeze rather than dollarization (Abdala and Hill 1996, 232). Neoliberal minister Cavallo reacted by taking over the agency,

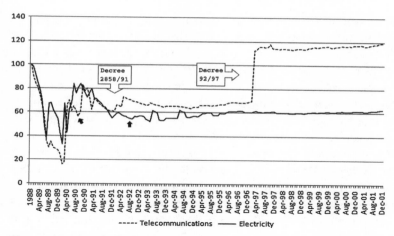

Figure 5.3 Residential Prices for Electricity and Telecommunications
Notes: From Gerchunoff et al. (2002). Black arrows mark onset of privatized management in both industries and the caption marks the dollarization and price rebalancing decrees.

whose board had been appointed by former minister of public works and allied expert Roberto Dromi. In pushing for the decree, he was also concerned about its fiscal effects, as the government was to underwrite the remaining shares of ENTEL in December of that year. Fiscal resources fostered his stabilization plan and increased neoliberal influence in the government.

Price dollarization, though, had negative effects on public opinion about privatization. The Ipsos-Mora y Araujo data on opinion about telephone privatization presented in Table 1.3 provides some information about the impact of this instance of regulatory redistribution across social classes. In the City of Buenos Aires, the probability that a respondent of low socioeconomic status favored privatization dropped from 0.57 in December 1990 (at the onset of private management) to 0.36 in July 1992 (the first time it was measured following the change in prices produced by Decree 2,858/91). For a respondent of medium socioeconomic status, the probability declined from 0.75 in December 1990 to 0.53 in July 1992 and for a high-status respondent from 0.87 to 0.74 during the same period. The effect on public opinion was negative, then, especially for lower- and middle-class consumers, for whom the income effects were stronger.

Despite this negative effect on consumer views, another instance of regulatory capture occurred when cross-subsidies were phased out, even though consumer mobilization and high public salience (Table 5.2) delayed the process for almost two years. Price rebalancing had been postponed at privatization to avoid the initial consumer outcry. The two providers agreed to keep cross-subsidies in return for a geographic extension of their monopolies to an area formerly served by a provincial cooperative they had acquired, along with licenses for mobile telecommunications in their areas (Decrees 344 and 506 of 1992). Yet a new CNT board, which had been selected through a process of public competition in October 1993, approved callback providers, which competed in long-distance communications and generated pressure to reduce long-distance prices in 1994 (Resolution 688). After Telefónica and Telecom lost their judicial appeal against this resolution, they presented a price-rebalancing proposal that established price hikes of up to 200 percent for local calls and reductions of up to 46 percent for domestic long-distance and 12 percent for international long-distance calls. An external report by NERA showed that, far from being price neutral, the implementation of such a proposal would have produced an extraordinary rent of U.S.$500 million for the providers (Abdala and Spiller 1999, 57).

Based on articles 42 and 43 of the new 1994 constitution, the consumer organization Consumer Action (ADELCO) filed a judicial injunction demanding consumer participation in the process through a public audience (Rhodes 2006, 85). As a result, the government called two public audiences on price rebalancing (and Cavallo participated in one of them), thereby increasing the public salience of the reform. However, public salience generated conflicting incentives for politicians depending on whether they wished to cater to residential users in the Buenos Aires metropolitan area, who were going to be hurt by higher prices for local communication, or to those in the interior provinces, who favored the proposed reduction in long-distance pricing. The PJ's electoral strongholds were in the underpopulated interior and the overpopulated Buenos Aires. Peronist governors and legislators from the interior whose constituencies relied more on domestic long distance favored price rebalancing, whereas the Peronist governor of the Buenos Aires province, Eduardo Duhalde, whose constituencies relied more on local communication, did not. In 1995, Cavallo agreed with Duhalde to postpone the decision regarding telephone prices until after the October election in order to prevent a backlash from his constituencies (*Ambito Financiero*, May 18, 1995).

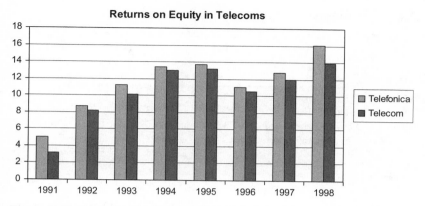

Figure 5.4 Profits by Telecommunications Providers
Source: Abdala and Spiller (1999, 66).

The CNT, meanwhile, rejected providers' proposal while demanding price reductions based on technology-driven productivity gains (Resolution 702 of 1995) and banning the use of the public network for data transmission (Resolution 1197 of 1995). Telefónica and Telecom reacted with a judicial injunction and lobbied the government, which put the CNT in a trusteeship and transferred the undersecretariat of telecommunications to the secretary of energy under neoliberal technocrat Carlos Bastos. Neoliberal technocrat Raúl Agüero was appointed as CNT trustee (*El Cronista Comercial*, May 18, 1995), and in 1996 the government made another proposal for price rebalancing favorable to providers' demands, calling the public audience with only one month's notice during the holiday season in a province distant from Buenos Aires. In February 1997, Menem issued Decree 92, which established the new price structure, including price reductions in long distance ranging from 56 to 71 percent, as well as hikes in local fixed costs of 50 percent and in local calls of 33 percent on average. According to Abdala and Spiller (1999, 68), providers took advantage of the increase in residential prices to pump up their profits, although price rebalancing should have been neutral for them, thereby generating regulatory capture. Although Figure 5.3 shows the aggregate effect of this decree on prices, Figure 5.4 identifies its positive effect on providers' profits.

Regulatory capture occurred in telecommunications regulation reform, despite the high public salience of the reform. *Clarín* published an average of seventeen articles on the reform per month in the six months between September 1996 and March 1997, peaking in February with sixty-two

Table 5.1. *Press Coverage in Telecommunications by Clarín*

Decree	Reform	Monthly Average of Articles	Number of Articles in Peak Month	Number of Articles in Front Pages
2585/91	Price dollarization	3	11	1
92/97	Price rebalancing	17	63	10
264/98	Partial liberalization	3	17	2
764/00	Total liberalization	15	29	7

Note: For all cases, the information refers to the five months before the decree and the one-month afterwards.

articles, nine of them front-page stories (see Table 5.1). Divisions between consumers gave providers the upper hand. Large users from interior provinces defended Decree 92/97 against the resistance of urban users in the metropolitan area. Peronist governors in Misiones, Salta, La Rioja, and Tierra del Fuego, along with business associations of Córdoba and Salta, filed judicial injunctions denouncing price discrimination and requesting the application of Decree 92/97.[19] By contrast, consumer associations, the city, and national ombudsmen (both headquartered in Buenos Aires) resisted price rebalancing by filling judicial injunctions based on complaints by residential users. Yet the interior provinces had been crucial in the 1995 reelection of Menem (Gibson and Calvo 2001), and the Supreme Court upheld the decree, reflecting its subservience to the executive (Helmke 2004).

The UCR and FREPASO, which relied heavily on voters from the Buenos Aires metropolitan area, rejected the decree but did not generate enough of an electoral threat to affect the outcome, because their division in 1995 facilitated Menem's electoral victory.[20] They would only come

[19] The Industrial Union of Córdoba's judicial injunction argued that as large users of long-distance service, its members had been hurt by the prior price structure and would benefit from price rebalancing. Small- and medium-size companies in the interior favored the new price structure because their markets were not circumscribed to their own urban area in contrast with the peers in the densely populated Buenos Aires metropolitan area. As a result, their association, the General Economic Confederation (CGE) supported the new price structure ("Las Pymes Hacen Números, *Telecomunciaciones y Negocios* año 7, no. 32).

[20] When they came together into the Alianza in August 1997, their leadership was formed by former president Raul Alfonsín (UCR, province of Buenos Aires), City of Buenos Aires mayor Fernando de la Rua (UCR), City of Buenos Aires representatives Rodolfo Terragno (UCR) and Chacho Alvarez (FREPASO), and Province of Buenos Aires senator Graciela Fernandez Meijide (FREPASO).

together in an electoral coalition in August 1997, two months before the October legislative elections, in which they received 57 percent of the vote in the City of Buenos Aires and 48 percent in the Province of Buenos Aires. Therefore, public salience could not deter regulatory capture, because the divided opposition reduced the threat of electoral competition for the PJ.

As the seven-year monopolies were scheduled to end in November 1997, the government had to regulate market liberalization. In a low-salience context, it issued Decree 264 only in March 1998. *Clarín* published an average of only three monthly articles about this regulatory change in the six months between November 1997 and April 1998, with only two articles on the front page (see Table 5.1). The regulation coincided with providers' preferences for market dominance, as it restricted competition to Telefónica and Telecom, subject to consumer presubscription, until November 1999 – assuming partial fulfillment of investment requirements. After November 1999, competition would open only to the two mobile providers – Movicom and CTI – in a joint venture with television cable companies and cooperatives, and market liberalization would happen only the following year.[21] In return for restricted competition, the government advanced some preferences for regulatory dominance: the four players had investment requirements imposed on them that emphasized rural coverage, subsidized rates for the poor, and pay phone access (Celani 2000, 39; Abeles et al. 2001, 240). Investment conditions included 640,000 new lines (15 percent in towns with more than 500 people and no phone line), 19,000 pay phones (half to be located in poor neighborhoods, hospitals, or bus terminals and 2,000 of them with subsidized fees), semipublic pay phones in towns with 80 to 500 people, and subsidized connection plans for poor users (Fiel 1999, 405–6; Abeles et. al 2001, 242). The emphasis on coverage benefited PJ constituencies at the expense of competitors rather than Alianza voters, who were more likely to have access and care about price effects.

In justifying partial liberalization, CNC president Roberto Catalán called attention to the need to expand coverage, mentioning legislators' request for service in smaller towns, and argued that having fewer players guaranteed their long-term sustainability. He cast the Chilean experience with competition in negative terms, arguing that it had led to widespread

---

[21] Movicom associated with Correo Argentino and Fecosur (Southern Federation of Telecommunication Cooperatives), whereas CTI joined with Multicanal (Clarín) and Fecotel (Northern Federation of Telecommunication Cooperatives).

provider bankruptcies (personal interview, Buenos Aires, May 11, 1999).[22] A study of Decree 264 concluded that "limits to competition, barriers to entry, [and] compulsory investment requirements suggest that the government thinks that it is in charge of inducing investment by using public policy rather than letting the market incentives work" (Institute for the Study of Argentine and Latin American Reality, or IERAL) 1999, 140).

Providers' preference for market dominance even at the expense of investment requirements was confirmed by the lack of competition for consumers after partial liberalization. A March 1999 survey by *La Nación* newspaper reported that half of the population was ignorant regarding the possibility of changing long-distance carriers (April 2, 1999). Additionally, Telefónica, Telecom, Movicom, and CTI explicitly supported Decree 264, echoing government arguments. Movicom's president, Mauricio Wior, argued that full liberalization would only bring temporary price reductions, would reduce investment, and would generate a dominant company. Similarly, CTI's president, Eduardo Menascé, suggested that full liberalization would reduce investment and produce market concentration (cited in Abdala and Spiller 1999, 72).

Potential competitors complained about market dominance because they had to wait until 2000 for full liberalization, even when they had invested in alternative networks, as had data service providers like Impsat, Compsat, and Keytech.[23] They denounced the fact that the four insider companies were also granted the new mobile PCS licenses and that interconnection prices were three times higher than in Chile, further contributing to market dominance (Abdala and Spiller 1999, 65).

The new Alianza administration inaugurated in December 1999 had not adopted the initial privatization reforms and thereby had fewer ties to first entrants than Menem's. It thus preferred market competition and regulatory dominance, like the Concertación in Chile. Henoch Aguiar was appointed secretary of communications. He was one of the competitively selected CNT directors fired by Cavallo for opposing price rebalancing, allowing callback competition, and banning the two main providers from

---

[22] At the end of his tenure in 1999, Roberto Catalán, who was a lawyer, served as secretary of government and legal affairs for La Rioja Peronist governor Angel Mazza, the trajectory of an allied expert.

[23] Ricardo Verdaguer, CEO of Impsat, complained that Decree 264 was discretional and biased, and that it had deleterious effects for competition. He argued that it sought to promote an oligopoly of two strong companies and two small ones, all of them selected discretionally (*Telecomunicaciones y Negocios*, año 9, no. 42, 23).

using their networks for data, and he explicitly defended competition as the crucial tool for the development of the sector (personal interview, December 2, 2000). As an attorney, he had represented cases against Decrees 92/97 and 264/98, and before his appointment he had publicly argued that the regulatory agency did not control providers and had criticized the lack of universal service, the high value of interconnection costs, and other limits to competition (Libro de Oro de las Telecomunicaciones, *Telecomunicaciones y Negocios*, 1999, 148).

On May 9, 2000, Aguiar presented his proposal for market liberalization without prior consultation with the incumbent providers. The proposal sought market competition, as it included a universal license with no investment requirements, disaggregation of the local loop, and a reduction of interconnection fees to 1.1 cents of dollar per minute, with interconnection obligations applying only to the "historic" companies (Telefónica and Telecom). Telefónica's general secretary and Telecom's vice president testified in Congress denouncing the asymmetrical requirements for universal service and general licenses without geographic obligations, which would favor the "creaming" of the richest consumers by entrants, who would not invest in expanding coverage as the first entrants had done (Bicameral Commission, July 25, 2000). They demanded higher interconnection prices, symmetrical obligations, and a subsidy of 3 percent of sales from the other companies for servicing areas that would not be profitable until 2021.

This time, though, providers were divided, as Movicom and CTI broke ranks with Telefónica and Telecom to join Impsat, Compsat, Keytech, Nextel, MetroRed, and ATT in supporting the proposal while requesting a lower interconnection fee and opposing the subsidies demanded by Telefonica and Telecom (Página 12, Cash supplement, June 25, 2000).[24] Representatives of all these companies testified in Congress and joined Aguiar's efforts to increase the public salience of the reform by participating in a press conference organized by him.[25] In the six months between Aguiar's announcement and the decree, *Clarín* published an average of fifteen

---

[24] Testifying for a Bicameral Commission, Roberto Pérez, the external relations manager of Movicom BellSouth, defended the proposal of June 9 while demanding a longer transition between the regime established by Decree 264 and the new one, as well as a lower universal service fee (as defined in Decree 264). Maximiliano Von Kesslstatt, regulations manager of CTI, also defended the original proposal while criticizing the increase in the universal service fee to 1% of sales (in addition to the existing 0.5% for the industry), as according to Decree 264 it was supposed to be lower until 2004 (Bicameral Commission, July 25, 2000).

[25] Personal interview with his advisor, Andrés Chamboulleyron (November 29, 2000).

articles per month on the issue, seven of them front-page articles, making this reform more salient than Decree 264/98 but less salient than Decree 92/97 (see Table 5.1). Unlike the cases of those decrees, though, the peak of articles in the month of June (with 29 articles, including 4 on the front page) happened prior to the decree, showing the deliberate use of media exposure by the secretary of communications to reduce providers' influence. In his testimony to Congress, Telefónica's president denounced such use of the media (Bicameral Commission, July 25, 2000, 4–5).

Telefónica and Telecom defended their views by emphasizing their prior investments and the importance of their companies in a contracting economy. The Ministry of the Economy, concerned with recession, pushed for a compromise that involve symmetrical obligations for interconnection for all providers, structure universal service with a pay or play scheme, and create regulations for providers with significant market share, in addition to dominant providers.[26] The pay or play scheme in particular allowed any company to qualify for the universal service subsidy generated by a 1 percent tax on sales if it was providing services in nonprofitable areas. Both that universal service fee and the CNC tax of 0.5 percent would be cancelled when providers served an area with teledensity lower than 15 percent, which included almost half of the provinces. However, subsidies and free prices for the two main incumbents required them to lose 20 percent of their income in their original area for local calls and two providers with a multicarrier system for long distance (art. 11). The market competition content of the decree was further strengthened by including representatives of all companies and consumers in the administration of a universal service fund.

The justification of Decree 764 of 2000 expressed partisan preferences for market competition and regulatory dominance. It claimed that regulation had to be used "to promote competition" and "defend consumers' interests" while endorsing universal service on the basis of the need "to guarantee access for all inhabitants of the country to the essential telecommunication services, regardless of their economic circumstances,

[26] Minister of the Economy Jose L. Machinea and the secretary of the defense of competition and consumer rights mediated in the relationship between the two main providers and Aguiar and were able to change the most conflictive clauses in the original proposal, according to personal interviews with Telecom regulations manager Jorge Otero (October 12, 2000) and with the telecommunications advisor of the secretary for the defense of competition, Marcelo Celani (October 27, 2000). The role of this secretary was also acknowledged by Telefonica's president, Fernandez Prida, in his testimony to the Bicameral Commission (July 25, 2000).

geographic location, or physical limitations." Showing policy makers' market-controlling preferences, the regulator received powers to define areas and services needing subsidies, impose interconnection obligations, and punish anticompetitive behavior.

Macroeconomic Crisis and Regulatory Reform

A comparison of the outcome of the 1999 electricity crisis in Chile and in Argentina suggests that microeconomic crises weaken providers' regulatory influence, regardless of institutional legacies. To test the effect of macroeconomic crises on regulatory influence and their impact on providers' legitimacy and consumers' stakes, this section focuses on regulatory reform in both sectors during the 2002 Argentine macroeconomic crisis.

The 2002 Argentine crisis generated strong incentives for redistribution to consumers. After Congress appointed PJ senator Eduardo Duhalde as interim president, it passed Law 25,561 of Public Emergency and Reform to the Exchange Rate System, which derogated the Convertibility Law on January 6, 2002. This law abolished the use of prices in dollars and indexation (art. 8), imposed the total renegotiation of contracts (art. 9), and allowed temporary price regulation by the executive (art. 13). The subsequent devaluation plunged the Argentine peso by more than 70 percent of its value, while an economic recession sent half of the population into poverty. As a result, a third of the population suspended paying for public services to deal with cash flow problems (Observatorio de Servicios Públicos, OPSM, Enrique Zuleta Puceiro, July 2002).

This regulatory change froze providers' income whereas the devaluation increased the cost of their imported inputs and debt service. Additionally, the law allowed discretionary regulation of previously nonregulated sectors, which was supplemented with investment obligations for contract renegotiation (Decree 292/02) and the inclusion of a consumer representative and the national ombudsman on the renegotiation committee (Decree 370/02), fostering conditions for regulatory dominance.

Meanwhile, providers' legitimacy declined markedly, probably heightened by prior instances of regulatory capture. In February 2002, 81 percent of the national population opposed providers' demand to "adapt" public-service prices to the new cost structure provoked by the devaluation, whereas 97 percent demanded total contract renegotiation and 81 percent believed that privatized providers had abused the lack of state control (Observatorio de Servicios Públicos, OPSM, Enrique Zuleta Puceiro,

September 2003). Consumers' associations explicitly framed their opposition to price hikes in terms of legitimacy. At a May 2002 meeting, for instance, consumer associations and the national and Buenos Aires ombudsmen demanded public audiences to increase the transparency of the contract renegotiation process and denounced the illegitimacy of Resolution 308 of the Ministry of the Economy, which suspended the application of sanctions for poor quality of service caused by the devaluation. The combination of both effects is clear in consumers' perception of public-sector prices as too expensive – a perception that grew between 2002 and 2005 despite rising inflation and frozen public-sector prices.[27]

In addition to the erosion of providers' legitimacy, political fluidity resulting from the crisis increased competitive pressures between the three Peronist candidates for president in 2003. Elected with only 23 percent of the vote, President Kirchner pushed for regulatory dominance after his inauguration, empowered by Law 25,790 from 2003, which delegated contract renegotiation and price agreements to the executive power. His administration emphasized the controlling role of regulatory agencies. His undersecretary of electric energy, Bautista Mareschi, argued that the state should not be passive and should include control beyond regulation (personal interview, June 22, 2006). The politically appointed heads of the two regulatory agencies also emphasized the importance of control of quality of service and consumer demands, explaining how their institutions were working together with consumer associations (personal interviews, June 21 and June 23, 2006). Moreover, residential prices continued to be frozen to attract the support of non-PJ middle-class voters, who had become politically independent due to the collapse of UCR and FREPASO. Hence, even as the economy grew 9 percent yearly and inflation increased 24 percent between 2003 and 2005, residential price renegotiation stalled.

Whereas price renegotiation was similar for both industries, other regulations changed due to sectoral differences. The elasticity of consumption was higher in telecommunications than in electricity, as were relative prices before the crisis.[28] Whereas unregulated telecommunications markets,

---

[27] The public perception that public-sector prices were expensive increased between September 2003 (57%), June 2004 (63%), and November 2005 (73%) (Observatorio de Servicios Públicos, OPSM, Enrique Zuleta Puceiro).

[28] In 2002, electricity consumption dropped by 6.8% and pay arrears reached 60%. By contrast, local telephone calls fell by 8.24% and domestic long-distance calls by 13%, and pay arrears reached 14% (Foster 2004, Table 1). Additionally, regulated prices were 40% higher in telecommunications than in electricity before the crisis (Winograd 2002).

such as that for mobile service, had boomed since 2004, electricity providers lacked nonregulated markets once the state took over the wholesale market.[29] Hence, in electricity, fixed prices increased demand but did not generate investment in capacity.[30]

As the PJ returned to a more statist position after 2002, partisan preferences for market-controlling regulations explain public investment in the expansion of transmission networks and generation capacity. First, Laws 27,882/03 and 25,957/05 returned to the Federal Electricity Transmission Plan to expand the transmission network, increased the tax paid to the National Fund for Electric Energy for wholesale market operations, and delegated investment decisions to the Federal Electricity Commission, whose president was the secretary of energy. Moreover, Law 26,095/06 allowed the government to establish new taxes for the expansion of energy infrastructure. Second, public investment in generation was an unintended consequence of low wholesale prices to keep residential prices frozen. Because it underpaid generators for their energy, even when subsidizing their fuel costs, the government acquired a debt with them, which was to be paid with the shares of two new 800 megawatts utilities built by the government. The construction would be financed by a new tax on wholesale market operations to solve the lack of private investment in generation (personal interview with Undersecretary of Electric Energy Bautista Marcheschi, June 22, 2006). In this case, regulatory dominance was detrimental to providers' preference for market competition, and they responded with no investment. In sum, the Argentine 2002 crisis, along with electoral fluidity, generated incentives for regulatory dominance by weakening providers' influence and increasing consumers' stakes.[31]

Meanwhile, the collapse of the convertibility system to sustain macroeconomic stability resulted in the vanishing influence of neoliberal technocrats and the increasing predominance of allied experts within the PJ,

---

[29] According to the CNC (June 2006), in 2002 the number of fixed lines declined by 4% and that of mobile lines by 3%. However, by 2005, the former had grown by 14% and the latter by 240%.

[30] Demand grew 15% in the two first years of Kirchner's administration, but installed capacity did not (CAF 2006).

[31] Price hikes for commercial and industrial users were applied in 2006, after Kirchner acquired control of Congress in 2005. Increases for the top 25% of residential consumers were implemented in 2008 after Kirchner's wife, Cristina Fernandez, had won the 2007 presidential election and the middle classes had proved impossible for the PJ to seduce – as shown by their support for rural protests against a tax decreed by President Cristina Fernandez de Kirchner.

thereby facilitating the return to the party's statist roots. These effects were similar across both sectors, regardless of the diverse providers' preferences produced by the combination of alternative networks and the original regulatory content of reforms. Hence, as in Chile, the institutional legacy of regulatory content slanted the playing field but was subject to subsequent modifications as a result of the incentives generated by political competition and partisanship.

Political Competition, Partisanship, and Institutional Legacies in Postreform Mexico

This section presents the expectations derived from the main hypotheses in Chapter 1 for postreform Mexico. It describes the evolution of political competition and the partisan preferences of incumbents, whereas the next section focuses on successful and failed regulatory efforts.

Political Competition

PRI president Salinas privatized Telmex in 1990. Subsequently, his party won the 1991 legislative elections, increasing its vote share from 51 to 61.5 percent and the electoral margin between it and the runner-up from 21 to 33 percent. Salinas's approval rating hovered around 80 percent during the second half of 1991 (CIDE 2008). Dominguez and McCahn (1996, 126–33) explain the PRI surge based on economic performance and prospective expectations of PRI strength. The PRI also won the 1994 presidential election, although an armed uprising and the assassination of the PRI presidential candidate marred the electoral campaign. Presidential approval ratings remained at 63 percent one month before the July election (CIDE 2008). The PRI substitute candidate, Ernesto Zedillo, received 50 percent of the vote, the same share as PRI legislative candidates, which gave him a 24 percent margin over the PAN runner-up (Figure 5.5) and marked low levels of electoral competition.

Shortly after Zedillo's inauguration in December 1994, Mexico suffered a macroeconomic crisis. Facing fiscal constraints and an economic slowdown, the government had increasingly relied on short-term debt denominated in pesos to sustain a fixed exchange rate. The collapse of this system brought a devaluation of the peso and a deep macroeconomic recession. By the end of 1995, inflation had grown 52 percent and GDP dropped 6.2 percent (or 9 percent in per capita terms), whereas unemployment had

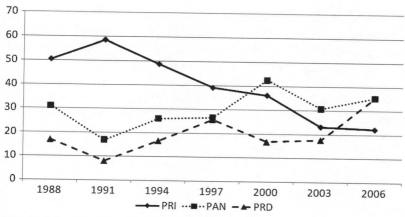

Figure 5.5 Electoral Competition in Mexico
Note: Presidential elections for 1988, 1994, 2000, 2006, and legislative election for 1991, 1997, and 2003.

almost doubled (Pastor and Wise 1997, 433; Wise 2003, 180). Presidential approval ratings had plunged to less than 36 percent by March of that year (CIDE 2008). The recovery was fast, however, aided by a U.S. bailout, and was reflected in improving approval rates for the president, which increased to 63 percent by July 1997.

In 1996, an electoral reform granted independence to the Federal Electoral Commission and controlled campaign financing, and in the legislative elections of 1997, the PRI legislative vote dropped to 39 percent and its electoral margin to less than 13 percent, while the combined vote share of its two contenders was more than 50 percent. A high level of electoral competition continued in the 2000 presidential election. In October 1999, 40.5 percent of voters intended to cast their ballots for the PRI candidate, Francisco Labastida, compared to 53.3 percent for his predecessor in May of 1994 and to 34.4 percent for PAN candidate Vicente Fox (Presidencia de la Republica/CIDE, 1989–2000). In July 2000, Fox received 42.5 percent of the vote to Labastida's 36 percent (Figure 5.5), and their legislative shares were 39.4 percent and 38 percent, respectively. The campaign for the 2003 legislative elections was also competitive. According to the Reforma group, the proportion of voters intending to vote for PAN declined from 47 percent in September of 2002 to 33 percent in June of 2003, whereas those intending to vote for the PRI grew from 34 to 38 percent, although Fox's approval rating had reached 64 percent by

May 2003.[32] In the end, the PAN received 30.6 percent of the vote, increasing its legislative electoral margin to 7.6 percent, as the PRI received 23 percent of votes and the PRD 18 percent. This result produced a divided Congress, which affected Fox's capacity to pass laws.

Thus, bouts of electoral competition occurred during the campaigns for the 1997, 2000, and 2003 elections after the 1996 reform allowed effective contestation. However, these campaigns did not coincide with the 1995 macroeconomic crisis, which increased the stakes of consumers. The conditions' lack of simultaneity should have reduced incentives for regulatory dominance in the postreform Mexican telecommunications sector.

Partisanship

The partisan preferences of the PRI, PAN, and PRD depended on their constituencies, ideological legacies, and role in the reform process. The PRI had adopted the reform and therefore should have preferred market dominance, subject to intraadministration tensions. That is, we should expect PRI policy makers to have sided with the providers who responded to their privatization calls, enhancing the credibility of their conversion to the market creed. By contrast, both the market-liberal PAN and the staunchly populist PRD could keep their original preferences for market competition and regulatory dominance, respectively.

Legislative positions during the congressional debate on consumer regulation, as well as electoral platforms, should provide indicators of these preferences. In the case of the PRI and PAN – the PRD was not formed until 1988 – the legislative debates over the 1976 Law of Consumer Protection, which created the Federal Agency for Consumers (PROFECO), can be used to assess long-term policy preferences by comparing partisan views with those of the 1992 reform to that consumer law. The 1976 law was an initiative of PRI labor leaders in response to rising prices. Secretary of Government Mario Moya Palencia and PRI legislators argued that there was an asymmetric relationship between consumers and retailers that justified state intervention to favor the weakest party.[33] Mexico's decision

---

[32] "Mexico Politics: President Fox Faces Declining Vote," *Financial Times*, July 2, 2003.

[33] Although there are numerous mentions of this asymmetry, the first one is by Labor Secretary Profirio Muñoz Ledo, who would later join the PRD (XLIX Congress, Diario No. 13, September 9, 1975, 17). Moya Palencia's speech is in XLIX Congress, Diario No. 9, September 26, 1975, 3.

to sign NAFTA in 1992 required a reform of PROFECO so that it would not control prices.[34] PRI legislators argued in favor of modifying the law, as NAFTA would increase the exposure of the weakest consumers, thereby requiring a stronger state role in the consumption relationship. Moreover, they added, the state should guarantee justice for consumers and promote citizen participation.[35]

The 1994 PRI platform provided no specifics regarding telecommunications (Curzio 1994), whereas the PRI's 2000 presidential program prioritized the need to expand the coverage of the telecommunications infrastructure and to include communities that were not profitable in that expansion. That is, the PRI retained a role for state rectorship and sought to pursue policies that defended mainly poorer consumers, who usually did not have access to telephones. Due to the PRI role in adopting the reforms, therefore, we should expect to find a PRI preference for market dominance in return for incentives for providers to service less-attractive populations, but with intraadministrative tensions due to the party's traditional preferences for regulatory dominance. Once the PRI lost the 2000 election, we should expect to find that internal tensions heightened as the party drifted back to more statist positions, like the Argentine PJ. And this shift is reflected by the preference for regulatory dominance in its 2003 electoral platform. The 2003 PRI platform promised to revise the telecommunications law to guarantee coverage for everyone and to protect consumers of these services. In electricity, it promised to defend the constitutional monopoly of the state over electric energy for generation, transmission, distribution, and supply as a public service. It opposed privatization of electricity and private participation while defending the vertically integrated monopoly of CFE and LyF (PRI 2003).

In contrast to the PRI, in 1975, PAN legislators argued that the role of the state was not to direct the economy but to improve the efficiency and efficacy of economic activities.[36] The party continued to express these views in the 1992 legislative debate. It argued that PROFECO should be a neutral agency that did not benefit any party in the consumption relationship, because according to the social market economy, economic freedom

---

[34] In 1988, the executive granted PROFECO authority to control prices in the context of a macroeconomic stabilization strategy.

[35] LV Congress, Diario No. 11, November 26, 1992, 1131, 1133, and 1988.

[36] PAN representative Margarita Prida de Yarza (XLIX Congress, Diario No. 31, November 28, 1975, 52).

only requires guarantees of competition, freedom of election, and private property.[37] PAN's 1994 electoral platform promised to revise the terms of the Telmex concession while promoting market liberalization (Curzio 1994, 277). Its 1997 electoral platform claimed that the state should have a subsidiary role while guaranteeing competition and preventing monopolies. It requested reforms in both sectors, including the modification of constitutional articles 27 and 28 to bring an end to the state monopoly on electricity generation, further private investment, and introduce market mechanisms (PAN 1997).

In his campaign for the presidency, Fox promised independence for the regulatory agency to promote transparency and stability in the rules of the telecommunications sectors (Reyes Heroles 2000, 24). He also called for "deregulation" in general and for increasing private participation in electricity generation while reversing PAN's support for privatization to win over PRD voters in a context of high electoral competition with the PRI, as explained in Chapter 2. The 2000 PAN legislative agenda included a proposal to reform electricity and the Federal Telecommunications Law. In electricity, it promised private investment and a competitive market. In telecommunications, the promised reform entailed increasing the autonomy of the regulatory agency, introducing interconnection regulation, imposing rules that would allow consumers to keep their phone numbers when changing carriers, formulating arbitrage procedures for conflicts in the sector, and defining clearer rules for transparency on prices. Thus, PAN policy makers, as right-wing true believers who had not adopted the reforms, preferred market competition. After PAN's arrival in power, its 2003 platform proposed a constitutional reform to the state monopoly on electricity (articles 27 and 28) to allow private participation in generation and market competition (PAN 2003).

PRD legislators only participated in the 1992 debate – the party was founded in 1988 – in which they insisted on the autonomy of consumer associations, which as unions were mostly dependant on the PRI. They also demanded the explicit inclusion of consumer protection as the main function of PROFECO in the bill.[38] Its 1997 electoral platform mentioned no reform in electricity or telecommunications, whereas its 2000 presidential program had no proposals for telecommunications but defended the state monopoly in electric energy (Alianza por Mexico 2000).

[37] LV Congress, Diario No. 11, December 14, 1992, 1,984.
[38] See debate in LV Congress, Diario No. 11, December 14, 1992, 1,981.

PRD legislators cared about residential prices. In a personal interview, PRD senator Sodi de la Tijera emphasized the importance of low prices in telecommunications (October 7, 2002), and the PRD had opposed price rebalancing due to its effects on local prices for residential consumers, according to former COFETEL head and undersecretary of telecommunications Javier Lozano (personal interview, January, 23, 2001). As the PRD represented statists who had left the PRI due to their refusal to convert to the market creed, we should expect the party to have preferred regulatory dominance and market-controlling regulations. As anticipated, its 2003 electoral platform continued to defend the state monopoly on electricity and to promote further regulation of private self-generation and the introduction of subsidies for low-income users. In telecommunications, it promised a stronger role for the state in the development of the sector, the control of market concentration, and the promotion of domestic investment (PRD 2003).

Institutional Legacies and Market Structure

Whereas electricity privatization had failed, as analyzed in Chapter 2, Telmex was privatized as a vertically integrated national monopoly with local, long-distance, and mobile services. By 1995, Telmex had a monopoly over local and long-distance service, whereas its subsidiary, Telcel, controlled 58 percent of the mobile market (Briceño ND, 7). Telmex's gross profits were 42.8 percent of revenue on average from 1991 to 1994 (Torre 2000, 16). The value of its shares peaked in January 1994 at U.S.$36.87, reflecting the high returns on the monopoly; CTC's shares peaked at the same time at U.S.$31.68. Whereas its monopolistic nature explains Telmex's preference for market dominance, the fact that the company that owned Telmex accounted for more than half the value of the Mexican stock exchange furthered its regulatory influence, because it could trade off favors and apply pressure across sectors of the government, as argued by Post (2007).

Telecommunications prices grew faster than coverage. In the 1990 to 1995 period, the number of fixed lines expanded from 5.19 million to 8.8 million, bringing teledensity from 3.8 to 6.6 per 100 inhabitants and extending coverage from 63 to 67 percent of urban households (Kuhlman et al. 2000, 14). In the period between the third quarter of 1991 and the last quarter of 1995, the installation cost for residential users increased by 59 percent, and the price of the basic service (with a monthly package of 100 calls) rose by more than 200 percent at a time when accumulated inflation was 85 percent (COFETEL 2000).

Even though limited access reduced the impact of price increases, consumer stakes should have grown when the 1995 macroeconomic crisis hit their income. Consumer associations were weak, however. The Mexican Association of Studies for the Defense of the Consumer (AMEDEC) was the only existing consumer association independent from the state. PROFECO's general manager for complaints, Adriana Campos (personal interview, December 11, 2000) justified the weakness of consumer associations, arguing that her institution's defense of consumers made these organizations less necessary. The head of AMEDEC, Arturo Lomelín, proclaimed its independence but admitted that the association had only a handful of members and that consumer mobilization was sporadic (personal interview, August 2, 2004). The weakness of consumers made regulatory dominance a less likely outcome and one that was increasingly dependent on electoral incentives rather than citizen organization.

Postreform Regulatory Redistribution

As Telmex's long-distance monopoly was set to expire in August 1996, the executive sent a bill to Congress to regulate the liberalization of the telecommunications market in April 1995. The bill was passed as the Federal Telecommunications Law in June. Telmex's preferences for market dominance differed from that of potential competitors, such as U.S.-based ATT and MCI, which favored market competition.

The timing of the reform coincided with the 1995 macroeconomic crisis, which increased consumer awareness of telecommunications prices and the influence of U.S. investors, because the U.S. government had provided a bailout loan of U.S.\$20 billion to Mexico. The macroeconomic crisis weakened the legitimacy of market-oriented reforms and telephone privatization. A national survey of August 1995 shows that almost half the respondents opposed the privatization of telecommunications, and only 37 percent thought that Telmex's service had improved with privatization. Moreover, 46.5 percent disagreed with Salinas's privatizations, 42 percent thought that privatization was bad for the population, and 44 percent believed that privatization benefited the wealthy (Cide, REC30895. PRG, August 29, 1995).

Consumer demands for regulatory dominance were muffled by the combination of Telmex's suspension of price rebalancing (it froze prices through 1995, a year of high inflation, at the request of the government) and the lack of coincidence between this crisis and a competitive electoral campaign, which gave politicians little incentive to demand regulatory redistribution to consumers. Demand was eroding, as more than a million lines had ceased service due to lack of payment that year (Javier Alvarado, personal interview, December 6, 2000), which gave Telmex a separate incentive to hold down prices. Still, the government was happy to have frozen prices when trying to control inflation. In return, the secretary of communications allowed Telmex to keep the rents derived from the differential between incoming and outgoing calls with the United States, thereby reducing the potential profits of competitors in long-distance service. This redistribution from competitors to Telmex (a case of market dominance) was agreeable to the PRI and Telmex.

The debate over the Federal Telecommunications Law pitted Telmex's preference for market dominance against foreign investors' preference for market competition, whereas PRI policy makers, who had a majority in Congress, continued to favor market dominance in return for coverage expansion, even when subject to intraadministrative tensions between allied and neoliberal experts. Allied experts supported market dominance, rewarding the domestic owners of Telmex while seeking to contain residential prices and expand coverage to benefit PRI constituencies. Neoliberal technocrats preferred market competition to signal their commitment to U.S. investors.[39] That is, they preferred full liberalization, whereas allied experts, such as Deputy Undersecretary Javier Lozano and Secretary Carlos Ruíz Sacristán, preferred gradual liberalization.[40]

The bill introduced to Congress proposed gradual liberalization. Competition would start in only sixty cities in 1997, with two types of renewable concessions for long-distance services: a residential one with coverage requirements and a commercial one with fewer requirements but higher interconnection fees. In all cases, companies had to provide long-distance service in at least three states. Javier Lozano justified the decision, arguing

---

[39] The intraadministrative debate was confirmed in the legislative debate by PRD representative Carlos Navarrete, who argued that the law resulted from the differences between neoliberal technocrats who wanted to please U.S. investors in the context of a high financial dependence, and allied technocrats, who were concerned with the risk of a total liberalization for the expansion of coverage and survival of companies (LVI Congress, Lower Chamber, Diario de Debates no. 3, May 17, 2001).

[40] Confidential interviews four (December 6, 2000) and five (January 21, 2001) suggest that the secretary of communications preferred to give only two or three long-distance concessions to limit the number of players in the market, avoid the cutthroat competition experienced in Chile, and bolster the stock market value of Telmex, due to its effect on the national economy.

that different interconnection prices generated incentives for expanding coverage (personal interview, January 23, 2001). Allied expert and former undersecretary of telecommunications Carlos Cassasus explained the three-state coverage obligation as a result of the PRI legislative pressures for investment requirements and defended it as a guarantee of the financial sustainability of entrants in the long-distance market that would help to prevent widespread bankruptcies (personal interview, December 8, 2000).

The law established that the bidding for mobile telecommunications spectrum (and wireless local loop) would entail ascending bids and investment requirements. The emphasis was on coverage. For the wireless local loop, investors were to include 30 percent of the total population in the area of service in three years and 50 percent in five years. In order to win the support of PRI legislators, moreover, the law established a limit to foreign capital investment at 49 percent of shares (art. 12).[41]

In the legislative debate, PRI senator Mauricio Valdés defended the executive bill, arguing that it would foster investment and technological development while keeping state sovereignty and rectorship. By contrast, PAN senator Emilio Goicochea criticized the private monopoly in telecommunications and demanded competition, emphasizing market liberalization. Meanwhile, PRD senator Héctor Sánchez complained that PRD proposals were ignored, whereas PRD representatives Carlos Navarrete and Luis Sánchez Aguilar criticized the risks to national sovereignty of allowing foreigners to own cellular licenses and denounced the bill as following "orders from the US Congress" in return for the bailout loan.[42]

PRI partisan preferences for expanding coverage also brought the secretary to create a program for the expansion of rural coverage, which delegated considerable discretion to the regulator. Article 50 gave the SCT the obligation to establish programs of social coverage and forbade the interruption of services in any locality with a single provider. The program for the expansion of rural telephone coverage was paid for directly through the budget rather than through providers' taxes, as was the Chilean Telecommunications Development Fund.[43] During Zedillo's

---

[41] Cellular service was exempted, because the mobile company Iusacell had already sold its company to Southern Bell before the passing of the law.

[42] See LVI Congress, Senate, Diario de Debates no. 17, April 26, 1995, and LVI Congress, Lower Chamber, Diario de Debates no. 3, May 17, 2001.

[43] According to Carlos Escalante from local provider Axtel, the local party bosses controlled the distribution of those phones (personal interview, January 19, 2001).

administration, telephones reached more than 31,000 towns of less than 500 people – about two-thirds of which were directly served by the government and another third by Telmex (SCT 2000, 279, Dirección de Telefonía Rural de Telecomunicaciones).

The market-dominant character of the Federal Telecommunications Law blended with some potential for regulatory dominance in the considerable discretion given to COFETEL to define the conditions for concessions, which was criticized by an OECD (Organization for Economic Cooperation and Development) report on Mexican regulations (2000, 89). Due to its power in the economy and its capacity to negotiate with the government, Telmex accepted the discretion provided that COFETEL, but it successfully resisted its originally proposed autonomy.[44] The law also established the obligation of interconnection and granted enforcement powers to the regulator, including the levying of fees if parties did not agree (art. 41 and 42). Whereas Telmex local prices had been regulated by price caps since 1997 according to the terms of the original concession, the law also obliged competitors to register their prices with the regulator and established regulated prices for cases of dominant market power (art. 63). In sum, the law restricted foreign investment, established investment requirements on entrants, and gave discretion (but not autonomy) to the regulator, in line with both PRI's and Telmex's preferences. Explaining Telmex's position, Telmex regulations manager Ramírez Alvarado argued that entrants should have the same investment requirements Telmex had had, and he justified different interconnection prices and treatment for local providers, such as Axtel, in terms of these providers' larger investment requirements (personal interview, January 16, 2001).

Limited competition benefitted Telmex. By 2000, Telmex's share of long-distance calls had reached 80 percent, in contrast to 10 percent for Avantel and 8 percent for Alestra. By then, domestic long-distance prices had declined 20 percent in 1994 pesos (and remained constant in dollars), whereas the cost of calling the United States had declined by a third (Gil Hubert 2000, 39, 49, 52, 54). Additionally, Telmex gross profits continued to be 35.3 percent on average for the 1995–9 period (Torre 2000, 16), and by 2000 its local revenues per line were twice as large as those of Chilean CTC and Telefónica of Argentina; interconnection fees accounted

---

[44] Confidential interview four (December 6, 2000) and interview with Secretary Ruíz Sacristán (January 18, 2001).

for a much larger proportion of those revenues than in the other two cases (Avantel 2000).

The 1995 law displayed an instance of market dominance rather than regulatory dominance, despite the macroeconomic crisis, because a low level of public salience and the absence of a competitive election reduced consumer influence. The public salience of the reform was low thanks to the suspension of price rebalancing, which according to then-secretary Ruíz Sacristán increased Telmex's influence in the policy-making process as it helped confront the inflationary crisis (personal interview, January 18, 2001).[45] Between January 17 and June 29, there were 39 articles on the liberalization of the telecommunications market in eight major Mexican newspapers, for a monthly average of 6.5 articles, peaking at 11 in April – many fewer than were printed to address electricity privatization in 1999. Low salience enhanced Telmex's influence.

Telmex's two main competitors – Avantel and Alestra – preferred full liberalization, and they were involved in judicial conflicts with Telmex over interconnection and billing.[46] Avantel led the judicial strike against Telmex for its lack of a single interconnection fee, denounced Telmex's dominant position to the Anti-Trust Commission, and denounced Mexico to the U.S. trade representative in light of the World Trade Organization (WTO) regulations on dominant suppliers.[47] Telmex's regulatory influence delayed COFETEL's declaration of dominance until 2000, even though the Anti-Trust Commission had established Telmex's dominant position in five markets (local telephones, interconnection, domestic long distance, international long distance, and long-distance resale) two years ealier. As in Chile, the conflict between providers generated a demand for regulatory reform.

The new PAN administration of Vicente Fox was inaugurated in December 2000, and he faced providers' demands for regulatory reform. The National Chamber of the Electric, Telecommunications, and

---

[45] A neoliberal technocrat working for him suggested regulatory capture by Telmex as rules changed after a meeting between Secretary Ruíz Sacristán and Carlos Slim (confidential interview no. 4, December 6, 2000).

[46] Avantel was owned by MCI Worldcom (45%) and Banamex (55%), while Alestra was owned by ATT (49%), Alfa group (25.6%), and Bancomer (25.4%).

[47] Between 1998 and 2000, Telmex and Avantel were the two companies with the largest number of cases in the Mexican courts. In 2000, Telmex had fifty-four cases and Avantel had twenty-four. Most of the Telmex cases were injunctions against regulatory acts, whereas Avantel litigation protested Telmex's anticompetitive behavior (See "Compiten en amparos Telmex and Avantel," Reforma, October 5, 2000).

Information Technology Industry (CANIETI), which represented telecommunications providers except for Telmex, presented a document to President Fox shortly after his inauguration requesting a reform to the Federal Telecommunications Law. The proposal emphasized the need to reduce regulatory discretion and foster competition by establishing a universal service fund rather than charging higher interconnection costs to promote the expansion of coverage. It also suggested the need to open all cities in the country to long-distance competition, apply regulations on dominance of markets as well as new mechanisms to denounce anticompetitive behavior, define interconnection fees according to long-term incremental costs, unbundle the local loop, and convene a public discussion of the proposals for new regulations (CANIETI 2000). The group's market competition preferences coincided with those of the PAN.

PAN preferences for market competition were strongly sustained by Senator Corral and Representative Goicochea in the telecommunications commissions of both chambers. To the post of secretary of telecommunications, however, Fox appointed the head of his campaign and former Telmex manager Pedro Cerisola, showing how the tensions between partisan preferences and providers' regulatory influence grew in the postprivatization period.

In March 2001, under the initiative of PAN legislators, the Mexican Congress called a public discussion in order to elaborate a new Federal Telecommunications Law. The original proposal called for the use of technical conditions rather than revenue maximization in the bidding of spectrum, COFETEL independence, asymmetric regulations for the dominant carrier, and obligations for interconnection, including the unbundling of the local loop and explicit subsidies for universal service. The proposal divided the industry, with Telmex and its suppliers opposing it and Telmex's competitors supporting it (or even demanding more stringent conditions on the dominant carrier). In congressional testimony, Telmex representatives argued that the new conditions on the dominant carrier would be deleterious to coverage and infrastructure investment, benefit the entrant carriers, and punish the only carrier that had previously invested in the industry and could be the motor of industry development. Telmex complained that dominance regulation included areas in which it was the only carrier due to service obligations rather than investment decisions it had made. It added that the proposed regulations promoted the entry of less-efficient carriers, while the rules on dominance gave undue regulatory discretion to COFETEL. By contrast, the CANIETI, which was dominated by Telmex's competitors, and especially Alestra, Avantel, and Iusacell, defended asymmetric rules for the dominant carrier, the unbundling of the local loop, and COFETEL independence.

Although PAN legislators supported the more competitive proposal, PRI legislators were divided. PRI senators supported the proposal, but in April 2002 PRI representative Jesus Orozco and PRD representative Victor Ochoa Camposeco presented an alternative bill with rules on dominance and local loop unbundling that followed Telmex's preferences.[48] The comparison of this bill with Telmex's proposal to the bicameral commission shows a remarkable similarity in the fine print. The rules banning and punishing bypass of local networks were copied almost verbatim, and so were the rules on interconnection, which was to take consideration of capital costs and could vary geographically and be suspended for lack of payment. Also remarkably similar was the wording on the regulation of market dominance, which could only be applied to companies that limited supply and set prices above competitive levels, and which could not be applied at all in markets opened to competition. The bill also eliminated the intervention of the Federal Anti-Trust Commission to assessments of possible anticompetitive behavior as a result of market concentration, by using the same wording as in the Telmex proposal (Orozco and Ochoa Camposeco 2002; Telmex 2002).

When the proposal prepared by the legislative commission was announced in August 22, 2002, it included regulation on dominant market position for any company with more than 25 percent of the income in a market. There was also an explicit prohibition on interrupting services due to interconnection conflicts unless such interruptions were ruled to be acceptable by the COFETEL, and there were no sanctions to be applied for bypassing the network. The proposal established a social telecommunications fund for expanding coverage and included a chapter on consumer rights, including rights to transparent and public pricing and to privacy (CPT 2002). Telmex achieved important concessions, however. Instead of long-term incremental costs, interconnection fees were to be agreed upon between the parties; in addition, there was no mention of unbundling the

---

[48] Personal interviews with PAN senator Javier Corral (October 8, 2002), PAN representative Emilio Goicochea (April 16, 2001), and former undersecretary Javier Lozano (October 8, 2002). Lozano explained that PRI representative Miguel Orozco depended on Telmex support for his gubernatorial campaign in the state of Colima.

local loop, no autonomy given to COFETEL, weak regulation of the dominant supplier, and no definition of numerical portability, while foreign investment was limited to appease PRI supporters (personal interview with PAN senator Javier Corral, October 8, 2002).[49]

On interconnection, the final proposal reflected an agreement between Telmex and its competitors, which, facing regulatory uncertainty, continued using both the courts and technological alternatives to foster competition. After Avantel had obtained COFETEL's declaration of dominance, to which Telmex responded with a judicial injunction, it turned to using alternative networks to bypass Telmex's. It also refused to pay accumulated debts for interconnection, forcing Telmex to the courts. In the end, Telmex reached a commercial compromise with Avantel, Alestra, Marcatel, and Telnor, setting an interconnection rate of 0.975 cents per minute for 2002, which was 22 percent lower than the previous rate of 1.25 cents.

Despite compromises in the final proposal, Telmex rejected it immediately, and its spokesperson publicly said that the bill would never become a law while explicitly criticizing the dominance rules.[50] The bill never reached the floor, stalling in Congress, and the silence of President Fox and Secretary of Communications (and former Telmex manager) Carlos Cerisola suggests that Telmex lobbying the executive power was instrumental in this outcome.[51]

Thus, the PANist preference for market competition was hindered by Telmex's preference for market dominance. Low public salience facilitated providers' regulatory influence. As shown in Table 5.2, *La Jornada* and *El Universal* published around two articles monthly on average and a single front-page story in August, when news peaked, about the proposal. Moreover, the strong position of a single dominant actor in Mexico – with the regulatory leverage given by its control of other economic areas – further facilitated the maintenance of the status quo. According to Senator Javier

---

[49] According to PAN senator Javier Corral and Fox undersecretary of telecommunications Jorge Alvarez Hot, the PAN preference for banning limits on foreign capital was abandoned because it would have killed the proposal due to PRI and PRD opposition (personal interview, October 8 and 10, 2002 respectively).

[50] See the speech of Arturo Elias Ayub, Telmex manager of communications and public relations, in "Genera conflict proyecto de Ley de Telecomunicaciones," *El Universal*, August 23, 2002.

[51] See also Javier Lozano, "Las Telecomunicaciones ne la LVIII Legislatura: la crónica de un fracaso," in IDET (Right to Telecommunications Institute), http://www.idet.org.mx/publicacctiones/artidet/Est2003LA02.htm (accessed January 18, 2004).

Table 5.2. *Mexican Press Coverage of Reform Discussions between March and December 2002*

	La Jornada		El Universal	
	Telecommunications	Electricity	Telecommunications	Electricity
Monthly Average	1.5	3	2.2	9.1
Peak month (august)	1	9	6	21
Front Pages in August	0	17	1	8

Corral, Telmex and the Carso Group waged the main opposition to the proposal (personal interview, October 8, 2002).[52]

In 2002, Fox also attempted an electricity reform that excluded privatization, as he had promised during the 2000 electoral campaign.[53] To avoid controversy, in 2001 he issued a decree permitting the private generators created by the 1992 reform to sell all their production to CFE. The Supreme Court declared the decree unconstitutional while pointing to the apparent unconstitutionality of the 1992 reform, bringing private investment to a halt (Carreón-Rodriguez et al. 2007, 208). As a result, the government presented an electricity reform bill, which modified articles 27 and 28 of the Constitution, as did Zedillo's reform bill. The bill opened generation to foreign and domestic private investment, keeping transmission and distribution for the state but creating a wholesale electricity market for users with a demand of more than 2,500 megawatts and requiring transparent subsidies in electricity pricing. The PRD rejected the proposal, denouncing the wholesale market, private participation, and the constitutional reform to allow it. Instead, it presented an alternative project that would have granted more autonomy to the state-owned electricity enterprises and increased subsidies to be paid from the general budget. In

---

[52] The Telmex legislative lobby was able to change the content of a tax bill in late 2001. To solve the fiscal deficit, the PAN and PRD in the Lower Chamber agreed on a special tax of wealth, which included telecommunications services except for local calls. However, the Telmex lobby in the Senate achieved the exclusion of long-distance calls and mobile calls made with prepaid cards, thereby shifting all its effect onto its mobile competitors, who depended more on contracted services.

[53] PAN senator Juan J. Rodriguez Prat and Undersecretary of Energy Planning Armando Jimenez explained the exclusion of privatization based on Fox's electoral promised (personal interviews, October 10 and 7, 2002, respectively).

justifying this position, PRD senator Demetrio Sodi de la Tijera argued that a wholesale market would weaken the state-owned enterprises by taking away rich clients who needed no subsidies. He also emphasized that small- and medium-sized companies had opposed the reform (personal interview, October 7, 2002). The association of small and medium companies, which consumed a third of electricity demand, denounced the proposal, whereas that of large industrialists supported it (CMIC 2002).

The PRI was divided over the reform, but the statist position prevailed. Senator Manuel Barlett presented an alternative bill opposed to private investment in generation and private access to the network while rejecting the wholesale market (personal interview, October 9, 2002). By contrast, another PRI faction led by Senator Genaro Borrego supported the reform, although arguing that it was technically weak and insufficient, as only large users would profit from it (personal interview, October 9, 2002). Despite multiple negotiations with Fox, in the end the PRI official position was against the reform. In a public document dated October 25, 2002, the PRI denounced Fox's bill for "weakening the state role," as well as for "favoring the interest of large consumers, discriminating against the small and medium industry, not transferring benefits for residential users or farmers and putting into public companies the obligation to serve more difficult and expensive markets" (PRI 2002, 18). That is, after the pressure of incumbency ended with its electoral defeat, the PRI returned to its statist roots, as the PJ did in Argentina. The association of electoral defeat with market-oriented reforms facilitated the shunning of neoliberal technocrats.

The electoral value of electricity privatization had already been proved in the 2000 election and was heightened by the salience of the reform, in contrast to the simultaneous reform of telecommunications. Between March and December 2002, an average of three articles appeared each month about electricity reform in *La Jornada* and nine in *El Universal*, including seventeen front-page stories in *La Jornada* and eight in *El Universal* during the peak month of August (see Table 5.2). Moreover, public opinion opposed both privatization and private participation in electricity for fear of price effects (Hernandez 2007, 33–5). A 2002 national survey showed that 60 percent of Mexicans opposed increasing private participation in electricity, while 64 percent opposed privatization and 63 percent thought that private participation would increase prices (Parametría 2002).

With the opposition of the PRD and the PRI, PAN could not win the support of the two-thirds of legislators needed for a constitutional reform.

As a result, legislative deadlock killed the electricity reform, whereas Telmex's influence had killed the telecommunications reform. The 2002 legislative session ended without either of the two reforms reaching the floor, effectively bringing reform efforts to a halt under the Fox administration.

Summary of Postprivatization Regulatory Redistribution

The comparison of regulatory politics in Chile, Argentina, and Mexico in the postprivatization periods illuminates the explanatory power of the main hypotheses on electoral competition and partisanship in the postreform period. Moreover, it generates insights into the effect of institutional legacies from the reform path and the durability of their impact.

In Argentina and Mexico, pragmatic converts adopted privatization reform and remained in power afterward; therefore, institutional legacies were market controlling, and policy makers remained obliged to the original providers, even when subject to intraadministration tensions. They were succeeded by policy makers with different preferences in both countries, however. Subsequently, market-controlling institutions generated concentrated telecommunications markets with providers that sought to maintain the status quo of market dominance. In the Argentine electricity sector, the effect was the opposite, as the privatized market was fragmented and providers preferred market competition, whereas Mexico failed to privatize its electricity sector.

Chilean reformers left a legacy of market-conforming reforms, but their successors were populists who converted out of power and preferred market competition and regulatory dominance. Market-conforming reforms produced a more competitive telecommunications market and generated providers who sought market competition. In electricity, these institutions allowed market concentration, and the main provider sought to keep its market dominance. These differences were reflected in postreform regulatory redistribution in both sectors.

The Argentine and Mexican telecommunications providers – Telefónica and Telecom in the former and Telmex in the latter – and the reformist administrations favored market dominance. This coincidence was reflected in Decree 268/98 in Argentina and the Federal Telecommunications Law in Mexico, both of which established partial liberalization in exchange for investment requirements. In Mexico, Telmex's influence was sufficient to overcome partisan preferences for market competition when it averted a liberalizing reform during the Fox administration. Telefónica and Telecom, by contrast, could not avert Decree 764/00, which followed the market competition preferences of the Alianza administration even when forcing the government to compromise on many issues, suggesting that policy makers were not straightjacketed by the institutional options decided at the time of reforms. By contrast, in the Chilean telecommunications sector, private providers' conflicts, which included judicial litigation, facilitated the outcome of market competition, which also was the government's preference. Providers' influence in the policy process, however, was illustrated by the erosion of partisan discipline during the debate on Law 3A and the need for an agreement between CTC and ENTEL to achieve legislative compromise.

Providers in all three countries also vied with consumers over income redistribution. Telmex was able to avert regulatory transfers to consumers, as the rural development program was paid for by the treasury, and even its delay in price rebalancing was compensated for with extraordinary rents from long-distance service. Similarly, the Chilean treasury paid into the Chilean Telecommunications Development Fund (1994) and its successor (2001). In Argentina, providers' regulatory influence allowed them to achieve regulatory capture through Decrees 2585/91 on price dollarization and 92/97 on price rebalancing. These companies, however, could not avert a national price freeze in 2002 that produced regulatory dominance due to a macroeconomic crisis, which generated strong income effects on consumers in a context of high political volatility. Their prior regulatory capture favored the subsequent shift toward regulatory dominance, as it had contributed to weaken their legitimacy and that of the original institutions established at the time of reform.

Electricity coverage was more extensive than that of telecommunications. In electricity, there were fewer alternative networks, such as mobile technology for telecommunications. These conditions increase the stakes for consumers who fear price effects on their income. These effects explained the PRI return to statism when Fox attempted to liberalize the Mexican electricity sector. In Argentina, providers in a fragmented electricity market preferred market competition, and so did policy makers, even when they disagreed about whether market-controlling or market-conforming measures would best foster this outcome. In Chile, Concertación preferences for market competition encountered Enersis resistance and led to compromise, reducing their impact significantly (as in DS 327) or moderately (as in the Short Law of 2004). Only when the government could act unilaterally, as it did when it sold Colbún or the gas pipelines, did it have an important impact on market structure, which over time reduced the regulatory influence of Enersis in the industry.

Consumers' influence grows (and providers' declines) when high public salience caused by an exogenous shock coincides with competitive elections; high salience by itself could not prevent regulatory capture in Argentine Decree 97/92, which established price rebalancing. Electoral competition in contexts of high public salience produced incentives for politicians to meet consumer demands in order to avoid electoral risks, regardless of partisan preferences. In the postreform period, these incentives reduced the regulatory influence of private providers and facilitated regulatory dominance, as happened in Argentina with ENRE's Resolution 292. This resolution established sanctions that transferred income from providers to consumers, which had a substantive effect on Edesur's bottom line. A similar context of crisis combined with electoral competition allowed the passage of Chilean Law 19,613 in 1999. Even though powerful providers resisted regulatory dominance, the high salience caused by the crisis and the competitiveness of the upcoming presidential election brought incumbents and challengers to agree to request sanctions against providers and compensation for consumers. Yet the effect on providers' bottom line was more immediate in Argentina, where the regulator already had sufficient sanctioning power due to the market-controlling character of the original reform.

Whereas the trends in regulatory redistribution in all three countries support the hypotheses about electoral competition and partisanship, they also provide insights into the effects of original reform choices. The original reform content – market controlling or market conforming – had different effects in each sector. In all cases, though, it shaped the market structure after privatization and therefore the predominant preferences of private providers, who became important policy players in the postreform period. Even though the original reform biased the playing field, it did not necessarily bind politicians forever. Partisan preferences and consumer pressures can help change the market structure. Hence, the policy effects derived from original choices regarding privatization shape regulatory outcomes but do not determine them.

Partisan mechanisms for policy influence subsisted in the postreform period and were still subject to intraadministration conflicts in the case of populists who had adopted market-oriented reforms. These mechanisms, however, were also subject to providers' pressures, including lobbying in

Congress, as in the case of Law 3A and the failed Mexican telecommunications reform for which legislators sided with company proposals; or in the executive, as in the case of Argentine Decree 764/00, when lobbying the Ministry of the Economy facilitated compromise; or in the case of the Chilean electricity Short Law, when government officials were associated with providers. Erosion of partisan discipline, bills resembling providers' proposals, and personal connections with companies are indicators of channels of provider pressure.

Finally, the origin of capital is crucial to understanding Mexican regulatory politics in telecommunications, and it was a consequence of reform content. That the firm controlling Telmex's management was Mexican heightened its policy influence. It made allied experts and PRI politicians more concerned about Telmex's future than they were about companies controlled by foreign owners, who got more attention from neoliberal technocrats. In Argentina, where the original providers were controlled by foreign capital, allied experts were more distrustful of them than were neoliberal technocrats. The origin of capital did not affect regulatory reforms in Chile, however, where domestic companies were sold to foreign investors during the studied period without obvious regulatory effect.

6

A Multilevel Analysis of Market Reforms in Latin American Public Utilities

This book builds on a new generation of comparative studies of Latin American market-oriented reforms that focus both on specific policies and increasingly on those policies' medium-term effects rather than on the adoption of general reform packages.[1] Seeking to understand policy decisions and their consequences for subsequent political dynamics, this study shows that despite the appearance of policy convergence around the privatization of public utilities in Latin America at the end of the twentieth century, political incentives were crucial in explaining the timing and the content of policy decisions in telecommunications and electricity, two technically complex and capital-intensive sectors. This chapter summarizes the empirical findings of the previous four chapters while explaining the advantages provided by the research design of this book to identify causal mechanisms. It concludes by drawing lessons from the effects of electoral competition and partisan linkages in public-utility reform for the more general literature on Latin American policy making. Moreover, it discusses the implications of cross-sectoral reform legacies for our understanding of institutional evolution in the region.

Bringing the Pieces Together in a Multilevel Analysis of Policy Making

The research design used to study public-utility reforms and policy making in the aftermath of these reforms in the preceding chapters is based on

[1] For instance, comparative studies of social security reform include Madrid (2003), Brooks (2008), and Weyland (2006); comparative analyses of labor policies include Murillo (2005), Murillo and Schrank (2005), and Cook (2007). New comparative studies focusing on post-reform effects include Post (2007) for water privatization and O'Neill (2007) for social security.

a multimethod approach that combines a duration analysis of reform adoption with comparative case study research for regulatory content and postreform regulatory redistribution. Whereas this combination permits testing hypothesized effects and their causal mechanisms, increasing the internal validity of results, it limits the explanatory scope of the study to Latin America. The cross-sectoral nature of the study, though, suggests that beyond these two industries, the political dynamics of other public services should be similar. This research design also controls for external financial pressures, technological demands, and institutional constraints in the quantitative analysis while keeping national- and sectoral-level variables constant in the qualitative comparison. The postreform case studies seek both to test the longitudinal explanatory power of the main hypotheses – by allowing variation in the main independent variables keeping the national context constant – and to investigate the medium-term effects of regulatory legacies on policy making.

The study of reform adoption is based on duration analysis of all reform instances in Latin America between 1985 and 2000. Chapter 2 tests the effect of political competition on reform adoption while controlling for important variables reflecting the effect of political institutions, technological demands, external financial constraints, and government ideology. The quantitative analysis does not illuminate the causal mechanisms triggered by the main variables, however. Case studies of electricity and telecommunications reform in Argentina, Chile, and Mexico are used to illuminate these effects on policy makers' incentives to respond to either voters or footloose capital. Case selection allows tracing those effects while controlling for political regime, which shapes the conditions for political competition, including challengers' oversight and capacity to replace incumbents, as well as media coverage. Nondemocratic regimes in Chile and Mexico curtailed political competition and freedom to express dissent. In Argentina, however, political competition varied while democracy was constant, and challengers enjoyed the benefit of a free press.

In Chapter 3, the comparative research method is used to control for variables constant at the national level (such as national institutions) and at the industry level (such as technological differences) while testing the effect of partisan incentives on policy content. The partisan mechanisms driving different choices for regulatory content are traced to constituencies, ideological preferences, and delegation to allied experts, which generated tensions with neoliberal technocrats in the case of populists converted to the market creed. To control for the impact of market size, the case studies based on the three middle-income countries are supplemented by an analysis of electricity and telecommunications reform in two small open economies of Central America: El Salvador and Panama.

Table 6.1 summarizes how the research design points to the impact of reformers' identity as the explanation for the type of regulatory content adopted, regardless of diversity in national institutions and political regime.[2] Populists who had pragmatically converted to the market creed chose market-controlling regulations, and right-wing true believers chose market-conforming ones. Political institutions, thus, are complementary rather than substitutive of partisan arguments, because the former explain constraints and the latter explain preferences. In addition to the general reform patterns in the case studies, the statistically significant correlation between the partisan identity of reformers and reform content in all eighteen Latin American countries presented in Chapter 3 points to the same direction.

Case studies by sector provide controls for the effect of technology, which developed faster in telecommunications than in electricity and has been used to account for sector-level patterns (Levi-Faur 1999; Bartle 2002). Jordana and Levi-Faur (2005) argue, for instance, that the involvement of sectoral experts makes the adoption of regulatory agencies more likely in the same sector in another country than in the same country in another sector. Similarly, studying electricity and telecommunications in the EU, Levi-Faur (1999) emphasizes the effect of different technological characteristics in each sector for explaining the pace of liberalization under EU directives. Yet even though technology shapes the possibilities available to policy makers, providers, and consumers, technological differences cannot account for the choices made regarding regulatory content in the case studies shown in Table 6.1, because reformers chose a similar regulatory content across both sectors in Argentina, Chile, Mexico, El Salvador, and Panama.

External financial pressures, measured in terms of fiscal shortage and Moody's credit ratings, which affect the cost of public borrowing, prompted the conversion of populists to the market and constrained policy makers' options. These pressures vary over time even within the same

---

[2] Thatcher (1999) and Vogel (1996) suggest that national institutions and bureaucratic legacies are crucial to explaining regulatory outcomes in public utilities, whereas Haggard and Kaufman (1992; 1995) suggest that political regime affects macroeconomic policy making in Latin America.

Table 6.1. *Regulatory Content of Public-Utility Reform*

Countries	Electricity			Telecommunications		
	Government	Regime	Type	Government	Regime	Type
Argentina	Populist convert	Democracy	Market controlling	Populist convert	Democracy	Market controlling
Chile	Right-wing	Authoritarian	Market conforming	Right-wing	Authoritarian	Market conforming
Mexico	Populist convert	Authoritarian	Market controlling	Populist convert	Authoritarian	Market controlling
El Salvador	Right-wing	Democracy	Market conforming	Right-wing	Democracy	Market conforming
Panama	Populist convert	Democracy	Market controlling	Populist convert	Democracy	Market controlling

country, but they are not sufficient to explain reform content. Because creditors demanding fiscal resources were less concerned about the fine print of regulatory content, the degree of financial duress does not map well to the type of regulatory content adopted, as shown in Figure 6.1. The lines show the fiscal position of the five countries subjected to case study in this volume, while the points show these countries' Moody's ratings for public bonds, with higher values reflecting better ratings.

Chile decided to pursue privatization reform while not under any financial strain and chose a market-conforming content, against the World Bank's resistance. When Panama and El Salvador decided to privatize telecommunications in 1996, however, both countries were under financial duress, although the pressures were stronger in El Salvador. El Salvador's deficit was 2.5 percent of GDP, and its Moody's rating the following year was a paltry Baa3. Panama's deficit was 0.66 percent of GDP, and it was granted a Baa1 on its bonds the following year. Yet El Salvador chose market-conforming reforms like those adopted by financially flexible Chile, whereas Panama opted for market-controlling reforms like those of Argentina and Mexico, which had similarly adopted telecommunications privatization under harsh financial conditions. In 1990, Argentina's fiscal deficit was 0.35 percent of GDP and Mexico's 2.5 percent, whereas their credit ratings were poor: the former received a B3 in May 1989 and the latter a Ba2 in December 1990. In short, although financial pressures generated incentives for reform adoption, technology defined available

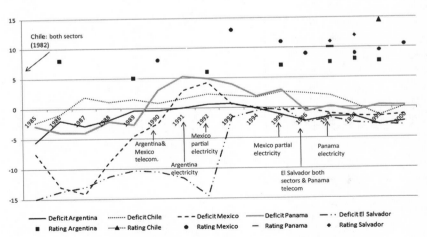

Figure 6.1 Financial Conditions at the Time of Privatization Decision.

options, and institutions shaped opportunities for and constraints on policy makers in charge of reform, these policy makers' agency was crucial in shaping their choices regarding regulatory content.

The historical analysis in Chapters 4 and 5 has two goals: to further test the effects of political competition and partisanship in Argentina, Chile, and Mexico – controlling for national context in the longitudinal comparison of case studies – in the aftermath of reforms and to identify patterns for policy feedback effects derived from the original reforms. In these chapters, the research design controls for the impact of technological differences across both sectors and for regulatory legacies, which were market controlling in Argentina and Mexico and market conforming in Chile. Comparative case studies evaluate the impact of the original institutions adopted at the time of reform to define whether market-oriented reforms generated a critical juncture in terms of subsequent policy making in public utilities by using two dependent variables: (a) regulatory redistribution between consumers and providers and (b) regulatory redistribution between incumbent providers and their competitors.

In the studied cases, political competition continued to generate incentives for politicians to seek redistribution to consumers, regardless of partisan preferences, political institutions, and regulatory legacies. In the postreform period, however, political competition had to be combined with an environment in which regulatory reform had high public salience before politicians would become aware of the electoral risks involved in not considering consumer preferences. Taking redistribution between consumers and providers as a dependent variable, Table 6.2 shows that the combination of political competition and high salience (mostly produced by crises) generated redistribution to consumers in the Argentine electricity (1999 and 2002) and telecommunications (2002) sectors and in the Chilean electricity sector (1999). By contrast, neither salience nor electoral competition alone were sufficient to empower consumers' distributive demands, as shown by the lack of regulatory dominance either in the 1999 Chilean telecommunications sector – despite competitive elections – or in the 1995 Mexican telecommunications sector – despite a macroeconomic crisis. Moreover, neither divided government nor the legacy of regulatory institutions seems to have affected the direction of redistribution.

Table 6.2 also illuminates intersectoral differences. Most instances of regulatory dominance occurred in electricity rather than telecommunications, regardless of relative changes in prices in the two sectors. The more extensive coverage of electricity in all three countries increased the

Table 6.2. *Consumer Pressure for Redistribution of Providers' Income in the Aftermath of Reforms*

Electricity

	Electoral Competition	Salience	Divided Government	Regulatory Legacy	Redistribution
Argentina	Yes (1999 electricity)	Yes (crisis)	Yes	Controlling	Yes (sanctions)
	Yes (2002 crisis)	Yes (crisis)	Yes	Controlling	Yes (price freeze)
Chile	Yes (1999 electricity)	Yes (crisis)	Yes	Conforming	Yes (sanctions)
Mexico					

Telecommunications

	Electoral Competition	Salience	Divided Government	Regulatory Legacy	Redistributoion
Argentina	No	No	No	Controlling	No (price dollarization)
	No	Yes (media)	No	Controlling	No (price rebalancing)
	Yes (2002 crisis)	Yes (crisis)	Yes	Controlling	Yes (price freeze)
Chile	Yes	No	Yes	Conforming	No
Mexico	No	Yes (1995 crisis)	No	Controlling	No (price compensated with long-distance rents)

electoral value of income effects in this sector. Moreover, residential consumers have alternative options in telecommunications – as shown by the faster regional growth of mobile rather than fixed-line phones – but they do not usually have a meaningful choice of their electricity provider. That is, when consumers' market options were reduced, the likelihood of political action grew, suggesting that exit and voice were alternatives, as found long ago by Hirschman (1970).

In the aftermath of reforms, the effect of providers' regulatory influence on policy outcomes weakened the policy impact of partisan incentives more than of those derived from political competition. Partisan preferences continued to respond to constituencies' distributive preferences, policy makers' ideological viewpoints, and their different endowment of allied experts. Yet in the postreform period, partisan preferences were not only subject to political compromise but also to providers' pressures to defend or improve the status quo. As partisan incentives prevailed in an environment of low electoral competition, they were more likely to apply to contexts of low salience in which providers' asymmetry of resources vis-à-vis consumers was greater.

Even when partisan preferences did not direct regulatory outcomes, variation in the partisan identity of the government generated certain expected changes in policy makers' preferences. Pragmatic populist reformers were loyal to first entrants, sustaining preferences for market dominance in the Argentine and Mexican telecommunications sectors while requiring that some of the associated rents be invested in expanding coverage to benefit less well-off constituencies. By contrast, when pragmatic populists had not reformed and converted out of power, they attempted to promote market competition with more success and regulatory dominance with less success in the Chilean telecommunications sector. The right-wing PAN, which had not reformed, tried to promote market competition as well, but it was constrained by the preference of the first entrant (Telmex) for market dominance.

In the studied cases, moreover, regulatory legacies affected the preferences of providers in an unintended way. Telecommunications technology allowed options for technological competition to develop relatively rapidly through alternative networks in a way that electricity technology did not. As a result, in telecommunications, a market-conforming regulatory framework favored market competition, whereas market-controlling regulations facilitated market dominance by the incumbent provider. As electricity remained a monopoly except for all but large users with access to the wholesale market, market-conforming regulations facilitated the un-checked concentration of property and market dominance. By contrast, market-controlling regulations checking property transfers promoted market competition between providers. In sum, the first entrants to priva-tized markets had diverse preferences regarding regulatory redistribution depending on the contingent combination of technology and institutional choices about market structure. Regulatory outcomes, in turn, varied according to the combination of policy makers' and providers' preferences and their capacity to force each other to compromise when they disagreed.

These findings show that whereas the ideology of the incumbent may not have prevented populists from converting to the market creed, it still shaped their regulatory preferences. The relative ideologies of the chal-lenger and incumbent affected the credibility of political competition, while partisan ideological legacies shaped policy choices despite the con-straints imposed by international financial institutions and volatile financial markets. After deploying their capital, private providers acquired a large stake in the status quo, and their regulatory preferences were specific and influential because they had a strong effect on their bottom lines. Their influence constrained partisan policy preferences, especially when reformers were still in power, but it did not erase the effects of partisanship or political competition on the definition of policy makers' preferences.

The Search for Causal Mechanisms

Because political competition and partisanship are crucial variables for a systematic understanding of policy makers' agency, it is important to identify the mechanisms they trigger that shape policy makers' incentives, leading to the studied outcomes. The case studies are crucial for unveiling the causal mechanisms that produced the hypothesized effect (Gerring 2007, 48).[3] Case studies in Chapters 2 through 5 trace the processes that led to particular policy decisions, linking them to causal mechanisms derived from the hypothesized effects.

The concept of political competition includes the incentives generated by marginal differences in power between incumbent and challengers, along with those derived from relative ideology. Its effects include dissuad-ing incumbents, making challengers oppose incumbents, and broadening

---

[3] On the importance of the search for causal mechanisms to explain processes that generate correlations, see Elster (1998), Gerring (2007), and McAdam, Tarrow and Tilly (2001).

the public debate and potential electoral costs for all players. The threat of replacement makes incumbent policy makers afraid of pursuing electorally costly policies, as was the case for PRI politicians when President Zedillo tried to privatize electricity. Challengers take advantage of the opportunity for "monitoring" incumbents by denouncing market reforms, whereas their relative ideology affects their credibility among voters as an alternative to incumbents. In Argentina under Alfonsín, for instance, Peronist legislators had credibility in opposing the privatization of ENTEL due to their previous statist past, even if Peronists would latter privatize the company.

Moreover, political competition heightens the attention paid by incumbents (trying to avoid being unseated) and challengers (eager not to miss their chance) to public-utility reforms. By endogenously raising public salience and broadening the policy debate to include previously unaware voters, it increases the electoral stakes of policy choice (Baumgartner and Jones 1993, 18). The opposition of the PRD and SME in Mexico, for example, contributed to raising the salience of electricity reform to the point of making it affect electoral behavior in the 2000 election.

In the postreform period, political competition in combination with crises generated incentives for regulatory redistribution to consumers by making issues salient and thereby electorally useful to attract marginal voters. The electricity crises of Chile and Argentina in 1999 generated regulatory reforms against providers' preferences because competitive presidential elections were taking place that year, although nonreformers were in power in the former country, and reformers were in charge in the latter. In both cases, incumbents and challengers demanded redistribution to consumers through sanctions and compensation for rationing, regardless of their ideological differences.

Similarly, in the Dominican Republic, after the price of oil went up in 2002 – at the same time that a major banking crisis and currency devaluation were affecting the economy – the government refused to transfer the higher cost of electricity production to consumers. Subsequent blackouts increased public discontent with the distribution company. Facing an upcoming competitive election, President Hipólito Mejía renationalized electricity in October 2004 (paying high-value compensation to providers). His decision was popular because the company was blamed for the blackouts. Mejía was able to use the expansion of coverage and subsidized prices as part of his electoral capital, moreover, although it was not sufficient to get him reelected.

Crises by themselves increased salience and weakened providers' legitimacy, but they did not necessarily bring redistribution to consumers in the absence of electoral competition. The Brazilian 2001 electricity crisis did not bring President Fernando Henrique Cardoso, who had adopted market reforms, to confront providers. Brazilian 2001 blackouts were provoked by drought, although the challenger Workers' Party blamed them on electricity privatization. Rationing weakened support for market reforms but did not provoke any major regulatory reform in the absence of electoral incentives (Ruffin 2002).[4] Instead, the government created a crisis committee and used market mechanisms, such as a rationing quota that could be traded, and a system of surcharges and prizes for heavy residential users, to deal with blackouts (Inter-American Development Bank 2001, 174).

In short, consumers' most useful policy tool was their vote in competitive elections. Their organization was not nearly as effective in compensating for their asymmetry of resources vis-à-vis providers. Organized consumers in Argentina were able to use the media and the judiciary to raise public salience to a much larger extent than their Chilean counterparts. Yet consumers in both countries were more likely to achieve regulatory redistribution when politicians of different partisan persuasions and with diverse roles in the reform process perceived that such a policy would have valuable electoral payoffs.

Partisan preferences, in turn, shaped the regulatory content of reform. Partisanship engenders policy preferences for regulatory content based on its distributive effects on core constituencies, the way in which these effects are perceived by policy makers, and politicians' choices of personnel to delegate technically complex choices. Although true believers and pragmatic converts adopted market reforms, they chose different regulations for the same sectors. Partisan legacies included the viewpoint from which distributive inferences were made. Latin American policy makers inherited shared sets of historical references (especially in their assessment of institutional effects) based on their prior perceptions and experiences. They relied on those schemas in making inferences about policy consequences and in defining their allied experts. Allied experts, in turn,

---

[4] Ruffin (2002, 7) reports that the crisis eroded public support for privatization in Brazil. He writes that in 1998, a majority of Brazilians agreed that privatization was beneficial, but in 2001 negative views prevailed, with the largest group (40% of respondents) being very critical of privatization. Cardoso, though, had won reelection in 1998 with a margin of twenty percentage points over his challenger, and the following elections were more than a year and a half away.

internalized these distributive preferences associated with politicians' constituencies while proposing to politicians the technical options that would satisfy them. As a result, experts were not necessarily homogenizing agents imposing the same technical model across countries. Although they agreed on the possible technical options, they sometimes disagreed about which one to promote based on the short-term consequences of those options. That is, contrary to the literature on the role of Latin American technocrats in bringing about policy convergence, this study shows that technocrats can generate (and justify) diverse regulatory options.

Partisan delegation to experts shaped regulatory content, as shown by the contrast between Guatemalan and Salvadorian true believers and Argentine and Mexican converted populists in the privatization of telecommunications. Guatemalan privatizer Manuel Ayau and Salvadorian Manuel Mena Lagos were committed to free markets and had worked together. Manuel Ayau was influential in the choice of a reform format by Mena Lagos, as he was hired as an advisor to work on the Salvadorian process. In choosing a reform model from Pablo Spiller's proposal, they picked the regulations that would reduce regulatory discretion, such as arbitration, which removed the need for strict price controls and reduced the need of a regulator with discretionary power (Bull 2005, 70–1).

By contrast, allied experts in Argentina and Mexico came to opposite decisions when looking at the pioneer experience of Chile with telecommunications competition, as described in Chapter 5. Argentine CNC head Roberto Catalán referred to Chile's competitive experience when defending gradual liberalization as a tool for preventing concentration and promoting investment in coverage. His defense of partial liberalization resonated remarkably with that of the former Mexican secretary of transportation and communication Carlos Ruíz Sacristán, although teledensity in Chile grew twice as much as in Mexico and one and a half times more than in Argentina in the 1990s.

Politicians also introduce their own bias when interpreting the new information that they receive from experts based on prior experience and ideological legacies. That is, even when political parties changed their policies, the way in which they did so was always partial and contingent on how these policies were presented to them and how they interpreted their options. Thus, policy makers' incentives for changing the status quo were derived from their constituencies and ideology, even when they delegated the methodology to allied experts who "persuaded" them regarding the distributive effects of technical choices.

The immediate price effects on constituencies, for instance, generated diverse preferences for price rebalancing in telecommunications. Chilean reformers undertook price rebalancing before privatization, and by 1994 there was no difference in subscription charges for residential and business users, according to ITU. By contrast, Argentine PJ reformers and their Mexican counterparts delayed price rebalancing and included investment requirements to expand coverage, which were absent in Chile. According to the same source, the business subscription rate in Argentina was three times as large as the residential one until 2000, when competition between providers was allowed. In Mexico, after privatization, the business rate doubled the residential rate until 1996, when long-distance competition was allowed.

Diverse partisan linkages to core constituencies also shaped the distribution of subsidized shares at privatization. In Argentina and Mexico, worker-subsidized shares were administered by the labor union, which designated a director in the board, but they did not benefit military officers as in Chile, where the navy and the army received 10 percent of ownership in CTC and ENTEL, respectively.

Ideological legacies also brought politicians to adopt different views of state institutions. When Brazilian PT president Luiz Inacio Da Silva (Lula) replaced reformer Fernando Henrique Cardoso in 2003, the government changed its regulatory preferences. The Brazilian Workers' Party (PT) used electricity and telecommunications for policy differentiation, emphasizing regulatory control and a proconsumer attitude. In electricity, the PT government "implemented a new model based on a mixture of public and private investment under close government control and supervision." Rufin and Romero describe this model: "The key measures, specified in two government decrees, have been the substantial demise of the wholesale market in favor of a single-buyer system for distributors, the use of long-term contracts to attract private capital for the construction of facilities planned by a new government entity, and a renewed role for public funding and construction of generation facilities through the federal development bank (BNDES) and the federal electricity company (Eletrobras), respectively" (2005, 23).

In telecommunications, the PT had criticized privatization and the fragmentation of the Telebras monopoly, as well as the independence of the regulatory agency (Rhodes 2006, 123–6). At the onset of Lula's first administration, the new Brazilian minister of communications and many other government authorities put pressure on the regulatory agency to use a different index for price rebalancing. When the agency followed preexisting rules, the minister went to the media and encouraged consumers to challenge the regulatory agency's decision in court (Rossi de Oliveira 2003).

Finally, the effect of institutional legacies was conditional on the technological development of alternative networks, and it affected the advantages of first entrants in the privatized markets. Where institutional legacies allowed property concentration, they facilitated the emergence of dominant players with incentives to resist competition in order to keep their initial rents. This effect, however, was not homogenous across sectors. It was conditional on technological alternatives and institutional legacies of the original reform content. The emergence of dominant players slanted the field of subsequent policy making by imposing diverse baselines for policy makers, regardless of their preferences. Remarkably, these effects held when the regulatory structure varied quite dramatically, as in Argentina (with the CNT becoming the CNC and multiple takeovers of the agency by the executive), and when it was quite stable, as in Chile, despite the fact that regulators were political appointees. This effect, however, was not necessarily path dependent, in the sense that policy makers' preferences could change the market structure, though the diverse paths of initial privatization created difficulties in doing so.

Political Incentives and Latin American Policy Making

Financial pressures led incumbents to adopt market-oriented reforms regardless of their ideological preferences, but popular views on macroeconomic stabilization and structural reforms differed even if these policies were bundled together. Weyland (2002a) shows that hyperinflation generated popular support for market-oriented reforms, and Remmer (2003) and Lora and Olivera (2005) demonstrate the negative electoral impact of inflation in Latin America since the 1980s – and the negative effect of structural reforms in the latter case. As politicians wanted to avert the short-term costs of market reforms on their electoral survival, they bundled together macroeconomic stabilization and structural reforms such as privatization.

The effects of policy bundling were dual. On the one hand, privatization (especially in public utilities, due to the value of assets) facilitated stabilization by providing fiscal revenue that replaced seigniorage as trade liberalization generated competition on prices. On the other hand, the popularity of lowering inflation was explicitly associated with less popular market-oriented reforms in the hope that institutional changes would produce subsequent modifications of economic behavior and expectations. That is, reform advocates expected that as the Latin American public observed the better functioning of public services – especially in access and quality – or the improved access to imported goods that followed market reforms such as privatization and trade liberalization, they would be persuaded of the value of these reforms in their daily lives. Argentine technocrat Domingo Cavallo exemplifies this view:

As a political strategy when I was appointed minister of the economy, I merged the Ministry of Public Works into a single Ministry of Economy and Public Works so as to link the convertibility with privatization, economic liberalization, and improvements in economic efficiency. That is, all the reforms were linked to inflation, and this link facilitated the support of public opinion and Congress. . . . I did not look at public opinion surveys, because if you ask the people if they are in favor of privatization, they oppose. It is necessary to ask about service, quality, and access. The decision of how to improve efficiency is made by policy makers, not the people. The means are chosen by the policy maker. The people want to improve access and quality but do not know how. The [public] opinion on privatization results from an ideological campaign developed in the late 1980s. Once the reform takes place and results can be observed, the people support it (personal interview, May 6, 2003).

The interaction between political competition and crises' effects on policy legitimacy, which shaped policy making in public utilities, therefore has broader implications. Powerful first entrants shaped the legitimacy of market reforms and facilitated the erosion of public support when these policies faced subsequent crises. The high economic volatility of the region continued after market-oriented reforms, increasing the risks of crises and shortening politicians' time horizons. Henisz and Zelner (2005) identify the effect of crisis in eroding the legitimacy of new market-oriented institutions, which lack sufficient time for consolidation in the developing world. Political competition is crucial, however, to providing incentives for viable politicians to attempt regulatory redistribution at the expense of private investors when crises increase consumer stakes and attention. It is the combination of consumer monitoring with electoral payoffs that makes politicians respond to crises by shifting the blame to providers or taking credit for promoting regulatory redistribution as a solution.

These findings contribute to the literature on new Latin American democracies, which suggests that newly enfranchised citizens had their policy influence curtailed to applauding or throwing away the incumbent, with a consequent decline in politicians' accountability and public enthusiasm for democracy.[5] This literature recognizes the "vertical accountability" of politicians to voters in fixed-term presidential systems but emphasizes the weakness of "horizontal accountability" (O'Donnell 1994) or even suggests that there is only retrospective accountability based on the performance of politicians who may have lied in their electoral campaigns (Stokes 2001).

This book finds that electoral mechanisms are more useful to consumers than self-organization, and not because market-oriented reforms weaken consumers' capacity for collective action, as argued by Oxhorn and Ducatenzeiller (1998) or Kurtz (2004) more generally. Consumers were more organized in Argentina than in Chile and Mexico, and the timing of democratization is probably the best explanation for this difference, as argued by Rhodes (2006). Votes were more influential than consumer organization in achieving regulatory redistribution to consumers, however, because providers had an easier time than did consumers in organizing their policy influence.

The Argentine consumer associations, born mostly as a result of market-oriented reforms, were able to heighten public salience and promote judicial injunctions, thereby serving as monitoring "fire alarms" (McCubbins and Schwartz 1984). They therefore contributed to fostering what Peruzzotti and Smulovitz (2006) called "societal accountability" by increasing the public salience of an issue – what Peruzzotti and Smulovitz call "exposing and denouncing" it – and including it on the public agenda. Yet the effectiveness of this strategy is conditioned on the political consequences for public officials failing to react to public pressure, as Peruzzotti and Smulovitz argue more generally for other forms of societal accountability based on nongovernmental organizations and media actions in Latin America (2006, 16). Hence, even in Argentina, where consumers' organization was strong, their influence was heightened when it could be channelled through votes.

This book also contributes to the literature on partisan policy making in Latin America. The fact that governments of different ideological

---

[5] Hagopian (2005) shows that the third wave of democratization was the broadest and longest in the region, with very few setbacks (notably Peru and Haiti), and yet has been accompanied by profound citizen dissatisfaction with democratic performance. Public opinion, though, supported democracy as the best form of government, even when it was dissatisfied with its performance, whereas this disappointment decreased when the economies of the region improved after 2002 (Latinobarometro 2005).

traditions adopted market reforms in Latin America during the last two decades of the twentieth century gives fodder to arguments about the end of partisan policy making. Across the region, incumbents adopted market reforms whether they were right-wing true believers or pragmatic populist converts. Because politicians adopted free-market policies whether they had promised these or populist policies in their electoral campaigns, it has often been assumed that they also changed their parties' policy preferences (Corrales 2002). There is evidence, however, that presidents' who converted to free-market preferences made no effort to extend these preferences to the party rank-and-file in Argentina (Levitsky 2003), and that they failed to do so in Mexico (Baena Paz 2003; Reveles Vazquez 2003), which explains the subsequent return to statist roots of the PJ and the PRI.

Some blame the lack of consistent partisan policy making in Latin America on political parties that, traditionally, had been more ideologically fluid and patronage-prone than their European counterparts (Conniff 1999; Foweraker et al. 2003). Others point to weakly institutionalized party systems and fragile democratic institutions to explain the lack of accountability for politicians' campaign promises and party labels (O'Donnell 1994, 64; Mainwaring and Scully 1995, 25). For still others, the apparent lack of consistency in parties' policy making in Latin America is not a regional malaise but a worldwide epidemic: the literature on globalization heralds the end of partisan policy preferences as all governments move toward implementing the same policies in order to attract footloose capital (Strange 1996; Simmons 1999). This study shows that partisan preferences mattered for Latin American public-utility policy making, however, even in a period characterized by an apparent convergence toward market-oriented reforms.

In stressing the importance of partisan preferences for shaping the content of technically complex microeconomic policies, moreover, this study contributes to the emerging literature showing the effects of partisan policy making on the distribution of public and private goods in Latin America. Remmer (2002), Kaufman and Segura Ubiergo (2001), and Huber et al. (2008) identify partisan policy making in macroeconomic and social policies in Latin America. Rosas (2005) shows the importance of economic policies for defining interparty competition in the late 1990s.[6] Calvo and Murillo (2004) and Magaloni, Diaz Cayeros, and Estevez (2007)

---

[6] Using surveys of legislators in 1997, he shows that economic policies explain ideological positions in interparty competition in Argentina, Bolivia, Chile, Costa Rica, Mexico, and Uruguay.

242

demonstrate that political parties can generate distributive expectations to keep their partisan loyalties by using both private and public goods.

In short, partisan policy preferences did not disappear in late-twentieth-century Latin America. Even in the ideologically fluid Latin American parties, partisan policy preferences subsisted amid policy convergence caused by the pressure of capital scarcity. Even if all governments adopt reforms with the same label, it matters who the incumbent is who pursues such policies, thanks to the citizens' choice in the ballot box. This effect, however, is conditional upon having an incumbent who carries partisan legacies, as shown by the difficulties in coding reforms under President Alberto Fujimori in Peru, discussed in Chapter 3. In the new century, the crisis of political parties in the Andean countries has provoked the emergence of new political organizations with few ties to the past and therefore made legacies less useful in defining the preferences of governing coalitions.

Policy Feedback Effects and Weak Institutions

In the studied cases, policy feedback effects resulting from the interaction between the original reform content and interindustry differences in technological development were not necessarily path dependent. Institutional choices slanted the playing field, generating different market structures and thereby diverse stakes for the first entrants to these privatized sectors. These effect, however, were contingent on the technological availability of alternative networks in each sector. The original institutional choices underwent both incremental and dramatic modifications, and their provisions were not always enforced. Whereas Argentina imposed a regulatory turnaround in electricity after the 2002 crisis, Chilean policy makers incrementally changed the governance of their electricity sector. By contrast, in Mexico, the power of Telmex, itself the result of rules that fostered the company's market dominance, explains the failure of telecommunications reform under Fox and therefore institutional resilience. Weak enforcement is another mechanism that shapes regulatory effects. Whereas the independence of the Argentine CNT was guaranteed in its bylaws and the selection mechanism for the members of its board, a takeover by the government in order to impose its preferred regulations demonstrated that the CNT's informal regulatory independence was weak. Similarly, in Mexico, although there were no formal limits on local competition after privatization, the secretary of communication systematically refused licenses for Telmex competitors, producing a de facto monopoly in that market for the first years after privatization.

Theories of institutional development that do not account for institutional weakness cannot explain the coexistence of both incremental and dramatic change, as well as de facto change through variation in enforcement. The durability produced by mechanisms of reproduction driven by institutional effects usually assumes strong institutions.[7] Even though the Latin American public-utility reforms were adopted in response to common financial incentives and followed the Chilean experience of privatization, as argued by Weyland (2006) for social security privatization, their subsequent evolution involved diverse circumstances and produced varied outcomes. Institutional evolution seems to have followed relative changes in power distribution and, as a result, resource asymmetries between private providers and consumers generated more dramatic instances of regulatory capture and dominance than they would have in a context of stronger institutions.

The Latin American literature recognizes problems of weak institutionalization in the region, and the historical analysis of institutions emphasizes the path dependence of coalitional effects.[8] In Latin America, thus, the sustainability of institutions, and even the enforcement of their powers, has depended on the continous capacity of coalitions to impose and sustain these rules. The lessons of findings on policy feedback effects in Latin America therefore are that the mechanisms of reproduction identified for the advanced countries by historic institutionalism, such as the mobilization of clienteles or the adaptation of strategies to the new rules of the game, do not necessarily work in the same way in Latin American public utilities.

In short, this study contributes to our understanding of political influence by Latin American citizens of new democracies, and it clarifies domains and mechanisms for partisan policy influence when policy makers are constrained either by capital scarcity or by the fear of investment withdrawal. It also illuminates policy feedback effects, allowing us to assess the effect of technological alternatives (and market options for consumers) on providers' influence over regulators as well as the impact of a context of institutional weakness on the durability of institutional effects.

---

[7] See Levitsky and Murillo (2009) for a critique of that literature on missing the impact of weak institutions on institutional development.

[8] Mainwaring and Scully (1995), O'Donnell (1994), Munck (2004), Weyland (2002b), Levitsky and Murillo (2009), and Helmke and Levitsky (2006) discuss weak institutionalization in the region. Collier and Collier (1991) and Mahoney (2003) provide good examples of historical analysis of critical junctures based on coalitional path dependency.

244

7

Conclusion

In analyzing public-utility reform under conditions of capital scarcity, this book demonstrates the effects of electoral competition and incumbent partisanship on Latin American public-utility reform. Electoral competition weakened the effect of the financial pressures that made incumbents adopt privatization and other market-friendly policies. When financial pressures prevailed in the absence of electoral competition, the partisan identity of reformers shaped the regulatory design of public-utility reforms. Extending the analysis longitudinally, this study also shows how electoral competition and incumbent partisan preferences, along with the industrial organization of privatized sectors, have shaped postprivatization regulatory redistribution between market actors.

The financial pressures generated by capital scarcity in the 1990s induced incumbent administrations to adopt market-friendly policies in Latin America except where electoral competition generated countervailing incentives. Incumbents perceived increasing electoral competition as signaling both discontent with the market-friendly policies they had adopted to please international financial markets and the rising viability of challengers. The credibility of challengers as carriers of a policy alternative to voters, however, depends on their ideology, which serves as a reputation mechanism for signaling prospective policies. The challenger's ideological position relative to the incumbent signals his or her policy credibility – challengers to the right of the incumbent are less credible in proposing alternatives to market-friendly policies. This insight is an important contribution to the literature on electoral policy effects, which focuses mostly on the ideology of incumbents.

The financial pressures generated by increasing capital mobility, especially when governments are cash strapped, weaken partisan policy differences, because incumbents with different ideological preferences are forced into pursuing the same policies to generate capital inflows. However, partisan preferences still shape the regulatory content of microeconomic policies based on the distributive consequences of different regulatory designs on party constituencies, as well as on the ideological frames within which politicians interpret institutional choices and on their delegation to different sets of experts. The role of experts, usually assumed to be responding to homogenizing epistemic communities, is crucial in explaining these partisan differences in regulatory design.

Finally, this study contributes to the literature on regulation by providing testable hypotheses about the direction of redistribution to market actors generated by different regulatory choices. By looking at the electoral and partisan incentives of policy makers and the way in which the industrial organization derived from original privatization reforms later shapes providers' preferences, it suggests four possible scenarios regarding the direction of redistribution between first-entrant private providers and their competitors, and between private providers and consumers.

This book's findings contribute to our understanding of policy making under the constraints created by increasing capital mobility, which are heightened by capital scarcity. Because Latin America was a capital-poor region, the conditions engendered by capital scarcity at the end of the twentieth century heightened the pressures and incentives generated by international financial markets favoring the adoption of market-friendly policies. Under other conditions, however, capital scarcity can generate pressure for convergence toward different policies – as shown by the shift toward the nationalization of financial systems in capital-rich countries in 2008. Even if financial constraints apparently erased partisan policy differences in Latin America at the end of the twentieth century, we should expect electoral and partisan effects to heighten when financial constraints decline. This seems to have been the case in Latin America when the commodities boom at the onset of the new century reduced the impact of international financial markets on domestic policy making.[1]

Electricity and telecommunications, as capital- and technology-intensive sectors consumed by broad sections of the population, provide ideal cases to test the tension between international financial constraints and domestic political incentives on incumbent administrations. This book's lessons should apply to other developing regions exposed to the pressures of

---

[1] This effect has been noted by Post (2007), Benton (2007), Weyland (2008), Kaufman (2008), and Murillo, Oliveros, and Vaishnav (forthcoming).

246

international markets and even to advanced industrial nations suffering deep financial constraints, as well as to other policy areas with broad effects on the population that have undergone market-friendly reforms. Further testing should confirm the systematic effects implied by this book in other policy areas and regions.

The Policy Effects of Electoral Competition under Conditions of Capital Scarcity

Analyzing contexts where capital scarcity constrains domestic policy making, this book shows that high levels of electoral competition, which depends on the viability and credibility of challengers, restrained policy makers from adopting policies designed to attract capital inflows by focusing politicians on middle-class consumers as swing voters.[2] The emphasis on credible electoral competition points to the importance of challenger ideology in contributing to a literature that, although incorporating the effect of international markets, has mostly focused on incumbent ideology.

The literature on macroeconomic policy making in advanced democracies points to the effect of increasing capital mobility in constraining domestic policy pressures derived from electoral competition and partisanship. Although electoral and partisan cycles in macroeconomic policy making were originally theorized more than three decades ago, and despite the addition of rational expectations to these theories (e.g., Alesina 1987), there is still no empirical consensus on whether partisan or electoral incentives prevail in advanced democracies when it comes to macroeconomic policy making (Franzese 2002a).[3] There is a consensus, however, that increasing capital mobility weakens domestic political pressures on monetary and fiscal policies.[4] Clark (2003, 170), for instance, finds support for

---

[2] The middle class is associated with an economic definition regarding its position in the distribution of income around the median but not with the sociological aspects of certain consumption and wealth patterns. Both definitions may not coincide for certain Latin American countries.

[3] Tufte's (1978) seminal article started the literature on electoral cycles of macroeconomic policy making in political science, while Hibbs (1977) played that role for the studies on partisan cycles.

[4] This literature also emphasizes the interaction of electoral and partisan incentives with those generated by domestic economic institutions (such as independent central banks and the organization of labor) and by political institutions (such as the electoral system and the number of parties in the government) (Franzese 2002b).

electoral rather than partisan effects on macroeconomic policy making through monetary expansion only when central banks are not independent and when capital mobility and fixed exchange rates have not eroded national monetary policy autonomy. Boix (2000), for his part, shows a decline over time in partisan effects for monetary and fiscal policy in advanced democracies due to the constraints imposed by increasing capital mobility.[5]

Although the literature on advanced democracies agrees about the constraints imposed by capital mobility on domestic macroeconomic policy making, Boix (1998) argues that political parties retain differences when it comes to microeconomic policy making, especially with respect to public investment in human and physical capital, taxation of high-income earners, privatization, and labor market policies.[6] By contrast, students of Latin American policy making find that partisan differences in macroeconomic and microeconomic policies eroded at the end of the twentieth century when incumbents pursued market-oriented reforms independently of their partisan identity, because the 1980s debt crisis heightened the financial constraints imposed by capital mobility.[7]

The combination of capital scarcity and balance of payments crises, produced by the 1980s debt crisis in Latin America, encouraged capital account liberalization, thereby deepening the constraining effects of capital mobility on partisan policy preferences.[8] The monetization of fiscal deficits produced very high inflation while depressing growth, creating an opportunity to replace previous policies of import substitution industrialization

---

[5] His work on partisan effects controls for the effects of an independent central bank and wage-bargaining institutions, as suggested by Iversen's research (1999). By contrast, Garrett (1998) suggests that despite capital mobility, partisan effects produce different macroeconomic outcomes, so that economic performance is better in countries with centralized wage bargaining and left-wing governments or with decentralized wage bargaining and right-wing governments.

[6] Recent studies of privatization in advanced economies, however, find that partisan differences regarding privatization policy eroded in the 1990s (Schneider et al. 2005) and are weakened by fiscal constraints (Obinger and Zohlnhofer 2005).

[7] See, e.g., Roberts (2008) for a general argument on partisan convergence on macroeconomic policies, Crisp and Johnson (2003) for the lack of effect of incumbent ideology on the adoption of structural reforms, and Biglaiser and Brown (2003) for a similar argument regarding privatization. See Stallings (1992) for an early formulation on the impact of international financial markets on domestic policy making in the aftermath of the Latin American debt crisis.

[8] In the wake of a balance of payments crisis, holders and generators of foreign exchange favor capital account liberalization because it provides an exit option against future government intervention, whereas it allows the government to increase its credibility vis-à-vis financial markets (Haggard and Maxfield 1996, 215).

248

with new policies embedded in monetarist principles. The attractiveness of these policies to Latin American politicians lay in their promises to control inflation and restore fiscal solvency while reopening access to international financial markets.[9] Latin America was amply rewarded by international financial markets during the 1990s, when country after country popped onto Wall Street screens as "emerging markets" attracting capital inflows.[10]

Taking into account the policy constraints created by international financial markets in Latin America at the end of the twentieth century, this book shows how viable and credible electoral competition weakens the policy effects derived from these financial constraints. Incumbents perceive declining electoral support as a sign of discontent with the policies they are adopting in response to capital scarcity. The ability of challengers to attract discontented voters, however, depends on their electoral viability and their credibility as carriers of a policy alternative. Challengers' ideology relative to incumbents is crucial in defining such credibility: only parties to the left of the incumbent based on their prior policy record can credibly criticize market-oriented policies. Identifying the role of challenger ideology in shaping the policy effects of electoral competition in the context of capital scarcity provides an important insight to the literature on electoral and partisan policy cycles, which focuses almost solely on the ideology of incumbents.[11]

The literature on electoral and partisan cycles takes for granted the salience of macroeconomic policies, but salience may vary across policy issues and even within policy issues across time. Due to the enormous flow of information received daily by politicians and voters, public attention is crucial to mobilize apathetic voters and generate electoral incentives. Its impact may be heightened by exogenous shocks or by the type of distributive policy consequences on a particular electoral coalition (Baumgartner and Jones 1993, 2005). When salience is high, electoral competition weakens the impact of financial pressures and the policy influence of

---

[9] Similarly, in explaining the spread of Keynesian ideas, Peter Hall (1989) emphasizes their resonance with immediate public problems and their impact on politicians' goals.

[10] In response to these policies, net autonomous capital inflows to the region grew from a negative U.S.$16.8 billion in 1985 to positive U.S.$62.3 billion in 2000 after peaking at U.S.$89.1 billion in 1997, according to CEPAL (2007).

[11] Kitschelt (2001), however, points to the location of challengers in analyzing the incentives of Western European social democratic parties to adopt unpopular pension reform in Europe.

partisan core constituencies, because it increases the incentives to bid for swing voters.[12]

In short, this study confirms the constraining effects of capital scarcity on domestic policy making. The effects generated by capital scarcity are counteracted, however, by the domestic incentives generated by electoral competition, which involves both electoral viability and ideological credibility for voters who are discontent with the policies pushed for by international financial markets. The fundamental tension for policy makers is between the pressures derived from (mostly external) wealth and the incentives generated by domestic voters.

Partisan Policy Makers, Allied Experts, and Regulatory Design

Although confirming that financial pressures brought Latin American governments of different partisan persuasions to adopt market-friendly policies in public utilities, this book also demonstrates how the partisan identity of incumbents shaped the regulatory content – and distributive consequences – of these microeconomic policies. Hence, the appearance of partisan convergence hides the importance of institutional choices as the locus for partisan distributive conflict.

The empirical findings of this study confirm, as we have seen, that the ideology of incumbents had no effect on the adoption of privatization policies in public utilities under the pressure of capital scarcity. However, partisan preferences did shape the regulatory design of the microeconomic policies adopted to attract capital inflows. Incumbents' prior policy records generate electoral coalitions with diverse distributive preferences, ideological frameworks (which politicians use as cues when updating their own understanding of technical ideas), and linkages with diverse sets of experts, to whom policy makers delegate complex technical choices. Each of these affects the choices made regarding the regulatory content of policies that carry the same name but have different distributive consequences.

In revealing partisan policy effects in the technically complex and capital-intensive public utilities, this study points to a previously neglected mechanism: the role of allied experts, who explain to politicians the benefits of diverse technical choices. Whereas the institutionalist literature on

---

[12] Swing voters, in turn, depend on the electoral rules, as shown by McGillivray (2003).

advanced countries emphasizes incentives derived from professional communities and bureaucratic careers, in Latin America experts' career trajectories do not necessarily go through the civil service but through political appointments – at least before privatization. After privatization, private-sector careers became available to them, generating new incentives for regulatory capture that were similar to those pointed to by the literature on "revolving doors" and regulatory capture by special interests in the United States.[13] Hence, career incentives for experts may generate divergence within a single professional community.

Politicians' constituencies have different distributive preferences based on their market power. Politicians internalize these preferences to sustain their constituents' political support. The prior policies of a political party, which have nurtured its ties to constituencies, also generate an ideological legacy that affects policy makers' interpretation of technical ideas about institutional development. Policy makers' ideas carry normative views that shape their cognitive understanding of technical choices explained by experts. As a result, even when allied experts used their cognitive discourse to persuade politicians of the benefits of technical decisions, they needed to do so in terms of politicians' normative views (in turn shaped by their electoral coalitions). Therefore, delegation to allied experts – even when driven by asymmetries of information – reinforced the effect of constituencies' distributive preferences and ideological frameworks, because career incentives aligned experts' goals with those of policy makers at the time of market reforms.

In Latin America, the linkage between politicians and experts is crucial to understanding partisan influences on regulatory policy content in public utilities and suggests that a different dynamic for policy making holds there than in advanced democracies. Sectoral bureaucracies, which were deemed crucial for the institutionalist literature on public-utility reform in advanced countries, did not provide the crucial technical players in Latin America. Steve Vogel's (1996) study of telecommunications reform in Japan and the United Kingdom suggests – like this book – that state actors rather than organized interests had the reform initiative, which although labeled as "deregulation" in both countries led to differences in regulatory substance. Vogel argues that in the United Kingdom, the treasury, the

---

[13] For a summary of the literature on regulatory capture by special interests, see Levine and Forrence 1990. Weingast (1981) provides a model explaining regulatory subsystems involving "iron triangles" of legislators, regulators, and organized interests while suggesting conditions that weakened their influence.

Department of Trade and Industry, and Oftel bureaucrats had agendas that led to privatization and network competition. In Japan, the different policy orientation of bureaucrats in the administration reform council (Rinchō), the Ministry of Finance, and the Ministry of Post and Telecommunications explains a diverse pattern of reform. Similarly, Thatcher (1999) accounts for divergent patterns of telecommunications reform in France and Britain based on the legacy of 1960s reforms among the bureaucracies in charge of telecommunications. These reforms generated different preferences and capacities among each set of national bureaucracies, and thereby different reform paths.

Whereas the institutionalist literature on public-utility reform in advanced democracies emphasizes the role of state bureaucrats (as carriers of policy orientation) to explain diversity in the regulatory design of reforms, this book shows that politically appointed experts were the crucial technical players in Latin America. The weakness of Latin America bureaucracies – especially at the higher levels where reform decisions were made – increases the policy relevance of policy makers' ideas and those of the politically appointed experts they delegate decisions to. In a region where the average tenure of ministers was barely longer than a year and half during the 1990s (Martinez-Gallardo forthcoming), the sectoral experts in charge of technical choices face shorter time horizons than career bureaucrats in advanced democracies and are also more dependent on political appointments for career advancement. Their professional incentives therefore generate incentives for internalizing politicians' distributive preferences.

By building on career incentives, this argument contributes to our understanding of epistemic communities. Earlier studies of Latin American technocrats emphasized the linkages of U.S.-trained technocrats with their peers in international financial institutions and Wall Street, as well as between themselves, to explain their increasing policy influence in the region.[14] This study identifies different kinds of experts and associates them with the politicians who decide on their tenure based on prior partisan linkages or their value in signaling commitment toward

---

[14] This literature builds on Haas (1992) and was best exemplified in Latin America by the volume edited by Centeno and Silva (1998). Dominguez (1996) added political skills to the technical expertise of technocrats but did not question the assumption about the homogenizing effects of epistemic communities. The work of Sarah Babb (2001) moved this analysis forward by investigating the different ideas of Mexican experts and tracing them to diverse training and intraparty coalitions within the PRI-dominated bureaucracy.

the policies preferred by international financial markets.[15] Epistemic communities generated common cognitive discourses among experts. In Latin America at the time of market-oriented reforms, however, experts' professional incentives involved linkages defined by diverse normative ideas and prior career paths, which contributed to shaping the regulatory design of the studied policies. Admittedly, in the postprivatization period, the emergence of private-sector career options has reduced experts' reliance on political appointments for developing their careers while facilitating their capture by regulated companies. This finding resonates with the literature on regulatory capture in the United States, which also explores the effect of regulators' career incentives on regulatory outcomes. In both periods, therefore, experts can follow career options that should lead them to diverge from a common cognitive discourse, even while being limited by the ideational constraints imposed by epistemic communities.

To conclude, in understanding the diverse mechanisms that drive partisan shaping of institutional choices, this book goes beyond the usual emphasis on coalitional configuration and ideological commitments by focusing on the role of allied experts. The historic institutionalist literature on public-utility reforms in advanced democracies assumes bureaucratic autonomy, which explains bureaucrats' crucial agency in the process.[16] By contrast, Latin American technical decisions were made by experts who owed their tenure to political linkages at the time of reform. Whereas in the postreform period private career options compete with political linkages, both processes may generate a divergent view from the cognitive discourse established by epistemic communities.

The Politics of Redistributive Regulation: Lessons from Public Utilities

Longitudinal analysis of the pre- and postreform periods provides for variation in electoral competition and partisanship within the same national

---

[15] Schneider (1998) emphasizes the importance of signaling international creditworthiness when appointing these technocrats.

[16] Even in advanced democracies, Carpenter (2001) argues, civil service conditions are not sufficient to generate bureaucratic autonomy. Using the experience of the United States, he maintains that bureaucratic autonomy entails the combination of unique organizational capacities and political legitimacy embedded in cross-cutting political and social networks that reduce bureaucrats' dependence on elected officials. Huber and Shipan (2002), instead, argue that bureaucratic autonomy is conditional on politician's delegation, which in turn is associated with the alignment of their preferences.

institutional contexts while generating comparative hypotheses explaining the direction of regulatory redistribution. The economic literature on regulation does not provide clear predictions about the direction or magnitude of redistribution once Stigler's (1971) assumption of producer dominance is abandoned.[17] Similarly, the political science literature on regulation emphasizes the predominant channels for policy influence during the regulatory process (including regulators' career incentives) but does not provide predictions about the direction of redistribution.[18] The hypotheses proposed here can serve as a comparative tool for understanding other instances of regulatory redistribution by looking at policy makers' preferences based on political incentives and providers' preferences resulting from the industrial structure of each sector.

To understand postreform regulatory choices, this study focuses on four categories of regulatory redistribution between first-entrant providers and their competitors and between providers and consumers. Regulatory capture involves redistribution from consumers to first entrants, whereas market dominance entails redistribution from competitors to first entrants. First entrants lose, however, under regulatory dominance, when consumers benefit, and under market competition, when competitors win from redistribution. These four scenarios, which characterize the direction rather than the magnitude of regulatory redistribution, vary in their likelihood depending on the political incentives of policy makers and the preferences of private providers.

In the postprivatization period, the preferences of residential consumers are crucial in contexts of high salience and electoral competition. Electoral competition in combination with high salience – which is defined by a public attentive to the issue – generates regulatory dominance. High salience reduces the cost of monitoring regulators for residential consumers,

---

[17] Becker (1985) assumes that competition will reduce redistribution through regulation because rents are offset by deadweight costs, but there is empirical evidence of regulatory redistribution. Pelzman (1976) has a more nuanced model that includes the incentives of politicians/voters and regulated companies to capture the regulatory process, emphasizing organizational costs and benefits, but the model remains unspecified regarding predictions on the direction of redistribution.

[18] Wilson (1980), for instance, provides four different scenarios depicting the politics of regulation in the United States, but he does not provide testable hypotheses about the direction of redistribution through regulatory outcomes. Wilson (1980) and Weingast (1981) point to conditions that shape the bargaining power between business and consumers but not between businesses, such as in redistribution between first-entrant private providers and their competitors. Noll (1989), though, argues for the need to measure not just the stakes but also the gains in regulation.

whereas electoral competition makes politicians of diverse partisan persuasions coincide in seeking to attract possible swing voters among residential consumers.[19] Otherwise, the preferences of private providers and policy makers are critical in defining the possible regulatory outcomes.

Private providers' preferences are shaped by the industrial organization of the sector (either telecommunications or electricity in this study). In turn, the industrial organization results from the regulatory design chosen at the time of reform. This effect is different across the two studied sectors due to their diverse paths of technological innovation (and thereby access to alternative networks). The industrial organization of the sector affects the stakes, resources, and coordination of private providers in a particular sector. Concentrated industries favor providers' preference for market dominance, whereas industry fragmentation makes it more likely that private providers will prefer market competition. Hence, policy feedback effects derived from the original regulatory design and shaping regulatory outcomes were stronger on market outcomes affecting the industrial organization of the sector than on the working of regulatory agencies. Private providers' preferences, however, do not define regulatory outcomes by themselves: they interact with those of policy makers.

Partisanship continues to shape the preferences of incumbent policy makers in the postreform period unless they were responsible for the adoption of the market-oriented reforms. If they were the reformers, their ties to first entrants prevail due to reputational mechanisms (and probably rents generated during the reform process), which brings them to prefer either market dominance or regulatory capture, depending on their partisan ties. By contrast, for incumbent policy makers who have not introduced market-friendly reforms, partisanship explains their preferences for market competition (if right-wing) or a combination of regulatory dominance and market competition (if former populists).

In the absence of electoral competition, regulatory capture is more likely in cases in which the industry is concentrated and reforming policy makers are still in power. The probability of market dominance increases in cases of concentrated industry when reforming populist policy makers are in power. Market competition is more likely when the industry is fragmented and policy makers have not reformed – although if they are populists, it should be accompanied by efforts at regulatory dominance.

---

[19] Levine and Forrence (1990) similarly proposed that high salience reduced the costs of monitoring for the general public and therefore cut the "slack" of regulators favoring "general interest" regulation, but they do not consider the effects of electoral competition.

By clarifying the conditions that affect the regulatory leverage of first entrants in the privatization process, the focus on policy makers' incentives and private providers' preferences provides a testable argument regarding postprivatization patterns of regulatory redistribution.[20] This contribution is important, because prior instances of regulatory capture may have a cumulative effect on public opinion that shapes perceptions about the legitimacy of the new institutions and even private providers (Henisz and Zelner 2003).

In sum, electoral competition and partisanship had systematic effects on postprivatization regulatory redistribution, along with the industrial organization of privatized sectors, therefore explaining the distributive consequences of public-utility reform, which had a crucial effect on servicing citizens and generating infrastructure for development. These insights contribute to the political science and the economic literatures on regulation by providing testable hypotheses about the direction of regulatory redistribution between market actors that could be applied to other policy areas or countries.

Concluding Remarks: Extending the Argument

This book provides evidence of the countervailing policy effects generated by electoral competition and partisanship in public utilities, both at the time when capital scarcity generated pressures to adopt privatization and in the postprivatization period. Electoral competition makes policy makers pay more attention to residential consumers *qua* voters, whereas partisan coalitions generate different policy preferences based on their distributive effect, focusing politicians on core constituencies when their replacement risk is not at stake. This last section discusses the implications of this argument about political incentives on microeconomic policy making for other policy areas. The obvious extension of this argument is to other publicly provided services that are consumed massively and other policy areas, such as labor and social policies, which also experienced market-friendly reforms in response to conditions created by capital scarcity.

---

[20] By contrast, in analyzing the consequences of privatization in postcommunist countries, Hellman (1998) suggests that first-entrant advantages are conditional on the degree of contestation in the political system. Jones-Luong and Weinthal (2004) and Post (2007) emphasize the nature of ownership in understanding the influence of privatized companies vis-à-vis governments.

Conclusion

Policy reform in labor regulation during the period of capital scarcity in Latin America confirms the impact of partisan incentives in countries with strong organized labor legacies but provides less clear evidence of electoral effects (Murillo 2005; Murillo and Schrank 2005). Partisan effects point to the role of organized workers as core constituencies of labor-based or left-wing parties rather than potential swing voters. Latin American labor regulations affect workers in the formal sector, which typically are about half of the workforce, thereby reducing the scope of policy effects and the electoral impact of these policies (Murillo and Schrank forthcoming). Moreover, organized workers had previously established political alliances, making them into core constituencies of labor-based or left-wing political parties in countries where industrialization promoted the creation of labor-mobilizing political systems (Roberts 2002). Therefore, organized workers, or even workers in the formal sector, are more likely to influence the policy process as core constituencies than as swing voters. Although these conditions shaped the adoption of labor reforms, which were not generally a salient policy issue, Murillo and Schrank (2005) also provide evidence of partisan effects on institutional design, because reforms to collective labor laws were more likely to provide organizational gains for labor unions when their allies adopted these policies.

The findings from the literature on Latin American social policies can similarly be used to assess the scope of this book's argument, because these areas also experienced market-friendly reforms that increased private participation in response to financial strain. Although focusing on the impact of trade exposure and capital mobility, the findings of this literature are based on the study of two different types of expenditures: the evolution of social security expenditures on the one hand and expenditures on education and health as social services on the other hand. For the most part, social security in Latin America is employment based and contributory. Therefore, it covers only workers in the formal sector, which, as discussed in the preceding text, is more likely to have become a core constituency of the political party that fostered the original establishment of these policies. By contrast, public health and education services cover (albeit not with an even quality or density) the vast majority of the population. Beneficiaries of these services are not only likely to be poorer (as they cannot opt for private provision) but are also more evenly distributed among the electorate. Although the literature on social policy in Latin America does not generally control for the level of electoral competition, we should expect electoral incentives to be more predominant for education and health and for partisan pressures to emerge more clearly in social security – as they did in labor regulation. Yet the focus on expenditures, rather than on the nature of institutional design, that has been the main partisan effect emphasized in the literature on advanced welfare states does not permit an assessment of the effect of partisan incentives on policy content.[21]

In the absence of measures of electoral competition, it is important to note that democracy seems to have a consistent effect on expenditures in education and health across Latin America (Kaufman and Segura-Ubiergo 2001; Avelino et al. 2005; Segura-Ubiergo 2007). That is, a change in regime from authoritarian to democratic, which has an obvious impact on the possibility of electoral competition, generates greater spending in these areas. Kaufman and Segura-Ubiergo (2001) and Segura-Ubiergo (2007) also note the positive impact of "popularly based" presidents on social security expenditures across the region. They explain this effect based on the impact of these expenditures on organized workers, who are core constituencies of incumbent coalitions. Even though Segura-Ubiergo (2007) documents how globalization pressures reduce expenditures on social security, suggesting that capital scarcity generated incentives on incumbents that contradict those of partisanship, he does not analyze partisan effects on institutional design, such as the ones presented in this book. Further analysis of patterns of institutional design for social policies is necessary in order to test the cross-policy scope of this effect.

By providing testable hypotheses and empirical evidence for policy effects, this study opens a research path that can be applied to other policy areas and regions. That is, this book's lessons regarding the policy effects of electoral competition and partisanship, in particular under conditions of capital scarcity, can travel to other policy areas and regions. Identifying the mechanisms generated by the explanatory variables is crucial in testing these effects. Electoral competition should generate fear of replacement for incumbents while heightening challengers' voices. Partisanship, through constituencies' distributive preferences, ideological legacies, and allied experts, should shape the institutional design of the adopted policies. Finally, after privatization, private providers should become crucial policy

---

[21] In advanced democracies, partisanship has been used to explain different types of social policies (Esping-Andersen 1990; Huber and Stephens 2001) along with sectoral characteristics of crucial economic actors, such as the risks involved in a particular economic activity (Mares 2003).

actors whose incentives vary depending on the industrial organization of the sector.

To conclude, I want to call attention to this book's main lesson. The tension between the political incentives generated by voters and the economic incentives generated by either international markets or private corporations on policy makers is fundamental to our understanding of democratic policy making. Democracy does not promise voice – as provided by telephone service – or light – as supplied by electricity. This study provides evidence, however, that healthy electoral competition granted a voice to citizens, whereas the partisanship of elected officials casts a different light on policy choices. Both aspects influence the occurrence, design, and distributive outcomes of privatizations that have affected broad swathes of the Latin American population. These insights can be generalized to other policy areas. Their implication is that facilitating healthy electoral competition, reducing voters' information costs, and providing political parties with credible policy agendas should make voters' choices more meaningful in policy making. Therefore, the effect of democratic mechanisms in the resolution of distributive tensions in a way that benefits the majority of the citizenry depends on the ability of citizens to monitor policy makers, be able to replace them, and select politicians who have a long-term interest in keeping their support. Latin American democracies still have a long road to travel before they achieve empowered citizens who are crucial actors in the policy-making process, but only democratic regimes have opened the opportunity for the realization of such a promise.

References

Abdala, Manuel, and Alice Hill. 1996. "Argentina: The Sequencing of Privatization and Regulation." In *Regulations, Institutions and Commitment: Comparative Study of Telecommunications*, ed. Brian Levy and Pablo Spiller. Cambridge: Cambridge University Press.

Abdala, Manuel, and Pablo Spiller. 1999. *Instituciones, contratos y regulación en Argentina*. Buenos Aires: Temas.

Abeles, Martín, Karina Forcinito, and Martín Shorr. 2001. *El oligopolio telefónico argentino frente a la liberalización del mercado*. Buenos Aires: FLACSO-Universidad de Quilmes.

Acuña, Carlos. 1994. "Politics and Economics in the Argentina of the Nineties (Or, Why the Future No Longer Is What It Used to Be)." In *Democracy, Markets, and Structural Reform in Latin America*, ed. William C. Smith, Carlos H. Acuña, and Eduardo Gamarra. New Brunswick, NJ: North-South Center, Transaction Publishers.

Alesina, Alberto. 1987. "Macroeconomic Policy in a Two-Party System as a Repeated Game," *Quarterly Journal of Economics* 102: 651–78.

Alesina, Alberto, James Mirrlees, and Manfred J.M. Neumann. 1989. "Politics and Business Cycles in Industrial Democracies," *Economic Policy* 4, no. 8: 57–98.

Alianza por Mexico. 2000. *Plataforma Electoral 2000*, PRD, Convergencia, PAS, PT, PSN.

Altamirano, Carlos. 2002. "Ideologías, políticas y debate cívico." In *Los años peronistas (1943–55)*, ed. Juan Carlos Torre. Series Nueva Historia Argentina. Buenos Aires: Editorial Sudamericana, 207–55.

Altomonte, Hugo. 1996. "Energía y desarrollo en América Latina y el Caribe: Síntesis del estudio de caso sobre Chile." Working Paper. Santiago de Chile: CEPAL, May.

Altomonte, Hugo, and Graciela Moguillansky. 1999. "La crisis eléctrica en Chile: Del modelo a imitar al principios de los noventa al modelo a evitar en el 2000?" Working Paper. Santiago de Chile: CEPAL, June.

Aninat, Cristóbal, John Landregan, Patricio Navia, and Joaquín Vial. 2004. *Political Institutions, Policy Making Process and Policy Outcomes in Chile*. Unpublished manuscript. Washington, DC: Inter-American Development Bank.

Arias, Asunción, and Mario Carlos Damonte. 1998. "La visión de los grandes usuarios." In *Argentina. El Sector Eléctrico*. Buenos Aires: Manrique Zago Ediciones S.R.L.

Arriagada, Genaro. 1988. *Pinochet: The Politics of Power*. Boston: Unwin.

Arza, Camila. 2002. "La privatización de los servicios públicos y sus impactos distributivos." In *Privatizaciones y Poder Económico*, ed. Daniel Azpiazu. Buenos Aires: Universidad Nacional de Quilmes, 91–129.

Aspe, Pedro. 1993. *El camino mexicano de la transformación económica*. Mexico City: Fondo de Cultura Económica.

AVANTEL. 2000. "Comparative Revenue of Local Communication Companies." Internal Document. Mimeo. Mexico City.

Avelino, George, David Brown, and Wendy Hunter. 2005. "The Effects of Capital Mobility, Trade Openness, and Democracy on Social Spending in Latin America, 1980–1999," *American Journal of Political Science* 49, no. 3: 625–41.

Azpiazu, Daniel, ed. 2002. *Privatizaciones y poder económico*. Buenos Aires: FLACSO-Universidad de Quilmes.

———. 1999. "Privatizaciones en la Argentina. Regulación tarifaria, mutaciones en los precios relativos, rentas extraordinarias y concentración económica." Working Paper 7 (April). Buenos Aires: FLACSO-Universidad de Quilmes.

———. 1997. "Elite empresaria en la Argentina." Working Paper no. 7. Buenos Aires: FLACSO-Universidad de Quilmes.

Babb, Sarah. 2001. *Managing Mexico: Economists from Nationalism to Neoliberalism*. Princeton, NJ: Princeton University Press.

Bachelet, Michelle. 2005. "Programa de Gobierno de Michelle Bachelet, 2006–2010." Michelle Bachelet's Electoral Plataform. Centro de Estudios Miguel Enriquez, Archivo Chile. Santiago de Chile, Chile (October 18).

Badaraco, Ernesto. 1998. "La transformación del sector eléctrico argentino. La visión de los generadores." In *Argentina. El Sector Eléctrico*. Buenos Aires: Manrique Zago Ediciones S.R.L.

Baena Paz, Guillermina. 2003. "La participación de las bases en el PRI (un estudio del estado de México y un estudio nacional)." In *Partido Revolucionario Institucional. Crisis y refundación*, ed. Francisco Reveles Vázquez. Mexico City: Ediciones Gernika, 221–88.

Baker, Andy. 2007. *Consuming the Washington Consensus: Mass Responses to the Market in Latin America*. Unpublished manuscript.

———. 2003. "Why Is Trade Reform So Popular in Latin America? A Consumption-based Theory of Trade Preferences," *World Politics* 55, no. 3 (April): 423–55.

Barros, Robert. 2002. *Constitutionalism and Dictatorship*. Cambridge: Cambridge University Press.

Bartle, Ian. 2002. "When Institutions No Longer Matter: Reform of Telecommunications and Electricity in Germany, France, and Britain," *Journal of Public Policy* 22, no. 1: 1–27.

Basañes, C. Federico, Eduardo Saavedra, and Raimundo Soto. 2002. "Post-privatization Renegotiation and Disputes in Chile." In *Second-Generation Reforms in Infrastructure Services*, ed. F. Basañes and R. Willig. Washington, DC: Inter-American Development Bank, 51–88.

References

Bastos, Carlos M., and Manuel A. Abdala. 1995. *Transformacion del Sector Electrico Argentino*. Córdoba, Argentina: Editorial Pugliese Sena S.R.L.

Basualdo, Eduardo, Daniel Azpiazu, Martin Abeles, Camila Arza, Karina Porcinito, and Martin Schorr. 2002. "El proceso de privatización en la Argentina: La renegociación con las empresas privatizadas; Revisión contractual y supresión de privilegios y de rentas extraordinarias." Working Paper. Buenos Aires: Economy and Technology Area, FLACSO-Argentina, April.

———. 1993. *Agendas and Instability in American Politics*. Chicago: University of Chicago Press.

BCN. 2004a. Informe de comisión de Minería y Energía. Cámara Boletín No. 2, 922–08. http://sil.senado.cl/pags/index.html (accessed September 8, 2005).

———. 2004b. Primer informe de comisión de Minería y Energía del Senado. Boletín No. 2, 922–08. http://sil.senado.cl/pags/index.html (accessed September 8, 2005).

———. 2004c. Segundo informe de comisión de Minería y Energía del Senado. Boletín No. 2, 922–08. http://sil.senado.cl/pags/index.html (accessed September 8, 2005).

———. 1999. *Historia de la Ley. Compilación de Textos Oficiales del Debate Parlamentario. Ley No. 19,613*. Santiago de Chile: Biblioteca del Congreso Nacional.

———. 1994. *Historia de la Ley 19,302*. Compilación de Textos Oficiales del Debate Parlamentario. Santiago de Chile: Biblioteca del Congreso Nacional.

———. 1993. *Historia de la Ley 19,496*, Vols. 1–4, Santiago de Chile: Biblioteca del Congreso Nacional.

———. n.d. *Historia de la ley referencial*. Santiago de Chile: Biblioteca del Congreso Nacional. http://websinileg.bcn.cl/websinileg/hley/index.asp (accessed September 10, 2005).

Becker Gary. 1985. "A Theory of Competition among Pressure Groups for Political Influence," *Quarterly Journal of Economics* 98 (1985): 371–400.

Benton, Allyson. 2007. "Political Institutions, Hydrocarbons Resources, and Economic Policy Divergence in Latin America." Paper presented to Annual Meeting of the American Political Science Association, Chicago, August 30–September 2.

Bernstein, Juan Sebastián. 1999. "Racionamiento Eléctrico: Causas y Posibles Soluciones." *Puntos de Referencia* 209 (May): 1–11.

———. 1995. "Establecimiento de una política energética basada en el funcionamiento de los mercados competitivos y en la participación privada." Working Paper. Santiago de Chile: CEPAL.

Bicameral Commission for the Reform of the State and the Following of Privatization. Proceedings of Special Meeting in July 25, 2000, *Congress of the Nation of Argentina, Buenos Aires*.

Biglaiser, Glen, and David Brown. 2003. "The Determinants of Privatization in Latin America," *Political Research Quarterly* 56, no. 1 (March): 77–89.

Binder, Sarah A. 2003. *Stalemate: Causes and Consequences of Legislative Gridlock*. Washington, DC: Brookings Institution Press.

Birdsall, Nancy, and John Nellis. 2002. "Winners and Losers: Assessing the Distributional Impact of Privatization." Working Paper no. 6. Center for Global Development, May.

Bitran, Eduardo. 1998. "Regulación, privatización y competencia: Lecciones de la experiencia chilena." In *Qué hay de nuevo en las regulaciones? Telecomunicaciones, electricidad y agua en América Latina*, ed. Arthur Barrionuevo and Eugenio Lahera. Centro Latinoamericano de Administración para el Desarrollo. Buenos Aires: Eudeba, 31–60.

Bitran, Eduardo, and Raúl Sáez. 1994. "Privatization and Regulation in Chile." In *The Chilean Economy: Policy Lessons and Challenges*, ed. Barry Bosworth, Rudiger Dornbusch, and Raul Labán. Washington, DC: Brookings Institution Press, 329–78.

Bitran, Eduardo, and Pablo Serra. 1998. "Regulation of Privatized Utilities: The Chilean Experience," *World Development* 26, no. 6: 945–62.

———. 1994. "Regulatory Issues in the Privatization of Public Utilities: The Chilean Experience," *Quarterly Review of Economics and Finance* 34: 179–97.

Bitran, Eduardo, Antonio Estache, José Luis Guash, and Pablo Serra. 1999. "Privatizing and Regulating Chile's Utilities, 1974–2000: Successes, Failures, and Outstanding Challenges." In *Chile: Recent Policy Lessons and Emerging Challenges*, ed. Guillermo Perry and Danny M. Leipziger. Washington, DC: World Bank, 327–92.

Blyth, Mark. 2002. *Great Transformations: Economic Ideas and Institutional Change in the Twentieth Century*. New York: Cambridge University Press.

Boix, Carles. 2000. "Partisan Governments, the International Economy, and Macroeconomic Policies in OECD Countries, 1964–1993," *World Politics* 53: 38–73.

———. 1998. *Political Parties, Growth and Equality: Conservative and Social Democratic Economic Strategies in the World Economy*. Cambridge: Cambridge University Press.

Bonnet, Céline, Pierre Dubois, David Martimort, and Stéphane Straub. 2006. *Empirical evidence on satisfaction with privatization in Latin America: Welfare Effects and Beliefs*. Mimeo. Toulouse: IDEI.

Box-Steffensmeier, Janet M., and Christopher J.W. Zorn. 2001. "Duration Models and Proportional Hazards in Political Science," *American Journal of Political Science* 45, no. 4 (October): 972–88.

Boylan, Delia M. 2001. *Defusing Democracy: Central Bank Autonomy and the Transition from Authoritarian Rule*. Ann Arbor: University of Michigan Press.

Briceño, Arturo. n.d. Case Study: Fixed-mobile Interconnection in Mexico. http://www.itu.int/osg/sec/spu/ni/fmi/case_studies/ (accessed March 30, 2009).

Brooks, Sarah. 2008. *Social Protection and the Market: The Transformation of Social Security Institutions in Latin America*. New York: Cambridge University Press.

Brune, Nancy, and Geoffrey Garrett. 2000. "The Diffusion of Privatization in the Developing World." Paper presented at the APSA Annual Meeting, Washington, DC, August 31–September 3.

Buira, Ariel. 2003. "An Analysis of IMF Conditionality." G-24 Discussion Paper Series 22.

References

Bull, Benedicte. 2005. *Aid, Power, and Privatization: The Politics of Telecommunications Reform in Central America*. Cheltenham, UK: Edward Elgar.

Burgess, Katrina. 2004. *Parties and Unions in the New Global Economy*. Pittsburgh, PA: University of Pittsburgh Press.

CAF. 2006. "Argentina. Análisis del Sector Eléctrico," Corporación Andina de Fomento. Informes Sectoriales de Infraestructura 4, no. 1 (February).

Callaghy, Thomas. 1997. "Globalization and Marginalization: Debt and the International Underclass," special issue, The Global Economy, *Current History* 96, no. 613: 392–6.

Calvo, Ernesto, and Maria Victoria Murillo. 2005. "A New Law of Argentine Politics." In *Argentine Democracy: The Politics of Institutional Weakness*, ed. Steven Levitsky and Maria Victoria Murillo. University Park: Pennsylvania State University Press, 207–26

Calvo, Ernesto, and Maria Victoria Murillo. 2004. "Who Delivers? Partisan Clients in the Argentine Electoral Market," *American Journal of Political Science* 48, no. 4 (October): 742–57.

Cámara de Diputados. 1999. *Informe de la Comisión de Minería y Energía sobre la investigación de los hechos que han motivado el racionamiento de energía eléctrica en el país*. Valparaíso, Chile: Cámara de Diputados.

Camp, Roderic Ai. 2003. *Politics in Mexico*. Oxford: Oxford University Press.

CANIETI. 2000. "Propuesta del sector de telecomunicaciones para la nueva administracion del gobierno federal." Mexico City, January 18. Paper presented to the Joint Congressional Commission on Telecommunications Reform.

Canitrot, Adolfo. 1981. "Teoría y práctica del liberalismo. Política antiinflacionaria y apertura económica en la Argentina, 1976-1981," *Desarrollo Económico* 21, no. 82 (July–September): 131–89.

Canton, Darío, and Jorge R. Jorrat. 2001. "Economic Evaluations, Partisanship, and Social Bases of Presidential Voting in Argentina, 1995 and 1999," *International Journal of Public Opinion Research* 14, no. 4 (August): 413–27.

Carey, John. 2002. "Parties, Coalitions, and the Chilean Congress." In *Legislative Politics in Latin America*, ed. Scott Morgenstern and Benito Nacif. Cambridge: Cambridge University Press, 222–53

Carpenter, Daniel. 2001. *The Forging of Bureaucratic Autonomy*. Princeton, NJ: Princeton University Press.

Carreón Rodríguez, David G. Víctor, Armando Jiménez and Juan Rosellón. 2007. "The Mexican Electricity Sector: Economic, Legal, and Political Issues." In *The Political Economy of Power Sector Reform*, ed. David G. Victor and Thomas C. Heller. New York: Cambridge University Press: 175–214.

Carrera, Jorge, Daniele Checchi, and Massimo Florio. 2005. "Privatization Discontent and Its Determinants: Evidence from Latin America." Mimeo. University of Milan (March).

Casar, Maria Amparo. 1998. "Oscillating Relations: President and Congress in Argentina." In *Legislative Politics in Latin America*, ed. Scott Morgenstern and Benito Nacif. Cambridge: Cambridge University Press, 114–44.

Castelar Pinheiro, Armando, and Ben Ross Schneider. 1994. "The Fiscal Impact of Privatization in Latin America," *Quarterly Review of Economics and Finance* 34 (Summer): 9–42.

Catterberg, Edgardo. 1989. *Los argentinos frente a la política: Cultura política y opinión pública en la transición argentina a la democracia.* Buenos Aires: Editorial Planeta.

Celani, Marcelo. 2000. "Determinantes de la inversión en telecomunicaciones en Argentina." In *La Argentina de los noventa*, ed. Daniel Heymann and Bernardo Kosacoff. Buenos Aires: CEPAL-Eudeba, 9–56

Centeno, Miguel A. 1994. *Democracy within Reason.* University Park: Pennsylvania State University Press.

Centeno, Miguel A., and Patricio Silva. 1998. *The Politics of Expertise in Latin America.* Amsterdam: Macmillan Press.

Centro de Estudios Públicos (CEP). Studies in Public Opinion: Surveys from 1993 to 1999. http://www.cepchile.cl/enc_main.html (accessed October 1, 2005).

———. 1992. *El ladrillo: Bases de la política económica del gobierno militar chileno.* Santiago de Chile: Centro de Estudios Públicos.

CEPAL. 2007. *Anuario estadístico de America Latina y el Caribe.* Santiago: CEPAL.

Chong, Alberto. 2005. "Privatization in Latin America." Mimeo. Inter-American Development Bank.

Chong, Alberto, and Florencio López-de-Silanes. 2005. *Privatization in Latin America: Myths and Reality.* Washington, DC: Stanford University Press and the World Bank.

CIDE. 2000a. Encuesta de Privatización del Sector Eléctrico. Presidencia de la Nación. National Survey. February 1 (PRV10200).

———. 2000b. Encuesta de la Declaracion de Ernesto Zedillo Ponce de Privatización del Sector Eléctrico. Presidencia de la Nación. National Survey. August 15 (PRV10899).

———. 2008. National Home Surveys of the Office of the President of Mexico (1989–2000) and BGC Ulises Beltrán y Asociados (2001–2). National Sample.

CIDE/Presidencia de la Republica, 1989–2000, public opinión survey database.

———. 1995. Encuesta de Privatizacion Roll Económico. Presidencia de la Nacional. National Survey. August 29 (code REC30895.PRG).

Clark, William. 2003. *Capitalism, Not Globalism. Capital Mobility, Central Bank Independence and the Political Control of the Economy.* Ann Arbor: The University of Michigan Press.

Cleary, Matthew. 2006. "Explaining the Left's Resurgence," *Journal of Democracy* 17, no. 4: 35–49.

Clifton, Judith. 2000. *The Politics of Telecommunications in Mexico.* London: Macmillan.

CMIC. 2002. "Comision de Infraestructura: Sector Electrico." Mexico City. Paper presented to the Congressional Commission on Electricity Reform.

Collier, David, and Ruth Berins Collier. 1991. *Shaping the Political Arena: Critical Junctures, the Labor Movement, and Regime Dynamics in Latin America.* Princeton, NJ: Princeton University Press.

References

Comisión Nacional de Energía (CNE). 1999. *Crisis eléctrica*. Santiago de Chile: Comisión Nacional de Energía.

Concertación de Partidos por la Democracia. 1993. "Un gobierno para los nuevos tiempos: Bases programáticas del segundo gobierno de la Concertacion." Santiago de Chile.

———. 1989. "Programa de Gobierno." Santiago de Chile: Documentos La Época.

Conniff, Michael L. 1999. Introduction to *Populism in Latin America*, ed. Michael L. Conniff. Tuscaloosa: University of Alabama Press.

Cook, Maria Lorena. 2007. *The Politics of Labor Reform in Latin America*. University Park: Pennsylvania State University Press.

Coppedge, Michael. 1997. "A Classification of Latin American Political Parties." Working Paper no. 244. Helen Kellogg Institute for International Studies, University of Notre Dame, November.

Corrales, Javier. 2002. *Presidents without Parties: The Politics of Economic Reform in Argentina and Venezuela in the 1990s*. University Park: Pennsylvania State University Press.

Cox, D.R. 1972. "Regression Models and Life-Tables," *Journal of the Royal Statistical Society Series B (Methodological)* 34, no. 2: 187–220.

Cox, Gary, and Matthew D. McCubbins. 2001. "The Institutional Determinants of Economic Policy Outcomes." In *Presidents, Parliaments, and Policy*, ed. Stephen Haggard and Matthew D. McCubbins. New York: Cambridge University Press, 21–63.

CPT. 2002. "Ley Federal de Telecomunicaciones: Propuesta de reforma." Conferencia Parlamentaria de Telecomunicaciones, August 22.

Crisp, Brian, and Gregg Johnson. 2003. "Mandates, Power, and Politics." *American Journal of Political Science* 47, no. 1 (January): 128–42.

Cukierman, Alex, and Mariano Tommasi. 1998. "When Does It Take a Nixon to Go to China?" *American Economic Review* 88, no. 1 (March): 180–97.

Curzio, Leonardo. 1994. *La oferta electoral de los partidos politicos*. Mexico City: Triana Editores.

De la Garza Talavera, Rafael. 2003. "Del nacionalismo al liberalismo: la transformación ideológica del Partido de la Revolución." In *Partido de la Revolución Institucional: crisis y refundación*, ed. Francisco Reveles Vázquez. Mexico City: Editorial Gernika, 315–45.

Devlin, Robert, and Rosella Cominetti. 1994. "*La crisis de la empresa pública, las privatizaciones y la equidad social.*" Working Paper. Santiago de Chile: CEPAL.

Díaz, Carlos, Alexander Galetovic, and Raimundo Soto. 2000. "La crisis eléctrica 1998–1999: Causas, consecuencias, y lecciones," *Estudios Públicos* 80 (Spring): 149–92.

Di Maggio, Paul J., and Walter W. Powell. 1983. "The Iron Cage Revisited: Institutional Isomorphism and Collective Rationality in Organizational Fields," *American Sociological Review* 48, no. 2 (April): 147–60.

Domínguez, Jorge I. 1996. "Ideas and Leaders in Freeing Politics and Markets in Latin America in the 1990s." In *Technopols: Freeing Politics and Markets in Latin*

America in the 1990s, ed. Jorge I. Domínguez. University Park: Pennsylvania State University Press.

Domínguez, Jorge, and James McCann. 1996. *Democratizing Mexico.* Baltimore, MD: Johns Hopkins University Press.

Dornbush, Rudiger, and Sebastian Edwards. 1991. "The Macroeconomics of Populism." In *The Macroeconomics of Populism in Latin America*, ed. R. Dornbush and S. Edwards. Chicago: University of Chicago Press, 7–13.

Downs, Anthony. 1957. *An Economic Theory of Democracy.* New York: Harper.

Edwards, Sebastian. 1995. *Crisis and Reform in Latin America.* Oxford: Oxford University Press.

Eicheengreen, Barry, and Albert Fishlow. 1998. "Contending with Capital Flows: What Is Different about the 1990s." In *Capital Flows and Financial Crises*, ed. Miles Kahler. Ithaca: Cornell University Press, 1–22.

Eising, Rainer. 2002. "Policy Learning in Embedded Negotiations: Explaining EU Electricity Liberalization," *International Organization* 56, no. 1: 85–120.

Elster, Jon. 1998. "A Plea for Mechanisms." In *Social Mechanisms: An Analytical Approach to Social Theory*, ed. Peter Hedstrom and Richard Swedberg. Cambridge: Cambridge University Press, 45–73

Escolar, Marcelo, and Ernesto Calvo. 2002. *Transferencia electoral y reestructuración partidaria en la elección federal Argentina 2001: Categoría diputados nacionales.* Buenos Aires: UNDP Political Reform Program report.

Esping-Anderson, Gosta. 1990. *The Three Worlds of the Welfare State.* Princeton, NJ: Princeton University Press.

Etchemendy, Sebastián. 2009. "Models of Economic Liberalization: Regime, Power and Compensation in Spain, Argentina, Chile, and the Iberian-American Region," Manuscript. Universidad Torcuato Di Tella.

Fazio, Hugo. 1997. *Mapa actual de la extrema riqueza en Chile.* Santiago de Chile: Lom.

Fernández-Arias, Eduardo, and Ricardo Hausmann. 2000. "Is FDI a Safer Form of Financing?" *RES Working Papers* 4201, Washington, DC: Inter-American Development Bank, Research Department.

FIEL. 1999. *La regulación de la competencia y de los servicios públicos.* Buenos Aires: Fundación de Investigaciones Económicas Latinoamericanas.

Fisher, Ronald, and Alexander Galetovic. 2003. "Regulatory Governance and Chile's 1998–1999 Electricity Shortage," *Policy Reform* 6, no. 2 (June): 105–25.

Fischer, Ronald, and Pablo Serra. 2003. "Efecto de la privatización de servicios públicos en Chile: Casos sanitario, electricidad y telecomunicaciones." Mimeo. Universidad de Chile (June).

Fishlow, Albert. 1994. "Latin America and the United States in a Changing World Economy." In *Latin America in a New World*, ed. Abraham Lowenthal and Gregory Treverton. Boulder, CO: Westview Press, 65–78.

Fiske, Susan T., and Shelley E. Taylor. 1991. *Social Cognition.* 2nd ed. New York: McGraw-Hill.

References

Fontaine Aldunate, Arturo. 1988. *Los Economistas y el Presidente Pinochet*. Santiago de Chile: Zig-Zag.

Foster, Vivien. 2004. "Toward a Social Policy for Argentina's Infrastructure Sectors: Evaluating the Past and Exploring the Future," World Bank Policy Research Working Paper 3422 (October).

Foweraker, Joe, Todd Landman, and Neil Harvey. 2003. *Governing Latin America*. Cambridge: Polity.

Fox, Vicente. 2005. *Quinto informe de gobierno*. Mexico City: Presidencia de la República.

Franzese, Robert. 2002a. "Electoral and Partisan Cycles in Economic Policies and Outcomes," *Annual Review of Political Science* 5: 369–421.

Franzese, Robert. 2002b. *Macroeconomic Policies of Developed Democracies*. New York: Cambridge University Press.

Frei, Eduardo. 1999a. Discurso sobre la crisis eléctrica, 26 Abril de 1999. http://www.fundacionfrei.cl/nuevo/efr/discursos.html (accessed September 20, 2005).

———. 1999b. Mensaje presidencial 21 de Mayo 1999. http://www.camara.cl/hist/archivo/discurs/presi99.pdf (accessed September 21, 2005).

Frente para la Victoria. 2003. "Declaracion de Principios." Nestor Kirchner's Electoral Plataform. Buenos Aires, Argentina.

Frente para la Lealtad. 2003. "10 Propuestas para salir de la crisis." Carlos Menem's Electoral Plataform. Buenos Aires, Argentina.

Frieden, Jeffrey. 1992. *Debt, Development, and Democracy*. Princeton, NJ: Princeton University Press.

Frye, Timothy. 2006. "Partisan Politics in Transition Economies." Mimeo. Columbus: Ohio State University.

———. 2002. "The Perils of Polarization: Economic Performance in the Postcommunist World," *World Politics* 54: 308–36.

Galetovic, Alexander. 2003. "Integración vertical en el sector eléctrico: Una guía para el usuario," *Estudios Públicos* 91 (Winter): 199–232.

———. 2002. "*Transmisión y la 'ley corta.'*" *Puntos de Referencia, 265*. Santiago de Chile: Centro de Estudios Públicos, December.

Gargarella, Roberto. 2008. "The Accountability Function of Courts in New Democracies: The Cases of Argentina, Chile and Colombia." In *The Accountability Function of Courts in New Democracies*, ed. Roberto Gargarella, Siri Gloppen, Morten Kinander, and Bruce Wilson. Manuscript.

Garretón, Manuel Antonio. 1991. "The Political Opposition and the Party System under the Military Regime." In *The Struggle for Democracy in Chile*, ed. Paul Drake and Ivan Jaksic. Lincoln: University of Nebraska Press, 211–50.

Garrett, Geoffrey. 1998. *Partisan Politics in the Global Economy*. New York: Cambridge University Press.

Gerchunoff, Pablo, Esteban Greco, and Diego Bondorevsky. 2003. "Comienzos diversos, distintas trayectorias y final abierto: Más de una década de privatizaciones en Argentina, 1990–2002." Working Paper 34, Public Management Series. Santiago de Chile: CEPAL (April).

Gereffi, Gary, and Peter Evans. 1981. "Transnational Corporations, Dependent Development and State Policies in the Semiperiphery: A Comparison of Brazil and Mexico," *Latin American Research Review* 16, no. 3: 31–64.

Gerring, John. 2007. *Case Study Research*. Cambridge: Cambridge University Press.

Gervasoni, Carlos. 1998. "Del Distribucionismo al neoliberalismo: Los cambios en la Coalición Electoral Peronista durante el gobierno de Menem." Paper presented at the 1998 meeting of the Latin American Studies Association, Chicago, September 24–6.

Gibson, Edward. 1997. "The Populist Road to Market Reforms: Policy and Electoral Coalitions in Argentina and Mexico," *World Politics* 49 (April): 339–70.

Gibson, Edward, and Ernesto Calvo. 2000. "Federalism and Low-Maintenance Constituencies: Territorial Dimensions of Economic Reform in Argentina," *Studies in Comparative International Development* 35, no. 3 (Fall): 32–55.

Gil Hubert, Johanna. 2000. "La Interconexión en el sector de las telecomunicaciones en México a partir de la privatización de Telmex: Un análisis teórico y empírico." BA thesis, Economics Department, ITAM, Mexico City.

Gilardi, Fabrizio. 2004. "Institutional Change in Regulatory Policies: Regulation through Independent Agencies and the Three New Institutionalisms." In *The Politics of Regulation: Examining Regulatory Institutions and Instruments in the Age of Governance*, ed. Jacint Jordana and David Levi-Faur. Cheltenham, UK: Edward Elgar, 67–89.

———. 2002. "Policy Credibility and Delegation to Independent Regulatory Agencies: A Comparative Empirical Analysis," *Journal of European Public Policy* 9, no. 6: 873–93.

Gomez-Ibanez, Jose. 2003. *Regulating Infrastructure: Monopoly, Contracts and Distribution*. Cambridge, MA: Harvard University Press.

Greif, Avner, and David D. Laitin. 2004. "A Theory of Endogenous Institutional Change." *American Political Science Review* 98, no. 4 (November): 633–52

Grzymala-Busse, Anna. 2007. *Rebuilding Leviathan: Party Competition and State Exploitation in Post-Communist Democracies*. Cambridge: Cambridge University Press.

———. 2003. "Political Competition and the Politicization of the State in East Central Europe," *Comparative Political Studies* 36: 1123–46.

Guerrero, Isabel, Luis Felipe Lopez-Calva, and Michael Walton. 2006. "The Inequality Trap and Its Links to Low Growth in Mexico." Mimeo.

Haas, Peter. 1992. "Introduction: Epistemic Communities and International Policy Coordination," *International Organization* 46, no. 1: 1–35.

Hachette, Dominique, and Rulf Luders. 1993. *Privatization in Chile*. San Francisco: International Center for Economic Growth.

Haggard, Stephan, and Robert R. Kaufman. 1995. *The Political Economy of Democratic Transitions*. Princeton, NJ: Princeton University Press.

———. 1992. "Economic Adjustment and the Prospects for Democracy." In *The Politics of Economic Adjustment*, ed. Stephen Haggard and Robert Kaufman. Princeton, NJ: Princeton University Press, 319–50.

References

Haggard, Stephen, and Sylvia Maxfield. 1996. "The Political Economy of Financial Internationalization in the Developing World." In *Internationalization and Domestic Politics*, ed. Robert Keohane and Helen Milner. Cambridge: Cambridge University Press, 209–39.

Haggard, Stephen, and Matthew D. McCubbins, 2001. "Introduction: Political Institutions and the Determinants of Public Policy." In *Presidents, Parliaments, and Policy*, ed. Stephen Haggard and Matthew D. McCubbins. Cambridge: Cambridge University Press, 1–17.

Haggard, Stephen, and Gregory Noble. 2001. "Power Politics: Elections and Electricity Regulation in Taiwan." In *Presidents, Parliaments, and Policy*, ed. Stephen Haggard and Matthew D. McCubbins. Cambridge: Cambridge University Press, 256–90.

Hagopian, Frances. 2005. "Conclusions: Government Performance, Political Representation, and Public Perceptions of Contemporary Democracy in Latin America." In *The Third Wave of Democratization in Latin America: Advances and Setbacks*, ed. Frances Hagopian and Scott Mainwaring. Cambridge: Cambridge University Press, 319–62

Hall, Peter A. 1989. "Conclusion: The Politics of Keynesian Ideas." In *The Political Power of Economic Ideas: Keynesianism across Nations*, ed. Peter A. Hall. Princeton, NJ: Princeton University Press, 361–91

Hall, Peter A., and David Soskice, eds. 2001. *Varieties of Capitalism: The Institutional Foundations of Comparative Advantage*. Oxford: Oxford University Press.

Heckman, John, and Carmen Pages. 2000. "The Cost of Job Security Regulation: Evidence from Latin American Labor Markets," *Economia, the Journal of the Latin American Economic Association* 1 (Fall): 109–54.

Heller, William B., and Matthew D. McCubbins. 2001. "Political Institutions and Economic Development: The Case of Electric Utility Regulation in Argentina and Chile." In *Presidents, Parliaments, and Policy*, ed. Stephen Haggard and Matthew D. McCubbins. Cambridge: Cambridge University Press, 229–55

Hellman, Joel. 1998. "Winners Take All: The Politics of Partial Reform in Postcommunist Transitions," *World Politics* 50 (January): 203–34.

Helmke, Gretchen. 2004. *Courts under Constraints: Judges, Generals, and Presidents in Argentina*. New York: Cambridge University Press.

Helmke, Gretchen, and Steven Levitsky. 2006. *Informal Institutions and Democracy: Lessons from Latin America*. Baltimore, MD: Johns Hopkins University Press.

Henisz, Witold J. 2002. "The Institutional Environment for Infrastructure Investment," *Industrial and Corporate Change* 11, no. 2: 355–89.

Henisz, Witold J., and Bennet A. Zelner. 2005. "Legitimacy, Interest Group Pressures and Change in Emerging Institutions: The Case of Foreign Investors and Host Country Governments," *Academy of Management Review* 20, no. 3: 361–82.

———. 2003. "Legitimacy, Interest Group Pressures and Change in Emergent Institutions: The Case of Foreign Investors and Host Country Governments," *William Davidson Institute Working Papers Series 2003–589*, William Davidson Institute at the University of Michigan Stephen M. Ross Business School.

Henisz, Witold J., Bennet A. Zelner, and Mauro F. Guillen. 2005. "The World-wide Diffusion of Market-Oriented Infrastructure Reform, 1977–1999," *American Sociological Review* 70: 871–97.

Hernández, Cesar. 2007. *La reforma cautiva. Inversión, trabajo y empresa en el sector eléctrico mexicano.* Mexico City: CIDAC.

Hibbs, Douglas. 1977. "Political Parties and Macroeconomic Policy," *American Political Science Review* 71, no. 4: 1467–87.

Hillman, Amy J., Gerald D. Keim, and Douglas Schuler. 2004. "Corporate Political Activity: A Review and Research Agenda," *Journal of Management* 30, no. 6: 837–57.

Hinich, Melvin, and Michael Munger. 1994. *Ideology and the Theory of Political Choice.* Ann Arbor: University of Michigan Press.

Hirshman, Albert. 1968. "The Political Economy of Import-Substituting Industrialization in Latin America," *Quarterly Journal of Economics* 84 (February): 2–32.

———. 1970. *Exit, Voice and Loyalty: Responses to Decline in Firms, Organizations and States.* Cambridge, MA: Harvard University Press.

Hite, Katherine. 2000. *When the Romance Ended: Leaders of the Chilean Left, 1968–1998.* New York: Columbia University Press.

Holburn, Guy, and Pablo Spiller. 2002. "Interest Group Representation in Administrative Institutions: The Impact of Consumer Advocate and Elected Commissioners on Regulatory Policy in the United States." Unpublished manuscript.

Huber, Evelyne, Thomas Mustillo, and John D. Stephens. 2008. "Politics and Social Spending in Latin America," *The Journal of Politics* 70, no. 2 (April): 420–36.

Huber, Evelyne, and John Stephens. 2001. *Development and Crisis of the Welfare State.* Chicago: University of Chicago Press.

Huber, John, and Charles Shipan. 2006. "Politics, Delegation and Bureaucracy." In *The Oxford Handbook for Political Economy,* ed. Barry Weingast and Donald Wittman. Oxford: Oxford University Press, 256–73.

———. 2002. *Deliberate Discretion? The Institutional Foundations of Bureaucratic Autonomy.* New York: Cambridge University Press.

Hulsink, Willem. 1999. *Privatization and Liberalization in European Telecommunications: Comparing Britain, the Netherlands, and France.* London: Routledge.

Huneeus, Carlos. 2000a. *El régimen de Pinochet.* Santiago de Chile: Editorial Sudamericana.

———. 2000b. "Technocrats and Politicians in an Authoritarian Regime: The 'Odeplan Boys' and the 'Gremialists' in Pinochet's Chile," *Journal of Latin American Studies* 32 (May): 461–501.

IADB. 2005. *The Politics of Policies.* Economic and Social Progress in Latin America 2006 Report. Washington, DC: Inter-American Development Bank and David Rockefeller Center for Latin American Studies.

———. 2001. *Competitiveness: The Business of Growth.* Economic and Social Progress in Latin America 2001 Report. Washington, DC: Inter-American Development Bank.

References

IERAL. 1999. "Las regulaciones en la Argentina." Working Paper 22, IERAL.

Inostroza, Gabriel. 1995. "Control del estado y gestión empresarial en el sector eléctrico de Chile." Working Paper. Santiago de Chile: CEPAL, February.

Instituto Nacional de Estadística (INE). *Población de 15 años y más por situación en la fuerza de trabajo y tasa de desocupación. Total país, ambos sexos.* Series 1986–2004. http://www.ine.cl/03-empleo/9999.htm (accessed October 1, 2005).

Inter-American Development Bank. 2001. *Competitiveness: The Business of Growth.* Washington, DC: IPES, Research Department, Inter-American Development Bank.

Iversen, Torben. 1999. *Contested Economic Institutions: The Politics of Macroeconomics and Wage Bargaining in Advanced Democracies.* Cambridge: Cambridge University Press.

Iversen, Torben, and Anne Wren. 1998. "Equality, Employment, and Budgetary Restraint: The Trilemma of the Service Economy," *World Politics* 50 (July): 507–46.

James, Scott. 2000. *Presidents, Parties, and the State.* Cambridge: Cambridge University Press.

Jervis, Robert. 1976. *Perception and Misperception in International Politics.* Princeton, NJ: Princeton University Press.

Johnson, Gregg, and Brian Crisp. 2003. "Mandates, Power, and Politics," *American Journal of Political Science* 47, no. 1 (January): 128–42.

Jones, Bryan D., and Frank R. Baumgarner. 2005. *The Politics of Attention.* Chicago: University of Chicago Press.

Jones, Mark. 1997. "Evaluating Argentina's Presidential Democracy." In *Presidentialism and Democracy in Latin America,* ed. Scott Mainwaring and Matthew Shuggart. Cambridge: Cambridge University Press, 259–99.

Jones-Luong, Pauline, and Erika Weinthal. 2004. "Contra Coercion: Russian Tax Reform, Exogenous Shocks, and Negotiated Institutional Change," *American Political Science Review* 98, no. 1 (February): 139–52.

———. 2001. "Prelude to the Resource Curse: Explaining Oil and Gas Development Strategies in the Soviet Successor States and Beyond," *Comparative Political Studies* 34, no. 4 (May): 367–99.

Jordana, Jacint, and David Levi-Faur. 2005. "The Diffusion of Regulatory Capitalism in Latin America: Sectoral and National Channels in the Making of a New Order," *Annals of the American Academy of Political and Social Science* 598 (March): 102–24.

Kaufman, Robert. 2008. "The Political Left, the Export Boom, and the Populist Temptation." Mimeo. New York.

Kaufman, Robert R., and Joan M. Nelson. 2004. *Crucial Needs, Weak Incentives: Social Sector Reform, Democratization, and Globalization in Latin America.* Baltimore, MD: Johns Hopkins University Press.

Kaufman, Robert R., and Alex Segura-Ubiergo. 2001. "Globalization, Domestic Politics, and Social Spending in Latin America: A Time-Series Cross-Section Analysis, 1973–97," *World Politics* 53 (July): 553–87.

King, Gary, Robert Keohena, and Sidney Verba. 1994. *Designing Social Inquiry.* Princeton, NJ: Princenton University Press.

Kingdon, John W. 1995. *Agendas, Alternatives, and Public Policies.* New York: Harper Collins.

Kingstone, Peter. 2003. "Privatizing Telebrás: Brazilian Political Institutions and Policy Performance," *Comparative Politics* 36, no. 1 (October): 21–40.

Kitschelt, Hebert. 2001. "Partisan Competition and Welfare State Retrenchment: When Do Politicians Choose Unpopular Policies?" In *The New Politics of the Welfare State*, ed. Paul Pierson. Oxford: Oxford University Press, 265–302.

Klesner, Joseph. 2004. "The Structure of the Mexican Electorate: Social Attitudinal and Partisan Bases of Vicente Fox's Victory." In *Mexico's Pivotal Democratic Election*, ed. Jorge I. Domínguez and Chappell Lawson. Stanford, CA: Stanford University Press, 91–122

Kogut, Bruce, and J. Muir Macpherson. 2004. "The Decision to Privatize as an Economic Policy Idea: Epistemic Communities, Palace Wars, and Diffusion." Mimeo.

Kuhlmann, Federico, Marcio Wohlers de Almeida, Martin Abeles, Karina Forcinito, and Martín Schorr. 2000. "Privatization and Deregulation: Latin American Style." Paper presented at the 11th ITS European Conference, Lausanne, Switzerland, September 9–11.

Kurtz, Marcus. 2004. "The Dilemmas of Democracy in the Open Economy: Lessons from Latin America," *World Politics* 56 (January): 261–302.

———. 1999. "Chile's Neo-Liberal Revolution: Incremental Decisions and Structural Transformation, 1973–89," *Journal of Latin American Studies* 31, pt. 2 (May): 399–427.

Lagos, Ricardo. 1999. "Iniciar el siglo XXI con mas democracia y mas derechos," Ricardo Lagos's Electoral Plataform Bases Programáticas. Concertación de Partidos por la Democracia. Santiago de Chile. Chile (June 23).

La Época. Programa de Gobierno. 1989. *Concertación de Partidos por la Democracia.* Santiago de Chile.

Latintrack 2000. Public Opinion Tracking. Buenos Aires, Argentina.

Latinobarómetro. 2005. Informe Latinobarómetro, 1995–2005: Diez años de opinión pública. http://www.latinobarometro.org (accessed July 15, 2008).

———. 2003. Informe de prensa: resumen. http://www.latinobarometro.org/Upload/Informe-Resumen%20Latinobarómetro%202003.zip (accessed July 15, 2008).

———. 1998. 1998 Latinobarometer survey of Latin America data purchased at http://www.latinobarometro.org/(accessed July 20, 2008).

———. 1995. 1995 Latinobarometer survey of Latin America data purchased at http://www.latinobarometro.org/(accessed July 20, 2008).

Lawson, Chappell. 2004. Introduction to *Mexico's Pivotal Democratic Election*, ed. Jorge I. Domínguez and Chappell Lawson. Stanford, CA: Stanford University Press.

———. 2002. *Building the Fourth Estate: Democratization and the Rise of a Free Press in Mexico.* Berkeley: University of California Press.

References

Legisa, Juan. 2002. "Settlement of Disputes in the Power Sector in Argentina." In *Second-Generation Reforms in Infrastructure Services*, ed. F. Basañes and R. Willig. Washington, DC: Inter-American Development Bank, 133–45.

———. 1999. "Second Generation Issues in the Reform of Public Services," Mimeo, Interamerican Development Bank (October).

León, Samuel. 1990. "Del partido de partidos al partido de sectores." In *El Partido en el poder*. IEPES: Mexico City.

Levi-Faur, David. 2004. "On the 'Net Impact' of Europeanization: The EU's Telecoms and Electricity Regimes between the Global and the National," *Comparative Political Studies* 37, no. 1 (February): 3–39.

———. 2003. "The Politics of Liberalization: Privatization and Regulation-for-Competition in Europe's and Latin America's Telecoms and Electricity Industries," *European Journal of Political Research* 42: 705–40.

———. 1999. "The Governance of Competition: The Interplay of Technology, Economics, and Politics in European Union Electricity and Telecom Regimes," *Journal of Public Policy* 19, no. 2: 175–207.

Levi-Faur, David, and Jacint Jordana. 2005. "The Diffusion of Regulatory Capitalism in Latin America: Sectoral and National Channels in the Making of a New Order," *Annals of the American Academy of Political and Social Science* 598 (March): 102–24.

Levine, Michael, and Jennifer Forrence. 1990. "Regulatory Capture, Public Interest, and the Public Agenda: Toward a Synthesis," *Journal of Law, Economics, and Organization* 6: 167–98.

Levitsky, Steve. 2003. *Transforming Labor-based Parties in Latin America: Argentine Peronism in Comparative Perspective*. New York: Cambridge University Press.

Levitsky, Steven, and María Victoria Murillo. 2009. "The Causes and Implications of Variation in Institutional Strength," *Annual Review of Political Science* 11: 115–33.

———. 2003. "Argentina Weathers the Storm," *Journal of Democracy* 14, no. 4 (October): 152–66.

Levy, Brian, and Pablo Spiller. 1996. Introduction to *Regulations, Institutions and Commitment: Comparative Study of Telecommunications*, ed. Brian Levy and Pablo Spiller. Cambridge: Cambridge University Press.

Littlechild, Stephen C., and Carlos J. Skerk. 2004. "Regulation of Transmission Expansion in Argentina." Cambridge Working Papers in Economics 464. November.

Libertad y Desarrollo. 1993a. "Comentarios al Proyecto de Ley sobre los Derechos del Consumidor." Reseña Legislativa 155 (August). Santiago de Chile.

———. 1993b. "Telecomunicaciones: Hacia una Mayor Competencia," Temas Públicos 147 (June). Santiago de Chile.

Llanos, Mariana. 2002. *Privatization and Democracy in Argentina: An Analysis of President-Congress Relations*. New York: Palgrave.

Lodge, Milton, and Ruth Hammill. 1986. "A Partisan Schema for Political Information Processing," *American Political Science Review* 80, no. 2 (June): 505–20.

Lopreite, Débora Cecilia. 2001. "Ciudadanos o consumidores: Los dilemas institucionales del Defensor del Pueblo de la Nación Argentina." MA thesis, Public Administration, School of Economics, University of Buenos Aires, May.

Lora, Eduardo. 2001. " Structural Reforms in Latin America: What Has Been Reformed and How to Measure It." Working Paper 446. Washington, DC: Inter-American Development Bank, December.

Lora, Eduardo, and Mauricio Olivera. 2005. "The Electoral Consequences of the Washington Consensus," *Economia* (Spring): 1–45.

Lustig, Nora. 1992. "Equity and Growth in Mexico." In *Towards a New Development Strategy for Latin America*, ed. Simon Teitel. Washington, DC: Inter-American Development Bank, 219–58.

Madrid, Raul. 2003. *Retiring the State: The Politics of Pension Privatization in Latin America and Beyond*. Stanford, CA: Stanford University Press.

Magaloni, Beatriz. 2006. *Voting for Autocracy: Hegemonic Party Survival and its Demise in Mexico*. New York: Cambridge University Press.

Magaloni, Beatriz, and Alejandro Poire. 2004. "The Issues, the Vote, and the Mandate for Change." In *Mexico's Pivotal Democratic Election*, ed. Jorge I. Domínguez and Chapel Lawson. Stanford, CA: Stanford University Press, 293–319.

Magaloni, Beatriz, Alberto Diaz Cayeros, and Federico Estevez. 2007. "Clientelism and portfolio diversification: a model of electoral investment with applications to Mexico." In *Patrons, Clients, and Policies: Patterns of Democratic Accountability and Electoral Competition*, ed. Herbert Kitschelt and Steven Wilkinson. Cambridge: Cambridge University Press.

Mahoney, James. 2003. "Long-Run Development and the Legacy of Colonialism in Spanish America," *American Journal of Sociology* 109, no. 1 (July): 50–106.

Mainwaring, Scott, and Timothy Scully. 1995. "Introduction: Party Sytems in Latin America." In *Building Democratic Institutions: Party Systems in Latin America*. Stanford, CA: Stanford University Press, 1–34.

Manza, Jeff, and Fay Lomax Cook. 2002. "The Impact of Public Opinion on Public Policy: The State of the Debate." In *Navigating Public Opinion*, ed. Jeff Manza, Fay Lomax Cook, and Benjamin I. Page. New York: Oxford University Press, 17–32.

Mares, Isabela. 2003. *The Politics of Social Risk*. New York: Cambridge University Press.

Margheritis, Ana. 2002. "Policy Innovation and Leaders' Perceptions: Building a Reformist Consensus in Argentina," *Journal of Latin American Studies* 34: 881–914.

———. 1999. *Ajuste y reforma en Argentina, 1989–1995*. Buenos Aires: Nuevohacer.

Mariscal, Judith. 2002. *Unfinished Business: Telecommunications Reform in Mexico*. Westport, CT: Greenwood.

Mariscal, Judith, and Eugenio Rivera. 2005. "New Trends in the Latin American Telecommunications Market: Telefonica and Telmex," *Telecommunications Policy* 29: 757–77.

Martinez Gallardo, Cecilia. Forthcoming. "Cabinets and the Policy-Making Process." In *Political Institutions, Actors and Arenas in Latin American*, ed. Carlos Scartascini, Ernesto Stein, and Mariano Tommasi.

References

McAdam, Adam, Sidney Tarrow, and Charles Tilly. 2001. *Dynamics of Contention*. Cambridge: Cambridge University Press.

McCubbins, Matthew, and Thomas Schwartz. 1984. "Congressional Oversight Overlooked," *American Journal of Political Science* 28 (February): 165–79.

McCubbins, Mathew, Roger Noll, and Barry Weingast. 1987. "Administrative Procedures as Instruments of Political Control," *Journal of Law, Economics, and Organization* 3, no. 2 (Fall): 243–77.

McGillivray, Fiona. 2003. *Privileging Industry: The Comparative Politics of Trade and Industrial Policy*. Princeton, NJ: Princeton University Press.

McGuire, James. 1997. *Peronism without Perón*. Stanford, CA: Stanford University Press.

Megginson, William L., and Jeffrey M. Netter. 2001. "From State to Market: A Survey of Empirical Studies in Privatization," *Journal of Economic Literature* 39 (June): 321–89.

Meller, Patricio. 1996. *Un siglo de economía política chilena (1890–1990)*. Santiago de Chile: Editorial Andrés Bello.

Melo, José Ricardo. 1993. *"La liberalización y la privatización de las telecomunicaciones."* Manuscript, University of Chile.

Melo, José Ricardo and Pablo Serra. 1998. "Competencia y regulación en telecomunicaciones: la experiencia chilena,"*Perspectivas* 2, no. 1: 215–47. Santiago de Chile.

Menem, Carlos, and Roberto Dromi. 1997. *Reforma del estado*. Buenos Aires: Ediciones Ciudad Argentina.

Meseguer Yebra, Covadonga, and Fabrizio Gilardi. 2005. "What Is New in the Study of Policy Diffusion? A Critical Review." Mimeo. Mexico City.

Meseguer Yebra, Covadonga. 2002. *Bayesian Learning about Policies*. Madrid: Centro de Estudios Avanzados en Ciencias Sociales, Instituto Juan March de Estudios e Investigaciones.

MIDEPLAN (Ministry of Planning and Cooperation). 1998. Encuesta de Caracterización Socioeconómica Nacional 1998 (CASEN), Cuadros Vivienda. http://www.mideplan.cl/casen3/vivienda/cuadros1998.html (accessed September 18, 2005).

Milner, Helen V. 1988. *Resisting Protectionism: Global Industries and the Politics of International Trade*. Princeton, NJ: Princeton University Press.

Ministerio Secretaria General de Gobierno (MSGG). 1999. *Informe encuestas flash crisis eléctrica*. Santiago de Chile: Secretaria de Comunicación y Cultura, MSGG, May.

Moe, Terry. 1990. "The Politics of Structural Choice: Toward a Theory of Public Bureaucracy." In *Organization Theory: From Chester Barnard to the Present and Beyond*, ed. Oliver E. Williamson. New York: Oxford University Press, 116–53.

Moguillansky, Graciela. 1999. *La inversión en Chile: El fin de un ciclo en expansión?* Santiago de Chile: CEPAL.

Molano, Walter. 1997. *The Logic of Privatization: The Case of Telecommunications in the Southern Cone of Latin America*. Westport, CT: Greenwood.

Mora y Araujo, Manuel. 1980a. "Las bases estructurales del peronismo." In *El voto Peronista: Ensayos de sociología electoral Argentina*, ed. Manuel Mora y Araujo and Ignacio Llorente. Buenos Aires: Editorial Sudamericana, 397–440.

———. 1980b. "Introducción: La sociología electoral y la comprensión del peronismo." In *El voto Peronista: Ensayos de sociología electoral Argentina*, ed. Manuel Mora y Araujo and Ignacio Llorente. Buenos Aires: Editorial Sudamericana, 11–54.

Moreira, Carlos, and Pedro Narbondo. 1998. *"La reforma de las empresas públicas (1992–1994): Actores, diagnósticos y objetivos."* Working Paper no. 11. Department of Political Science, Universidad de la República, Montevideo.

Mosley, Layna. 2003. *Global Capital and National Governments*. New York: Cambridge University Press.

Munck, Gerardo. 2004. "Democratic Politics in Latin America: New Debates and Research Frontiers," *Annual Review of Political Science* 7 (May 2004): 437–62

Murillo, Maria Victoria. 2005. "Partisanship Amidst Convergence: Labor Market Reforms in Latin America,"*Comparative Politics* 37, no. 4 (July 2005): 441–58.

———. 2002. "Political Bias in Policy Convergence. Privatization Choices in Latin America," *World Politics* 54, no. 4 (July): 462–93.

———. 2001. *Labor Unions, Partisan Coalitions, and Market Reforms in Latin America*. New York: Cambridge University Press.

Murillo, Maria Victoria, and Andrew Schrank. 2005. "With a Little Help from My Friends: External and Domestic Allies and Labor Rights in Latin America,"- *Comparative Political Studies* 38, no. 8 (October): 971–99.

———. Forthcoming. "Labor Unions in the Policy making Process in Latin America." In *Actors in Latin American Policy making*, ed. Ernesto Stein and Mariano Tommasi. Washington, DC: Interamerican Development Bank.

Murillo, María Victoria, and Cecilia Martínez Gallardo. 2007. "Political Competition and Policy Adoption: Market Reforms in Latin American Public Utilities," *American Journal of Political Science* 51, no. 1 (January): 120–39.

Murillo, María Victoria, and Carmen Le Foulon. 2006. "Crisis and Policymaking in Latin America: The Case of Chile's 1998–99 Electricity Crisis," *World Development* 34, no. 9 (September): 1580–96.

Murillo, María Victoria, and Diego Finchelstein. 2004. "Privatización y Poder de Mercado: el caso de la generación de energía eléctrica en Argentina. Nota de investigación," *Desarrollo Económico* 44, no. 173 (April–June): 131–44.

Murillo, Maria Victoria, Virginia Oliveros, and Milan Vaishnav. Forthcoming. "Voting for the Left or Governing on the Left?" In *Latin American Left Turn*, ed. Steven Levitsky and Kenneth Roberts. Cambridge: Cambridge University Press.

Mustapic, Ana María. 2002. "Oscillating Relations: President and Congress in Argentina." In *Legislative Politics in Latin America*, ed. Scott Morgenstern and Benito Nacif. Cambridge: Cambridge University Press, 23–47.

Navia, Patricio. 2004. *Las grandes alamedas: El Chile post Pinochet*. Santiago de Chile: Tercera-Mondadori.

References

NERA (National Economic Research Associates). 1998. "Analysis of the Reform of the Argentine Power Sector: Final Report." New York, January.

Noll, Roger. 1999. "Telecommunications Reform in Developing Countries." Working Paper 99–10, AEI – Brookings Joint Center for Regulatory Studies, November.

———. 1989. "Economic Perspective on the Politics of Regulation." In *Handbook of Industrial Organization*, vol. 2, ed. Richard Schmalensee and Robert D. Willig. London: Elsevier Science Publishers, 1253–87.

Noll, Roger, and Bruce Owen. 1983. *The Political Economy of Deregulation: Interest Groups in the Regulatory Process*. Washington, DC: American Enterprise Institute.

Obinger, Herbert, and John Zohnhofer. 2005. *"Selling Off the 'Family Silver': The Politics of Privatization in the OECD, 1990–2000."* Center for European Studies Working Paper no. 121. Harvard University, Cambridge, MA.

Observatorio de Servicios Públicos (OPSM -Enrique Zuleta Puceiro). 2002. Monitor de Tendencias Económicas y Sociales. Opinión Pública, Servicios y Mercados (July).

———. 2003. Monitor de Tendencias Económicas y Sociales. Opinión Pública, Servicios y Mercados (September).

Ochoa Camposeco, Victor, and Jesus Orozco. 2002. "Iniciativa de Ley Federal para el Desarrollo de las Telecomunicaciones," April. Congreso de la Union. Mexico City.

O'Donnell, Guillermo. 1994. "Delegative Democracy?" *Journal of Democracy* 5 (January): 55–69.

OECD. 2000. *Reforma regulatory en México*. Vol. 1. Paris: OECD.

Olson Mancur. 1965. *The Logic of Collective Action: Public Goods and the Theory of Groups*. Cambridge, MA: Harvard University Press.

O'Neil, Shannon. 2007. "The Rise of the Regulatory State: Post-Privatization Politics in Latin America." Paper presented at Latin American Studies Association International Congress XXVII, Montréal, Canada.

Orenstein, Michael. 2001. *Out of the Red: Building Capitalism and Democracy in Post Communist Europe*. Ann Arbor: University of Michigan Press.

Orozco, Jesús and Víctor Manuel Ochoa Camposeco. 2002. "Propuesta de Reforma a la ley Federal de Telecomunicaciones." Comisión de Telecomunicaciones. Cámara de Diputados. Mexico City, Mexico.

Ostiguy, Pierre. 1998. *Peronism and Anti-Peronism: Class-Cultural Cleavages and Political Identity in Argentina*. PhD diss., University of California, Berkeley.

Oxhorn, Philip, and Graciela Ducatenzeiler. 1998. *What Kind of Democracy? What Kind of Market? Latin America in the Age of Neoliberalism*. University Park: Pennsylvania State University Press.

Palermo, Vicente and Marcos Novaro. 1996. *Política y poder en el gobierno de Menem*. Buenos Aires: Grupo Editorial Norma Ensayo.

Palermo, Vicente, and Juan Carlos Torre. 1992. *"A la sombra de la hiperinflación. La política de reformas estructurales en Argentina."* CEPAL, Buenos Aires, unpublished manuscript.

References

PAN. 2003. "Legislative Program 2003." Mexico City, IFE.

———. 1997. Plataforma Legislativa 1997–2000, January 13.

Parametría. 2002. National Home Surveys. Electricity Reform. Parametria SA de CV, Mexico City, Mexico (June 15–13).

Pastor, Manuel, and Carol Wise. 1997. "State Policy, Distribution, and Neoliberal Reform in Mexico," *Journal of Latin American Studies* 29, no. 2 (May): 419–56.

Pelzman, Sam. 1976. "Toward a More General Theory of Regulation," *Journal of Law and Economics* 19: 211–40.

Peruzzotti, Enrique, and Catalina Smulovitz, eds. 2006. *Enforcing the Rule of the Law: Social Accountabity in the New Latin American Democracies.* Pittsburgh, PA: University of Pittsburgh Press.

Petracci, Mónica. 1998. "La calidad de los servicios públicos privatizados—luz, agua, gas y teléfono: Evaluada por el ciudadano-usuario." Dirección Nacional de Estudios y Documentación, Instituto Nacional de Administración Pública (INAP). Buenos Aires.

Petrazzini, Ben Alfa. 1995. *The Political Economy of Telecommunications Reform in Developing Countries: Privatization and Liberalization in Comparative Perspective.* Westport, CT: Praeger.

Pierson, Paul. 1994. *Dismantling the Welfare State? Reagan, Thatcher, and the Politics of Retrenchment.* Cambridge: Cambridge University Press.

———. *Politics in Time: History, Institutions, and Social Analysis.* Princeton, NJ: Princeton University Press.

Piñera, José. 1990. *La revolución laboral en Chile.* Santiago de Chile: Zig-Zag.

Piñeira, Sebastián. 2005. "Compromiso de Gobierno de Sebastián Piñeira. Primeros 120 días." Sebastián Piñeira's Electoral Plataform. Santiago de Chile, Chile.

Pop-Eleches, Grigore. 2008. "Crisis in the Eye of the Beholder: Economic Crisis and Partisan Politics in Latin American and East European International Monetary Fund Programs," *Comparative Political Studies* 41, no. 9 (September): 1179–1211.

Post, Alison. 2007. "Bargaining for the Long-Term in Volatile Economies: The Regulation of Water and Sanitation Concessions in Latin America." Paper presented for the Latin American Studies Association Meeting, Montreal, September 5–8.

PRD. 2003. "Party for a Democratic Revolution: Legislative Program, 2003–2006." Mexico City, IFE.

PRI (Institutional Revolutionary Party). 2003. "Unidad y Congruencia: Plataforma Electoral 2003." PRI National Political Committee, Mexico City. January 13, IFE.

———. 2002. "Analisis y presentación de criterios para la discusión de reformas del sector eléctrico nacional." Aprobado por unanimidad en la comisión permanente del consejo político nacional del PRI.

———. 2000. *Federal Electoral Program, 2000–2006.* Mexico City.

Proyecto de Elites Latinoamericanas (PELA). 1994–2005. Manuel Alcántara, Director. Salamanca, Spain: Universidad de Salamanca.

References

Przeworski, Adam. 1991. *Democracy and the Market*. Cambridge: Cambridge University Press.

Przeworski, Adam, Michael E. Alvarez, Jose Antonio Cheibub, and Fernando Limongi. 2000. *Democracy and Development: Political Institutions and Well-Being in the World, 1950–1990*. New York: Cambridge University Press.

Rehren, Alfredo. 2000. "Clientelismo político, corrupción y reforma del estado en Chile." Working Paper no. 305. Centro de Estudios Publicos, Santiago de Chile.

Remmer, Karen. 2003. "Elections and Economics in Contemporary Latin America." In *Post-Stabilization Politics in Latin America*, ed. Carol Wise and Riordan Roett. Washington, DC: Brookings Institution, 31–55.

———. 2002. "The Politics of Economic Policy and Performance in Latin America," *Journal of Public Policy* 22, no. 1: 29–59.

———. 1998. "The Politics of Neoliberal Economic Reform in South America, 1980–94," *Studies in Comparative International Development* 33 (Summer): 3–29.

Reveles Vázquez, Francisco. 2003. "La lucha entre fracciones priistas en la selección de candidatos presidenciales." In *Partido Revolucionario Institucional: Crisis y refundación*, ed. Francisco Reveles Vázquez. Mexico City: Ediciones Gernika, 79–152.

Reyes Heroles, Federico. 2000. *Hacia la Presidencia en el 2000*. Mexico City: Fondo de Cultura Economica.

Rhodes, Sybil. 2006. *Social Movements and Free-Market Capitalism in Latin America*. Albany: State University of New York Press.

Rios Figueroa, Julio. 2007. "Fragmentation of Power and the Emergence of an Effective Judiciary in Mexico, 1994–2002," *Latin American Politics and Society* 49, no. 1 (Spring): 31–57.

Rivera, Eugenio. 2000. "Competencia y regulación de los servicios de utilidad pública en Chile: una perspectiva institucional." In *El estado y el sector privado: Construyendo una nueva economía en los años 90*, ed. Oscar Muñoz Gomá. Santiago de Chile: Dolmen-FLACSO, 155–98.

Roberts, Kenneth. 2008. "Party Systems and Electoral Volatility during Latin America's Transition to Economic Liberalism." Mimeo. Ithaca, NY.

———. 2002. "Social Inequalities without Class Cleavages in Latin America's Neoliberal Era," *Studies in Comparative International Development* 36: 3–33.

Rodrik, Dani. 1998. "Why Do More Open Economies Have Bigger Governments?" *Journal of Political Economy* 106, no. 5 (October): 997–1032.

Rodrik, Dani. 1996. "Understanding Economic Policy Reform," *Journal of Economic Literature* 34, no. 1 (March): 9–41.

Rogozinski, Jacques. 1997. *La privatización en México: Razones e impactos*. Mexico City: Trillas.

Rojas Bolaños, Manuel, and Carlos Sojo. 1995. *El malestar con la política: Partidos y elites en Costa Rica*. San José: FLACSO.

Romero, Carlos. 1999. "Regulaciones e inversiones en el sector electric." Texto de Discusión 5, Centro de Estudios Económicos de la Regulación. UADE, Buenos Aires, Argentina (June).

Rosas, Guillermo. 2005. "The Ideological Organization of Latin American Legislative Parties: An Empirical Analysis of Elite Policy Preferences," *Comparative Political Studies* 38, no. 7 (September): 824–49.

Rossi de Oliveira, Andre. 2003. "The Future of Privatization and Regulation in Brazil." Paper presented at the conference Progress and Challenges of Rendering Infrastructure in Latin America, Universidad del Pacífico, Lima, Peru, October 2.

Rozas, Patricio. 1999. "La crisis eléctrica en Chile: Antecedentes para una evaluación de la institucionalidad reguladora." Serie Recursos Naturales e Infraestructura No. 5. Santiago de Chile: CEPAL.

Rufin, Carlos. 2003. *The Political Economy of Institutional Change in the Electricity Supply Industry*. Cheltenham, UK: Edward Elgar.

———. 2002. "Political Economy of the Brazilian Electricity Sector." Report presented to the Inter-American Development Bank. http://faculty.babson.edu/crufin/ (accessed June 8, 2005).

Rufin, Carlos, and U. Srinivasa Rangan. 2004. *Institutional Change in the Electricity Industry: Initial Evidence*. Unpublished manuscript. Babson College, January.

Rufin, Carlos, and Evanán Romero. 2005. "Evaluating the Sustainability of Privatization and Regulatory Reform: Brazil in Comparative Perspective." Paper presented at the Brazil in Interdisciplinary Perspective conference, Cornell University, Ithaca, NY, April 29–30.

Saavedra, Eduardo. 2005. *Marco Regulatorio de los Servicios Basicos en Chile*. IDEAS. http://ideas.repec.org/p/ila/ilades/inv167.html (accessed September 28, 2006).

Sábato, Jorge. 1971. *Segba, cogestión y Banco Mundial*. Buenos Aires: Juárez.

Saiegh, Sebastian. 2006. *"Patterns of Successful Statutory Policy Making around the World."* Mimeo. San Diego: University of California, San Diego.

Salinas, Carlos. 1994. *Sexto informe de gobierno*. Mexico City: Presidencia de la República.

Schamis, Hector. 2002. *Re-Forming the State: The Politics of Privatization in Latin America and Europe*. Ann Arbor: University of Michigan Press.

———. 1999. "Distributional Coalitions and the Politics of Economic Reform in Latin America," *World Politics* 51: 236–68.

———. 1991. "Reconceptualizing Latin American Authoritarianism in the 1970s: From Bureaucratic-Authoritarianism to Neoconservatism," *Comparative Politics* 23, no. 2 (January): 201–20.

Schenone, Osvaldo. 1991. "Public Sector Behavior in Argentina." In *The Public Sector and the Latin American Crisis*, ed. Felipe Larraín and Marcelo Selowsky. San Francisco: International Center for Economic Growth, 20–56.

Schneider, Ben Ross. 2004. *Business Politics and the State in Twentieth-Century Latin America*. Cambridge: Cambridge University Press.

———. 1998. "The Material Bases of Technocracy: Investor Confidence and Neoliberalism in Latin America." In *The Politics of Expertise in Latin America*, ed. Miguel Centeno and Patricio Silva. London: St. Martin, 77–95.

Schneider, Volker, Simon Fink, and Marc Tenbücken. 2005. "Buying Out the State: A Comparative Perspective on the Privatization of Infrastructures,"*Comparative Political Studies* 38, no. 6: 704–27.

References

Secretary of Communications and Transportation (SCT). 2000. *El sector comunicaciones y transporte, 1994–2000*. Mexico City: SCT.

Segura-Ubiergo, Alex. 2007. *The Political Economy of the Welfare State in Latin America*. New York: Cambridge University Press.

Serra, Pablo. 2002. "Regulación del sector eléctrico chileno,"*Perspectivas* 6, no. 1: 11–44.

Shoetters, Marcelo Alberto. 1999. " Preocupa la posible cartelización de la generación en el MEM? " Mimeo. Buenos Aires, Argentina.

Shugart, Matthew S., and John M. Carey. 1992. *Presidents and Assemblies: Constitutional Design and Electoral Dynamics*. Cambridge: Cambridge University Press.

Shugart, Matthew S. and Stephen Haggard. 2001. "Institutions and Public Policy in Presidential Systems." In *Presidents, Parliaments, and Policy*, ed. Stephen Haggard and Matthew D. McCubbins. New York: Cambridge University Press, 21–63.

Siavelis, Peter. 2002. "Executive-Legislative Relations in Chile." In *Legislative Politics in Latin America*, ed. Scott Morgenstern and Benito Nacif. Cambridge: Cambridge University Press, 79–113.

———. 2000. *The President and Congress in Postauthoritarian Chile: Institutional Constraints to Democratic Consolidation*. University Park: Pennsylvania State University Press.

Sigmund, Paul. 1990. "Chile: Privatization, Reprivatization, Hyperprivatization." In *The Political Economy of Public Sector Reform and Privatization*, ed. Ezra N. Suleiman and John Waterbury. Boulder, CO: Westview Press, 87–113.

Silva, Eduardo. 1996. *The State and Capital in Chile*. Boulder, CO: Westview Press.

Silva, Patricio. 1991. "Technocrats and Politics in Chile: From the Chicago Boys to the CIEPLAN Monks," *Journal of Latin American Studies* 23 (May): 385–410.

Simmons, Beth. 1999. "The Internationalization of Capital." In *Continuity and Change in Contemporary Capitalism*, ed. Herbert Kitschelt, Peter Lange, Gary Marks, and John Stephens. New York: Cambridge University Press, 36–69.

Simmons, Beth, and Zachary Elkins. 2004. "The Globalization of Liberalization: Policy Diffusion in the International Political Economy," *American Political Science Review* 98, no. 1 (February): 171–89.

Smith, Peter. 1980. "Las elecciones de 1946 y las inferencias ecológicas." In *El voto Peronista: Ensayos de sociología electoral Argentina*, ed. Manuel Mora y Araujo and Ignacio Llorente. Buenos Aires: Editorial Sudamericana, 165–89.

Spiller, Pablo, and Luis Viana Martorell. 1996. "How Should It Be Done? Electricity Regulation in Argentina, Brazil, Uruguay, and Chile." In *International Comparisons of Electricity Regulation*, ed. Richard J. Gilbert and Edward P. Kahn. Cambridge: Cambridge University Press, 82–125.

Stallings, Barbara. 1992. "International Influence on Economic Policy: Debt, Stabilization, and Structural Reform." In *The Politics of Economic Adjustment: International Constraints, Distributive Conflicts, and the State*, ed. Stephen Haggard and Robert Kaufman. Princeton, NJ: Princeton University Press, 41–88.

———. 1990. "The Role of Foreign Capital in Economic Development." In *Manufacturing Miracles: The Path of Industrialization in Latin America and East*

Asia, ed. Gary Gereffi and Donald L. Wyman. Princeton, NJ: Princeton University Press, 54–87.

Stallings, Barbara and Wilson Perez. 2000. *Crecimiento, Empleo y Equidad: el impacto de las reformas económicas en América Latina*. Mexico City: CEPAL/Fondo de Cultura Económica.

Stigler, George. 1971. "The Theory of Economic Regulation," *Bell Journal on Economic and Management Science* 2: 3–21.

Stokes, Susan. 2005. "Perverse Accountability: A Formal Model of Machine Politics with Evidence from Argentina," *American Political Science Review* 99, no. 3 (August): 315–26.

———. 2001. *Mandates and Democracy*. Cambridge: Cambridge University Press.

Strange, Susan. 1996. *The Retreat of the State*. Cambridge: Cambridge University Press.

Sturzenegger, Federico. 1990. "Description of a Populist Experience: Argentina, 1973–1976." In *The Macroeconomics of Populism in Latin America*, ed. Rudisher Dornbush and Sebastian Edwards. Chicago: University of Chicago Press, 77–120.

Subsecretaria de Economia. 2004. "*Indicadores de regulacion: Servicios de utilidad publica*." Ministerio de Economia, Santiago de Chile. http://www.economia.cl/aws00/Estatico/repositorio/Y/j/R/YjRiNWM0ZTZmNTMwZDQ1MjRiNj YONWM0MWZhNTFmMjg4YWRlN2ZmOA==.pdf (accessed October 1, 2005).

Székely, Gabriel, and Jaime Del Palacio. 1995. *Telefonos de México: una empresa privada*. Mexico City: Grupo Editorial Planeta.

Tabja, Rodrigo. 1996. "Organización industrial, legislación y tarificación en las telecomunicaciones de Chile. Un intento de Síntesis." Mimeo. Santiago de Chile.

Taylor, Shelley. 1982. "The Availability Bias in Social Perception and Interaction." In *Judgement under Uncertainty: Heuristics and Biases*, ed. Daniel Kahneman, Paul Slovic, and Amos Tversky. Cambridge: Cambridge University Press, 190–200.

Telecomunicaciones y Negocios. 1999. no. 42, year 9.

———. 1997. "Las Pymes hacen numerous," no. 32, year 7.

Teichman, Judith. 2001. *The Politics of Freeing Markets in Latin America*. Chapel Hill: University of North Carolina Press.

Telmex. 2002. "Propuesta de Telmex a la CPT." Mexico City. Mimeo.

Thatcher, Mark. 2002a. "Delegation to Independent Regulatory Agencies: Pressures, Functions and Contextual Mediation," *West European Politics* 25, no. 1 (January): 125–47.

———. 2002b. "Regulation after Delegation: Independent Regulatory Agencies in Europe," *Journal of European Public Policy* 9, no. 6: 954–72.

———. 1999. *The Politics of Telecommunications*. Oxford: Oxford University Press.

Thelen, Kathleen. 2004 *How Institutions Evolve: The Political Economy of Skills in Germany, Britain, the United States, and Japan*. Cambridge: Cambridge University Press.

References

———. 1999. "Historical Institutionalism in Comparative Politics," *Annual Review of Political Science* 2 (June): 369–404.

Torre, Juan Carlos. 1998. *El proceso político de las reformas económicas en América Latina*. Buenos Aires: Paidós.

Torre, Leonardo. 2000. *"Tarifas y penetración telefónica en México: Demanda insuficiente o poder de monopolio?"* Working Paper 18. Centro de Análisis y Difusión Económica (CADE), Monterrey (November).

Trends in Telecommunications Reforms. 1998. Geneva: International Telecommunications Union.

Tsebelis, George. 2003. *Veto Players: How Political Institutions Work*. Princeton, NJ: Princeton University Press.

Tufte, Edward. 1978. *Political Control of the Economy*. Princeton, NJ: Princeton University Press.

Ugalde, Luis Carlos. 2000. *The Mexican Congress: Old Player, New Power*. Washington, DC: CSIS.

UNDP. 2004. *Democracy in Latin America: Towards a Citizens' Democracy*. New York: United Nations Development Program.

Urbiztondo, Santiago. 2000. "El problema de los cortes de electricidad y posibles soluciones regulatorias." Mimeo. FIEL, March.

Urbiztondo, Santiago, Daniel Artana, and Fernando Navajas. 1998. "La autonomía de los nuevos entes reguladores argentinos," *Desarrollo Económico* 38 (Autumn): 7–40.

Valenzuela, Arturo. 1991. "The Military in Power: The Consolidation of One-Man Rule." In *The Struggle for Democracy in Chile*, ed. Paul Drake and Ivan Jaksic. Lincoln: University of Nebraska Press: 97–132.

Vergara, Pilar. 1981. "Las Transformaciones de las Funciones Económicas del Estado en Chile Bajo el Gobierno Militar," *Colección Estudios CIEPLAN* 5: 117–54.

Vernon, Raymond. 1971. *Sovereignty at Bay: The Multinational Spread of US Enterprises*. New York: Basic Books.

Victor, David, and Thomas Heller. 2007. *Introduction to the Political Economy of Power Sector Reform*, ed. D. Victori and T. Heller. New York: Cambridge University Press.

Vispo, Adolfo. 1999. *Los entes de regulación*. Buenos Aires: FLACSO-Norma.

Vogel, Steven K. 1996. *Freer Markets, More Rules: Regulatory Reforms in Advanced Industrial Countries*. Ithaca, NY: Cornell University Press.

Vreeland, James. 2003. *The IMF and Economic Development*. New York: Cambridge University Press.

Weingast, Barry. 1981. "Regulation, Reregulation, and Deregulation: The Political Foundations of Agency Clientele Relationships," *Law and Contemporary Problems* 44: 148–77.

Weldon, Jeffrey. 1997. "Political Sources of Presidencialismo in Mexico." In *Presidentialism and Democracy in Latin America*, ed. Scott Mainwaring and Matthew S. Shuggart. Cambridge: Cambridge University Press, 225–8.

Weyland, Kurt. 2008. "The Latin American Left: Destroyer or Savior of the Market Model?" Mimeo. Austin, TX.

———. 2006. *Bounded Rationality and Policy Diffusion: Social Sector Reform in Latin America*. Princeton, NJ: Princeton University Press.

———. 2005. "Theories of Policy Diffusion: Lessons from Latin American Pension Reform," *World Politics* 2: 262.

———. 2004. "Learning from Foreign Models in Latin American Policy Reform: An Introduction." In *Learning from Foreign Models in Latin American Policy Reform*, ed. Kurt Weyland. Baltimore, MD: Johns Hopkins University Press, 1–34.

———. 2002a. *The Politics of Market Reform in Fragile Democracies: Argentina, Brazil, Peru, and Venezuela*. Princeton, NJ: Princeton University Press.

———. 2002b. "Limitations of Rational-Choice Institutionalism for the Study of Latin American Politics," *Studies in Comparative International Development* 37, no. 1 (Spring): 57–85.

———. 1999. "Economic Policy in Chile's New Democracy," *Journal of Interamerican. Studies and World Affairs* 41, no. 3: 67–96.

———. 1998. "Swallowing the Bitter Pill: Sources of Popular Support for Neoliberal Reform in Latin America," *Comparative Political Studies* 31, no. 5 (October): 539–68.

Williamsom, John. 1994. *The Political Economy of Policy Reform*. Washington, DC: Institute for International Economics.

Wilson, Bruce. 1999. "Leftist Parties, Neoliberal Policies, and Reelection Strategies: The Case of the PLN in Costa Rica," *Comparative Political Studies* 32, no. 6: 752–79.

Wilson, James Q. 1980. "The Politics of Regulation." In *The Politics of Regulation*, ed. James Q. Wilson. New York: Basic Books, 357–447.

Winograd, Carlos. 2002. "Infraestructura y Servicios Públicos. Crisis Económica y Agenda Regulatoria." Mimeo. París: DELTA-Ecole Normale Superieure (September 11).

Wise, Carol. 2003. "Mexico's Democratic Transition: The Search for New Reform Coalitions." In *Post-Stabilization Politics in Latin America*, ed. Carol Wise and Riordan Roett. Washington, DC: Brookings Institution Press, 159–98.

World Bank. 2005. "Infrastructure in Latin America and the Caribbean: Recent Development and Key Changes." Washington, DC: World Bank.

———. 1991. "The Evolution, Situation, and Prospects of the Electric Power Sector in the LAC Countries." Washington, DC: World Bank and OLADE, August.

Yashar, Deborah. 2005. *Contesting Citizenship in Latin America*. Cambridge: Cambridge University Press.

Zedillo, Ernesto. 2000. *Sexto Informe de Gobierno*. Mexico City: Presidencia de la República.

Index

adoption, 3, 5, 8, 9, 13, 15, 17, 18, 20, 23, 25, 26, 28, 30, 38, 39, 40, 55, 56, 57, 59, 60, 63, 68, 69, 72, 73. *See also* policy adoption
Agua y Energía, 91, 96
Alestra, 215, 216, 218
Alfonsín, 8, 91, 92, 93
Alianza, 152, 175, 179, 181, 182, 188, 190, 192, 193
Allende, 81, 103
allied experts, 10, 16, 29, 35, 36, 37, 38, 48, 99, 100, 102, 103, 104, 106, 107, 108, 110, 116, 117, 124, 143, 151, 167, 176, 182, 183, 184, 194, 205
alternative networks, 51, 140, 155, 200, 206, 219, 223, 233, 239, 243
Alwyin, 151
ANTEL, 56, 139
Anti-Trust Commission, 117, 157, 166, 171, 173, 174, 175
ARENA, 127, 132, 139
Argentina, 1, 8, 9, 13, 14, 15, 19, 20, 22, 32, 33, 34, 49, 53, 55, 80, 85, 90, 91, 92, 94, 95, 97, 98, 103, 110, 113, 118, 120, 122, 123, 124, 126, 127, 132, 140, 141
asymmetric rules, 218
Avantel, 215, 216, 218

Bachelet, 151
Blancos, 56

Brazil, 9, 19, 33, 34, 40, 126, 132
bureaucracy, 22, 37, 78, 112, 123
bureaucratic expansion, 111, 112, 113, 116, 117, 118
bureaucrats, 252

Calderon Sol, 1
capital inflows, 142, 246, 247, 249, 250
capital scarcity, 3, 5, 7, 8, 9, 20, 21, 23, 24, 40, 101, 243, 244, 245
Cavallo, 107, 114, 115, 183, 184, 187, 192, 194
CFE, 84, 86, 108, 209, 220
challenger, 4, 25, 26, 27, 28, 43, 57, 59, 61, 68, 69, 72, 73, 78, 85, 87
Chile, 8, 9, 13, 14, 15, 18, 19, 22, 33, 34, 34, 49, 55, 80, 81, 83, 85, 91, 97, 98, 103, 106, 111, 113, 118, 125, 126, 127, 132, 140, 141, 144, 145, 146, 147, 149, 155, 156, 173, 175, 176, 178
Chilectra, 81, 112, 113, 153
Chilesat, 155, 166
Christian Democrats, 82, 104, 148, 150, 152
civil society, 6, 45
CNE, 19, 82, 111, 112, 115, 160
CNT, 94, 95, 120, 125, 194, 196, 197, 200, 239
COFETEL, 88, 90, 123, 125, 211, 212, 215

Index

Other Books in the Series *(continued from page iii)*